D0875767

Genocide on Settler Frontiers

When Hunter-Gatherers and
Commercial Stock Farmers Clash

War and Genocide

General Editors: Omer Bartov, Brown University; A. Dirk Moses, European University Institute, Florence/University of Sydney

There has been a growing interest in the study of war and genocide, not from a traditional military history perspective, but within the framework of social and cultural history. This series offers a forum for scholarly works that reflect these new approaches.

"The Berghahn series Studies on War and Genocide has immeasurably enriched the English-language scholarship available to scholars and students of genocide and, in particular, the Holocaust."
—Totalitarian Movements and Political Religions

Genocide on Settler Frontiers

When Hunter-Gatherers and
Commercial Stock Farmers Clash

Edited by Mohamed Adhikari

berghahn
NEW YORK • OXFORD
www.berghahnbooks.com

Published by
Berghahn Books
www.berghahnbooks.com

©2015 Berghahn Books
This version of *Genocide on Settler Frontiers* is
published by arrangement with UCT Press.

Not for sale in South Africa, Namibia, Botswana, Zimbabwe,
Zambia, Swaziland, Lesotho, Malawi, Uganda or Kenya.

©2014 UCT Press

Library of Congress Cataloging-in-Publication Data
Genocide on settler frontiers: when hunter-gatherers and commercial stock farmers
clash / edited by Mohamed Adhikari.
    pages cm. – (Studies on war and genocide; 22)
Originally pulished in 2014 as Genocide on Settler Frontiers by UCT Press.
Includes bibliographical references and index.
ISBN 978-1-78238-738-1 (hbk.: alk. paper) – ISBN 978-1-78238-739-8 (ebook)
1. Indigenous peoples – Violence against – History. 2. Indigenous peoples – Violence
against – South Africa – History. 3. Indigenous peoples – Violence against – Australia
– History. 4. Genocide – South Africa – Cape of Good Hope – History. 5. Genocide –
Australia – History. I. Adhikari, Mohamed. II. Title.
 GN380.G46 2015
 364.15'1 – dc23

                                                                    2014039958

British Library Cataloguing in Publication Data

A catalogue record for this book is available from the British Library.

Printed on acid-free paper.

ISBN: 978-1-78238-738-1 hardback
ISBN: 978-1-78238-739-8 ebook

For Rafiq and Zaheer
and in loving memory of my grandmother, Nazeema

Table of Contents

Acknowledgements

This project was conceptualised in mid-2010 as I was completing my manuscript on the genocidal destruction of Cape San societies. Writing a paragraph placing the Cape San case in global perspective brought home to me just how destructive settler colonialism had been of indigenous peoples, especially hunter-gatherers. It also occurred to me that in all the cases that immediately came to mind—Tasmania, Queensland, the Yuki of California, the Plains Indians, the Selk'nam of Tierra del Fuego, among others—one had hunter-gatherer societies annihilated by commercial stock farmers. Wondering about the specific dynamic of conflict between these two groups, I thought that an edited book on the subject would be a worthwhile project as the phenomenon was global, the topic too wide and the issues too intricate for me to handle on my own, and because no-one else appeared to have done such a a study.

It was apparent that I would have to cold canvass academics across the globe working on related issues since I did not have the time or resources to organise a conference on the subject, nor was I part of some ready-made network of scholars interested in the topic. Because I expected my requests for contributions to be ignored or to elicit polite refusals from busy academics, I was hesitant about setting the ball rolling. I was, at the same time, aware of a clear counter example to my hypothesis that when commercial stock farmers invaded the lands of hunter-gatherer peoples the outcome was 'invariably genocide', namely, that the Ghanziland San of western Bechuanaland were neither exterminated nor suffered mass violence when Boer stock-farming settlers from the Cape occupied their territories from the late nineteenth century onwards. The existence of a contrasting case in itself was not a problem, as I was not intending to make absolute claims in this respect and recognised that an opposing example would shed valuable light on the subject. Indeed, I soon came to regard the inclusion of this counter example as essential to the proposed project. I knew from background reading to the Cape San study that Mathias Guenther, the doyen of San studies, was the expert on the Ghanzi case. Facing these uncertainties, I decided that if I could get Mathias to contribute a chapter on why the Ghanzi San did not suffer genocide, I would commit to the project.

When I with some trepidation wrote to Mathias, whom I had never met nor communicated with before, I not only got a positive response, but generously long emails explaining some of the intricacies of the Ghanzi case and commenting on my vague initial observations about it.

So, a huge thank you to Mathias Guenther, for without his enthusiasm and willingness to participate, this project would most likely have been stillborn. I then started approaching other possible contributors and am happy to say that most of them agreed to author chapters, with some recommending colleagues interested in the subject. In this regard, I am particularly grateful to Robert Gordon, who put me in contact with several potential contributors. The odd polite refusal nothwithstanding, within a matter of weeks I had a viable project.

And so, a second huge thank you to contributors for responding positively to my cold canvassing and for their genial cooperation throughout the production of this volume. I also wish to express my appreciation to those who participated in the workshop around the book which was held at the University of Cape Town (UCT) in December 2012. Throughout the compilation of this volume, I particularly enjoyed the chatty emails and frequent back-and-forths on subjects ranging from how to get rid of wasp nests to the quality of semester abroad students that American universities disgorge each year. A common saying among academics is that editing a collection of essays calls for both the arts of persuasion and coercion. It was, however, cheerful collegiality that marked this enterprise.

I am enormously appreciative of the congeniality and proficiency of the UCT Press team that collaborated with me in the production of this book. Sandy Shepherd, publisher of UCT Press, supported this project from the time I outlined my ideas to her in late 2010, and has played an important role in the realisation of this undertaking, not least of which was securing Berghahn Books as co-publisher. Sandy has been a dream to work with— creative, resourceful, energetic, flexible, and unflagging good humour are some of her qualities that immediately come to mind. Lee-Ann Ashcroft did a sterling job as editor, and project manager, Willemien Jansen, was superb at keeping the publishing process on track.

Some of the editing and writing of the introductory chapter towards the end of the project was done while on a month-long fellowship at Stanford University. I am greatly indebted to Tim Stanton, director of Stanford's Bing Overseas Studies Programme (BOSP) in Cape Town for nominating me for this fellowship, and to Stanford University's Humanities Center for hosting me during this most pleasant and productive interlude. I would also like to extend my thanks to the anonymous reviewers whose reports helped us improve the manuscript. It is with gratitude that I acknowledge funding from the National Research Foundation as well as from UCT's University Research Committee, without which this research would not have been possible.

Along the way, this project was facilitated, and my life enriched, by a host of dear friends and family members. While working on this volume, I twice visited the San Francisco Bay Area. On both occasions my friend Jonathan Winters offered me warm hospitality, and on the latter visit helped me gather material for my next project. I valued the opportunity of bouncing ideas off Sherry Stanton, who for three years helped me teach my BOSP course, Genocide: African Experiences in Comparative Perspective. Kamiel, Fiekkie-Leila, Kittycaaaat, Mr Scabbers and Max helped liven things up and Skipper, after more than a decade of keeping us all waiting, finally came through and did his thing.

I dedicate this book to the memory of my grandmother who effectively raised me. The contents of her large and eclectic bookcase kept me occupied for a good deal of my childhood and adolescence, and the encouragement to read was a formative influence on my life. Her constant counsel that 'education is something that no-one can ever take from you', which had a particular salience in apartheid South Africa, has stayed with me. As always, this book is also dedicated to my sons Rafiq and Zaheer, whose love and warmth keep me grounded and are a constant reminder of what really matters.

Notes on the Contributors

Mohamed Adhikari is an Associate Professor in the Department of Historical Studies at the University of Cape Town. He has published widely on coloured identity and politics in South Africa. His recent books on the subject include *Not White Enough, Not Black Enough: Racial Identity in South Africa's Coloured Community* (Double Storey and Ohio University Press, 2005); *Burdened By Race: Coloured Identities in Southern Africa* (UCT Press, 2009); and *Against the Current: A Biography of Harold Cressy, 1889–1916* (Juta, 2012). He now works primarily in the field of settler colonial genocide and published *The Anatomy of a South African Genocide: The Extermination of the Cape San Peoples* (UCT Press and Ohio University Press, 2010).

Tony Barta is a Research Associate at La Trobe University, where he taught European and Australian history and founded the History and Film programme. In addition to his pioneering work on genocide in Australia, he has written on twentieth-century Germany and nineteenth-century genocidal ideology. His overview of genocide scholarship in Australia is in Dan Stone (ed) *The Historiography of Genocide* (Palgrave Macmillan, 2008). He is completing *The Destruction of Peoples: On Colonialism and Genocide,* to be published by Bloomsbury.

Edward Cavanagh is the Trillium Foundation scholar at the University of Ottawa. In addition to a number of scholarly articles in the fields of history and law, he has published two books, the most recent being *Settler Colonialism and Land Rights in South Africa* (Palgrave Macmillan, 2013). He is the co-founder and managing editor of the journal *Settler Colonial Studies*, and with Lorenzo Veracini, he is currently preparing the *Routledge Handbook of the History of Settler Colonialism*. He specialises in comparative histories of colonialism, settler colonialism and imperialism. He is also interested in legal history, in particular corporations and property.

Ann Curthoys is an Honorary Professor in History at the University of Sydney, and formerly an Australian Research Council professorial fellow. She has written widely on questions of Aboriginal history, genocide theory and race relations in colonial and modern Australia, as well as on issues of historical theory and writing. Her books include *Freedom Ride: A Freedom Rider Remembers* (Allen & Unwin, 2002); with John Docker, *Is History Fiction?* (University of Michigan Press, 2005); with Ann Genovese and

Alexander Reilly, *Rights and Redemption: History, Law, and Indigenous People* (University of New South Wales Press, 2008); and with Ann McGrath, *How to Write History that People Want to Read* (Palgrave Macmillan, 2009). She has co-edited over a dozen major collections of essays on diverse topics, including women's historical writing; transnational approaches to history; and myth, memory, and indigenous histories. She has also edited a special issue of the *Journal of Colonialism and Colonial History* (13:1) on settler self-government and indigenous peoples.

Robert Gordon is Professor of Anthropology at the universities of Vermont and the Free State, and Visiting Professor at the University of Cologne. He has done fieldwork in southern Africa and Papua New Guinea. His books include *Law and Order in the New Guinea Highlands*; *The Bushman Myth and the Making of a Namibian Underclass*; and *Picturing Bushmen: The Denver African Expedition of 1925* as well as several edited volumes, the most recent being *Re-inventing First Contact*, co-edited with Joshua Bell and Alison Brown and published by the Smithsonian.

Mathias Guenther is Professor Emeritus in the anthropology programme at Wilfrid Laurier University in Waterloo, Ontario from where he retired in 2007. He conducted field work among the Naro and =Au//eisi in the Ghanzi district of Botswana from 1968 to 2007, as well as archival work in Namibia. His broad research interests are socio-cultural change, social organisation, ethnohistory, religion, cultural revitalisation, myth, folklore and art among Kalahari Bushman communities. His publications include *The Nharo Bushmen of Botswana: Tradition and Change* (Helmut Buske, 1986); *Tricksters and Trancers: Bushman Religion and Society* (Indiana University Press, 1999); and *Kalahari and Namib Bushmen in German South West Africa: Ethnographic Reports by Colonial Soldiers and Settlers* (Rüdiger Köppe, 2005).

Sidney L. Harring holds both PhD and law degrees from the University of Wisconsin. He is the author of two books on the legal history of indigenous peoples of Canada and the United States, namely, *Crow Dog's Case: American Indian Sovereignty, Tribal Law, and United States Law in the Nineteenth Century* (Cambridge Univeristy Press, 1994) and *White Man's Law: Native People in Nineteenth Century Canadian Jurisprudence* (University of Toronto Press, 1998). Professor Harring has taught in Malaysia, Namibia and Sweden, held three Fulbright professorships, and three National Endowment for the Humanities fellowships. He held the Law Foundation of Saskatchewan's distinguished professorship in law at the University of

Saskatchewan while he did research on Indians and law on the Canadian prairies.

Jared McDonald is a post-doctoral research fellow in the Department of Historical Studies at the University of Johannesburg, where he also teaches. He recently completed his PhD at the School of Oriental and African Studies (SOAS), University of London. McDonald's primary research interest focuses on indigenous responses to British colonialism in the Cape Colony during the nineteenth century. His other research interests include interactions between Christian missions and 'First Nations'; settler colonialism and genocide; 'childhood' and child labour; and the work of the London Missionary Society in southern Africa.

Nigel Penn is a Professor in the Department of Historical Studies at the University of Cape Town. His research interests include early colonial society at the Cape and the history of indigenous Khoisan societies of southern Africa. His books include *The Forgotten Frontier: Colonist and Khoisan on the Cape's Northern Frontier in the Eighteenth Century* (University of Ohio Press, 2005) and *Rogues, Rebels and Runaways: Eighteenth Century Cape Characters* (David Philip, 1999). He co-edited *Britain at the Cape, 1795–1803* with Maurice Boucher (Brenthurst Press, 1992) and *Written Culture in a Colonial Context: Africa and the Americas 1500–1900* with Adrien Delmas (UCT Press, 2011).

Lyndall Ryan is an Honorary Conjoint Professor in the School of Humanities and Social Sciences at the University of Newcastle. She has published widely on settler violence on the Australian colonial frontier before 1850. Her books include *The Aboriginal Tasmanians* (Allen & Unwin, 1981), an edited collection with Philip Dwyer, *Theatres of Violence: Massacre, Mass Killing and Atrocity throughout History* (Berghahn Books, 2011), and *Tasmanian Aborigines: A History since 1803* (Allen & Unwin, 2012).

Lorenzo Veracini is an Associate Professor at the Swinburne Institute for Social Research in Melbourne, Australia. His research focuses on the comparative history of colonial systems and settler colonialism. He has authored *Israel and Settler Society* (Pluto Press, 2006) and *Settler Colonialism: A Theoretical Overview* (Palgrave Macmillan, 2010). Lorenzo is managing editor of *Settler Colonial Studies*.

xiv

Chapter One

'We are Determined to Exterminate Them': The Genocidal Impetus Behind Commercial Stock Farmer Invasions of Hunter-Gatherer Territories

Mohamed Adhikari
University of Cape Town

In 1830, Willem Barend, a citizen of the Griqua state of Philippolis in the Transorangia region north of the Cape Colony, was reported to have expressed a determination to kill all San hunter-gatherers because they preyed on Griqua cattle. Within a few years, his resolve had effectively become reality through persistent Griqua raiding and massacring of San communities within reach of their commandos.[1] In 1860, H.L. Hall, notorious Indian hunter and stock manager for Judge Serranus Hastings, one of the largest landholders in northern California, went on a killing spree of Yuki Indians in the Eden Valley area, openly boasting that he had deliberately provoked conflict with them, and had recruited a posse consisting of men prepared to slay all Yuki they came across. The Yuki people suffered demographic collapse when settlers invaded their lands in the mid-1850s, declining from perhaps 12 000 to no more than 300 by the mid-1860s, reflecting a commensurate slump in Californian Indian society.[2] Carl Lumholtz, Norwegian ethnographer, travelled extensively through Queensland in the early 1880s, publishing an account of his experiences in 1889. He reported that: 'In Northern Queensland I often heard the remark: "The only treatment proper for the blacks is to shoot them all ... They are unwilling to work" I have heard colonists say, "and hence they are not fit to live".' During the latter half of the nineteenth century, Queensland's pre-colonial Aboriginal population of over 250 000

---

[1] Cavanagh E. *Settler Colonialism and Land Rights in South Africa: Possession and Dispossession on the Orange River.* Houndmills: Palgrave Macmillan, 37–39, and Cavanagh's chapter below. 'Commando' is a southern African term for armed, mounted militia units.

[2] Carranco L. & Beard E. 1981. *Genocide and Vendetta: The Round Valley Wars and Northern California.* Norman: University of Oklahoma Press, 62–63; Madley B. 2008. 'California's Yuki Indians: defining genocide in Native American history'. *Western Historical Quarterly,* 39, no. 3, 304, 329.

suffered attrition of over 90 per cent.[3] What most powerfully binds these diverse examples of exterminatory violence is that the victims were hunter-gatherer peoples, and the main perpetrators commercial stock-farming settlers linked to the industrialising and globalising Western economy.

A few years ago, while writing and researching the annihilation of Cape San society,[4] largely by Dutch-speaking stock farmers through the eighteenth and nineteenth centuries, and trying to locate that episode in global historical context, I was struck by how destructive European settler colonialism had been of hunter-gatherer societies generally, whether in southern Africa, Australia or the Americas. Pursuing this line of thought further, it appeared to me that a particular subset of settler colonial confrontations—those in which livestock farmers linked to the global capitalist market clashed with hunter-gatherers—were particularly catastrophic in their outcome. The frequency with which encounters of this kind resulted in the near complete destruction of forager societies raises the question why this particular form of settler colonial conflict seems to have been overwhelmingly predisposed to eradicatory violence.

The tendency towards genocide in this category of conflict is even more marked if one takes into account that the definition of genocide that I use is more stringent than that of the United Nations Convention on Genocide (UNCG), the one applicable in international law. The definition used in this introduction and the next chapter is that genocide is 'the intentional physical destruction of a social group in its entirety or the intentional annihilation of such a significant part of the group that it is no longer able to reproduce itself biologically or culturally'.[5] Survivors are usually reduced to forced labour or utter destitution, and subject to cultural suppression and purposeful marginalisation—in some cases even legislated exclusion from mainstream society as, for example, outlined in Sid Harring's case study

---

3   Lumholtz C. 1979. *Among Cannibals: Account of Four Year's Travels in Australia, and Camp Life with the Aborigines of Australia*. Firle, Sussex: Caliban Books, first published London,1889, 373; Evans R. 2013. 'Foreword', in *Conspiracy of Silence: Queensland's Frontier Killing Times*, T. Bottoms. Sydney: Allen & Unwin, xix–xx.

4   Adhikari M. 2010. *The Anatomy of a South African Genocide: The Extermination of the Cape San Peoples*. Cape Town: UCT Press.

5   This definition is adapted from the one provided in *Anatomy of a South African Genocide*. See especially pages 12–13 for elaboration on its meaning and scope. For further introductory discussion on the concept of genocide, see Jones A. 2011. *Genocide: A Comprehensive Introduction*. London: Routledge, ch. 1; Shaw M. 2007. *What is Genocide?* Cambridge: Polity Press, ch. 2; Stone D. 2008. *The Historiography of Genocide*. New York: Palgrave Macmillan, especially the opening chapter, Curthoys A. & Docker J. 'Defining genocide', 9–41.

of Plains Indians in Canada. This definition is more demanding than its UNCG equivalent in that it requires higher levels of violence and social devastation for an episode of mass violence to be recognised as genocide.

It is possible to identify a number of shared features in conflicts between hunter-gatherers and market-oriented stock farmers in European settler colonies across the globe that served to intensify hostilities and tilt the balance towards exterminatory violence. This analysis explores those factors that I consider to be fundamental to promoting genocidal outcomes in clashes of this kind. While there were many other contributors to eradicatory violence between hunter-gatherers and commercial stock farmers, and each conflict was unique, the primary facilitators identified here were not only common to cases globally, but also instrumental in escalating the violence to genocidal levels.

The nature of commercial stock farming

In the first instance, the nature of commercial stock farming itself was a major contributor to the escalation of bloodshed to genocidal levels. One of the crucial dynamics at play in pastoral settler colonies was the rapid occupation of sweeping expanses of land characteristic of capitalist stock farming, especially when entering 'virgin' territory.[6] The repercussions for hunter-gatherer peoples of the invasion of their land by commercial stock farmers contrasted markedly to those by other kinds of farmers.

Commercial stock farmers had a significantly different impact on hunter-gatherer communities to invading subsistence pastoralists such as the Khoikhoi (Hottentot) or Herero peoples of southern Africa, for example. The absence of sizeable market outlets or opportunities to trade in traditional societies meant that there were low limits to the economic surplus that could be realised. And because subsistence herders tended to farm in more sustainable ways, their need for land and other resources was limited. For such peoples, stock also had substantive aesthetic and social value, which mitigated their management mainly for economic benefit. Commercial stock farmers, on the contrary, were driven primarily by profit, treated stock as commodities and sought to maximise economic returns. Linked to world markets, they were generally

---

6   Newly invaded territories were, of course, seldom 'virgin' as often portrayed in settler discourse because they were usually inhabited. Francis Jennings' remark that such land 'was more like a widow than a virgin' is apt. See Jennings F. 1975.*The Invasion of America: Indians, Colonialism, and the Cant of Conquest.* Chapel Hill: University of North Carolina Press, 30.

incentivised to produce as much as possible, whatever the environmental and human cost, particularly during economic booms. Thus when subsistence herders entered the lands of hunter-gatherers, conflict was far less intense as invasions were more gradual, conflict localised and the impact less destructive of foraging activities. Although such interaction tended towards displacement of hunter-gatherers and often resulted in bloodshed, it also included incorporation, clientship and even symbiosis. With commercial stock farmers, however, the incursions were much more rapid, intent on thoroughgoing and permanent confiscation of land and resources, and far less compromising in dealing with indigenous resistance.

Commercial stock farming also had a different dynamic to that of colonising crop growers. Whereas agriculturalists tended to be sedentary, marking out longer term occupancy of land with fences and hedges, and tending to expand incrementally and contiguously, commercial stock farmers needed extensive pastures and were inclined to be on the move. Though crop farming was locally more destructive of indigenous societies because it supported denser populations and occupied land more comprehensively and permanently,[7] the impact of stock farming extended much more swiftly over larger areas, and was nonetheless devastating to hunter-gatherer communities living there. Stock keepers were usually engaged in a constant search for pasture and water, particularly in drier environments and when entering territory for the first time. Indeed, dry spells and drought accelerated their dispersal beyond the fringes of colonial settlement. Frontier stock farmers were generally not bound by the confines of ranches, even where they laid formal claim to such holdings. On pastoral frontiers, registered farms were often used as bases from which flocks and herds were moved in transhumant fashion and vast stretches of countryside were treated as communal grazing or open range. Distance from ports and markets was far less of a concern to stock farmers than their crop-growing counterparts, as in most cases their produce was capable of carrying themselves to desired destinations. This was especially true of animals raised for meat.

---

[7]   For an extended analysis of the impact of agriculture on genocidal thinking and practice globally, see Kiernan B. 2007. *Blood and Soil: A World History of Genocide and Extermination From Sparta to Darfur*. New Haven: Yale University Press, as a whole and especially 29–33, 166–68, 252–53. For detailed discussion on incompatibilities between foraging and farming lifestyles, and the exterminatory violence that often results, see Brody H. 2000. *The Other Side of Eden: Hunters, Farmers and the Shaping of the World*. New York: North Point Press as well as Docker J. 2008. *The Origins of Violence: Religion, History and Violence*. London: Pluto Press, ch. 1.

Case studies across the temperate colonial world confirm that settler advances were relatively slow and conflict with indigenes limited until colonies turned to large scale pastoral farming. Few colonies were established as pastoral ventures from the start and it was generally growing demand from the metropole or some sector of the global trading network that sparked the shift to commercial stock farming. Indeed, in many temperate zone colonies, it was the ready adaptation of imported livestock to the environment that made farming with them economically viable and attractive to settlers.[8] Increasing demand for their produce, especially as the industrial revolution progressed through the nineteenth century, encouraged stock keepers to expand their flocks and herds, as well as formal landholdings and to move into new territory beyond the limit of colonial settlement. Economic booms usually set in motion spectacular frontier advances and the rapid stocking of land, especially with cattle and sheep, but also with pigs, goats, horses and other domesticated animals. For example, leading historian of the destruction of Queensland's Aboriginal societies, Raymond Evans, comments that with the onset of pastoral farming in that colony around 1840, 'the frontier did not merely spread; it galloped'. He estimates that at the height of the land rush of the early 1860s, the Queensland pastoral frontier advanced by as much as 300 kilometres annually.[9] Similarly, in Tasmania, as Lyndall Ryan demonstrates, conflict with Aborigines was muted and localised until the colony entered its pastoral phase in 1817. After that, grazing land was very quickly occupied and leading Tasmanian farmers shifted their operations across the Bass Strait to the Port Philip District (later Victoria), from about 1834 onwards where indigenous societies were destroyed within 15 years.[10] Similar trends are observable in southern Africa and North America. In the former it was in particular the incorporation of the Cape Colony into the British Empire and the opening up of new markets that stimulated pastoral production. In the latter it was westward migration from within the United

---

[8]   Crosby A. 2004. *Ecological Imperialism: The Biological Expansion of Europe, 900–1900.* Cambridge: Cambridge University Press, 172–73, 187.

[9]   Evans R. 2004. '"Plenty shoot 'em": the destruction of Aboriginal societies along the Queensland frontier', in *Genocide and Settler Society: Frontier Violence and Stolen Indigenous Children in Australian History,* ed. A.D. Moses. New York: Berghahn Books, 163; see also Bottoms T. 2013. *Conspiracy of Silence: Queensland's Frontier Killing Times.* Sydney: Allen & Unwin, 17–18; Loos N. 1982. *Invasion and Resistance: Aboriginal–European Relations on the North Queensland Frontier.* Canberra: ANU Press, 29.

[10]   Ryan L. 2012. 'White settler massacres of Aborigines in Tasmania (1820–1835) and Victoria (1835–1851): a comparative analysis'. Unpublished paper presented at the conference Invariably Genocide? When Hunter-gatherers and Commercial Stock Farmers Clash, University of Cape Town, 6 December 2012, 5–6.

States, immigration from Europe, and growing demand from the settled eastern areas of the continent that drove the pastoral frontier.

On occasion, it was the discovery of minerals, most dramatically gold rushes, that extended frontiers precipitately and spelt doom for hunter-gatherer communities across entire regions. The attendant growth in stock farming to help feed the explosive increase in population was usually an important ingredient in the devastation of indigenous societies far beyond the mining centres themselves, its impact felt long after the rush had subsided. This is evident in a significant way with the 1850s copper mining boom in the northern Cape, more so with gold rushes that took place in Australia, particularly Queensland, from the late 1850s onwards, and most spectacularly with the Californian gold rush that started in the late 1840s. Newly built infrastructure to support the mining economy made former wilderness areas much more accessible to settlers. Even where mineral deposits were soon exhausted, some prospective miners remained behind, turning to hunting, logging, crop growing or commonly pastoralism, as a means of living, permanently displacing indigenous peoples.[11]

Not only did stock farmers shift frontiers rapidly and occupy the best land, they also commandeered resources critical to the survival of hunter-gatherer communities. Commercially farmed herds and flocks consumed large amounts of grazing and water, and often exceeded the carrying capacity of the land. This damaged the ecosystem, at times altering it permanently for the worse. Invasion by commercial stock farmers had an immediate, and usually devastating, impact on the region's foraging societies, whose seasonal migrations were disrupted and whose food supplies and other foundations of life were severely compromised. The introduction of large numbers of domesticates undermined indigenous hunting, fishing and gathering activities to the extent that communities would soon be suffering malnutrition or even be facing starvation. Conflict was almost unavoidable as both hunter-gatherers and stock farmers were in direct competition for the same environmental resources, especially land, water and game. Foraging bands suddenly found that they were denied access to sacred locales, traditional hunting grounds and watering places such as springs, pools and river frontages. Livestock contaminated and exhausted water supplies, trampled edible plants, disrupted foraging activities and displaced herds of game, a primary source of food for hunter-gatherer

---

[11]   See, for example, Adhikari, *Anatomy of a South African Genocide*, 74; Palmer A. 2000. *Colonial Genocide*. Adelaide: Crawford House, 92, 95; Lindsay B. 2012. *Murder State: California's Native American Genocide, 1846–1873*. Lincoln: University of Nebraska Press, 135, 146.

peoples. Importantly, colonists decimated herbivore populations—whether antelope in Africa, bison in North America, kangaroos in Australia or guanaco in Latin America—and other wild animals with their guns, permanently depleting a key resource. Hungry bands thus often had little option but to target settler stock for sustenance.[12]

The result, almost inevitably, was spiralling levels of violence as afflicted indigenous peoples resisted encroachment and settlers in turn retaliated, usually with excessive and indiscriminate force. Hunter-gatherer communities typically resisted settler incursions using guerrilla tactics of raiding and maiming stock, slaying herders isolated out in the pastures, and attacking farmsteads, usually at night. Stock farmers responded with individual acts of slaughter, informal militia activity, and on occasion, teamed up with colonial state forces in retaliatory offensives. Such conflicts often culminated in open warfare and exterminatory onslaughts on the part of colonial society. The weakness of the colonial state and its tenuous control over frontier areas gave settlers, who had access to arms, wide discretion to act against indigenes. Frontier pastoral societies, being land hungry, having relatively low labour requirements and being difficult to administer, were prone to exterminatory violence when faced with indigenous resistance. This was particularly the case when their opponents were hunter-gatherers whose labour was not highly valued, and whose sparse settlement and peripatetic lifestyle invited thoughts of eradication.

There was another significant way in which the nature of stock farming itself helped amplify violence against indigenous peoples. Given the need for extensive landholdings or a transhumant lifestyle to graze and water animals, stock-keeping settlers were widely dispersed in small numbers across open landscapes. They were thus vulnerable not only to attack, but also to severe economic setbacks from hunter-gatherer retaliation. It was not uncommon for commercial stock farmers to be heavily indebted and threatened with bankruptcy by downward fluctuations in commodity prices or recessionary conditions. This set up an anxiety-ridden existence for stock-farming communities, making them susceptible to over-reaction to threats and rumours of danger, as well as to pre-emptive violence against perceived enemies. They were usually suspicious of all indigenes, and fearful of raids, revenge attacks, uprisings or collusion with indigenous

---

[12] See, for example, Watson P. 2004. 'Passed away? The fate of the Karuwali', in *Genocide and Settler Society*, ed. A.D. Moses, 177–78; Madley, 'California's Yuki Indians', 314–15; Adhikari, *Anatomy of a South African Genocide*, 34, 36–37; Macdonald T. 2012. 'Settlers, missionaries, and sheep among the Yamana and Selk'nam of Tierra del Fuego'. Unpublished paper in possession of the author.

servants. Frontier stock keepers seldom went about their business unarmed and were constantly alert to the possibility of indigenous aggression. They expected trouble and this easily became a self-fulfilling prophecy. Situations of pervasive anxiety punctuated with sporadic violence are likely to give rise to extreme othering of enemies.[13] Hunter-gatherers were vulnerable to the harshest forms of racial stereotyping by settlers because their lifestyle placed them at the polar opposite of colonial societies' perception of themselves as 'civilised' and part of humanity's highest incarnation. To this heady brew of anxiety, fear and racial contempt one needs to add vengeance in the wake of indigenous resistance. This made for volatile passions among stock-farming communities that often spilt over into exterminatory rhetoric and mass violence towards indigenous peoples. Chronic tension and uncertainty weakened settler restraints against violence towards and the killing of foragers, especially where their labour was not deemed essential. It is no surprise that in pastoral settler societies, shoot-on-sight vigilantism, informal militia activity and even state-sponsored eradicatory drives were common, as the case studies in this book demonstrate.

International capitalist markets

A second dynamic tipping the balance towards exterminatory violence was that access to world markets and a concomitant desire among colonists to accumulate wealth encouraged both intensive exploitation of natural resources for short-term gain as well as a resort to annihilatory practices to eliminate obstacles or threats to the colonial project, be they vegetation, animals or indigenous peoples. This impulse, though present from the very start of European colonisation—very evident, for example, in the colonisation of the east Atlantic islands in the two centuries prior to Columbus' voyages to the Americas[14]—intensified markedly with European industrialisation and the rapid growth of world markets through the nineteenth century. Settler rapacity, excited by opportunities for profit during economic booms, often proved deadly for indigenous communities. Many frontiersmen in newly established colonies, often

---

[13] For discussion of how anxiety and fear of attack intensified racial animosities of settlers in unfamiliar landscapes, see Veracini L. 2010. *Settler Colonialism: A Theoretical Overview.* New York: Palgrave Macmillan, 81; Newton-King S. 1999. *Masters and Servants on the Eastern Cape Frontier, 1760–1803.* Cambridge: Cambridge University Press, ch. 7; Lindsay *Murder State,* chs 2 & 3; Bottoms, *Conspiracy of Silence,* 43–44, 90.

[14] See, for example, Mercer J. 1980. *The Canary Islanders: Their Prehistory Conquest and Survival.* London: Collings; Crosby, *Ecological Imperialism,* ch. 4; Abulafia D. 2008. *The Discovery of Mankind: Atlantic Encounters in the Age of Columbus.* New Haven: Yale University Press, chs 4 & 5.

referred to as settlers in the literature and who often became settlers, were in fact sojourners in mindset in that it was their intention to make a quick fortune at any cost and return home to a life of leisure. Ensuing busts and retreat of pastoral frontiers seldom resulted in much of a reprieve for hunter-gatherer communities as in many cases severe or irreparable damage to their communal lives had already been inflicted, frustration and desperation incited callous behaviour towards indigenes, and it was usually only a matter of time before abandoned land was re-occupied.

The case studies in this collection confirm that the degree to which settler pastoral economies participated in international trade, together with demand for the commodities they produced, were roughly proportional to the rapidity of indigenous dispossession and levels of violence perpetrated. Thus in both Tasmania and Victoria, key suppliers of wool to burgeoning British markets, Aboriginal societies were effectively destroyed within 15 years of the onset of the pastoral economy, as Lyndall Ryan shows, whereas at the Cape, where the market for pastoral products was limited, the process was more incremental. This correlation is also apparent in the North American studies of Tony Barta and Sid Harring, where accelerating immigration and growing markets dictated the pace at which the pastoral frontier moved westwards and indigenous societies were displaced. A stark contrast is presented by colonial Bechuanaland (modern-day Botswana) where the market was insignificant and colonial institutions more protective of indigenous rights. Mathias Guenther explains in some detail why the characteristic pattern of mass violence towards hunter-gatherers was replaced by a relatively benign form of paternalism in this case. In neighbouring German South West Africa (today Namibia), Robert Gordon, however, demonstrates that an acute shortage of labour throughout the booming economy after the colonial wars of 1904–1908, was not enough to prevent the ruthlessly oppressive colonial regime from implementing decidedly genocidal policies towards sections of the hunter-gatherer population.

The privatisation and commodification of natural resources, especially land, a defining characteristic of capitalist economies, undermined foraging societies fundamentally. Systems of land tenure based on personal entitlement, exclusive usage, fixed boundaries, registration of title deeds, alienability and permanent settlement were completely foreign to hunter-gatherer world views[15] and effectively excluded them from legal ownership

---

[15] As Tony Barta eloquently put it with regard to Australian Aborigines, the land was 'something to which they in many profound ways belong, rather than something which belongs to them'. Barta T. 'Decent disposal: Australian historians and the recovery of genocide', in *The Historiography of Genocide*, ed. D. Stone. Houndmills: Palgrave MacMillan, 303.

of vital resources. Privatisation generally meant the permanent loss of such resources and that settler claims were backed by the legal apparatus, and ultimately, the armed might of the colonial state. While colonial states were often weak and had little control over frontier regions, their access to superior military technology allowed them to concentrate their fire-power and thus impose their will at particular times and places. Economic and political imperatives invariably resulted in the colonial state supporting settler interests and condoning land confiscations, even in cases where both metropolitan and local governments tried to curb frontier violence and restrain settler aggression. The case of Tasmania, where both Governor Arthur and the Secretary of State tried to mitigate settler violence and acknowledged that the dying out of Aborigines would be an 'indelible stain' on the record of the British Empire, provides a good example.[16]

Their ability to claim legal title to natural resources in many instances gave settlers cause for going on the offensive against indigenous peoples and, no doubt, reason for justifying such violence to themselves. Although different legal regimes applied to different colonies, and conditions varied considerably, it is nonetheless possible to generalise broadly about the role of colonial law in spurring frontier violence and indigenous dispossession in settler societies.[17] Significantly, the absence of the rule of law on the frontier favoured settlers who had superior firepower and were generally able to confiscate land and resources as well as perpetrate violence against indigenes with a fair degree of impunity. The absence of the rule of law also aided in the suspension of conventions, scruples and moral codes that might otherwise have tempered settler violence. Much of this violence was committed with the knowledge and connivance of the colonial state or elements within it. And when the rule of law was eventually implemented with the closing of the frontier, it was heavily biased in favour of settlers. Not only were indigenes routinely and explicitly disadvantaged by the legal system, but settlers also had significant control over its institutions and day-to-day operation. The law was instrumental in both confirming settler claims to the land and consolidating their control of indigenous labour. As Lisa Ford put it: 'Settler violence, then, was clothed in law—a law which in important respects settlers constituted and controlled'.[18]

---

16   Reynolds H. 2004. 'Genocide in Tasmania', in *Genocide and Settler Society*, ed. A.D. Moses, 144.
17   I am thankful to Edward Cavanagh for drawing my attention to the significance of the role of law on settler colonial frontiers.
18   Ford L. 2010. *Settler Sovereignty: Jurisdiction and Indigenous People in America and Australia, 1788–1836*. Cambridge, Mass.: Harvard University Press, 85. See also Kercher B. 1995. *An Unruly Child: A History of Law in Australia*. St Leonards: Allen & Unwin, 1–18.

The access that frontier communities had to world markets, their metropole and settled parts of colonies also meant the availability of resources, technologies and ideologies that made mass violence towards indigenes all the easier to perpetrate, and extermination all the more comfortable to contemplate. Ships carrying men and supplies with which to settle and conquer; guns and ammunition with which to kill; horses and wagons with which to transport goods; centralised political institutions through which to organise dispossession and mass violence, and an array of tools and machines, the sophistication of which indigenous societies could not hope to match, were among the more obvious advantages frontier settler society derived from continued contact with its Western wellsprings. Less tangibly, such contact helped reinforce the ideological underpinnings of violence perpetrated against indigenous peoples. Cultural and religious chauvinism, ideas of European racial superiority and entitlement, as well as jingoistic imperialism, were fortified by continued settler contact with their European and colonial hubs, and played important parts in promoting violence towards indigenes. Where colonies gained complete independence, even through war and revolution, settler communities nonetheless continued to derive great power from their metropolitan connections.

Racial ideologies

A third common characteristic favouring exterminatory violence was the influence of Western racist thinking that dehumanised the hunter-gatherer way of life as an utterly debased form of existence, comparable in many respects to that of animals, and proof of their racial inferiority. Foragers were cast as the lowest of the low in the racial hierarchy, with particular groups at times the object of speculation that they formed the 'missing link' between humans and animals. Hunter-gatherers were generally perceived as not owning their territories but merely inhabiting them, much as animals do, because they were allegedly not making productive use of it. Though modulated by local imperatives, the generalised image of unused land occupied by dangerous, godless savages bereft of morality, reason or any form of refinement, and importantly, obstructing the advance of 'civilisation' and economic development, usually underlay settler rationales for both land confiscation and accompanying mass violence.[19] Stereotyped as immune to 'civilising' influences, and their labour unsuited to settler

---

[19]   Levene, M. 2005. *Genocide in the Age of the Nation State, Volume II: The Rise of the West and the Coming of Genocide.* New York: I.B. Taurus, 47; Kiernan, *Blood and Soil*, 280–81, 342, 362.

needs, hunter-gatherer populations were often regarded as expendable. Exceptions arose in cases where hunter-gatherer labour was essential to the well-being of the colonial economy, as demonstrated by Ann Curthoys' chapter on Western Australia. However, as Robert Gordon's study indicates, racially motivated exterminatory urges sometimes did trump the economic interests of the colony.

One of the consequences of racial thinking was that supposed racial traits were generally regarded as inherent, the entire 'race' being judged in terms of them. Blanket racial condemnation of 'the savage' helped foster indiscriminate as well as exterminatory violence. Commercially based pastoral settlers across the globe seem to have had little difficulty justifying the killing of indigenous women and children as well, and did so in remarkably similar fashion, claiming that the women bred bandits, and that children grew up to become enemies. Griqua, Willem Barend, reportedly said of the San that '... we are determined to exterminate them [as] the children grow up to the mischief and the women breed them'; Californian H.L. Hall justified his extirpatory actions by claiming that '... a knit (sic) would make a louse'; and Carl Lumholtz recounts that a Queensland farmer found it 'severe but necessary' to shoot 'all the men he discovered on his run, because they were cattle killers; the women because they gave birth to cattle killers; and the children because they would in time become cattle killers'. 'Nits make lice' reasoning was an inexorable part of racist discourse.[20]

Racist theorising, especially from the latter part of the nineteenth century when Social Darwinism became popular, often anticipated the dying out of 'the savage', conceiving of it within a meta-narrative of an all-encompassing racial struggle for the survival of the fittest through which humanity would progress to its full potential. This brand of thinking further encouraged violence against indigenes and fostered an extirpatory attitude within frontier society as their demise was seen as inevitable, the outcome of an inexorable law of nature. The extirpation of indigenes could thus be interpreted positively as being in step with nature and ridding humanity of an encumbrance, and racial war could be romanticised as a

---

[20] Carranco & Beard, *Genocide and Vendetta*, 63; Cavanagh, *Settler Colonialism*, 37; Lumhotz, *Among Cannibals*, 373. See also Stannard D. 1992. *American Holocaust: The Conquest of the New World*. Oxford: Oxford University Press, 131; Churchill W. 1992. *A Little Matter of Genocide: Holocaust and Denial in the Americas, 1492 to the Present*. San Francisco: City Lights Books, 229; Barta T. 2007. 'Mr. Darwin's shooters: on natural selection and the naturalising of genocide', in *Colonialism and Genocide*, eds A.D. Moses & D. Stone. London: Routledge, 27.

means of achieving this advancement.[21] Because forager subsistence needs were by and large irreconcilable with those of the settler economy, colonial society viewed the foraging way of life as one to be eliminated, whether neutralised through segregation in reserves, forced acculturation into some subordinate status in the colonial order or outright extermination. In many cases the forces propelling settler expansion radicalised over time in ways that favoured the most extreme of these options. Where commercial stock farming was the mainstay of the colonial economy, they nearly always did.

Although often cast in racial terms and shot through with racist rhetoric, genocidal struggles between hunter-gatherers and commercial stock farmers were not primarily racial in character. They were essentially about incompatible ways of life vying for the same scarce resources and the right to occupy particular areas of land. Racist ideology played essentially enabling and justificatory roles in these conflicts. Racism provided a rationale for dispossessing indigenes, and their dehumanisation made it easier to ignore their suffering and to exploit, kill or exterminate them.[22] That economic competition rather than race was at the heart of these conflicts is demonstrated by Edward Cavanagh's chapter on the Griqua, a mainly Khoikhoi-speaking people in the northern Cape. After successfully turning from subsistence to commercial pastoralism in the 1810s and 1820s as a result of market opportunities opened up by British occupation of the Cape Colony, the Griqua became as enthusiastic and deadly slaughterers of the San as European colonists, and effectively cleared the Transorangia region of hunter-gatherer bands.

---

[21] See Brantlinger P. 2003. *Dark Vanishings: Discourse on the Extinction of Primitive Races, 1800–1930.* Ithaca: Cornell University Press; McGregor R. 1997. *Imagined Destinies: Aboriginal Australians and the Doomed Race Theory, 1880–1939.* Melbourne: Melbourne University Press; Finzch N. 2007. '"It is scarcely possible to conceive that human beings could be so hideous and loathesome": discourses of genocide in eighteenth- and nineteenth-century America and Australia', in *Colonialism and Genocide*, eds A.D. Moses & D. Stone London: Routledge, 12–13; Dippie B. 1982. *The Vanishing American: White Attitudes and US Indian Policy.* Lawrence: University Press of Kansas; Gallois W. 2013. *A History of Violence in the Early Algerian Colony.* New York: Palgrave Macmillan, 14.

[22] For an extended analysis of the dehumanisation of racial others, see Smith D.L. 2011. *Less than Human: Why We Demean, Enslave, and Exterminate Others.* New York: St Martin's Press. For further reflection on the matter, see Scheper-Hughes N. 2002. 'Coming to our senses: anthropology and genocide', in *Annihilating Difference: The Anthropology of Genocide*, ed. A.L. Hinton. Berkeley: University of California Press, 369–74; Chirot D. & McCauley C. 2006. *Why Not Kill Them All? The Logic and Prevention of Mass Political Murder.* Princeton: Princeton University Press, 81–87; Lindqvist S. 1992. *Exterminate All the Brutes.* London: Granta Books, 9, 130, 140.

Superior military technology

A fourth contributor to genocidal outcomes in clashes with hunter-gatherers was the advanced military technologies available to insurgent pastoral settlers, which gave them huge advantages in situations of conflict. Superior technologies of war both aided processes of dispossession and played a role in escalating violence to exterminatory levels. Not only did this disparity in military power make mass violence easier to perpetrate, but meant that colonial forces, both formal and informal, could act with relative impunity. This technological gap also helped confirm settler views that their enemies were racially inferior.

Most obviously, firearms gave settlers and their surrogates massive military ascendancy over hunter-gatherer adversaries. Even the relatively primitive front-loading muskets available prior to their replacement by rifles in the latter half of the nineteenth century, were far superior to the stone-age weapons used by hunter-gatherers. Muskets had a range much greater than that of forager weapons such as spears, darts, or bows and arrows— at least double the distance of the last-mentioned, which had the furthest reach. This allowed colonists to pick off enemies from a safe distance. Guns fired in volleys were particularly effective when the enemy was massed together. From the mid-nineteenth century onwards the availability of much more accurate and rapid-firing rifles greatly tilted the balance in favour of colonists. Pistols were used in closer engagements, as were sabres and knives.

Horses not only gave colonial fighters the ability to cover long distances rapidly, but also manoeuvrability and advantages of height in close skirmishing. Jared Diamond describes the horse as 'of incalculable military value' in pre-industrial times, the equivalent of 'the tank, the truck and the jeep of warfare'.[23] Horses were particularly effective in flat, open country with low scrub, and were invaluable in situations requiring hot pursuit. The combination of guns and horses amplified the settler military advantage in warfare for, as historian William Keleher Storey explains, the pairing allowed colonial forces to travel like cavalry and attack like infantry. Small contingents of armed, mounted settler militia were thus able to defeat much larger throngs of indigenous fighters on foot using traditional weapons.[24] Not surprisingly, both guns and horses

---

23 Diamond J. 1992. *The Third Chimpanzee*. New York: Harper Collins, 237; Crosby, *Ecological Imperialism*, 23–24.

24 Storey W. 2008. *Guns, Race and Power in Colonial South Africa*. Cambridge: Cambridge University Press, 36; Lindqvist, *Exterminate All the Brutes*, 48–49; Swart S. 2012. *Riding High: Horses, Humans and History in South Africa*. Johannesburg: Wits University Press, 13, 19, 27; Swart S. 2007. 'Riding high: horses, power and settler society in southern Africa, c.1654–1840', in *Breeds of Empire: The Invention of the Horse in Southeast Asia and Southern Africa*, eds G. Bankoff & S. Swart. Copenhagen: NIAS Press, 123–50.

became emblematic of European racial ascendancy in colonial situations, featuring prominently in symbolic displays of settler power. Packs of dogs trained for hunting, herding and guarding against intruders were commonly part of the settler armoury.[25]

Also, frontier stockmen were a hardy breed. They were toughened by long periods spent outdoors in uncomfortable conditions and in the saddle. Hunting both for the pot and for sport, together with the carrying of guns for protection, meant that most were adept at handling firearms. Two ubiquitous settler skills on pastoral frontiers, marksmanship and horsemanship, complemented each other, enhancing the proficiency with which they were able to kill indigenes when their energies were channelled in that direction.

For all these advantages, some stock-farming communities nevertheless had difficulty quelling hunter-gatherer resistance, even when they went on the offensive. The basic reasons for this were that frontier areas were vast, pastoral settlers thin on the ground, environments often hostile, and the target populations sparse, mobile, self-reliant and exceedingly well adapted to their surroundings. Even where settlement was sparse, settler communities or the colonial state were usually able to assert their dominance at times and places of their choosing by concentrating their fire-power. This allowed relatively small groups of armed colonists to confiscate land, destroy bands, defend strategic nodes, and for colonial states to force targeted indigenous peoples to do their bidding.

Also, colonial fighters needed coordination and discipline through some form of training and tactical deployment. It is for this reason that settlers and colonial administrations formed militias and paramilitary groups such as the commandos of the Cape Colony, the roving parties of soldiers, policemen and settlers in Tasmania, the Native Police forces of Victoria, New South Wales and Queensland, and volunteer companies of Indian hunters of California such as the Eel River Rangers that operated in Mendocino County, northern California. Conflict on pastoral frontiers in many instances radicalised to the extent that settler violence became indiscriminate, and virtually every indigene a potential victim irrespective of age or gender. In such cases it was not unusual for settler paramilitary forces, such as those mentioned above, to operate as mobile death squads, scouring the countryside for natives to kill.[26]

---

25 Van Sittert L. & Swart S. 2008.*Canis Africanis: A Dog History of South Africa*. Leiden: Brill, 7.

26 For Cape commandos, see Penn N. 2005. *The Forgotten Frontier: Colonist and Khoisan on the Cape's Northern Frontier in the 18th Century*. Cape Town: Double Storey, ch. 5; Adhikari, *Anatomy of a South African Genocide*, 39–59, 72–75; for Queensland's Native Police, see Richards J. 2008. *The Secret War: A True History of the Queensland Native Police*, chs 1–2; for the Eel River Rangers, see Carranco & Beard, *Genocide and Vendetta*, ch. 5, and Lindsay, *Murder State*, ch. 5.

Demographic imbalances

Demographic imbalances played a significant role in the genocidal destruction of indigenous societies in various ways. Most obviously, the sheer weight of numbers and resources that settler colonial projects were able to muster would in time, and with continued immigration, overwhelm hunter-gatherer societies, which by their very nature were sparsely populated. With the coming of the industrial age and the possibility of what James Belich refers to as 'explosive colonisation',[27] as occurred in the American west and the Melbourne hinterland, these imbalances became very stark indeed. Tony Barta's characterisation of this unequal struggle as objectively embodying 'relations of genocide' in which hunter-gatherer society was 'subject to remorseless pressures of destruction inherent in the very nature of the society' is apt.[28]

The communicable diseases interlopers carried, to which indigenes had low immunity, compounded these inequalities. Their low population densities and itinerant lifestyles did not spare foraging societies from the devastating repercussions of virgin soil epidemics. As an elderly San hunter reminisced about the impact of smallpox on indigenous communities: wherever it spread, 'there are no people left, only stones'.[29] Disease often wreaked a toll greater than direct killing, and sometimes entire communities were severely compromised even before direct contact was made. The effects of contagious disease were commensurately greater in those societies suffering land confiscation, malnutrition, mass violence, forced labour and the psychological traumas of invasion. Colonisation and contagion fed off one another, a deadly pairing that buttressed racist theorising about the inevitable demise of the 'savage'.

A significant demographic imbalance almost inherent to the colonial frontier was that severely skewed gender ratios in settler society led to excessive sexual violence towards indigenous women. The more remote and undeveloped the frontier, as pastoral frontiers tended to be, the greater

---

[27] Belich J. 2009. *Replenishing the Earth: The Settler Revolution and the Rise of the Anglo-World*. Oxford: Oxford University Press, 9, 178–79; see also Barta T. '"They appear actually to vanish from the face of the earth": Aborigines and the European project in Australia Felix'. *Journal of Genocide Research*, 10, no. 4, 520; Mann M. 2005. *The Dark Side of Democracy: Explaining Ethnic Cleansing*. Cambridge: Cambridge University Press, 72, 82.

[28] Barta T. 1987. 'Relations of genocide: land and lives in the colonisation of Australia', in *Genocide in the Modern Age: Etiology and Case Studies of Mass Death*, eds I. Walliman & M. Dobkowski. New York: Syracuse University Press, 240; see also Maybury-Lewis D. 2002. 'Genocide against indigenous peoples', in *Annihilating Difference*, ed. A. Hinton, 44–45.

[29] Phillips H. 2012. *Plague, Pox and Pandemics: A Jacana Pocket History of Epidemics in South Africa*. Aukland Park: Jacana Media, 37.

gender disparities were likely to have been. On some pastoral frontiers, the ratio between settler men and women was as high as 10:1. What is more, frontier stockmen tended to be a hard, uncompromising and rough lot who behaved in sexually predatory ways towards indigenous women in particular. This, together with racial stereotyping of indigenes as barely human, led to rampant sexual violence towards native women and the spread of venereal disease. Assault, abduction, rape and sexual slavery of indigenous women by settler men were common on many frontiers. Venereal infection was sometimes so widespread it was a major hindrance to the biological reproduction of indigenous communities. Not only were infected women often unable to conceive or bear foetuses to term, but sexually transmitted diseases by themselves sometimes killed large proportions of populations, on occasion surpassing other diseases and direct killing in impact.[30] These factors had severe repercussions for hunter-gatherer communities as their populations were sparse and they reproduced at relatively slow rates because of the necessary wide spacing between siblings. Sexual violence and venereal disease were thus of central import to the implosion of indigenous societies.

The nature of hunter-gatherer society

Finally, the nature of hunter-gatherer society itself contributed to genocidal outcomes when faced with an aggressive settler pastoral presence. Whereas the hunter-gatherer way of life in many ways was extremely resilient, it in other ways was vulnerable when under sustained attack or when it faced prolonged disruption of economic activity. Hunter-gatherer society was inherently resilient because it consisted of small social groups scattered over large areas, often in inhospitable and remote landscapes. It was, in addition, extremely flexible, mobile, superbly adapted to the environment, and able to live off the land. On the other hand, because hunter-gatherer communities by and large subsisted off the current offerings of nature, were dependent on seasonal cycles of regeneration, and produced virtually no surplus, the severe ecological disruption and despoilment caused by invading commercial stock farmers represented an immediate and acute threat to their foundations of life.

Foraging societies were also vulnerable to genocidal outcomes in other ways when faced with prolonged, systematic violence. Because of its

---

[30]   Cook N. 1998. *Born to Die: Disease and New World Conquest, 1492–1650.* Cambridge: Cambridge University Press; Alchon S. 2003. *A Pest in the Land: New World Epidemics in a Global Perspective.* Alburquerque: University of New Mexico Press; Hays J. 1998. *The Burdens of Disease: Epidemics and Human Response in Western History.* New Brunswick: Rutgers University Press, ch. 4; Broome R. 2010. *Aboriginal Australians: A History Since 1788.* Crows Nest: Allen & Unwin, 63–66.

small scale and relative lack of social differentiation, almost any form of organised violence against foraging peoples took on the aspect of total war, and bloodshed or child confiscation to any appreciable degree started assuming genocidal proportions at the level of the band and of socio-linguistic groupings. That there was likely to be a blurring of distinctions between warriors and non-combatants in hunter-gatherer society, and that settler violence was often indiscriminate rather than targeted at fighters or stock raiders, made this doubly so. It was not unusual for entire indigenous communities to be held responsible for the actions of a few individuals, for one community to pay for the acts of another, and for collective punishments in the form of massacres and random killings to be meted out to people known to be innocent.[31] In the case of hunter-gatherers, colonial violence thus easily degenerated into 'total war on a local scale'.[32]

That hunter-gatherers were unable to fight in any other way except by using guerrilla tactics, contributed to the escalation of violence against them. Settlers tended to see their stealth attacks, arson and maiming of stock as dishonourable forms of warfare which in turn fuelled unrestrained responses.[33] Settlers had difficulty adapting traditional European means of warfare to dealing with hunter-gatherer adversaries. As Henry Reynolds noted: 'There were no forts to besiege, villages to attack, crops to burn, or wells to poison. Nor did there appear to be any chiefs or leaders with whom to negotiate'.[34] Colonists thus had to find new ways of countering hunter-gatherer resistance. It is not surprising that settlers at the Cape, in North America, Australia, and probably elsewhere in the world, developed the strategy of forming roving paramilitary detachments whose favoured tactic was to surround sleeping hunter-gatherer camps under cover of darkness and attack at dawn. The need for fresh approaches also resulted in such ill-conceived experiments as the 'Black Line' offensive governor George Arthur organised against surviving Tasmanian Aborigines in 1830.

There is another important way in which the small-scale social structure of foraging societies was an inherent weakness. The dispersed format of their social order meant that hunter-gatherer fighters were routinely

---

31 For some examples, see Lindsay, *Murder State*, 26, 200, 204, 206; Palmer, *Colonial Genocide*, 52; Mann, *Dark Side of Democracy*, 96; Evans, 'Plenty shoot 'em', 155–57; Rowley C. 1970. *The Destruction of Aboriginal Society*. Harmondsworth: Penguin, 39–40; Bottoms, *Conspiracy of Silence*, 39, 41, 50, 63, 66–67, 106–07.

32 Moses A.D. 2008. 'Empire, colony, genocide: keywords and the philosophy of history', in *Empire, Colony, Genocide: Conquest, Occupation, and Subaltern Resistance in World History*, ed. A.D. Moses. New York: Berghahn Books, 26.

33 Madley B. 2004. 'Patterns of frontier genocide 1803–1910: the Aboriginal Tasmanians, the Yuki of California, and the Herero of Namibia'. *Journal of Genocide Research*, 6, no. 2, 173.

34 Reynolds, 'Genocide in Tasmania', 147.

outnumbered in hostile engagements, even when attacked by relatively small militia or paramilitary units because individual hunting bands seldom had more than eight or ten men of fighting age, and often no more than four or five. Forager bands, though they did not have hereditary leaders, were on occasion able to combine fighting forces under the command of temporary war chiefs. They were, however, unable to sustain such initiatives for long as the lack of centralised political structures must have made coordination difficult. More to the point, hunter-gatherers did not produce enough of a surplus to maintain anything resembling an army in the field.

The small-scale social structure of forager societies also meant that women and children usually found themselves in the frontline of fighting and thus extremely vulnerable to being slaughtered or captured. Being taken prisoner, which in most cases meant serving as forced labour or being integrated into colonial society in some subservient status, was an integral part of the genocidal process because it was as destructive of indigenous society as killing its members. A common pattern in settler mass violence towards hunter-gatherer communities was to slay the men, take those women not killed as domestic and sexual drudges, and to value children as sufficiently malleable to be trained for a life of servile labour. As Jared McDonald convincingly argues, child abduction played a central role in the genocidal destruction of hunter-gatherer societies at the Cape. The dispersed social structure of foraging peoples was an asset for as long as intruding settler societies lacked the strength or the will to embark on systematic killing campaigns against them. It appears to have become a decided liability when settler societies went on concerted, eradicatory drives.

Those bands forced onto marginal land beyond the range of colonial settlement or in the interstices of farms lived miserable lives and were vulnerable to extinction in a range of ways. Some managed to live off a combination of foraging and stock theft for a while. This was a dangerous option as it invited deadly reprisal from settlers. Many were in time forced into the service of farmers, usually on detrimental terms dictated by employers. Where hunter-gatherer bands were forced into the territories of neighbouring communities, it often resulted in internecine conflict between indigenous groups, weakening them further. In drier areas, bands displaced to remote, marginal land might succumb some years after their displacement because with the coming of the next drought, there was every possibility they would find themselves stranded without food or water.[35]

---

[35]   Adhikari, *Anatomy of a South African Genocide*, 57.

The social dislocation caused by incessant conflict and displacement from ancestral land severely undermined the cultural and biological reproduction of hunter-gatherer societies. The intensely spiritual lives of hunter-gatherer communities were usually closely tied to specific sites and aspects of the landscape, and for them, in the words of Nigel Penn, 'to lose the land was to lose literally everything'.[36] Also, the necessarily lengthy spacing between siblings in hunter-gatherer society meant that procreation was more easily disrupted and difficult to maintain in times of severe and prolonged upheaval than in farming communities. This wide spacing meant that it also took a long time for bands and socio-linguistic groupings to recover from demographic setbacks as hunter-gatherer women rarely bore more than four children in their lifetimes.[37] The stress accompanying the sundering of their world could only have reduced the fertility of hunter-gatherer women. This could have happened in direct ways, such as people deciding not to have children or resorting to abortion and infanticide, or indirectly, through the physiological impacts of stress and poor nutrition reducing women's ability to conceive and bring foetuses to term.

The observation that the nature of hunter-gatherer society itself contributed to genocidal outcomes in conflict with commercial stock farmers is not in the least meant to put blame on the victims, nor to diminish either the agency of foraging societies engaged in frontier conflict, or the reality that settler society at times had a rather tenuous hold on power. Nor are these comments to be read as lending any credence to specious doctrines such as *terra nullius* or *vacuum domicilium* and other justifications for violence and dispossession used by imperial establishments. It was, after all, their resistance that usually precipitated extirpatory offensives against hunter-gatherers. This line of argument is intended rather to indicate that, in the final analysis, such struggles were inherently very uneven and that the assault on the land, lives and culture of hunter-gatherer peoples had a decided tendency towards exterminatory violence.

* * * * *

Case studies are broadly arranged in geographic and temporal sequence. The collection kicks off with my chapter on the destruction of the San

---

[36] Penn N. 1996. '"Fated to perish": the destruction of the Cape San', in *Miscast: Negotiating the Presence of the Bushmen*, ed. P. Skotnes. Cape Town: UCT Press, 88. Although he was referring specifically to the Cape San, his comments apply to hunter-gatherer society generally.

[37] Diamond, J. 1999. *Guns, Germs and Steel: The Fates of Human Societies*. New York: Norton, 89.

(Bushman) societies in the Cape Colony during the eighteenth and nineteenth centuries because it is the earliest of the cases and provides useful context for contributions on the San that follow. Cape San society was almost completely annihilated as a result of land confiscation, massacre, forced labour and cultural suppression that accompanied colonial rule. The first part of this chapter analyses the dynamic of frontier conflict between the San and settler under Dutch colonial rule during the eighteenth century. The basic pattern was one of incursion into San territory by Dutch-speaking pastoral farmers known as trekboers, San retaliation in the form of cattle raids and farm attacks, followed by colonial retribution by armed, mounted, state-sanctioned militia units known as commandos, as well as indiscriminate murder and massacre by farmers. Conflict intensified through the eighteenth century, with all-out war on the frontier for nearly three decades from about 1770 onwards. The chapter demonstrates both the exterminatory intent underlying settler violence as well as the complicity of a weak colonial state in these depredations, most clearly evident in its sanctioning of the root-and-branch eradication of the San in 1777. Whereas Dutch colonial violence against the San was exterminationist, British policies were eliminationist in that they sought to extinguish San society through assimilation, or 'civilising' in colonial parlance. Despite relatively benevolent British colonial policies from 1798 onwards, the San way of life within the Cape Colony was nevertheless extinguished during the course of the nineteenth century through incremental encroachment on their land, enforced labour incorporation and periodic massacre. This chapter holds that the near extermination of Cape San society constitutes genocide.

Next, Jared McDonald spotlights the much neglected topic of the experience of captured San children in the Cape Colony. One reason for this lack of attention has been that the evidence is sparse and scattered, but McDonald has done an excellent job of tracking down relevant sources. He contends that after San resistance had effectively been broken along the north-eastern frontier in the latter decades of the eighteenth century, an increasing number of San children were captured to satisfy the growing labour needs of the expanding European pastoral economy. McDonald concentrates on the trade in San children during the early decades of the nineteenth century and their forced assimilation into trekboer society— or 'taming' as it was known. McDonald interprets the process as one of culturecide, which he characterises as the eradication of the culture of victims who survive exterminatory violence, a practice integral to the genocidal process. Drawing on comparisons with Australian and Latin American examples during the same period, he demonstrates the importance of culturecide to San experience of genocide on the Cape's north-eastern frontier, especially after British occupation of the colony in 1806. The British introduced legislation to regulate the employment of Khoikhoi labourers and the treatment of slaves and their descendants, but tended to be silent on the San. In this context, 'tamed' San children had an ambiguous legal status exploited by commercial stock farmers who presented them as 'Hottentot' rather than 'Bushman' to gain tighter control over such workers. The capture and virtual enslavement of their children was fundamental to the obliteration of Cape hunter-gatherer identities and cultures.

In chapter Four, Edward Cavanagh examines the annihilation of San society in the Transorangia region at the hands of Griqua polities formed there in the early decades of the nineteenth century. By demonstrating that the struggle was fundamentally economic in nature, Cavanagh seeks to subvert the 'simplistic, colour-coded binary' that often informs studies of frontier conflict. As competition for resources between indigenous and colonial economic systems intensified along the southern African frontier during the early nineteenth century, it was not only trekboers, but also Bantu-speaking, Khoikhoi, 'Bastaard' and Griqua pastoralists that came into conflict with the San hunter-gatherers who raided their stock. Retributive campaigns against the San became commonplace and some of these offensives, notably on the part of the Griqua, were exterminatory in character. The chapter first outlines the nature and scale of the Griqua pastoral economy which by the 1820s had grown to become the envy of many competing settler farmers. Next it provides an account of the slaughter of the San communities in the Transorangia region between the 1820s and 1850s by commandos mobilised by the Griqua states, centred on Griquatown and Philippolis respectively. The diaries of missionaries and travellers, along with many pointed observations by *landdrost* (magistrate) Andries Stockenström reveal the degree to which Griqua commandos perpetrated exterminatory violence against the San. Concluding that this case constitutes genocide, Cavanagh cautions against racial reductionism that often informs studies of frontier conflict.

Robert Gordon's chapter, which focuses on the divergent experiences of two foraging communities in German South West Africa (GSWA), demonstrates that not all hunter-gatherer peoples were necessarily perceived in similar ways by colonisers. Contrasting perceptions could be of fundamental importance to their experience of colonisation, and indeed, even to their survival. Gordon points out that while the Namibian San, viewed as irredeemable outlaws of little value as workers, faced genocidal onslaught from the colonial establishment, another hunter-gatherer people, the Damara, did not, because they were viewed as useful labourers. What makes this comparison particularly tantalising is that it represents an inversion of pre-colonial perceptions in terms of which the San were valued as guides and for their hunting skills, whereas Damara were regarded as marauders who deserved to be exterminated. The German onslaught against the Namibian San came in the wake of the 1904–1908 genocidal wars against the Herero and Nama, when pastoral settlement moved into San territory north and north-east of Hereroland. Resistance to this invasion resulted in the colonial state and settlers embarking on a policy of *Ausrottung* (extermination) against Bushmen. After identifying several mutually reinforcing factors that fuelled the tendency for settler violence against indigenes, Gordon explains how an exaggerated emphasis on ceremonialism and on the letter of the law regulated and routinised relations of violence in the colony. He goes on to demonstrate how an excessive reliance on the dubious speculations of academics about the racial dispositions of indigenous peoples contributed to divergent perceptions of the San and Damara in early twentieth century GSWA.[38] Academic discourse presented the San as incorrigibly criminal and incapable of being 'civilised', and thus deserving of a final solution such as extermination or deportation, whereas Damara, though 'primitive', were portrayed as 'born servants, capable of continuous and challenging labour'. Gordon argues that it was in particular the San's supposed lack of any concept of property that singled them out for *Ausrottung* in colonial eyes. However much they maligned San labour, both the colonial state and settlers hunted and captured the San for use as workers on farms and in the copper mines. This genocide in the making was ended in 1915 when South African forces invaded Namibia as a result of the outbreak of the First World War.[39]

In an explicit counter example to the hypothesis that initially set this project in motion, Mathias Guenther shows that colonial relations between the San of the Ghanzi region in western Bechuanaland (present-day Botswana) and incoming white pastoral settlers in the late nineteenth and early twentieth centuries were largely peaceful, even cordial. Instead of genocidal conflict over resources as occurred in other parts of southern Africa, relations between Boer pastoral settlers and Bushman hunter-gatherers soon stabilised into patterns of patronage, with Boers as patrons and the San as labour-rendering clients. In their initial interactions, which included competition for resources, Boer and San transformed the potential

---

[38]   See Stone D. 2007. 'White men with low moral standards? German anthropology and the Herero genocide', in *Colonialism and Genocide*, eds A.D. Moses & D. Stone, for mutual influences between German anthropology and colonial experience in Namibia.

[39]   See Gordon R. 2009. 'Hiding in full view: the "forgotten" Bushman genocides of Namibia'. *Genocide Studies and Prevention*, 4, no. 1, 29–57.

for mass violence into forms of accommodation. Importantly, ecological and economic factors, including the aridity of the Ghanzi region and the isolation of the Boers, forced them to combine a foraging life style with their inchoately commercial cattle-ranching practices. Because hunter-gatherer bands occupied a different ecological niche to that of Boers, they were able to share Ghanziland with its aboriginal inhabitants. Firstly, extensive tracts of unfenced land between settler farms offered enough foragable foods to allow Bushmen to continue their traditional lifestyle. Secondly, the region was relatively rich in game and the Ghanzi Boers were not eradicatory in their hunting practices, leaving the San with a major source of sustenance largely intact. This, together with Boer need for San labour, and many San over time becoming dependent on Boers for food, allowed an opportunity for relations of clientship to develop. The potential for violence arising from both white supremacism and economic exploitation was mitigated by their similar lifestyles, and mutual obligations from their patron–client arrangement helped forge close emotional bonds between Boer and Bushman. With Boers living in Bushman-style wattle-and-daub huts, settler children being reared by San nannies, as well as farmers becoming fluent in San languages and developing extensive knowledge of San cultural practices, the potential for violence was dampened. Guenther, in addition, contends that a strong humanitarian impulse, stemming from both the missionary presence and oversight by the League of Nations, limited violent tendencies in the Bechuanaland Protectorate. The key factor explaining the exceptional outcome in Ghanziland was that although they had access to markets, the Ghanzi Boers, because of their isolation and the semi-desert environment, were more in the nature of subsistence pastoralists than capitalist ranchers.

Nigel Penn's chapter, which compares frontier conflict between hunter-gatherers and settler stock farmers at the Cape in the eighteenth and nineteenth centuries with that between hunter-gatherers and pastoralists in Australia, serves as a convenient transition between case studies in the two regions. On the one hand, because of his detailed coverage of the Cape's northern frontier, Penn provides a useful summation of developments in the annihilation of the Cape San. On the other, his general survey of the Australian situation fulfils the role of an introduction to the detailed regional Australian studies that follow. Penn sets out to explain why these frontiers were so violent and why the hunter-gatherer societies of both regions were virtually exterminated by pastoral settlers. The main similarity he discerns between the two is that both involved violent competition for environmental resources. Although the Cape frontier was one of Dutch colonial expansion in the eighteenth century, in the nineteenth century both the Cape and Australia were part of the British

Empire. The chapter attempts to explain why in both cases British authorities, despite humanitarian motives and policies, were powerless to stop the genocidal destruction of hunter-gatherer societies under their jurisdiction.

In chapter Eight, Lyndall Ryan compares the settler pastoral invasions of Tasmania (1817–1832) and Victoria (1835–1851), which in both cases led to the eradication of more than 80 per cent of their Aboriginal populations within 15 years. She challenges interpretations that consider the virtual extinction of Tasmanian Aborigines as an aberration, and the virtual disappearance of Aboriginal Victorians as the result of inadvertently introduced European diseases by pointing to the dire impact of pastoral land seizures on the Aboriginal populations of the two colonies. She also questions why it is that many historians accept Tasmania, but not Victoria, as an example of genocide. The chapter compares the various methods of land appropriation in the two colonies, their ties to the global economy, and colonial interaction with indigenous populations, dealings marked by racism, settler senses of entitlement and annihilatory violence. The pastoral invasion of Victoria was more rapid and violent than in Tasmania as these squatters were more experienced colonisers, more numerous, better resourced and better prepared for dealing with Aboriginal resistance. Importantly, rapid growth in the demand for pastoral products in the industrialising world at this time meant that larger fortunes were at stake. Ryan focuses in particular on the role of massacre in the decimation of Aboriginal populations in the two colonies, using a comparative statistical approach to reveal new aspects of the genocidal nature of these cases. She concludes that in Australia, when stock farmers invaded the lands of hunter-gatherers, genocide was a predictable outcome, except in instances where Aboriginal labour was needed, such as in the Northern Territory.

This is precisely the point of departure of Ann Curthoys' contribution on the fate of the Aboriginal peoples of Western Australia, where the labour of indigenous peoples was 'not merely useful but essential'. She compares the repercussions that employment in the pastoral, as opposed to the pearling, industry held for Aboriginal society to help tease out the implications demand for Aboriginal labour might hold for understanding the relationship between settler colonialism and genocide. She demonstrates that whereas the treatment of indigenous labour in pearling approximated that of genocide, that of the pastoral industry, though harsh, did not. Pearling involved a regimen of 'brutality and death ... [that] helped destroy certain groups and their relation to country ... [through] the destruction of emotional and family ties including the taking of children'. Pastoralism, on the other hand, although it 'relied on a powerful mix of dispossession and forced labour ... and significant amounts of ill treatment ... provided a space for some forms of cultural and physical survival'. Curthoys on this basis suggests the need to rethink the argument that settlers were interested only in appropriating land. In the extensive cattle farming regions of Western Australia, where imported and immigrant labour was scarce, colonists were more dependent on Aboriginal labour and had an interest in preserving this workforce. This was important not only for the survival of hunter-gatherer peoples, but is also significant for our understanding of the relationship between settler colonialism and genocide.

In chapter Ten, Tony Barta focuses on the dispossession of hunting peoples in a large section of the Great Plains north of Texas, known as 'Indian Territory', first by commercial stock farmers and later a deluge of settlers moving westward—what Edmund Burke anticipated as 'hordes of English Tartars ... a fierce and irresistible cavalry'. From the early nineteenth century, waves of stock-farming settlers in the region forced Indians off their land and into reserves. A period of coexistence ensued in which enterprising Indians were able to fashion a degree of autonomy for themselves by leasing reservation land to overstocked cattlemen. While the cattle industry destroyed traditional Indian society, it provided some opportunity to those prepared to move with the times. Barta argues that the invasion by stock farmers in this case was not genocidal in the sense of physically obliterating Indian societies, but rather that it displaced them to reserves and eliminated resistance to settler encroachment. Whatever promise this symbiotic relationship held was erased by the subsequent flood of immigration westward, mainly by homesteaders but also by all manner of refugees and fortune seekers from within the United States itself, and later in the century by even greater numbers of European immigrants. The westward surge intensified in the wake of the 1862 Homestead Act that allocated 160 acres of land to new settlers. The US government was complicit in the havoc that befell Native American society 'not by murder but by a ruthless policy of privatisation' of Indian reserves. In one of the clearest examples of explosive colonisation, smallholders came in sufficient numbers to complete the destruction of Indian society that the earlier incursion of stock farmers did not.

In the penultimate chapter, Sidney Harring argues that the demographic collapse experienced by Native American societies of the Canadian prairies, which were opened to white settlement in the late nineteenth and early twentieth centuries, constitutes genocide. Unlike the US frontier, the settlement of the Canadian west was more carefully regulated, with

Canadian First Nations removed to reserves after a series of numbered treaties were negotiated with them. This land was then sold to settlers, initially mainly stockmen who later turned to crop and mixed farming. The reserves, predictably, were overcrowded and poverty stricken. They were completely unsuited to the kind of agriculture that was expected to sustain these populations and eventually result in their acculturation to Canadian society. Any possibility of continuing the hunting life of old ended with the obliteration of the buffalo herds by the late 1880s. Hunger, alcoholism, disease, depression and generally poor living conditions on reserves led to the Plains Indian population being reduced by half between 1870 and 1900. Harring explains that although direct killing of Indians was limited, the annihilation of Native American society nonetheless constitutes genocide in terms of the UNCG definition. While forced cultural assimilation, or ethnocide, was the stated objective of Canadian policy, it was the government's failure—and later its refusal—to act when Indians started starving on reserves that makes it guilty of genocide. Surviving Indian peoples tried various ways of adaptating to their dispossession, but under the 1876 Indian Act and subsequent amendments, were relegated to an inferior status that kept them on the fringes of prairie society. These structures of subordination have been maintained through to the present, marginalising Native American peoples.

Finally, Lorenzo Veracini's contribution serves both as a conclusionary chapter as well as to provide theoretical reflection on the main theme of the book by drawing together many of its diverse strands in the development of its argument. Veracini regards settler colonialism as consisting of two inter-related transfers. Firstly, colonists physically occupy indigenous land and transfer to it an attachment as their new home, thereby becoming settlers rather than being mere sojourners or migrants. Secondly, to gain exclusive control of its resources, indigenous peoples are physically coerced or transferred from the land. The colonised are also discursively detached from the land in a variety of ways to help legitimate settler claims. Hunter-gatherer communities are particularly vulnerable to both forms of transfer as they are sparsely settled, militarily susceptible to attack and lead migratory lifestyles. This fragility is compounded by the specific nature of stock farming, especially when hunter-gatherer labour is not needed by the colonial economy. Veracini argues that a crucial part of consolidating settler claims to the land is the discursive indigenisation of settlers and the concomitant nomadisation of indigenes. By presenting settlers as inherently sedentary, and indigenes, especially hunter-gatherers, as 'pathologically mobile', settler colonial societies globally sought to legitimate their dispossession and, where necessary, their extermination of indigenous peoples.[40]

Conclusion

While there have clearly been many other contributors to mass violence between hunter-gatherer peoples and invading commercial stock farmers, the cumulative effect of the six fundamental factors identified here go a long way towards explaining why, in sustained clashes between these two groups, exterminatory violence was not so much an aberration as normative.

A factor inherent to situations of commercial stock farmers occupying the domains of hunter-gatherers not addressed directly, but implicit in much of the discussion so far, is the nature of settler colonialism itself. Unlike other forms of colonial domination, settler colonialism is much more focused on the permanent confiscation of land and seizure of resources, and therefore on the complete dispossession of indigenous peoples within those areas that settlers claim for themselves. Settler colonial situations are therefore much more prone to mass violence towards indigenous peoples, as well as to violent indigenous resistance to the occupation of their land. Hunter-gatherer communities who resisted settler encroachment have, in addition, been more susceptible to exterminatory violence than other forms of indigenous society. They were despised as the most 'primitive' of peoples, their way of life an anachronism destined for extinction, and sometimes even seen as deserving of that fate. Their sparse populations made extermination more thinkable to interlopers who sought permanent solutions to the 'problem' of indigenous resistance, and their nomadic lifestyle invited settler justification for their dispossession on the basis that they did not really own the land and could not lay legitimate claim to it. In cases where their labour was superfluous to the needs of the colonial economy, foraging peoples were particularly susceptible to extirpatory campaigns. The situation was accentuated in the pastoral industry which had relatively low labour requirements, needing a small, dispersed labour force with skills that foragers had to be taught, and that colonisers often considered them incapable of learning. In other instances, although settlers disparaged hunter-gatherer labour as unsuited to their requirements, they nonetheless made extensive use of such workers, usually captives, or people in one or other way coerced into working for farmers.

---

40 See Brody, *Other Side of Eden*, 152–53; Day D. 2008. *Conquest: How Societies Overwhelm Others*. Oxford: Oxford University Press, 77, 161–62, 165; Docker, *Origins of Violence*, 34–36.

These arguments are not meant to suggest that settler colonialism is inherently genocidal as has sometimes been claimed, and as Lemkin seemed to imply,[41] but that it tends to be particularly violent. It is also not suggested that settler colonialism is inherently genocidal towards hunter-gatherer peoples, but that in cases where commercial stock farmers invaded the lands of foraging societies it was generally so. The inclusion in this volume of several examples that challenge absolute claims in this regard is an unequivocal indication of this. In the clearest of these cases, Ghanziland, there is no question of genocide having been perpetrated, essentially because the market for settler produce was so small and their profit motive so attenuated that its pastoral economy was closer to a traditional than capitalist mode of production. Although Guenther presents a counter example to the general pattern outlined in this book, it confirms a key contention of the project, namely, that it is the extent of access to capitalist markets and the operation of a profit motive that are the key drivers of mass violence in these cases.[42] In partial counter examples, Gordon shows how one section of the hunter-gatherer population in German South West Africa was targeted for genocidal persecution, while another was not; and Curthoys demonstrates how one sector of the West Australian economy, pearling, was genocidal in its impact while stock farming was not. Tony Barta, in addition, argues that the process of destruction started by commercial stock farmers was devastating to Indian societies, but not genocidal, their ultimate shattering accomplished by the subsequent invasion of large numbers of homesteaders. The key question is for how long the symbiosis between cattlemen and Indians could have continued. My guess is not for very long. Given time, ranchers were likely to have dispossessed Indians as completely as their Canadian counterparts were busy doing.

---

[41]   Lemkin R. 1944. *Axis Rule in Occupied Europe: Laws of Occupation, Analysis of Government, Proposals for Redress*. New York: Columbia University Press, xi, 79–80; Docker J. 2008. 'Are settler colonies inherently genocidal? Rereading Lemkin', in *Empire, Colony, Genocide*, ed. A.D. Moses, 97; Moses A.D. 'Genocide and settler society in Australian history', in Moses, *Genocide and Settler Society*, 27; Finzsch N. 2008. '"The Aborigines … were never annihilated, and still they are becoming extinct": settler imperialism and genocide in nineteenth-century America and Australia', in *Empire, Colony, Genocide*, ed. A.D. Moses, 253.

[42]   In addition to his chapter in this collection, see Guenther M. 1993. '"Independent, fearless and rather bold": a historical narrative on the Ghanzi Bushmen of Botswana'. *Journal of the Namibian Scientific Society*, 44, 25–40; Guenther M. 2002 'Independence, resistance, accommodation, persistence: hunter-gatherers and agro-pastoralists in the Ghanzi veld, early 1800s to late 1900s', in *Ethnicity, Hunter-Gatherers and the 'Other': Association or Assimilation in Africa*, ed. S. Kent. Washington: Smithsonian Institution Press, 87–104.

The international market for pastoral commodities was the main driver of conflict between hunter-gatherers and commercial stock farmers, and the level of demand for these products the main determinant of the intensity of hostilities. It was *ultimately* this market's ability to absorb large quantities of merchandise and create the prospect of substantial wealth for producers that helped spur immigration to colonies, and that propelled stock farmers into the lands of indigenous peoples. This was what stoked ruthlessly exploitative attitudes to land and labour, a sense of entitlement to resources among settlers, and a determination that nothing would stand in their way of creating personal prosperity.[43] The most significant *proximate* factor giving impetus to genocidal violence in settler colonies was indigenous resistance. It was this threat to their subsistence, personal ambitions and at times to the colonial enterprise as a whole, that precipitated exterminatory attitudes, actions and policies within the settler establishment. It is not surprising that settlers reacted with extreme hostility, and in concert, when they perceived their lives and livelihoods to be at risk. It was equally predictable that colonial and metropolitan governments would support the settler cause or allow violence they instigated to take its course when the economy suffered or the colonial project itself was under threat. It was the settler population rather than the colonial state that tended to be the main perpetrators of violence when commercial stock farmers overran the territories of hunter-gathering peoples, as these states tended to be weak, were often hampered by metropolitan constraints, and because the initiative in frontier regions generally lay with settlers. Although these were civilian-driven rather than 'state-led' genocides,[44] there were significant degrees of state collusion in such violence, even where policy makers were repelled by settler aggression. The degree of state collusion in such violence was by and large dependent on the degree of settler control of the state.

The preceding analysis, and the volume as a whole, attempts to demonstrate that where pastoralists producing for capitalist markets invaded the territories of hunter-gatherers, the global economic system tended to bring together the practices of metropolitan and colonial governments, the interests of providers of capital and consumers of commodities, and the agency of colonial actors ranging from governors to graziers in remote

---

[43] In a survey of American genocides, Alfred Cave, in my opinion, correctly concludes that 'Native American groups, which for one reason or another, could not be integrated into the colonial economy were the most likely to be the earliest victims of genocide'. See Cave A. 2008. 'Genocide in the Americas', in *Historiography of Genocide*, ed. D. Stone.

[44] See Palmer, *Colonial Genocide*, 3, 199; Levene, *Rise of the West*, 95.

outposts in ways that almost invariably fostered exterminatory violence towards those peoples whose territories they overran.[45] The fate of the Cape San, Australian Aborigines, as well as hunter-gatherer peoples who once inhabited substantial swathes of the Americas, testifies to this.[46]

---

[45]   Wolfe P. 2008. 'Structure and event: settler colonialism, time and the question of genocide', in Moses, *Empire, Colony, Genocide*, 104.

[46]   The broad thesis of this volume certainly applies to Latin America and other parts of the world. Unfortunately, two commissioned case studies, one on the Pampa-Patagonia region and one on Tierra del Fuego, did not materialise. Illness robbed this collection of a study on Queensland, while a comparison of Zimbabwean and Kenyan experiences did not come to fruition either. Attempts at securing Asian case studies came to nought.

Chapter Two

'The Bushman is a Wild Animal to be Shot at Sight': Annihilation of the Cape Colony's Foraging Societies by Stock-Farming Settlers in the Eighteenth and Nineteenth Centuries[1]

Mohamed Adhikari
University of Cape Town

In 1998 David Kruiper, the leader of the ≠Khomani San people who today live in the Kalahari Desert in the furthest reaches of South Africa's Northern Cape province, lamented of his people: 'We have been made into nothing'.[2]

The ≠Khomani San are a tiny remnant of the foraging communities that once inhabited most of the area that currently constitutes South Africa. Whereas Kruiper was voicing his concern about the marginalisation of the ≠Khomani San in post-apartheid South Africa, his judgement applies even more literally to the fate of hunter-gatherer societies of the Cape Colony that were destroyed by the impact of European colonialism during the eighteenth and nineteenth centuries. Much of the dispossession and slaughter happened in the eighteenth century along the northern and north-eastern frontiers under Dutch East India Company (DEIC, also VOC for its Dutch title, the *Verenigde Ooste-Indische Compagnie*) rule, with continued displacement and killing under the relatively benign auspices of British imperialism through the nineteenth century. The main agents of destruction were Dutch-speaking pastoralists whose murderous land-grabbing and ecologically damaging farming practices ensured the virtual extermination of the Cape San peoples.

The terms 'San' and 'Bushman' are used to refer to the hunter-gatherer peoples of southern Africa who were the earliest human inhabitants of the

---

[1] This chapter is a condensed version of Adhikari M. 2010. *The Anatomy of a South African Genocide: The Extermination of the Cape San Peoples*. Cape Town: UCT Press.

[2] Crwys-Williams J. comp. 1999. *Penguin Dictionary of South African Quotations*. Sandton: Penguin, 62.

region. They lived in small, loosely knit, family-based bands of usually between 10 and 20 people. These groups were sometimes as small as five or six, or as large as 30, but hardly ever exceeded 50 members. At the start of European colonisation, their number in what was to become the Cape Colony was in all probability no more than 50 000. Individual bands roamed within a defined territory determined usually by the availability of water, following game and harvesting seasonally available plant foods. While a variety of edible plants formed the mainstay of their diet, game was crucial to the welfare of the San. Smaller animals were snared while larger ones, most typically buck, were shot with poison-tipped arrows. Spears and clubs were also used. There was a fairly clear-cut gendered division of labour in San society in that men were hunters and women did most of the gathering. In coastal and riverine environments, fish and shellfish complemented their diet. They also gathered fruit, berries, honey and insects such as locusts, caterpillars and termite larvae. Anthropologist Alan Barnard indicates that the San had 'a traditional knowledge ... of several hundreds of different species of plants, as well as their seasonal locations, their ecological associations with other species, and how to prepare them as foods or medicines. They may [have known] a hundred species of animal as well, their migration patterns, their social behaviours and psychologies, ... [and] their life cycles'.[3]

The San were not culturally homogeneous. Apart from regional variations in social customs, cosmology, rock art styles and material culture, they spoke a wide variety of languages, many of which were mutually unintelligible. Although they shared a similar mode of subsistence, San economies differed considerably depending on the natural environment, and changed as groups moved from one ecological zone to another. They lived in makeshift shelters or in caves and used a range of stone and bone tools fashioned to serve as arrow heads, knives, axes, harpoons, scrapers, needles and other implements. The San are probably best known for their exquisite paintings on cave walls and rock faces.

---

[3]   Hewitt R. 2008. *Structure, Meaning and Ritual in Narratives of the Southern San.* Johannesburg: Witwatersrand University Press, 14–26; Smith A., Malherbe C., Guenther M. & Berens P. 2000. *The Bushmen of Southern Africa: A Foraging Society in Transition.* Cape Town: David Philip, 5–9; Tobias P. ed. 1978. *The Bushmen: San Hunters and Herders of Southern Africa.* Cape Town: Human & Rousseau, chs 2–3; Barnard A. 1992. *Hunters and Herders of Southern Africa: A Comparative Ethnography of Khoisan Peoples.* Cambridge: Cambridge University Press, ch. 1.

They had names for hunting bands and for larger cultural and linguistic groupings, but not for hunter-gatherers generally. Anthropologist Mathias Guenther stresses that the 'key features of Bushman society, its organization, and its institutions and ethos [were] flexibility, adaptability and diversity, fluidity and amorphousness, ambivalence and ambiguity'. This versatility was necessary for the effective exploitation of migratory game and unevenly distributed plant food supplies that resulted from localised and unpredictable rainfall patterns.[4] Thus, although the concept of San is in one sense a colonial construct and an invented social category, specialist foraging communities did share a distinctive economy and way of life as opposed to pastoralists and cultivators.[5]

The labels 'San' and 'Bushman' are controversial because they are pejorative and their meanings contested. There is a good deal of confusion in the historical record itself about the identities of indigenous peoples and the names applied to them. 'Bushman' is ambiguous because it was used by colonists to describe hunter-gatherer communities as well as pastoralist Khoikhoi peoples (Hottentots) who had lost their cattle or, indeed, anyone, including runaway slaves, renegades and destitute colonists who resorted to foraging. Often colonists did not, or were unable to, distinguish between the San and Khoikhoi without stock, and at times it was in their interest to conflate the two. There was a degree of mixing and inter-marriage between the San and other indigenous peoples, and they were known to be taken up as clients by Khoikhoi. Sometimes dispossessed Khoikhoi joined hunter-gatherer communities or resisted colonial encroachment in alliance with them. In such cases, the use of 'Khoisan' makes eminent sense. Because 'Bushman' has historically been a highly pejorative term in the South African context, scholars from the 1960s started using 'San' as an alternative. But this term is also problematic because it is a disparaging Khoikhoi designation applied to hunter-gatherers. In recent years, some scholars have reverted to the use of 'Bushman' because existing San communities often prefer this name. I favour 'San' because it is not gendered, less pejorative, less ambiguous in denoting aboriginal hunter-gatherer

4   Guenther M. 1999. *Tricksters and Trancers: Bushman Religion and Society*. Bloomington: Indiana University Press, 13, 26.
5   Wilmsen E. 1996. 'Decolonising the mind: steps toward cleansing the Bushman stain from southern African history', in *Miscast: Negotiating the Presence of the Bushmen*, ed. P. Skotnes. Cape Town: UCT Press, 185–90; Jolly P. 1996. 'Between the lines: some remarks on "Bushman" ethnicity', in *Miscast*, ed. P. Skotnes, 197–210; Smith et al, *Bushmen*, 14–15; Lewis-Williams D. & Pearce D. 2004. *San Spirituality: Roots, Expressions and Social Consequences*. Cape Town: Double Storey, 209–21.

peoples, and currently is the term most widely accepted by leaders and organisations representing the San people.[6]

Colonial expansion through the eighteenth century

By the start of European colonisation, the San had largely been displaced to drier, more rugged interior areas by Khoikhoi pastoralists and Bantu-speaking cultivators, both of whom had migrated into the region about two thousand years ago. The first European colonial settlement in southern Africa came in 1652 when the DEIC set up a refreshment station at Table Bay. The colony soon started spreading because the VOC in 1657 decided that allowing independent farmers to work the land was the most expeditious way of meeting its need for agricultural produce. The opening of an agrarian frontier, together with natural population increase and immigration, ensured the expansion of colonial frontiers. By the end of the 1670s, the indigenous peoples of the Cape Peninsula and the immediate interior, mainly Khoikhoi herders, were subjugated and dispossessed of their land and livestock. This opened the way for the settlement of the fertile Stellenbosch and Paarl districts, as well as the Swartland area encompassed by the Berg River. It took roughly half a century for most of the arable south-western Cape to be occupied by European farmers.

From the early eighteenth century, Dutch-speaking, semi-nomadic pastoralists known as trekboers rapidly infiltrated the dry Cape interior, the greater part of which was only suitable for transhumant pastoralism. Population growth and a lack of economic opportunity in the more settled areas fuelled this expansion. From 1714, the VOC started issuing grazing rights to extensive 6 000-acre farms beyond the arable freehold areas in return for an annual rental. This was the origin of the Cape's loan farm system, a form of leasehold which had the effect of accelerating movement into the interior and dispersing the population into tiny isolated groupings across the landscape. 'Trekboer', which means 'migrant farmer' in Dutch, refers to the need for these pastoralists to move around with their flocks and herds in

---

6   See, among others, Gordon R. & Douglas S. 2000. *The Bushman Myth: The Making of a Namibian Underclass.* Boulder: Westview Press, 4–6; Guenther M. 1986. '"San" or "Bushmen?"', in *The Past and Future of !Kung Ethnography: Critical Reflections and Symbolic Perspectives,* eds M. Biesele, R. Gordon & R. Lee. Hamburg: Helmut Buske Verlag, 27–33; Wright J. 1996. 'Sonqua, Bosjesmans, Bushmen, abaThwa: comments and queries on pre-modern identifications'. *South African Historical Journal,* 35, 16–29; Hitchcock R., Ikheya K., Biesele M. & Lee R. eds. 2006. *Updating the San: Image and Reality of an African People in the 21st Century.* Osaka: National Museum of Ethnology, 4–6; Barnard, *Anthropology and Bushmen,* 5–16, 138–40; Wilmsen E. 1989. *Land Filled With Flies.* Chicago: University of Chicago Press, xv, 27–30.

search of seasonally available grazing and water, using their loan farms as a base. Several families might share a loan farm to reduce costs and for greater security. The poorest stockmen tended to live wayfaring lives out of tented wagons, looking for grazing and hopeful of finding a place to settle. Even the more prosperous farmers with well-watered loan farms needed to engage in a degree of transhumance. Hardy and resourceful, but vulnerable because of their isolation, trekboers were generally ruthless in their appropriation of natural resources and their treatment of indigenous peoples.[7]

The decision by the DEIC government in 1700 to lift its ban on livestock trading between colonists and Khoikhoi was not only a major impetus for expansion into the interior, but also for violence against indigenous peoples. This policy change and the resultant push into the hinterland held dire consequences for the pastoralist Khoikhoi peoples occupying the winter rainfall area of the south-western Cape and even those further north in Namaqualand. Freebooting settlers saw this as an opportunity to enrich themselves and set up as stock farmers. Within a few years most Khoikhoi in the region were stripped of their herds by marauding gangs of colonial raiders spreading murder and mayhem. Independent Khoikhoi society in the region had effectively been destroyed by the time the VOC re-introduced the prohibition on livestock trading in 1725.[8]

Their land occupied and cattle seized by Dutch-speaking interlopers, Khoikhoi society along the frontier zone rapidly disintegrated. Some dispossessed Khoikhoi resorted to hunter-gathering, while others migrated beyond the frontier. A number became stock raiders, sometimes in collaboration with the San. Epidemics, in particular the smallpox outbreak of 1713, took a huge toll on Khoikhoi society. Importantly, many Khoikhoi were also taken up as workers by farmers. Their labour was valued by trekboers because Khoikhoi had intimate knowledge of the natural environment and were skilled at animal husbandry. Useful also as hunters, trackers and guides, some became trusted servants. While it initially often suited destitute Khoikhoi to work for farmers in return for part payment

---

[7] Guelke L. 1984. 'Land tenure and settlement at the Cape, 1652–1812', in *History of Surveying and Land Tenure in South Africa*, eds C. Martin & K. Friedlander. Cape Town: University of Cape Town, 18–24; Guelke L. 1989. 'Freehold farmers and frontier settlers, 1657–1780', in *The Shaping of South African Society*, eds R. Elphick & H. Giliomee. Cape Town: Maskew Miller Longman, 84–94; Elphick R. & Malherbe V. 1989. 'The Khoisan to 1828', in *Shaping*, eds R. Elphick & H. Giliomee, 11–18; Giliomee H. 2003. *The Afrikaners: Biography of a People*. Cape Town: Tafelberg, 21, 31–32.

[8] Penn N. 2005. *The Forgotten Frontier: Colonist and Khoisan on the Cape's Northern Frontier in the Eighteenth Century*. Cape Town: Double Storey, 38–41, 54; Mostert N. 1992. *Frontiers: The Epic of South Africa's Creation and the Tragedy of the Xhosa People*. London: Pimlico, 171.

in livestock—just as it suited farmers to pay such servants in kind—their status deteriorated through the course of the eighteenth century. As options for leading an independent lifestyle diminished for Khoikhoi, so farmers were able to assert greater control over such workers by paying subsistence wages, denying them the right to keep stock, confiscating their animals and retaining children so as to tie parents to the farm. By the end of the century, most Khoikhoi in the employ of farmers were in effect forced labourers little better off than serfs.[9]

As they moved beyond the cultivable south-western Cape from about 1700 onwards, colonists started coming into growing conflict with hunter-gatherer peoples. The dynamic behind the confrontation with the San tended to be different to that with Khoikhoi. Whereas traditional Khoikhoi society crumbled in the face of colonial conflict, the San society proved to be much more resilient. The basic reason for this is clear enough. The Khoikhoi's pastoralist way of life was fragile when faced with the superior military force at the disposal of trekboers and was relatively easily undermined by stock raids or by depriving them of access to grazing or water. San bands were by comparison hardy and adaptable, being much more mobile and able to live off the land. Their being dispersed in isolated groups across an extensive and rugged terrain made it considerably more difficult for sparsely spread colonists to subjugate the San.[10]

Although these farmers did participate in the international capitalist economy by supplying meat and products such as soap, butter, hides and tallow to passing VOC fleets and the settlement at Cape Town, the trekboer economy was not principally driven by market forces, but by subsistence considerations. Because VOC demand for meat was limited, prices were set at levels favouring the company, and the environment was harsh, trekboers were not so much commercial ranchers motivated by profit than pastoralists with access to a substantial market through which they could dispense of surplus and procure the goods and services on which their way of life depended. Wagons, guns, ammunition and an array of tools and household goods were their main requirements. Frontier farmers were particularly dependent on contact with Cape Town for guns and ammunition, without

---

9   Elphick R. 1985. *Khoikhoi and the Founding of White South Africa*. Johannesburg: Ravan Press, 151–239; Elphick & Malherbe, 'Khoisan to 1828', 18–53; Elphick R. & Giliomee H. 1989. 'The origins and entrenchment of European dominance at the Cape, 1652–1840', in *Shaping*, eds R. Elphick & H. Giliomee, 529–37, 546–52.
10   Guelke L. & Shell R. 1992. 'Landscape of conquest: frontier water alienation and Khoikhoi strategies of survival, 1652–1780'. *Journal of Southern African Studies*, 18, no. 4, 820–22; Elphick, *Khoikhoi*, 170–74; Smith A. 1991. 'On becoming herders: Khoikhoi and San ethnicity in southern Africa'. *African Studies*, 50, no. 1, 51–52.

which they would not have been able to hunt, defend themselves or take the offensive against indigenous peoples. The absence of an overriding profit motive, however, did little to mitigate the ultimate fate of hunter-gatherer peoples on the Cape frontier as trekboer demographic growth and growing VOC demand for meat through the eighteenth century ensured colonial expansion into the interior and the destruction of indigenous societies. The dynamic behind the violence between trekboer and San thus had less to do with a voracious international market for meat than with the far older, more pervasive displacement and destruction of hunter-gatherer societies by farming communities.[11]

Because of the limited water resources of the Cape interior and the nature of transhumant pastoralism, the trekboer economy was expansive and a relatively small trekboer population appropriated large swathes of land. With a growing number of colonists entering the interior as farmers through the eighteenth century, and as the sons of trekboers set themselves up as independent stockmen, there was intensifying pressure on resources and a continuous drive to find new pastures. Trekboers, though thin on the ground—with no more than about 600 independent stockholders by 1770 and perhaps 1 000 by the end of the eighteenth century—were nevertheless able to control extensive tracts of land. Their superior military technology allowed them to take possession of scarce permanent water supplies, which in turn gave them dominion over the surrounding grazing. By establishing their farms around perennial springs and water holes in the parched landscape and being able to defend their occupation of these strategic nodes, trekboers were able to exercise power over an area of land incommensurate to their numbers and had a disproportionate impact on the lives of indigenous peoples.[12]

From 1700 onwards, settlers started moving across the Berg River into the Tulbagh basin about 100 kilometres from Cape Town. Here they encountered resistance, both from dispossessed Khoikhoi as well as from San stock raiders. By the early 1710s, pastoral farmers were migrating

---

[11]   Brody H. 2000. *The Other Side of Eden: Hunters, Farmers and the Shaping of the World.* New York: North Point Press, 6–7, 143–50; Newton-King S. 1999. *Masters and Servants on the Cape Eastern Frontier, 1760–1803.* Cambridge: Cambridge University Press, 20–25, 150–209; Mitchell L. 2009. *Belongings: Property, Family, and Identity in Colonial South Africa (An Exploration of Frontiers 1725–c.1830).* New York: Columbia University Press, 75–76, 90–91; Giliomee, *Afrikaners,* 33–34.

[12]   Ross R. 1989. 'The Cape of Good Hope and the world economy, 1652–1835', in *Shaping,* eds R. Elphick & H. Giliomee, 85; Ross R. 1994. 'The "white" population of the Cape Colony in the eighteenth century', in *Beyond the Pale: Essays on the History of Colonial South Africa,* ed. R. Ross. Johannesburg: Witwatersrand University Press, 127; Guelke & Shell, 'Landscape of conquest', 803–05, 816, 824.

northwards into the Olifants River valley and beyond that into the Bokkeveld across the Cedarberg mountains. The intrusion of trekboers into this region provoked concerted Khoisan resistance and it was not until 1739 that this frontier zone was closed when a series of major military campaigns by frontier farmers, organised by the VOC government, quelled indigenous opposition. From about 1740, the frontier advanced rapidly as trekboers started moving north and east of the Bokkeveld Mountains and beyond the Olifants River valley into the harsher environment of the escarpment formed by the Hantam, Roggeveld, Nieuweveld and Sneeuberg mountains. The escarpment marked the transition between the narrow coastal plains and the open expanses of the interior plateau as well as between the winter and summer rainfall areas. Farmers needed to be even more mobile in this environmental zone to exploit both summer and winter grazing to obtain year-round nourishment for their stock.[13]

Across the escarpment lay the Cape thirstland, an uninviting prospect for both San and frontier farmer. Over the next three decades, a growing number of trekboers established loan farms along the escarpment in the face of sporadic but intensifying resistance from the San and Khoikhoi refugees not prepared to retreat into the arid reaches of the Great Karoo and Bushmanland. By the late 1760s, pressure on resources reached critical levels, initiating sustained and coordinated Khoisan insurgency and guerrilla attacks against settlers along the length and breadth of the frontier. During the last three decades of the eighteenth century, a combination of ecological barriers and San resistance halted settler advances along the northern and north-eastern perimeters of the colony and in places even rolled it back. The stalling of the pastoral frontier precipitated a major crisis for trekboer society, which depended on continuous expansion to accommodate demographic growth. During this period trekboers, with the help of the VOC government, embarked on an exterminatory military offensive against the San.[14]

---

[13]   Van der Merwe P.J. 1937. *Die Noordwaardse Beweging van die Boere Voor die Groot Trek, 1770–1842*. The Hague: W.P. van Stockum, 1–10; Penn, *Forgotten Frontier*, 19–22.

[14]   Van der Merwe, *Noordwaardse Beweging*, ch. 2; Van der Merwe P.J. 1938. *Die Trekboer in die Geskiedenis van die Kaapkolonie*. Cape Town: Nasionale Pers, ch. 3; Newton-King, *Masters and Servants*, chs 4–6; Penn, *Forgotten Frontier*, ch. 4; Marks S. 1972. 'Khoisan resistance to the Dutch in the seventeenth and eighteenth centuries'. *Journal of African History*, 13, no. 1, 73–74.

The dynamic of frontier conflict between San and trekboer under VOC rule

Trekboers severely disrupted the lives of foraging communities that had been living in the Cape interior for thousands of years. San and trekboer were bound to clash because they were in direct competition for the same environmental resources, namely, water, game, grazing and access to land. San bands suddenly found that they were denied access to traditional watering places by trekboers who occupied springs and water-holes. Trekboer livestock muddied and contaminated water supplies, and destroyed plants on which the San subsisted. Overgrazing damaged and, in many areas, permanently changed the ecology. Colonists decimated herds of game, a primary source of food for the San, with their firearms and their stock consumed the grazing on which these animals fed. Trekboer hunting practices were extremely destructive for they not only shot game for sport, but destroyed herds of buck to make *biltong*, dried, salted strips of meat that became a staple of the frontier diet and was also sold in Cape Town. Because game usually followed a similar migratory pattern to that necessary for pastoralism, San and trekboer frequently competed for the same seasonal resources and habitations. The scarcity of game and the deterioration of the environment often gave the hungry San little option but to raid trekboer livestock. Trekboer destructiveness went beyond damaging the subsistence base of the San because the landscape, fundamental to San spirituality, was being desecrated and species of game, in particular eland, which were central to San belief systems, were being eradicated. The trekboer presence thus put San communities under enormous stress.[15]

During the eighteenth century, San responded to trekboer intrusion in one of two ways. The first was to withdraw. This was not an attractive option as it inevitably meant moving to more marginal and inhospitable terrain and perhaps encroaching on another, usually hostile, group's territory. There was little unoccupied land in the Cape interior except for that which was

---

[15] Sparrman A. 1975–77. *A Voyage to the Cape of Good Hope Towards the Antarctic Polar Circle Around the World and to the Country of the Hottentots and the Caffres from the Year 1772–1776*, ed. V.S. Forbes. Cape Town: Van Riebeeck Society, first published London: G.G. & J. Robinson, 1785–86, vol. 1, 238–39; vol. 2, 60; Thunberg C.P. 1986. *Travels at the Cape of Good Hope, 1772–1775*, ed. V.S. Forbes. Cape Town: Van Riebeeck Society, first published London: W. Richardson, 1793–95, 94, 197; Lichtenstein H. 1928, 1930. *Travels in Southern Africa in the Years 1803, 1804, 1805, 1806*, trans. by A. Plumptre. Cape Town: Van Riebeeck Society, first published London: Henry Colburn, 1812–15, vol. 1, 120–21; Neville D. 1996. 'European impacts on the the Seacow River valley and its hunter-gatherer inhabitants'. MA thesis, University of Cape Town, chs 4–5, 252–56; Newton-King, *Masters and Servants*, 97–101.

barely habitable. Antagonistic neighbours might include other San bands, Bantu-speaking peoples such as the Xhosa towards the east and Tswana in the north-east, or other pastoralist groups such as Khoikhoi, Griqua or Korana towards the north and along the Orange River. As with all hunter-gatherers, the San had a deeply spiritual connection to their territories and to particular features in the landscape and would abandon their domains only as a last resort. While on the one hand, colonial invasion resulted in a degree of cooperation among indigenous peoples against a common enemy, on the other, it also gave rise to intensified conflict between them as groups were displaced and pressure on resources mounted. There is evidence that the time-honoured tradition of reciprocity whereby San groups allowed other bands access to their territory in times of need, broke down as a result of the stresses brought about by settler land seizures.[16]

A second, increasingly more common reaction was for the San to resist trekboer encroachment. This included raiding or killing trekboer stock, slaying herders, destroying crops and attacking farmsteads which were sometimes burnt down. Not content with killing the enemy, San raiders might torture or mutilate victims, mainly Khoikhoi herdsmen. The San usually attacked at night, striking where trekboers were most vulnerable, their herds. Stock raiders under pressure from pursuing farmers usually maimed or killed the animals to deny them to their foes. The motives for these offensives generally went beyond plundering stock. They were also intended to drive trekboers from the land. These attacks were at first sporadic and small scale, but became ever more frequent and coordinated through the eighteenth century.[17]

It is apparent that through the eighteenth century San bands increasingly coalesced to fight off colonial intrusion and that they were often joined by dispossessed Khoikhoi. These larger attacking parties drew on kinship and cultural ties to mobilise against a mortal threat to their way of life. Although San bands, because of their small size and egalitarian structure, did not have hereditary chiefs, they must have developed some form of temporary collective leadership to coordinate joint resistance. Khoisan raiding gangs that attacked farms and rustled cattle were sometimes several hundred strong, especially in the latter decades of the eighteenth

16   Smith et al, *Bushmen*, 44; Lewis-Williams & Pierce, *San Spirituality*, 51–53; Penn N. 1996. '"Fated to perish": the destruction of the Cape San', in *Miscast*, ed. P. Skotnes, 88, 91.

17   Szalay M. 1995. *The San and the Colonization of the Cape, 1770–1879: Conflict, Incorporation, Acculturation*. Köln: Rüdiger Köppe Verlag, 17–18; Penn, *Forgotten Frontier*, ch. 3; Van der Merwe, *Noordwaardse Beweging*, 10–12; Green L. *Karoo*. 1955. Cape Town: Howard Timmins, 31; Mostert, *Frontiers*, 220–21.

century. There was also a degree of collaboration between San attackers and farm servants, many of whom were captives or coerced into working for farmers. Increasingly Khoisan deserters stole guns, lead shot, powder and even horses where the opportunity presented itself. In some cases it was farm servants who instigated attacks or acts of sabotage. Masters' fear of betrayal goes a long way towards explaining their pervasive cruelty towards servants and why desertion was so severely punished.[18]

, Colonists responded to San attacks with individual acts of slaughter and massacre of bands. They also organised retaliatory raids by armed, mounted militia units known as commandos. Beyond the limited reach of the VOC garrison in Cape Town, the commando was the main institution of military force at the Cape under Dutch rule and the main instrument of war against indigenous peoples. Whereas initially commandos were organised by the DEIC and consisted of company soldiers and servants as well as colonists, by 1715, officially sanctioned commandos consisting entirely of colonists and their dependents, and led by frontier farmers, were being formed. The institution evolved through the eighteenth century to meet the military needs of trekboer society.[19]

Commandos mobilised men between the ages of 16 and 60. Members were organised by district, elected their own officers and were required to attend annual drills. These militias mounted state-sanctioned, punitive expeditions led by *veldwachtmeesters* (field sergeants), officials who represented the government at local level. *Veldwachtmeesters*, usually the VOC government's only agents in outlying districts, were themselves frontier farmers. They were appointed by, and answerable to, the *landdrost*, the chief administrator of the district, who was far removed from the frontier. *Veldwachtmeesters* thus had a good deal of freedom to act and often did so in their own interests. They had the authority to raise commandos on their own and only needed to report their activities to the *landdrost* afterwards. The VOC government provided commandos with powder and shot, and gave instructions regarding its aims and conduct. Instructions were often cursory and ignored by commandos. In addition to its principal

---

18 Stow G. 1964. *The Native Races of South Africa: A History of the Intrusion of the Hottentots and Bantu Into the Hunting Grounds of the Bushmen, the Aborigines of the Country.* Cape Town: Struik; first published London: Swan Sonnenschein, 1905, 32–33; Newton-King, *Masters and Servants*, 42, 64, 89, 107–08; Marks, 'Khoisan resistance', 74; Van der Merwe, *Noordwaardse Beweging*, 19–20.

19 Elphick, *Khoikhoi*, 121–33; Marks, 'Khoisan resistance', 64–67; Roux P. 1925. *Die Verdedigingstelsel aan die Kaap Onder die Hollands Oosindiese Kompanjie, 1652–1795.* Stellenbosch: publisher unknown, 151; Elphick & Malherbe, 'Khoisan to 1828', 25.

functions of defending trekboer society and crushing indigenous resistance, commandos served as a means of acquiring forced labour.[20]

Unofficial commandos, that could be mobilised rapidly and that in effect allowed farmers to take the law into their own hands, were a common occurrence along the frontier. Unofficial commandos were posses formed on an ad hoc basis, usually for the purpose of hot pursuit, but also for land grabs, pre-emptive attacks against the San considered a threat or for razzias to round up forced labour. From the point of view of the frontier farmer it was essential that they be allowed to react immediately to San attacks and cattle raids. While leaders of unofficial commandos were required to submit a report to the *veldwachtmeester* upon their return, it is clear that there were many forays by trekboers against Khoisan that went unreported. Historian Nigel Penn estimates that several hundred such unofficial sorties were mounted along the northern frontier during the course of the eighteenth century. Though most informal commandos consisted of smaller parties in pursuit of stock raiders, there were some substantive, informal expeditions as deadly as any of the official commandos.[21]

Besides being necessary for countering the guerrilla tactics of the Khoisan, this flexibility and devolution of authority served the interests of the VOC. It allowed the DEIC to withdraw from military activity on the frontier by giving colonists a free hand in dealing with indigenous peoples. Being a commercial enterprise concerned with its bottom line and with servicing its maritime empire, the VOC was more loathe than most colonial governments to bear the costs of frontier conflict. The commando system fulfilled its need for cheap frontier defence because trekboers bore the greater part of its overall cost. Members were not paid and brought their own provisions. They used their own guns, horses and wagons, all of which were costly items and suffered severe wear and tear on commando. Although it tried to curb, and in some cases punished, trekboer excesses against indigenes, the VOC generally overlooked the abuses of commandos because the system suited its interests so well. Frequent warnings against unnecessary bloodshed

---

[20] For discussion of the commando as an institution on the Cape frontier, see Roux, *Verdedigingstelsel*, 139–202; Penn, *Forgotten Frontier*, 108–54; Legassick M. 1989. 'The northern frontier to c.1840: the rise and decline of the Griqua people', in *Shaping*, eds R. Elphick & H. Giliomee, 361–63; Katzen M. 1982. 'White settlers and the origin of a new society, 1652–1778', in *Oxford History of South Africa*, eds M. Wilson & L. Thompson. Cape Town: David Philip. See also Boeseken A.J. 1944. 'Die Nederlandse kommissarisse en die 18de eeuse samelewing aan die Kaap', in *Archives Year Book of South African History*. Pretoria: Government Printer, 81.

[21] Penn, *Forgotten Frontier*, 35; Van der Merwe, *Noordwaardse Beweging*, 65; A 39-1863. Cape of Good Hope Official Publications. *Message From His Excellency the Governor, With Enclosures, Relative to the Affairs of the Northwestern Districts of the Colony*, 10.

indicates that the company was well aware of excessive cruelty towards the San by trekboers. The VOC nevertheless abetted settler violence by recognising individual trekboer title to land confiscated from indigenous peoples and derived an income from it through the loan farm system. The further colonists moved from Cape Town, the more tenuous VOC control over subjects became and the greater the degree of lawlessness.[22]

As frontier conflict escalated through the eighteenth century, going on commando for a few weeks a year became a way of life for trekboers and their dependents. From 1739, the VOC made commando service compulsory for frontier farmers, but allowed them to send substitutes, often a Khoikhoi servant. Wealthier farmers or those not directly threatened were usually not eager to go on commando. Some evaded commando duty and many sent surrogates. Farmers resented these arduous tours of duty because it consumed valuable resources, and exposed them to danger. It moreover removed them from their farms and families, left vulnerable to attack and insubordination by servants. Trekboers nevertheless went on commando because they perceived there to be little alternative to eliminating or containing the threat posed by the San. There were some advantages to going on commando: it held out the promise of augmenting their workforce with captives, the possibility of gaining a share in recovered livestock and of opening up new areas for settlement. Official commandos against the San generally operated in early spring. Not only was this a time when there was enough water and fodder for horses in the veld, but it was also a quiet period in the agricultural cycle that made it easier for crop growers to join these expeditions. An added advantage was that from August through to October it was still cold enough for San bands to light fires for warmth, making it easy to locate their camps.[23]

The more immediate dynamic of the encounter between San and settler on the frontier was thus one of trekboer encroachment, San retaliation and trekboer retribution—an escalation that culminated in commando raids usually conducted with local exterminatory intent. Another longer term cycle of violence that can be identified through the eighteenth century is of trekboers encroaching in phases on successive ecological zones as they moved further into the interior. After entering a new zone, environmental

---

22   Marais J.S. 1968. *The Cape Coloured People, 1652–1937.* Johannesburg: Witwatersrand University Press, 17; Newton-King, *Masters and Servants,* 66, 109–10; Van der Merwe, *Noordwaardse Beweging,* 26–29, 49, 57.
23   Moodie D. ed. 1960. *The Record: Or a Series of Papers Relative to the Condition and Treatment of the Native Tribes of South Africa.* Cape Town: Balkema, first published Amsterdam: 1838 and 1842, 62–63; Barrow J. 1801–04. *Travels Into the Interior of Southern Africa in the Years 1797 and 1798.* London: Cadell & Davies, vol. 1, 235.

pressures grew over time as more and more farmers moved into the area. This resulted in intensified Khoisan resistance to the point where trekboers felt seriously threatened, giving rise to concerted, state-aided, trekboer offensives that led to the comprehensive defeat of Khoisan resisters and the closure of that frontier zone. A period of relative calm on the frontier ensued as trekboers started colonising new areas further inland. The peaks of violence in this longer term pattern can be observed in the early 1700s in the Tulbagh basin, the late 1730s in the Bokkeveld region, the mid-1750s in the Roggeveld, and then for over three decades from about 1770 along the entire escarpment.[24]

In the spiral of attack and counter-attack in these frontier confrontations, trekboers enjoyed huge military advantages. Most obviously, this superiority rested on trekboer access to firearms. Though cumbersome by modern standards, their flintlock rifles were nevertheless far superior to the stone-age weapons of the San. Whereas San arrows could accurately be shot at a distance of 60 or 70 metres, the front-loading muskets of the colonists were effective at more than twice that range. This commonly allowed trekboers to pick off adversaries from a safe distance. Muskets fired in volleys were extremely effective when opponents were massed and allowed relatively small commandos to inflict severe casualties on much larger Khoisan raiding parties. Most trekboers also carried pistols and sabres. The San were able to acquire a few guns from absconding servants by raiding farm houses or taking them from armed Khoikhoi herders. They were not able to use guns to great effect partly because it took some skill and practice to use them properly and because they did not have reliable supplies of ammunition or flints. Importantly, the speed and power of horses gave trekboers major advantages in mobility, in covering longer distances rapidly, in closer encounters, and for hot pursuit. The combination of guns and horses was particularly potent in the open country of the northern frontier. Few San tried to steal or ride horses themselves, but killed them whenever they got the opportunity.[25]

---

24 Newton-King, *Masters and Servants*, 63–71; Penn, *Forgotten Frontier*, 19–22.

25 Storey W. 2008. *Guns, Race and Power in Colonial South Africa*. Cambridge: Cambridge University Press, 35–40; Sparrman, *Voyage to the Cape*, 2, 111–12; Mentzel O.F. 1944. *A Geographical and Topographical Description of the Cape of Good Hope, 3*, ed. H. Mandelbrote. Cape Town: Van Riebeeck Society; first published Glogau: Christian Friedrich Günther, 1787, 217–18, 309; Guelke & Shell, 'Landscape of conquest', 810; Penn, *Forgotten Frontier*, 111, 134, 189, 193, 203, 225, 229; Moodie, *Record*, V, 33–34; Lye W.F. ed. 1975. *Andrew Smith's Journal of His Expedition Into the Interior of South Africa, 1834–36: An Authentic Narrative of Travels and Discoveries, the Manners and Customs of Native Tribes, and the Physical Nature of the Country*. Cape Town: A.A. Balkema, 22, 284; Mostert, *Frontiers*, 222; Newton-King, *Masters and Servants*, 107–08.

From about 1770 through till the late 1790s, official commandos against the San were organised annually, often more frequently, and generally consisted of between 40 and 100 armed men on horseback. The preferred modus operandi of the commando was to locate the San camps by means of their fires, surround the sleeping kraal under cover of darkness and then attack at dawn. The small size of hunting bands, which rarely had more than eight males of fighting age, meant that the San were outnumbered in most hostile engagements. With the advantages of guns, horses, numerical superiority and surprise on their side, San encampments stood little chance against commando attacks. While many bands were exterminated in this way, it was not always that easy for commandos. It was difficult to hide their presence in open country and the San sometimes lived in naturally fortified locations. The San could retreat to remote, inhospitable areas where horses often could not follow, and where it became difficult to track them over stony ground. Mountainous country provided greater opportunities for defence as the San could take refuge in caves or behind boulders. This could result in protracted stand-offs in which the San usually came off second best if trekboers were prepared to lay seige to them. The San on occasion rolled boulders down onto advancing trekboers from high ground. But mountains also held perils for the San as they were sometimes caught up against sheer cliff faces or the edges of precipices, or were cornered in gorges.[26]

In commando raids San men were, with few exceptions, put to death on the spot, while many women and especially children were taken captive. Adult males were killed because they were regarded as extremely dangerous and as having little economic value. They were perceived to be irredeemable savages who could not be schooled in productive activity. The chances for escape and revenge on the frontier were simply too great for many farmers to contemplate taking them as forced labourers. San men were regarded as particularly menacing because they gave no quarter in combat and generally fought to the death. San fighters often displayed remarkable fearlessness, throwing themselves into suicidal assaults against attacking commandos in the vain hope of allowing women and children a chance to escape. This is not to romanticise the San response as the historical record is clear about the ferocity of their resistance. Surrender seems not to have been an option many San men considered, and was rarely on offer by commandos. Nigel

---

[26]   Smith et al, *Bushmen*, 44–45; Lye, *Andrew Smith's Journal*, 22–23; Van der Post L. 1958. *Lost World of the Kalahari*. London: Hogarth Press, 44–45; Penn N. 1991. 'The /Xam and the Colony, 1740–1870', in *Sound From the Thinking Strings: A Visual, Literary, Archaeological and Historical Interpretation of the Final Years of /Xam Life*, ed. P. Skotnes. Cape Town: Axeage Private Press, 33.

Penn partly attributes their uncompromising resistance to the San's bond to their territory being of such an intensely spiritual nature that 'to lose the land was to lose literally everything'.[27]

Women and children were also often massacred. Trekboers were not beyond smashing the heads of children against rocks or skinning the breasts of women they had killed to make tobacco pouches. While South African historical scholarship has hitherto been silent on the matter because of the nature and paucity of the evidence, there is every likelihood that captive women were sexually abused.[28] Women not killed were taken as servants in trekboer households or as concubines for Khoikhoi dependents. Female captives had added value in that their offspring would in time augment the farmer's labour supply.[29]

San children were prized because they were seen as tractable and more easily assimilated into the trekboer economy as menial labourers. They could, from a young age, be trained to work as herders and to do a variety of tasks around the household. The vulnerability of child captives and children born into captivity made them an ultra-exploitable class of labourers. From 1775, what was effectively a system of child slavery became institutionalised by the VOC through the apprenticeship system whereby Khoisan children were bound to masters till the age of 25. Since few San knew their precise ages and the colonial state was hardly in a position to police the situation on the frontier, farmers were generally able to coerce apprentices to remain in their employ till they were much older, in many cases for life. The bartering and gifting of the San, especially children, was a common practice on the frontier. The San assimilated to trekboer society as forced labourers were usually referred to as 'Hottentots' and in time many came to see themselves as such, helping to efface identification with a foraging way of life. This was particularly the case with child captives for whom their experience as hunter-gatherers may have been little more

---

27   Penn, 'Fated to perish', 87–89; Moodie, *Record*, V, 33; Gall S. 2001. *The Bushmen of Southern Africa: Slaughter of the Innocent*. London: Chatto & Windus, 68; Jeffreys M. 1978. 'An epitaph to the Bushmen', in *Bushmen*, ed. P. Tobias, 92–93; Green, *Karoo*, 25, 31; Van der Post, *Lost World*, 43–44.

28   Researchers largely depend on *veldwachtmeester* reports for information on eighteenth century commando raids. These reports are terse, self-serving and generally amount to little more than tallies of casualties. Stow, *Native Races*, 48 makes passing reference to such abuse.

29   BPP VII.425, 1837. British Parliamentary Papers. 1966. *Report of the Select Committee on Aborigines (British Settlements)*, facsimile reprint. Cape Town: Struik, 28; Mentzel, *Cape of Good Hope*, 309; Gall, *Bushmen*, 60; Eldridge E. 1994. 'Slave raiding across the Cape frontier', in *Slavery in South Africa: Native Labour on the Dutch Frontier*, eds Eldridge E. & Morton F. Boulder: Westview Press, 94.

than a hazy memory. Captured San were subject to a grim regime of unremunerated labour, and physical as well as psychological abuse, with virtually no protection against the arbitrary power of masters. They were slaves in every sense except that they could not be sold openly.[30]

As clients and servants of trekboers, Khoikhoi were frequently complicit in violence against the San and many participated in commando raids. One reason for this animus was that it was usually Khoikhoi servants who bore the brunt of San attacks and many were killed while looking after farmers' herds. Those Khoikhoi dependents who were allowed to keep stock were equally threatened by San raids. Often farmers who were reluctant to go on commando sent Khoikhoi servants instead. Some commandos, particularly in the latter part of the eighteenth century, had a majority of Khoikhoi members. There was some incentive for Khoikhoi to go on commando in that they often got a share of the spoils, albeit smaller than that of trekboers. They might get some of the recovered livestock or captured San women as sexual partners. Khoikhoi were skilled scouts and trackers, and were routinely sent into dangerous situations where trekboers were not prepared to risk their own skins. Many Khoikhoi participants, in the words of Nigel Penn, probably made the calculation that '[i]t was better to be a low-status member of a commando than a defenceless object of its wrath'.[31] The relationship between the San and Khoikhoi was, however, complex. Independent Khoikhoi pastoralist communities beyond the colonial frontier were often in conflict with the San who raided their stock. The San were sometimes also taken up into Khoikhoi society as clients and it was not unusual for dispossessed Khoikhoi to join the San in resisting colonial intrusion.[32]

Racism was an important determinant in the extreme violence visited upon the San. From the outset, colonists regarded the San to be racially inferior. They were usually judged to be on the very lowest rung of the racial hierarchy, certainly below the despised Khoikhoi. Being hunter-gatherers, the San appeared to be living in a feral state not far removed from animals. It appeared to many that the San did not even have a fully developed

---

30   Malherbe V.C. 1991. 'Indentured and unfree labour in South Africa: toward an understanding'. *South African Historical Journal*, 24, 15–16; Philip J. 1828. *Researches in South Africa*. London: James Duncan, 2, 50, 265–68, 276–77; Barrow, *Travels*, 146–47, 280, 290–92; Stow, *Native Races*, 48; Morton F. 1994. 'Slavery and South African historiography', in *Slavery in South Africa*, eds E. Eldridge & F. Morton, 3; Theal G.M. comp. 1897–1905. *Records of the Cape Colony*, 9. London: Clowes Printers, 257.

31   Penn, *Forgotten Frontier*, 139.

32   Newton-King, *Masters and Servants*, 61, 106–07, 131–33; Smith et al, *Khoikhoi*, 26, 28; Penn, *Forgotten Frontier*, 18, 57, 90, 161.

faculty for language. Phenotypical differences, their degree of nakedness, apparent lack of religion or social organisation beyond the family put them at the polar opposite of the European ideal of humanity—or as Johannes Kicherer, who led the first mission to the San alleged, 'on a level with brute creation'. Not surprisingly, the San as well as other indigenous peoples were referred to as 'schepselen' (creatures). Settler racial attitudes were pithily summed up by landdrost Alberti from Uitenhage in 1805: 'According to the unfortunate notion prevalent here, a heathen is not actually human, but at the same time he cannot really be classed among the animals. He is, therefore, a sort of creature not known elsewhere. His word can in no wise be believed, and only by violent measures can he be brought to do good and shun evil'.[33]

This dehumanisation made it easier for colonists to justify occupying San land, enslaving and killing them, though economic competition in a situation of acute resource scarcity was the fundamental reason behind trekboer violence towards the San. Because of their nomadic way of life, the San were seen as not owning the land but to be ranging across it, much as animals do. It is supremely ironic that European interlopers who had travelled thousands of miles across the ocean and pressed hundreds of miles inland viewed the San, who had been living in their ancestral territories for centuries, if not millenia, as racially inferior because of their migratory lifestyle and used this as justification for confiscating their land. Their fierce resistance only intensified the fear and hatred felt towards the San. Trekboer isolation and small numbers fed their insecurity as well as disregard for the lives or suffering of the San. Some frontiersmen shot the San with impunity, arbitrarily, and often on sight. As conflict intensified through the eighteenth century, trekboer society also developed an exterminatory attitude towards the San—that they were little better than vermin and San society as needing, even deserving, to be eradicated. By the 1770s it was apparent that indigenes were killed for no other reason than that they were thought to be San.

Writing in 1775, traveller Anders Sparrman related: 'Does a colonist at any time get sight of a Bushman, he takes fire immediately, and spirits up his horse and dogs, in order to hunt him with more ardour and fury than he would a wolf or any other wild beast'. Louis de Grandpré, a French

---

33 Du Toit A. & Giliomee H. 1983. *Afrikaner Political Thought: Analysis and Documents, 1780–1850*. Cape Town: David Philip, 84; Guenther M. 1980. 'From "brutal savages" to "harmless people": notes on the changing Western image of the Bushmen'. *Paideuma*, 26, 127–30; Marais, *Cape Coloured People*, 15; Chidester D. 1996. 'Bushman religion: open, closed and new frontiers', in *Miscast*, ed. P. Skotnes, 53–54; Mostert, *Frontiers*, 175; Kicherer J. 1804. *Narrative of His Mission to the Hottentots and Boschemen With a General Account of the South African Missions*. London: T. Williams, 7–8.

army officer who visited the Cape in 1786–1787, accused trekboers of being even more bloodthirsty than the conquistadors because 'they have hunted the Boschis as one would hunt hares; their dogs are trained for it'. A quarter of a century later John Barrow, private secretary to Lord Macartney, described how 'the name of Bosjesman is held in horror and detestation; and the farmer thinks he cannot proclaim a more meritorious action than to murder one of these people'. In 1927, W.M. Macmillan, generally acknowledged as the leading South African historian of his generation, summarised these attitudes concisely in *The Cape Colour Question*: 'The well-established colonial tradition came to be that the Bushman is a wild animal to be shot at sight; and unhappily it was on this inadequate theory that the Bushman of earlier days was usually dealt with and destroyed'.[34]

Commandos thus often hunted San bands with the express intention of completely clearing particular areas of them. It was not unusual for larger commandos to kill several hundred San in expeditions lasting several weeks. The largest of these state-sponsored operations, the General Commando of 1774 which mobilised about 250 men in an attempt to purge the entire frontier zone of San, reported 503 San killed and 239 taken captive. Commandos habitually under-reported casualties to mask the violence perpetrated. Referring to the north-eastern frontier, Colonel Collins, who toured the interior in 1808–1809 on behalf of the governor to advise him on how to end frontier violence, reported that a former commando leader had informed him 'that within a period of six years the parties under his orders had either killed or taken prisoner 3,200 of these unfortunate creatures; another has stated to me that the actions in which he had been engaged had caused the destruction of 2,700'. George Thompson, an English merchant who travelled through the interior in 1823, spoke to a Commandant Nel, who told him that 'within the last thirty years he had been upon thirty-two commandos against the Bushmen, in which great numbers had been shot, and their children carried away into the colony. On one of these expeditions, not less than two hundred Bushmen were massacred'. Government records of the Graaff-Reinet magistracy show that in the last decade of Dutch rule, commandos killed

---

34   Sparrman, *Voyage to the Cape*, vol. 2, 111; vol. 1, 194, 200–01; Johnson D. 2007. 'Representing the Cape "Hottentots" from the French Enlightenment to post-apartheid South Africa'. *Eighteenth Century Studies*, 40, no. 4, 543; Macmillan W.M. 1968. *The Cape Colour Question: A Historical Survey*. Cape Town: Balkema, 27.

at least 2 504 San and took 669 prisoner, a set of statistics historian P.J. van der Merwe correctly describes as 'definitely very incomplete'.[35]

While commandos generally operated with local exterminatory intent, 1777 marked a radicalisation in the attitude of the VOC government towards the San. Whereas the governor previously gave instructions to commandos to subdue only hostile San and take captives as they deemed fit, for the first time in 1777 the Cape government explicitly sanctioned the extermination of San wherever and whenever they were encountered. Up to that point, the Cape government held some hope that the San threat could be contained either through a show of force, as with the General Commando, or through some peace initiative, such as negotiating with San leaders. By 1777, it appears to have lost hope of any such outcome as a result of escalating San attacks in the preceding years. This policy shift was of greater symbolic import than of practical significance in that the governor was not so much implementing a harsher killing regimen than sanctioning what was already happening on the frontier. Under pressure from frontier farmers to act decisively against intensifying San offensives, the governor and Council of Policy were prepared to leave the San to the mercy of commandos by acceding to requests of commando leaders that they be given the freedom to deal with the San as they saw fit.[36]

Although settlers enjoyed great advantages in this conflict, it was not at all easy for trekboers to defeat the San comprehensively or annihilate San society completely. Trekboers were thin on the ground and commandos could operate only sporadically, at most for a few weeks at a time. Significantly, San society consisted of a large number of small social units scattered over a vast, often inhospitable, landscape. In addition, the San resisted fiercely and used guerrilla tactics successfully. Though they had suffered severe loss of land and life by the end of the eighteenth century, and though their ability to reproduce biologically and culturally had been severely compromised, the San peoples of the Cape Colony were far from vanquished.

Attrition under British colonial rule

The dynamic of frontier violence against the San changed at the end of the eighteenth century soon after the British took control of the Cape Colony.

---

35   Van der Merwe, *Noordwaardse Beweging*, 12, 27–32, 53; Penn, *Forgotten Frontier*, 112–25; Moodie, *Record*, V, 7; Theal, *Records of Cape Colony*, 7, 35–36; Marais, *Cape Coloured People*, 18; Thompson G. 1968. *Travels and Adventures Through Southern Africa*, vols 2 & 3. Cape Town: Van Riebeeck Society, first published London: Henry Colburn, 1827, 6.

36   Moodie, *Record*, III, 50–70, 72; Van der Merwe, *Noordwaardse Beweging*, 41; Smith et al, *Bushmen*, 47.

When the British occupied the Cape in 1795, they were disconcerted by the incessant frontier violence not only out of humanitarian concern but also because they wanted to maintain social order and because of the high cost of such conflict. Meat production had been severely affected by the chaos on the frontier and an increasing number of farmers had defaulted on their loan farm rentals. The British administration realised that despite trekboer complaints of depredations by the San, it was really the San who were the victims. The British favoured a policy of assimilation, what they thought of as 'civilising' the San and encouraging them to lead settled lives as pastoralists, servants and farm labourers. The San were therefore encouraged to become pastoralists not only because it was regarded as appropriate for that natural environment, but also because stock-keeping was seen as the next step up in the evolutionary ladder from hunter-gathering.

The British administration tried a three-pronged approach to putting an end to the relentless violence against the San. Starting with a proclamation issued by Governor Macartney on 24 July 1798, the British encouraged farmers to make gifts of livestock to San. *Veldwachtmeesters* were to collect sheep and goats from farmers through voluntary subscription and distribute them among the San. In addition to this being a gesture of goodwill and a practical step in short-circuiting the cycle of violence that had fomented frontier conflict for decades, it was also hoped that it would encourage the San to abandon foraging and become pastoralists. Besides providing for their immediate subsistence and tiding them over in times of drought, thereby removing their need to raid trekboer stock, the gifts of livestock were meant to 'impress them with a sense of the benefits arising from permanent property, preferable to casual and predatory supplies' as Macartney's proclamation put it.[37]

Secondly, the British promoted missionary activity among hunter-gatherer communities as another way of 'taming' them and teaching them the benefits of a sedentary existence. The San were regarded as lacking both the intellectual means and the moral principles for independently fashioning a 'civilised' way of life for themselves, and missionaries as best equipped to overcome these deficiencies. Missionaries from the London Missionary Society, which had been founded in 1795, arrived at the Cape at the end of March 1799 and set up its first mission to the San at Blydevooruitzicht Fontein one day's journey beyond the north-east border of the colony in August of that year. While the missionary project was couched in terms

---

37 Theal, *Records of Cape Colony*, 7, 116–17; Van der Merwe, *Noordwaardse Beweging*, 67–68; Spilhaus M. 1966. *South Africa in the Making, 1652–1806*. Cape Town: Juta, 251.

of the 'upliftment' and 'moral redemption' of the San, it was predicated on breaking down their way of life and altering their world view.[38]

Thirdly, the Cape government declared the area known as Bushmanland, the northern Cape between the colonial boundary and the Orange River, to be a reserve for the San and forbade colonists from entering the area. By the early nineteenth century, Bushmanland was in effect the last refuge of independent Cape San society essentially because trekboers regarded the semi-desert of the northern Cape as being of little use to them except for hunting and occasional pasturage.

These measures were meant to provide the San with some protection against settler violence and to encourage them to abandon their hunter-gathering lifestyle. The British administration tried to curb violence against the San with threats of criminal action against perpetrators and warnings that ammunition supplies would be cut off. It also issued an injunction that San not be molested and that commandos against them cease—except in cases where San aggression justified their use for self-defence. It was this qualification that allowed for continued state-sanctioned violence against the San and the organisation of official commandos against them. Although San casualties as a result of commando activity were considerably lower under British rule than in the preceding 30 years, they were nevertheless significant.[39] Intermittent informal commando activity and vigilantism continued to take a toll of San life.

All three British initiatives to 'civilise' the San failed. First, making them gifts of livestock did not work because the plan, though well intentioned, was ill conceived and patchily implemented. Although some farmers were prepared to try the experiment in the hope of breaking the cycle of violence, many were reluctant to participate in the scheme. Over the next two decades, several thousand sheep and goats, but also cattle, were donated to San communities along the frontier, both for immediate consumption and to encourage them to take up herding. Some farmers also tried to help the San by shooting game for them. The gift-giving scheme failed mainly because the San were most likely to eat the animals they got than try and farm with them in the semi-desert of the northern Cape. Not only did they need the food desperately, but San society was extremely egalitarian and everyone had an obligation to share food with the rest of the community rather than selfishly retaining it for

---

38   McDonald J. 2009. 'Encounters at "Bushman Station": reflections on the fate of the San of the transgariep frontier, 1826–1833'. *South African Historical Journal*, 61, no. 2, 382–83; Szalay, *San and Colonization*, ch. 4; Penn N. 2007. '"Civilizing" the San: the first mission to the Cape San, 1791–1806', in *Claim to the Country: The Archive of Wilhelm Bleek and Lucy Lloyd*, ed P. Skotnes. Johannesburg: Jacana Media, 90–91; Philip, *Researches*, vol. 2, chs 1–3.

39   Theal, *Records of Cape Colony*, 17, 507–08; 19, 19–20; 31, 1–55; Van der Merwe, *Noordwaardse Beweging*, 88–90; Szalay, *San and Colonization*, 23.

farming. For such groups, an ongoing threat was their vulnerability to raids by other San and the array of stock-keeping peoples on the frontier, including unscrupulous trekboers. There were nevertheless reports of a few San bands who managed to retain small flocks for a while. What is apparent though, is that few willingly discarded foraging as a way of life.[40]

Second, attempts at converting the San to Christianity had little success as few showed interest in abandoning their world view in favour of missionary teachings. This was not because the San were incapable of cultural adaptation or of understanding the Christian message as has often been alleged, but because they preferred their own way of life. The missionary effort itself was sporadic, with eight failed mission stations aimed specifically at the San being established between 1799 and 1846 along the north-eastern frontier. They all closed within a few years because of extreme isolation, inadequate funding from the LMS and because they attracted few San converts. Drought, repeated stock theft and the antagonism of indigenous peoples, including independent San bands, also played a role in their closure. Missionaries, in addition, faced hostility from settlers for not only did they occupy desirable land and water resources, but they were seen as depriving farmers of scarce labour. Farmers regarded mission stations as havens for deserters and shirkers, and as undermining settler control by educating indigenous peoples and filling their heads with seditious ideas. 'Meddling missionaries', moreover, roused the ire of government officials for challenging colonial policy.[41]

---

[40]   Theal, *Records of Cape Colony*, 34, 437–38; Stockenström A. 1964. *The Autobiography of the Late Andries Stockenström*, Cape Town: Struik; first published Cape Town: Juta, 1887, 1, 230; Van der Merwe, *Noordwaardse Beweging*, 69–73, 245; Lichtenstein, vol. 1, *Travels in Southern Africa*, 104–05; MacCrone I.D. 1937. *Race Attitudes in South Africa: Historical, Experimental and Psychological Studies*. London: Oxford University Press, 124–25; McDonald J. 2007. '"When shall these dry bones live?": interactions between the London Missionary Society and the San along the Cape's north-eastern frontier, 1790–1833'. MA thesis, University of Cape Town, 64; Szalay, *San and Colonization*, 30, 36–37, 42; Stow, *Native Races*, 47, 205, 393.

[41]   Du Plessis J. 1965. *A History of Christian Missions in South Africa*. Cape Town: Struik, 106, 209; Theal G.M. 1919. *Ethnography and Condition of South Africa Before AD 1505*. London: Allen & Unwin, 25–26, 76–77; Schoeman K. 1993. 'Die Londonse Sendinggenootskap en die San: die stasies Toornberg en Hepzibah, 1814–1818'. *South African Historical Journal*, 28, 230, 232–33; Schoeman K. 1993. 'Die Londonse Sendinggenootskap en die San: die stasies Ramah, Konnah en Philipolis, 1816–1828'. *South African Historical Journal*, 29, 132, 141–43; Guenther, *Tricksters and Trancers*, 89–91, 209–11, 224; Macmillan, *Cape Colour Question*, 129–32; McDonald, 'When shall these dry bones live?', 71–72, 79, 97, 112; Stockenström A. 1964. *The Autobiography of the Late Sir Andries Stockenström, Sometime Lieutenant-Governor of the Eastern Province of the Colony of the Cape of Good Hope*. 2 volumes. Cape Town: C. Struik., vol. 1., 212–14; Walker E. 1957. *A History of Southern Africa*. London: Longmans Green, 97.

As for the Bushmanland reserve, trekboers simply ignored this proclamation. Policing the isolated frontier areas of the Cape Colony was an impossible task for the colonial government and it was not capable of maintaining the area as a reserve for the San. Colonial hunting parties regularly traversed the territory, depleting the game and robbing the San of a major source of food. Farmers continually encroached on land occupied by the San, pushing them into the more marginal areas. In times of drought, farmers would move beyond the colonial borders in search of grazing, making temporary incursions into San territory. When it suited them, farmers used the area as communal grazing land, their stock damaging the ecology and undermining San subsistence.[42]

While British initiatives for peace had some success in reducing lawlessness and turbulence on the frontier, it failed to eliminate violence against the San. The unremitting warfare of the last decades of Dutch rule gave way to a fragile and uncertain peace punctuated by periodic bloodshed. More settled conditions on the frontier served only to spur further settler penetration of the interior. Although some San groups were 'pacified' by the new approach, others remained hostile. Violence on the frontier continued sporadically through the first half of the nineteenth century, with the San raiding trekboer stock and farmers retaliating with both formal and informal commandos against them.[43]

Under the false peace of British rule there were divergent tendencies in the destruction of San society on the northern and north-eastern frontiers during the first half of the nineteenth century. The predominant trend along the north-eastern frontier was for the incorporation of the surviving San into colonial society as a servile underclass. The farmers' need for labour and diminishing possibilities for pursuing a foraging lifestyle in this more densely populated region promoted this outcome. Intense commando activity in this region over the preceding decades had also sapped San resistance. Along the drier, sparsely settled northern frontier, and beyond in Bushmanland, it was still possible for independent San bands to subsist as hunter-gatherers, though such an existence became more and more precarious.

---

[42]   Findlay D. 1977. 'The San of the Cape thirstland and L. Anthing's "special mission"'. BA Hons thesis, University of Cape Town, 23–24; Penn, 'Fated to perish', 81–82; Van der Merwe, *Noordwaardse Beweging*, 153–54.

[43]   Freund W. 1989. 'The Cape under the transitional governments, 1795–1814', in *Shaping*, eds R. Elphick & H. Giliomee, 331–32; Neville, 'Seacow River valley', 257; Van der Merwe, *Noordwaardse Beweging*, 107–14.

Along the north-eastern frontier, the San in the early nineteenth century by and large had little option but to enter the service of farmers to survive. Others were coerced into becoming farm labourers. Where the possibility still existed, some moved beyond the advancing tide of colonial settlement, inevitably to barely habitable terrain. A few bands might for a while have eked out a living by combining foraging on unused land between white farms with livestock theft. Hunting bands under pressure sometimes opted for the compromise of handing over children to farmers in return for a few sheep or goats, feeding the well-established practice of the bartering and exchange of the San children. It was not unusual for groups of San first to enter the service of farmers as clients while still practising a degree of foraging. Over time the tendency was for such groups to become tied to farmers through threats of violence, the retention of women and children on the farm, and growing dependence on farmers for food. The San generally worked as herders, but were also employed as guides, hunters and trackers because of their intimate knowledge of the terrain and its ecology. Many were also used as domestic labourers. A small number of the San ended up in frontier towns where they lived by occasional labour or as vagrants.[44]

After 1810, San resistance, which had stalled colonial penetration north of the Sneeuberg since the 1770s, gave way under continued pressure and stock farmers were able to press on, resulting in the Orange River being proclaimed the new colonial boundary in the north-east in 1824. The efforts of the British administration to maintain peace notwithstanding, periodic commandos against the San continued to be organised into the 1830s by frontier officials who were given the discretion to do so to protect settler interests. These later commandos on the north-eastern frontier seemed more concerned with acquiring captive labour than with extermination.[45]

Along the northern frontier, independent San society continued to be undermined by settler incursions into Bushmanland, which further diminished the San's options for leading a foraging existence. As frontier farmers infiltrated areas occupied by San, there were ongoing disputes over specific parcels of land and access to water resources. Farmers often

[44]   Theal, *Records of Cape Colony*, vol. 11, 326–28, 365–67; 35, 325–26; Philip, *Researches*, vol. 2, 265–68, 276–77; Szalay, *San and Colonization*, 79–80, 84–94; Van Sittert L. 2004. 'The supernatural state: water divining and the Cape underground water rush, 1891–1910'. *Journal of Social History*, 37, no. 4, 916; Wright J. 1971. *Bushman Raiders of the Drakensberg, 1840–1870: A Study of Their Conflict With Stock-Keeping Peoples in Natal*. Pietermaritzburg: University of Natal Press, 28; Stockenström, *Autobiography*, vol.1, 214–15.

[45]   Theal, *Records of Cape Colony*, vol. 19, 19–20; 17, 507–08; Legassick, M. 1989. 'The northern frontier to c.1840: the rise and decline of the Griqua people', in *Shaping*, eds R. Elphick & H. Giliomee,, 363; Neville, 'Seacow River valley', 257.

resorted to violence and the formation of informal commandos to settle disputes or to grab coveted land. Under conditions of insecure peace and unequal power, the San invariably found themselves on the back foot when trekboers took the offensive. The reality of settler penetration of Bushmanland was formally recognised by the colonial government pushing the northern boundary of the Cape Colony to the Orange River in 1847.[46]

In the northern Cape, significant numbers of San were also killed by Griqua, Bastard, Korana and other pastoralist groups. As Griqua and Korana gained access to firearms and horses through colonial contact and trade, they became more formidable enemies and also formed commandos to kill the San, who raided their stock. With the closing of the frontier some San were also taken up as forced labourers by them. In the first half of the nineteenth century, the San of the northern Cape found themselves greatly outnumbered and squeezed from north and south by pastoralists, who had access to superior technologies of war. With Griqua and Korana communities established along the Orange River and trekboers pushing up from the south, the San faced adversaries on two fronts and were increasingly hemmed into the drier parts of Bushmanland. What is more, trekboer pressure on Khoikhoi in Namaqualand and along parts of the Orange River forced some of these peoples into Bushmanland, putting further stress on the San. The degradation of the natural environment pushed famished San into stock raiding, followed almost inevitably by retaliation. This, together with periodic drought, led to the starvation and massacre of many San bands in Bushmanland during the nineteenth century. Others were forced to enter the service of farmers as virtual serfs.[47]

The discovery in the mid-nineteenth century that merino sheep were able to acclimatise to the semi-desert conditions of Bushmanland and the development of borehole technology to tap ground water held dire consequences for the San. As a result, the number of wool-bearing sheep in the northern Cape increased dramatically from the 1850s onwards. In addition, the 1850s copper mining boom in the Namaqualand gave rise to a demand for foodstuffs and an equally rapid growth in the number

---

46   Theal, *Records of Cape Colony*, vol. 31, 1–55; Findlay, 'San of Cape Thirstland', 23–24; Van der Merwe, *Noordwaardse Beweging*, 153–54.

47   A 39-1863, *Message From His Excellency*, 7; Ross R. 1975. 'The !Kora wars on the Orange River, 1830–1880'. *Journal of African History*, 16, no. 4 569; Ross R. 1976. *Adam Kok's Griquas*. Cambridge: Cambridge University Press, 23–25; McDonald, 'When will these dry bones live?', 53–54, 56, 92; Findlay, 'San of Cape Thirstland', 24.

of fat-tailed, indigenous sheep in the region. The semi-desert scrub of the northern Cape to which the surviving San had been confined now had economic value, guaranteeing further settler encroachment on Bushmanland.[48]

These commercial opportunities and growing environmental pressures precipitated a series of massacres of San bands by intruding Boer and Bastard farmers in the 1850s and 1860s which brought an effective end to independent San society in Bushmanland. In 1861 Louis Anthing, resident magistrate and civil commissioner of Namaqualand, received complaints of San bands having been slaughtered in Bushmanland by informal commandos over the preceding decade. Sympathetic to the plight of the San, Anthing relocated to Kenhardt for several months to investigate these claims. In 1863, he produced a government report documenting some of the atrocities. Despite collecting evidence of several massacres of San bands over the previous decade and proposing measures for protecting the remaining San, nothing came of his efforts because of the unwillingness of the Cape government to incur the necessary expenditure. Anthing estimated that there were no more than 500 San left in the whole of Bushmanland by the early 1860s. He also noted that besides those murdered, many died from starvation and dehydration, especially in times of drought, due to the destruction of game and their diminished access to natural resources.[49]

The final throes of primary resistance by the San within the Cape Colony came during the Korana wars of 1868–1869 and 1878–1879 along the middle reaches of the Orange River when remnant groups of !Xam-speaking San joined forces with Korana against encroaching white farmers and the colonial forces supporting them. Although the pastoral Korana were generally hostile towards hunter-gatherers, who preyed on their livestock, by the late 1860s, both were under sufficient pressure from white farmers taking control of grazing lands along the southern bank of the Orange River for them to be pushed into an alliance against their common enemy. In both conflicts, a number of !Xam, including women and children, were killed by colonial forces and a substantial number died from starvation as a result of drought and disruption caused by the conflict. Those taken prisoner were

---

[48]   Smith et al, *Bushmen*, 57; A 39-1863, *Message From His Excellency*, 9; A 30-1880. Cape of Good Hope Official Publications. *Papers Connected With Affairs on the Northern Border of the Colony of the Cape of Good Hope*, 35; Smalberger, J.M. 1975. *A History of Copper Mining in Namaqualand. 1846–1931*. Cape Town: Struik, 2

[49]   Findlay, 'San of Cape Thirstland', ch. 4; A 39-1863, *Message From His Excellency*, 7–9, 11.

indentured to farmers, while some fighters were sentenced to hard labour at the Breakwater Prison at the Cape Town docks.[50]

Conclusion

Despite relatively benevolent British colonial policy, the San society within the Cape Colony was nevertheless extinguished during the course of the nineteenth century in an incremental process of encroachment on their land, enforced labour incorporation and periodic massacre. A few independent bands managed to survive on the edge of the Kalahari Desert, giving rise to a common contemporary misconception of the San as a 'desert people'. Despite a recent resurgence in numbers due to the Khoisan revivalist movement, today no more than 1 500 people identify as being of Cape San descent.[51]

In the case of the Cape San peoples, the destruction of their societies was not simply an inadvertant consequence of land alienation and blind pursuit of selfish economic interests by colonists. It was rather the intentional, even consciously desired, outcome of a sustained eradicatory drive rooted in Cape settler society's vision of itself, its future and the nature of humanity— and is therefore genocide.[52]

---

[50] Strauss T. 1979. *War Along the Orange: The Korana and the Northern Border Wars of 1868–69 and 1878–79*. Cape Town: Centre for African Studies, University of Cape Town, 37, 43–44, 53, 68–69, 111; Dooling W. 2009. 'Reconstructing the household: the northern Cape Colony before and after the South African War'. *Journal of African History*, 50, no. 3, 403–05; A 30-1880, *Affairs on the Northern Border*, 35.

[51] Today there are about 7 500 people in South Africa who identify as San. Of these about 6 000 are recent immigrants from Namibia and southern Angola who accompanied the retreating South African army of occupation at the end of the 1980s. See Chennels R. & du Toit A. 2004. 'The rights of indigenous peoples in South Africa', in *Indigenous Peoples' Rights in Southern Africa*, eds R. Hitchcock and D. Vinding. Copenhagen: IWGIA, 98; Besten M. 2009. '"We are the original inhabitants of this land": Khoe-San identity in post-apartheid South Africa', in *Burdened By Race: Coloured Identities in Southern Africa*, ed. M. Adhikari. Cape Town: UCT Press; Comaroff J.L. & Comaroff J. 2009. *Ethnicity, Inc.* Chicago: University of Chicago Press, 86–98.

[52] For detailed argument about the genocidal nature of this conflict, see Adhikari, *Anatomy of a South African Genocide*, ch. 4. Here 'intentional' is used in the juridical sense of perpetrators being reasonably expected to foresee the consequences of their actions.

Chapter Three

'Like a Wild Beast, He Can be Got for the Catching': Child Forced Labour and the 'Taming' of the San along the Cape's North-Eastern Frontier, c.1806–1830[1]

Jared McDonald
University of Johannesburg

In 1825 while on a journey through 'Bushman country',[2] John Philip, the superintendent of the London Missionary Society (LMS) in the Cape Colony, came into contact with several San[3] communities. Reporting his conversations with these people, some of whom were living among farmers 'in a state of nature', he noted that 'their heaviest complaints were those that were occasioned by the manner in which they were robbed of their children'.[4] In March 1842, 17 years after this observation, while undertaking a tour of inspection of the LMS' missions beyond the Orange River, Philip was met by a 'Bushman ambassador' at Philippolis. The purpose of this ambassador's visit to the Griqua mission was to request that a missionary be sent to reside at his kraal.[5] He informed Philip that his kraal had 100 guns in their possession and that those around them knew they were 'always ready to defend [their] property, and [their] children'. In relaying this encounter to the directors of the society in London, Philip observed: 'Had we gone to search for Bushmen we [would] not have expected to find them, except in a state of separation, in places inaccessible to any, but to such as made a trade

---

1   I would like to thank Wayne Dooling, Edward Cavanagh and Mohamed Adhikari for their helpful comments and insightful suggestions on earlier drafts of this chapter.

2   This was a generic name for the semi-desert region which lay beyond the Cape's escarpment of the Nieuweveld, Roggeveld and Sneeuberg ranges.

3   'San' is used here to denote the Cape's hunter-gatherer communities, for whom the terms 'Bushmen' or 'Bosjesmen' were used by writers and observers in the eighteenth and nineteenth centuries. Given the pejorative connotations of 'Bushmen', San is employed instead. The label 'San' is, however, not without detractors.

4   Philip, J. *Researches in South Africa: Illustrating the Civil, Moral and Religious Condition of the Native Tribes*. London: James Duncan, vol. 2, 268. See also Cape Archives (hereafter CA), Clerk of the Legislative Council (hereafter LCA), 6/19, J. Philip, tour of inspection, 1825.

5   Kraal refers to the basic social unit of San society, which was made up of mobile, extended family foraging groups. The size of such groups varied, influenced by rainfall patterns and availability of food and game.

of hunting Bushmen for their children'.[6] The exchange with the 'Bushman ambassador' confirmed for Philip that the eradication of the San continued through both outright killing and child abduction. In his influential and widely read book, *Researches in South Africa* which was published in 1828, Philip had previously highlighted the propensity of frontier farmers to capture the San children and detain them as labourers. In describing the fate of the San children, Philip argued that life for a Bushman child was like that of a 'wild beast', in that 'he [could] be got for the catching'.[7]

References to the kidnapping and trading of San children along the Cape's north-eastern frontier zone during the early nineteenth century appear with regularity in both missionary and colonial archives of the period. This chapter explores the extent to which the capture and compulsion into a forced labour regime of its children contributed to the demise of Cape San society, and its significance relative to the other ways in which San society was destroyed, particularly the exterminatory activities of commandos.[8]

The use of child labour at the Cape was common practice in the early nineteenth century and already had a long history there. Children born of slave mothers were automatically enslaved. Dating back to the early eighteenth century, children born to a Khoisan[9] mother and slave father were classified as 'Bastaard-Hottentots', and farmers were entitled to indenture such children born on their farms until they turned 25.[10] The contemporary Western conviction that children ought to be protected and nurtured originated in the mid- to late-nineteenth century. Victorian Britain began to emphasise the role of the family in society and initiated the modern predilection for the sanctity of childhood. The use of child labour at the Cape in the early nineteenth century was in keeping with common labour practice in pre-industrial society, including Europe, where it was

---

6   Council for World Mission Archive (hereafter CWMA), Fiche 1598, J. Philip to directors of the LMS, 15 March 1842. In addition to Philippolis, Philip also visited Bethulie, Griquatown and Colesberg on this particular tour of inspection.

7   Philip, *Researches*, vol. 2, 263.

8   For further detail on the role of commandos on the Cape frontier, see Penn, N. 2005. *The Forgotten Frontier: Colonist and Khoisan on the Cape's Northern Frontier in the Eighteenth Century.* Cape Town: Double Storey Books, 108–54; Adhikari, M. 2010. *The Anatomy of a South African Genocide: The Extermination of the Cape San Peoples.* Cape Town: University of Cape Town Press, 39–43.

9   Khoisan is a combination of Khoikhoi and San. Its wide use in South African and Cape historiography points to difficulties in determining whether individuals were Khoikhoi or San. The incorporation of both pastoralists and hunter-gatherers into the Cape economy, especially during the nineteenth century, resulted in a blurring of the two categories.

10   Viljoen, R. 2005. 'Indentured labour and Khoikhoi "equality" before the law in Cape colonial society, South Africa: the case of Jan Paerl, c.1796'. *Itinerario*, 29, no. 3, 60.

taken for granted that children should work.[11] British colonial authorities at the Cape, however, did recognise that child labourers were vulnerable to ill treatment. It was also apparent to the British that some San children were being captured on the frontier and sold in the colony, thus resulting in their enslavement.

In South African historiography, a clear distinction has been drawn between Khoisan and slave statuses. Chattel slaves who came from a wide variety of regions within the Indian Ocean trading network were imported to service the labour needs of the Dutch East India Company (DEIC, also VOC)[12] as well as that of the emerging settler economy at the Cape. The importation of slaves began a few years after the VOC established its refreshment station at Table Bay in 1652 and continued through until 1807, when the slave trade was abolished throughout the British Empire. The VOC had insisted early on that the Khoisan were not to be enslaved. It would, however, be too simplistic to draw a neat distinction between 'free' Khoisan and chattel slaves for as Malherbe has observed, differences between slavery, indenture, contract labour and apprenticeship were blurred in early nineteenth century Cape society. This was especially true of the San children on settler farms, though early nineteenth century British authorities were themselves uncertain whether these children were being treated as slaves.[13]

Histories of European forms of bonded labour, and especially of the Atlantic slave trade, have tended to regard the label 'slave' as synonymous with 'chattel'. Yet, recent scholarship increasingly acknowledges that forms of bondage were diverse, especially outside of the Atlantic world. Slaves were not always, and not only, chattels, and a definition of slavery that places greater emphasis on the experience of 'social death' for its victims proves more helpful in an analysis of this sort. Orlando Patterson, eminent historian

---

[11]   González, O.E. & Premo, B. eds. 2007. *Raising an Empire: Children in Early Modern Iberia and Colonial Latin America.* Albuquerque: University of New Mexico Press, 2–3; Cunningham, H. 2006. *The Invention of Childhood.* London: BBC Books; Cunningham, H. 1995. *Children and Childhood in Western Society since 1500.* Harlow: Pearson Education Limited; Hetherington, P. 2002. *Settlers, Servants and Slaves: Aboriginal and European Children in Nineteenth Century Western Australia.* Nedlands: University of Western Australia Press, 1; Breuil, B.C. 2008. 'Precious children in a heartless world: the complexities of child trafficking in Marseilles'. *Children and Society,* 22, 226.

[12]   VOC stands for its Dutch equivalent, *de Verenigde Oost-Indische Compagnie.*

[13]   Ross R. 1983. *The Cape of Torments: Slavery and Resistance in South Africa.* London: Routledge, 43; Malherbe V.C. 1991. 'Indentured and unfree labour in South Africa: towards an understanding'. *South African Historical Journal,* 24, no. 1, 5. For a related analysis of farm labour and slavery, see Russell M. 1976. 'Slaves or workers? Relations between Bushmen, Tswana and Boers in the Kalahari'. *Journal of Southern African Studies,* 2, no. 2, 178–197.

of slavery, has highlighted three features distinctive of the institution, namely, extreme violence, natal alienation and dishonour. Together, they subject the slave to 'social death', which entails their subservience being maintained by brute force, their alienation imposed by severing ties to natal groups and locales, and their being denied an independent social existence. All three features can be reconciled with the experience of San children taken captive on the Cape frontier.[14]

Whether removed from their parents by force, or given up by their parents out of desperation, San children were legally bonded or apprenticed to farmers until adulthood. They were required to serve their masters faithfully and productively, and as with slaves and other bonded servants, they were subject to corporal punishment if they did not perform their duties as expected.[15] They could not legally be traded, although this did occur, and their status may not have been inherited by their offspring, yet forced removal from their natal communities and subsequent bondage amounted to 'something like slavery'.[16]

After the second British occupation of the Cape in 1806, local authorities were prepared to facilitate the apprenticeship of San children to farmers. Rather than being concerned that San children were used as labourers, the British colonial administration at the Cape was worried about how San children were being procured. The prospect that children were being captured and enslaved along the Cape frontier in the years following the abolition of the slave trade was embarrassing to the colonial government. In an attempt to monitor the procurement of child labour, elaborate rules were introduced to regulate the apprenticeship system. These measures proved ineffective as the colonial state lacked the capacity to curb the frontier practice of kidnapping San children and using them as forced labourers.

---

[14] Campbell G., Miers S. & Miller J.C. eds. 2009. *Children in Slavery Through the Ages.* Athens: Ohio University Press, 2, 3; Blagbrough, J. 2008. 'Child domestic labour: a modern form of slavery'. *Children and Society*, 22, no. 3, 179–190; Patterson, O. 1982. *Slavery and Social Death: A Comparative Study.* Cambridge, Mass.: Harvard University Press, 2; Newton-King, S. 1999. *Masters and Servants on the Cape Eastern Frontier.* Cambridge: Cambridge University Press, ch. 7; Mason, J. 2003. *Social Death and Resurrection: Slavery and Emancipation in South Africa.* Charlottesville: University of Virginia Press, 7–9.

[15] The apprenticeship or *inboekseling* system was legalised by the VOC government in 1775. It had existed for at least half a century before this. The term 'apprenticeship' is misleading as apprentices were not taught 'trades', but exploited as unskilled labour. Indenture would be a more appropriate term, the system resembling slavery in key ways.

[16] This phrase alludes to Shirleene Robinson's 2008 study *Something like Slavery? Queensland's Aboriginal Child Workers, 1842–1895.* Melbourne: Australian Scholarly. For a discussion of how modern practices of forced child labour are analogous to slavery, see Degirmencioglu S.M., Acar H. & Acar Y.B. 2008. 'Extreme forms of child labour in Turkey'. *Children and Society*, 22, no. 3, 191–200.

That most San children in the employ of colonists came to be treated as 'Hottentot'[17] was encouraged by local Dutch-speaking officials, who were themselves farmers, as 'Hottentot' status meant to be 'in the permanent and servile employ of white settlers'.[18]

The vulnerability of the San child captives accentuates the larger tragedy that befell the Cape's hunter-gatherers. As in other colonial settings, in particular in Latin America and Australia, 'kidnappings and raids of rebellious indigenous neighbours' was a hallmark of the settler frontier. The upheaval accompanying frontier violence meant that children were subject to abandonment, destitution and forced migration which facilitated 'the circulation of children' in settler society.[19] Understanding the conditions under which San children were incorporated into settler society as forced labourers sheds new light on the destruction of the community to which they belonged. Using the lens of San child forced labour brings into sharper focus processes of cultural genocide that complemented the physical destruction of Cape San society.

San and settler on the Cape's north-eastern frontier

The early nineteenth century heralded a crucial period in the San's struggle for survival on the fringes of the expanding Cape Colony. Their formidable resistance to the encroachment of settler stock farmers in the north-eastern reaches of the Cape frontier during the closing decades of the eighteenth century had been weakened by the time of the first British occupation in 1795.[20] Extensive loss of land and resources curtailed the San's ability to resist

---

[17] 'Hottentot' was a pejorative term initially used by Europeans to refer to indigenous pastoralists encountered at the Cape. By the early nineteenth century, the label had a wider resonance, increasingly applied to any servile labourer not chattel. In this way most San incorporated into the colonial economy came to be regarded as 'Hottentot'.

[18] Dooling W. 2005. 'The origins and aftermath of the Cape Colony's "Hottentot Code" of 1809'. *Kronos,* 31, 53.

[19] Shelton L. 2007. 'Like a servant or like a son? Circulating children in northwestern Mexico', in *Raising an Empire,* eds O.E. González & B. Premo, 232.

[20] The north-eastern Cape frontier, which had reached the escarpment by the late eighteenth century, was a crucial zone for both San and colonist. For millennia, San had traversed the escarpment following seasonal rainfall patterns. The consolidation of European settlement along this divide meant that the San were faced with the prospect of being confined to the more arid interior, dramatically disrupting their transhumant hunter-gatherer lifestyle. Penn has argued that this was the main reason why San resistance against settler encroachment beyond the escarpment was so fierce. See Penn, *Forgotten Frontier,* 82–85; Penn N. 1996. 'Fated to perish: the destruction of the Cape San', in *Miscast: Negotiating the Presence of the Bushmen,* ed. P. Skotnes. Cape Town: University of Cape Town Press, 82.

further settler advances, but they remained undefeated. For trekboers,[21] the commando system proved the most effective means of dispossessing the Cape's indigenous peoples and opening up new territory for stock farming. Several thousand San were killed by commandos, especially in the last three decades of the eighteenth century. The San were not, however, completely eradicated from the north-eastern frontier zone during this time. The scale of destruction wrought by commandos meant that by the early nineteenth century San opposition had been reduced to isolated acts of guerrilla-style resistance. Large-scale, collective resistance, such as that which had occurred during the 'Bushmen Wars' of the 1770s and 1780s, was no longer possible as the social fabric of San society had been too radically disrupted. Nonetheless, attacks by San groups on frontier settler homesteads continued into the nineteenth century and even small bands were capable of inflicting severe losses on stock farmers. Such resistance was regarded as criminal by farming communities and the removal of the San from the land seen as the only means of securing the frontier.[22]

While the commando system of the late eighteenth century had the full sanction of the VOC, the institution was reluctantly retained by the British administration which inherited the ongoing conflict between settler and San on the north-eastern frontier. The British were eager to resolve the conflict and check wanton destruction of San life. The first such effort was undertaken by Governor George Macartney, whose proclamation of 1798 set out a conciliatory course for future relations between the colony and San. However, in spite of the best intentions of the authorities in Cape Town, frontier hostilities continued.[23]

What followed over the next 30 years was the introduction of legislation intended by the British to quell violence on the frontier and bring the San to 'peaceable' means. Under British rule at the Cape, the San continued to be pursued and murdered by commandos along the north-eastern frontier. At

---

21 Trekboers were transhumant pastoralists who were at the forefront of settler encroachment into the Cape interior. See Van der Merwe P.J. 1995. *The Migrant Farmer in the History of the Cape Colony, 1657–1836*, trans. by R.G. Beck. Athens: Ohio University Press.

22 Adhikari, *Anatomy*, 86; Giliomee H. 1981. 'Processes in development of the southern African frontier', in *The Frontier in History: North America and Southern Africa Compared*, eds H. Lamar & L. Thompson. New Haven: Yale University Press; House of Commons Parliamentary Papers (HCPP), 50 of 1835, no. 6, *Reports and Papers relating to Depredations of, and Expeditions against, the Bushmen, from 1817 to 1824, in the Districts of Graaff Reynet, Cradock, Beaufort, Worcester and Clanwilliam*, 56; Newton-King, *Masters and Servants*, 146.

23 Dooling W. 2007. *Slavery, Emancipation and Colonial Rule in South Africa*. Scottsville: University of KwaZulu-Natal Press, 60; McDonald, J. 2007. 'When shall these dry bones live? Interactions between the London Missionary Society and the San along the Cape's northeastern frontier, 1790–1833'. MA thesis, University of Cape Town, 28–30.

the same time, remnant groups of San who survived commando raids were incorporated into the colony's labour market and increasingly subsumed under the category of 'Hottentot'. Former hunter-gatherers and herders came to constitute an important source of labour for frontier stock farmers. Survivors were distributed among those trekboers who had participated in the commando to help satisfy their growing labour needs. San children, in particular, were sought after as herders and domestic servants. In spite of their vilification as 'wild' and 'dangerous', it was widely acknowledged in settler society that if 'tamed', the San could make useful labourers. Trading in San children became common practice among frontier stock-farming communities. The forced assimilation, or 'taming', that followed the capture of San children constituted what sociologist Robert van Krieken, who has written on Australia's 'stolen generations', refers to as 'cultural genocide'— the eradication of the culture of those who survive the physical destruction of their social group by being forcibly assimilated into colonial society.[24]

Cultural genocide was a crucial factor in the destruction of Cape San identity, especially after the second British occupation in 1806. Legislation was introduced in subsequent years to regulate the employment of Khoisan labourers and the treatment of slaves and their descendants. Though well intentioned, this legislation reinforced, rather than diminished, the ambiguous legal status of abducted San children and was deftly exploited by stock farmers. Ambiguities stemmed from the inability of colonial authorities to enforce this legislation on the north-eastern frontier. This region was sparsely populated by settlers who occupied large tracts of grazing land. Distances between farms were considerable and the authority of the government tenuous. Magistracies lacked the necessary oversight to ensure compliance by stock farmers. This meant that settler

---

[24] Van Krieken has highlighted the relevance of 'cultural genocide' to debates around Australia's 'stolen generations' and the applicability of genocide as a label to describe what happened to Aboriginal children in the early twentieth century. He supports an understanding of genocide that goes beyond mass slaughter and argues that very often intent to destroy 'in whole or in part' was met by assimilationist objectives in settler colonies. Van Krieken R. 2004. 'Rethinking cultural genocide: aboriginal child removal and settler-colonial state formation'. *Oceania*, 75, no. 2, 125–51; Van Krieken R. 2008. 'Cultural genocide reconsidered'. *Australian Indigenous Law Review*, 12, 76–81. See also Card, C. 2003. 'Genocide and social death'. *Hypatia*, 18, no. 1, 63–79. For Khoisan labour on the frontier, see Ross, *Cape of Torments*, ch. 4; Guenther,M.G. 1977. 'Bushman hunters as farm labourers'. *Canadian Journal of African Studies*, 11, no. 2, 195–203; Magubane Z. 1996. 'Labour laws and stereotypes: images of the Khoikhoi at the Cape in the age of abolition'. *South African Historical Journal*, 35, no. 1, 115–34; Cloete H. 1852. *Three Lectures on the Emigration of the Dutch Farmers from the Colony of the Cape of Good Hope, and Their Settlement in the District of Natal.* Pietermaritzburg: J. Archbell & Son, 19.

abuse of regulations relating to San child labour continued well into the nineteenth century.[25]

A dearth of documentary sources means it is difficult to reconstruct the experience of captured San children in any detail. Most children disappeared from the records once they were apprenticed. Many appear only fleetingly as names in registers of apprenticeship. Sometimes their age at the time of their apprenticeship was recorded. This was almost always an estimate and often understated, so that children could be apprenticed for longer. In a few instances, the names of their mothers and place of birth were noted by officials. This tended to happen when San children were either voluntarily placed with farmers by parents no longer able to ensure their children's survival, or when recruiters ventured beyond the frontier to seek San children to take back to the colony.[26]

Commandos and the capturing of the San

Slaves at the Cape were not only imported from across the Indian Ocean trading network, but also acquired along the colony's frontiers. European slaving on the north-eastern frontier was motivated by the desire both to procure labour as well as to eradicate the threat posed by San communities, especially to stock farmers. Colonists constantly complained of labour shortages. This was particularly true of settlers residing in the extensive frontier district of Graaff-Reinet. With chattel slaves concentrated in the south-western Cape, where wine and grain farming dominated the economy, settlers in the interior relied on Khoisan to meet their labour needs. In the late 1790s, John Barrow, for example, while touring the frontier districts on behalf of the government, reported that farmers made use of 'Hottentot' labour as it was too expensive to purchase slaves. He estimated that in the whole of the Graaff-Reinet district there were no more than 700 slaves, but put the number of 'Hottentots' at 10 000. Given the prolonged conflict and concomitant slave-raiding in this district over the preceding two decades, it is highly likely that a sizeable portion of the 10 000 'Hottentots' were 'tamed' San. It was in the context of frontier conflict between European stock farmers and hunter-gatherers during the eighteenth century that forced labour akin to slavery emerged and became an accepted part of frontier life for colonists, so much so that a group of Graaff-Reinet settlers who had gone

---

25   Dooling, *Slavery*, 58–101; Van der Merwe, *Migrant Farmer*, 155.
26   See, for example, CA, Graaff-Reinet Magistrate (hereafter 1/GR), 15/71, *Register der Aanbesteeding van Bosjesmen Kinderen*, 1823; Philip, *Researches*, vol. 1, 180.

into rebellion against the VOC government in 1795 demanded the right to trade the San captives openly and to bind them to service for life.[27]

Newton-King provides the most detailed analysis of the scale on which the San were captured and enslaved, arguing that the labour regime which emerged in the closing decades of the eighteenth century in the eastern districts was 'consistent with the concept of slavery'. Those trekboers who sought land and pasturage in the Cape interior brought with them ideas about labour that were shaped by the slave economy of the western Cape. Newton-King argues that 'slaving was a by-product of a commando's activities', its most important objective being to destroy enemies, captive labourers being 'a valuable perquisite'. Commandos seldom engaged in either slave-raiding or extermination, but usually in both simultaneously.[28]

The VOC sanctioned both the taking of San captives as well as the killing of those who resisted the settler advance. This meant that the numbers of San killed and the ratio to those taken captive depended on the whim of those leading the commandos. In some instances, men and women were murdered and their children carried away. In other cases, men were killed and considerable numbers of women and children taken prisoner. It is apparent that the destruction of San bands continued into the nineteenth century. For example, writer and poet, Thomas Pringle, recorded the 1821 experience of a Cradock field-commandant: 'The kraal was surprised, the males consigned to indiscriminate slaughter, and such of the women and children as survived the massacre were carried into captivity'. It appears that the priority of this commando was to eradicate the threat of this San kraal and only secondarily to take advantage of what labour could be procured. Both the killing of San adults and the capture of San children served to eliminate the hunter-gatherer threat to settler livestock and livelihoods. On occasion, San children were also killed by commandos. A frightful glimmer into the heartlessness of commando attacks on the San is revealed by *Landdrost* Maynier, who had been 'made acquainted with the most terrible atrocities … such as ordering the Hottentots to dash out against the rocks the brains of infants in order to save powder and shot' because they were so

---

27   Eldredge E.A. 1994. 'Slave raiding across the Cape frontier', in *Slavery in South Africa: Captive Labour on the Dutch Frontier*, eds E.A. Eldredge & F. Morton. Pietermaritzburg: University of Natal Press, 93; Marais, J.S. 1944. *Maynier and the First Boer Republic*. Cape Town: Maskew Miller, 64–66; Barrow J. 1968. *An Account of Travels into the Interior of Southern Africa in the Years 1797 and 1798*. New York: Johnson Reprint Corporation, vol. 1, 163; Benton L. 2002. *Law and Colonial Cultures: Legal Regimes in World History, 1400–1900*. Cambridge: Cambridge University Press, 174. See also Legassick M. 1969. 'The Griqua, the Sotho-Tswana and the missionaries, 1780–1840: the politics of a frontier zone'. PhD thesis, University of California, Los Angeles, 132–48.

28   Newton-King, *Masters and Servants*, 120.

young as to be a burden to the commando. A 'Dutch colonist' told Pringle about a commando he had served on in his youth. After the commando had 'destroyed a considerable kraal of Bosjesmen' and the firing had ceased, it was discovered that 'five women were still living'. Their lives were initially spared, as some of the farmers 'wanted a servant for this purpose, another for that'. When it was determined that the five women were hindering the progress of the commando on its return to the colony, Carl Krotz, the leader, ordered they be shot. Four of the women were murdered on the spot, but one 'who clung on to a farmer' was spared. It was said that she was taken back to the colony by him and that she 'served him long and faithfully', eventually dying while still in the service of his family.[29]

Regardless of the intentions of individual commandos on the north-eastern frontier, the overarching goal was to eliminate the San threat to stock farming, and the capture of San children was a crucial element of this broader campaign. The apparent discrepancy between frequent massacring of the San, and stock farmers' need for labour, was not as contradictory as it may seem. By forcibly incorporating San children into the pastoral economy of the frontier, commandos not only helped destroy San society, but procured much-needed labour. The abduction and assimilation of San children was as injurious to San society as physical destruction. Newton-King estimates that by 1795, 'upwards of 1 000 war captives' were working for farmers of the Graaff-Reinet district and that by 1798, captives constituted one-eighth of the total population of servants.[30] While it is not possible to determine how many of these captives were children, it is safe to assume that the majority were, given the clear propensity of commandos for killing adults and taking children prisoner. Also, children were less likely to have engaged directly in fighting and so would have had a better chance of survival and being taken prisoner. San women would have accounted for the second largest category of captives.

While the closing decades of the eighteenth century represent the high point of commando activity, San resistance nonetheless continued well into the nineteenth century, providing the British administration with

---

29 Bradlow E. & Bradlow F. eds. 1979. *William Somerville's Narrative of His Journeys to the Eastern Cape Frontier and to Lattakoe, 1799–1802.* Cape Town: Van Riebeeck Society, 60; Pringle, T. 1835. *Narrative of a Residence in South Africa.* London: Edward Moxon, 238, 242; HCPP, 425 of 1837. *Report from the Select Committee on Aborigines (British settlements); with the minutes of evidence, appendix and index,* 27; Eldredge, 'Slave raiding', 97; Lye W.F. ed. 1975. *Andrew Smith's Journal of His Expedition Into the Interior of South Africa, 1834–36: An Authentic Narrative of Travels and Discoveries, the Manners and Customs of the Native Tribes, and the Physical Nature of the Country.* Cape Town: Balkema, 284.
30 Newton-King, *Masters and Servants,* 117–18.

justification for continued use of commandos. Although perturbed by the commando system, there was no viable alternative for checking San depredations on the frontier. Official commandos were, however, more strictly regulated under British rule. For example, in February 1822, a request to send out a commando of 150 men to pursue San stock thieves was declined by the *landdrost* of Graaff-Reinet. Due to the drought which had afflicted the region, the *landdrost* argued that the thieves had been 'urged on by want' and 'driven to desperation'. As such, he did not think that the thefts which had occurred warranted a commando. Unofficial commandos organised by disgruntled farmers, without the knowledge of local officials and sometimes with their collusion, continued to attack San kraals.[31]

In the Graaff-Reinet district, between 1813 and 1824, 21 official commandos were despatched 'against the Bosjesmen' with the *landdrost*'s sanction. During this period, 97 San were reported killed and 280 taken prisoner. The ratio of those taken captive to those killed is telling, especially when compared with commando figures for other districts. Between 1797 and 1824, 14 commandos from Stellenbosch district declared only 22 captives, while the 18 commandos that set out from the Worcester district during the same period claimed that no prisoners were taken. These figures ought to be treated with caution as they are likely to be significantly lower than the actual numbers killed or captured. That only three San are recorded as having been wounded by Graaff-Reinet commandos between 1813 and 1824 appears especially dubious. These figures do, however, illustrate that commandos continued to take significant numbers of captives on the north-eastern frontier through to the beginning of the 1820s.[32]

The previous decade had seen the British administration introduce a codified system of labour recruitment in the colony. The two most significant pieces of legislation to affect the Khoisan in this regard were the Caledon or 'Hottentot' Code of 1809 and the Apprenticeship Law of 1812. The 'Hottentot' Code effectively coerced all Khoisan living in the colony into the service of settlers, requiring that all 'Hottentots' carry a pass indicating that they were in employment and that they had a fixed place of abode. Any colonist could demand to see any 'Hottentot's' pass. Those without a pass were designated vagrants and could be placed in the service of farmers by *landdrosts* and field-cornets. The Apprenticeship Law is of greater relevance to the treatment of captive San children as it allowed farmers to apprentice

31   Barrow J. 1968. *Account of Travels*, vol. 1, 237; HCPP, 50 of 1835, no. 5. *Proclamations and Orders, Relative to Commandos and Institutions, from 1796 to 1824*, 53–54; HCPP, 50 of 1835, no. 6. *Reports and Papers*, 57.
32   HCPP, 50 of 1835, no. 6, 56; Dooling, *Slavery*, 62.

'Hottentot' children, who had been born to parents in their service, for 10 years once they reached the age of eight. This act gave legal sanction to farmers' belief that they were entitled to the labour of children who had been born on their properties, reflecting the slave-holding mentality which pervaded labour relations in the colony. Because farmers were entitled to the labour of slave children, so too did they feel entitled to the labour of 'Hottentot' children.[33]

This apprenticeship law had important repercussions for San identity because farmers were able to extend the regulations that applied to 'Hottentot' children to San children. While apprenticeship placed obligations on the master for the care of servants, the system of child apprenticeship also made it possible for farmers to conflate deliberately the status of captive San children with that of 'Hottentot' children. Masters were expected to provide for the basic needs of apprentices, including sufficient, 'wholesome' food, suitable shelter and decent clothing. Child apprentices were also to be instructed in the 'Christian religion' and the 'English language'.[34] Articles of apprenticeship recorded the name and approximate age of the child, along with the 'trade' in which the apprentice would be instructed. These were hardly trades as nearly all children were used as herders or domestic servants. For children separated from their communities and held in settler custody, the humane intentions of the apprenticeship system led to a cruel irony. While it was meant to ameliorate their lot, the assimilation of San children as apprentices into the settler economy also served to eradicate their identity as hunter-gatherers.

The 'cruel barbarous custom' and trafficking in San children

On 5 May 1817, Andries Stockenström, the *landdrost* of Graaff-Reinet district, wrote to Lieutenant-Colonel Christopher Bird, the colonial secretary to the Cape governor, Lord Charles Somerset, to draw his attention to what he termed a 'cruel barbarous custom'. Stockenström's letter conveyed his aversion at the prevalence of this 'custom' on the frontier, stressing that it required 'the immediate interference of Government':

The cruel barbarous custom so prevalent among the Bosjesmen of murdering or exposing such of their children as they cannot provide for, or parting with them on

---

33   Magubane, 'Labour Laws', 117; Elbourne, E. 1994. 'Freedom at issue: vagrancy legislation and the meaning of freedom in Britain and the Cape Colony, 1799–1842'. *Slavery and Abolition*, 15, no. 2, 114–50; Dooling, *Slavery*, 64; Trapido S. 1990. 'From paternalism to liberalism: the Cape Colony, 1800–1834'. *International History Review*, 12, no. 1, 79.

34   CA, 1/GR 15/72. *Indentures of apprenticeship, instructions and discharges, 1813–1889*. See, for example, the indenture of 9 February 1837.

any terms whatever, has induced several farmers to procure some of those children, by giving their unnatural parents some trifles for them in exchange, for the purpose of keeping them as servants ... or some from a mere humane principle, only to save their lives ...[35]

The *landdrost* raised the matter with the governor at this time, owing to the arrival of 'two little Bosjesmen girls' in the town of Graaff-Reinet.[36] The girls had been brought through the village by Jacob Theron, a Cape Town merchant. Upon questioning him, Stockenström reported that Theron would not provide any details other than 'that he had got them at a Bosjesmen kraal, where he was told that they were orphans'. Stockenström had a reputation for being well disposed towards the San. This was apparent from a number of his official statements. In 1826, in response to questions from commissioners Colebrooke and Bigge, who were undertaking an inquiry into the 'Condition and Treatment of the Native Inhabitants of Southern Africa', Stockenström, for example, asserted that:

[t]he encroachments on the aborigines began at Cape Town, and never ceased to extend by degrees until the colonists had got to where they now are ... If the government had had sufficient knowledge of the interior and sufficient authority in it, when the first settlers came to the chain of the Sneeuw- and Neweld-bergen, and there had fixed the boundary ... the Bosjesmen might have remained in peaceable possession of the country beyond ...[37]

The *landdrost* was also a staunch advocate of missionary activity among the San. He argued that mission stations provided the most feasible means for instilling in San an appreciation for a sedentary lifestyle and agro-pastoral subsistence. Stockenström's humanitarian sentiments towards the San were at odds with attitudes within settler society at large. His position was closer to that of the Cape's evangelical lobby, in particular John Philip. However, like the missionaries, Stockenström thought little of the San's ancient ways of life. Given that the northward progression of the frontier was unlikely to be halted, in spite of the efforts of colonial authorities to control the movement of trekboers, the best that could be hoped for was the peaceful incorporation of the San into the colony. This explains Stockenström's pragmatic approach towards frontier San. The dispossession of land and resources which had fomented the 'Bushman Wars' of the late eighteenth century was set to

---

[35] HCPP, 202 of 1826-7. *Accounts of all commandos or expeditions against the Bonshmen, which have taken place at the Cape of Good Hope, since 1797; stating the number of Bonshmen killed, wounded and taken prisoner; stating also what had been done with the prisoners,* 23.

[36] HCPP, 202 of 1826-7, 24.

[37] HCPP, 50 of 1835, no. 8. *Papers relative to the measures taken for fixing the boundaries of the Colony of the Cape of Good Hope upon the eastern and northern frontiers,* 117.

continue apace. Yet, during the course of the early nineteenth century, it was intended that the San would be peacefully incorporated into settler society and help ease the labour shortage. Stockenström and the colonial government hoped this would be achieved without the violence and slaughter which had accompanied earlier contact.[38]

Life for the San along the Cape's north-eastern frontier became increasingly precarious during the 1820s as the spaces between colonial settlement diminished rapidly. There were few opportunities for them to sustain their hunter-gathering mode of existence. Some fled further into the interior, beyond the Orange River, where they entered into patron–client or hostile relations with emerging Griqua polities. Hemmed in by various agro-pastoral groups, many San who survived commando raids had little option but to enter into the service of trekboers. Although tied to settler society, such relations still afforded some San a limited degree of independence. Others were not prepared to make the socio-cultural adaptations expected of them by trekboers, colonial authorities and missionaries alike. The continuing resistance of such groups played into the hands of those most hostile towards the San. It legitimised continued use of commandos to attack kraals that had raided livestock. In some instances, San raiders wreaked havoc by murdering 'Hottentot' herders, setting fire to buildings and maiming those animals which could not be carried away. These acts of resistance struck fear into frontier settler society while inflicting heavy financial losses on farmers. Also, stolen livestock provided the San with continued independence in circumstances that would otherwise have meant a stark choice between surrender and starvation. It is in light of these dire circumstances that Stockenström's accusation of their 'cruel barbarous custom' needs to be seen. The devastation of San society on the north-eastern frontier was such that many parents were faced with the option of either killing their children to prevent further suffering, or handing them over to settlers for whatever they could get.[39]

Representations of San as unfit parents both fed upon and strengthened deep-seated settler antagonism to the hunter-gatherer way of life. Accusations of cruel treatment of their children were an important means by which the San were further dehumanised by settler society. Most importantly, it served as a convenient justification for the procurement of San children by frontier stock farmers under the guise of saving them from

---

38   HCPP, 50 of 1835, no. 8, 118.
39   HCPP, 50 of 1835, no. 7. Extract from Mr. C.J. Reyneveldt's Report of the Commission of Circuit to Lieut. General Sir J.F. Cradock, Cape of Good Hope, 28 Feb. 1812, 407; Van der Merwe, Migrant Farmer, 161.

their 'unnatural parents'. As in colonial Australia, many settlers believed that indigenous children were best moulded as servants in the workplace itself. For Cape colonists, the most effective way of assimilating San children as subservient labourers was to remove them from their parents, and the colonial state felt fully entitled to regulate indigenous parent–child relations. This was apparent in numerous laws passed by the Cape government during the early nineteenth century, including Ordinance 50 of 1828, the most significant piece of legislation to affect Khoisan under British rule. This ordinance granted Khoisan legal equality with settlers and afforded them greater freedom of movement by annulling pass legislation. While Ordinance 50 sought to remove former abuses in the child labour system, it nonetheless emphasised the colonial state's prerogative to manage Khoisan families and their labour.[40]

So pervasive were perceptions of San as unfit parents that in April 1824, the commissioners Colebrooke and Bigge, when obtaining evidence from Robert Moffat, prominent LMS missionary at Kuruman, felt inclined to inquire: 'Are the Bushmen in general attached to their children?' Moffat confirmed that they indeed were. He commented that although 'the practice is not yet extinct of obtaining Bushmen children by barter of sheep and goats, which children are permanently separated from their tribes and families' that 'many applications' for San children 'had been rejected by the parents'. According to Moffat, 'the price offered had been raised with a view to tempt them', in one case with which he was familiar, a cow had been offered as compensation.[41] In reply to questions from the Commissioners, Stockenström stated:

> ... *although it was impossible to maintain that these children were always well treated and decently brought up ... [it was] preferable that they should be received by the boors [sic] to being strangled or dashed to pieces by their parents from absolute want of food, or to being left exposed to the wild beasts ...*[42]

This sentiment was also expressed by Governor Somerset when he introduced legislation prohibiting settlers from bartering San children.

---

40 HCPP, 50 of 1835, no. 6, 56; HCPP, 339 of 1829. *Return to an address of the Honourable House of Commons, dated 5th June 1829; copy of the order in council relative to the natives of South Africa*, 4–5; Jacobs M.D. 2005. 'Maternal colonialism: white women and indigenous child removal in the American West and Australia, 1880–1940'. *Western Historical Quarterly*, 36, no. 4, 453–76; Haebich A. 2000. *Broken Circles: Fragmenting Indigenous Families, 1800–2000*. Fremantle: Fremantle Arts Centre, 69, 79.

41 HCPP, 50 of 1835, no. 9. *Evidence of Mr. Moffat, a missionary, resident with the Bichuana tribes at Latakoo, dated 20 April 1824*, 126–27.

42 Theal G.M. 1905. *Records of the Cape Colony, December 1827 to April 1831*, vol. 35. 'Report of J.T. Bigge upon the Hottentot and Bushman population of the Cape of Good Hope, and of the missionary institutions'. London: Government Printers, 326.

Similar representations of 'Hottentot' parents' unnatural feelings towards their children were also widely held among settlers and used to defend the apprenticeship system. John Philip argued that the claim 'that Hottentots are deficient in kindly affections to their children' was a regular justification for apprenticeship. To refute the 'unnatural parent' claim, Philip asserted that in his experience 'the Hottentots [were] remarkable for an excess of affection for their offspring'. San parents who had given up their children to farmers found their pleas for the return of their children refused when they were capable of providing for them again. Stockenström was so convinced of the scale of the abuse that he referred to the practice as a 'traffic' in 'Bosjesmen' children.[43] He informed Somerset that:

> ... this (as it is called) ancient custom is beginning to be seriously abused, that these children got in the above manner are transferred from one hand to another, and that payment is secretly taken; that many by these means are gradually taken from the frontier, brought into the inner districts, and passed off as orphans ...[44]

Somerset's 1817 proclamation

In August 1817, just three months after the matter of child trafficking had first been brought to his attention, Governor Somerset instituted several of Stockenström's recommendations, which the *landdrost* had proposed in his earlier letter to Bird. The governor issued an official proclamation regarding the apprenticing of San children. Somerset's proclamation set out a series of 'lenient principles' intended to regulate the practice. It affirmed that 'for some time past', the San had been 'in the habit of leaving their children' with farmers who, rather than maintaining them 'until reclaimed by their parents', had developed 'a tendency to abuse the best principles' of such arrangements. Further, members of the stock-farming community on the frontier had sought to 'induce savage parents, for paltry bribe, to divest themselves of their natural feelings, and sell their children, or by fraud or force, or even murder, to acquire possession of the children of others for the purposes of sale'. While designed to put an end to 'acts of so atrocious a nature', the proclamation did not outlaw the practice of procuring and apprenticing San children. Rather, it explained when procurement would be deemed appropriate and how the apprenticeship ought to be formalised.[45]

43   Philip, *Researches*, vol. 1, 178; HCPP, 202 of 1826-7, 23, 56.
44   HCPP, 202 of 1826-7, 57.
45   CA, Colonial Office (hereafter CO), 5881. *Proclamations for country districts, 1806–1820, Bosjesmen Children, 8 Aug. 1817.*

In terms of the proclamation, farmers were only allowed to apprentice San children if their lives were in imminent danger or they faced severe harm. It was also ordered that 'no inhabitant, without the previous knowledge of the field-cornet nearest to his residence, shall take, receive or give any gratuity for a child to his parents, guardians or others offering to dispose of such child'. In keeping with the kinds of regulations which were already in place for the apprenticing of 'Hottentot' children, it was stipulated that if acquired when under the age of five and then maintained by a farmer until the age of 10, such a child could be apprenticed for a further 10 years. If a child was acquired when older than five but younger than eight, and was maintained until the age of 12, then he or she could be apprenticed until the age of 22. It is hardly surprising that in spite of its reformist intentions, the proclamation was easily undermined and manipulated to serve the interests of farmers, particularly in outlying areas.[46]

The proclamation gave legal sanction to the intentional conflation of the statuses of San and 'Hottentot' children. Stockenström bears some responsibility for this. He had argued that San apprentices should be placed 'upon the same principle and under the same restrictions as [had] been established with respect to Hottentot children, by the Proclamation of 23 April 1812'. Likewise, he recommended that San orphans be bound to farmers as Hottentot children were, to 'place them by degrees in the same light with respect to the laws of the Colony as the Hottentots now stand'.[47] Herein lay a crucial means by which large numbers of 'Bushmen' came to be subsumed under the label 'Hottentots'. San children acquired in dubious ways were forced into the frontier stock-farming economy as apprentices and legally assimilated to 'Hottentot' status. Whereas in childhood they had been 'Bushmen', by adulthood they had become 'Hottentots'. While Somerset's proclamation of August 1817 appears to have done little to prevent procurement of San children as forced labourers by frontier farmers, it did provide them with the means to legitimise the practice.

In spite of the humanitarian intentions of the 1817 proclamation, the actions of Somerset's government with regard to relations between the San and the colony point towards the primary motive behind it, namely, quelling San resistance. This was apparent in his treatment of missions to the San, which had been regarded as a primary means of conciliation since the first British occupation. It was only in 1814, however, that a mission specifically for San was founded by the LMS in this region. Toornberg, as

---

46   CA, CO, 5881, 'Bosjesmen children'.
47   HCPP, 50 of 1835, no. 6, 57.

the site became known, was followed by the establishment of Hephzibah, another San mission further to the north, in 1816. By the beginning of 1817, it was estimated that the combined population of the two missions stood at 1 700. Many of the residents would have been San, although, as with most missions in the Cape interior at this time, it is likely that the population would have included 'Bastaards', Khoikhoi and Korana.[48]

However, in January 1817, Somerset ordered that Toornberg and Hephzibah be closed down. Believing all the residents of both missions to be San, Somerset feared that to have that many San congregated so close to the colonial boundary posed a threat to outlying farms. Growing tension between frontier stock farmers and LMS missionaries also influenced Somerset's decision. This tension revolved around stock farmers' need for labour. The missions were tolerated as long as the missionaries ministered to 'wild Bushmen'. Once the missionaries were accused of providing sanctuary to San farm labourers who had fled service in the colony, Somerset decided to act. Stockenström, only too aware of the pressing demands for labour in the Graaff-Reinet district, was likewise disappointed that this had been occurring. Writing to the head missionary at Toornberg, Erasmus Smit, Stockenström noted that '[c]ontinual complaints are sent in respecting persons who have run away from their masters being kept at your institution'. That 'tame Bushmen' were running away from Graaff-Reinet farms to seek refuge at Toornberg and Hephzibah undermined the main reason the colonial state supported missions to the San. For colonial authorities and stock farmers alike, the missions were supposed to help mould the San into a reliable source of labour. When mission stations became places of refuge for San fleeing European masters, this support was quickly withdrawn.[49]

It is apparent from Somerset's proclamation that his apprehensions stemmed not from the use of San child labour, but rather from how such labour was being acquired and whether the children were being treated as slaves. Somerset conveyed these sentiments to Stockenström in May 1822,

---

48 Schoeman K. 1993. 'Die Londense Sendinggenootskap en die San: die stasies Toornberg en Hephzibah, 1814–1818'. *South African Historical Journal*, 28, no. 1, 221–34; Philip, *Researches*, vol. 2, 21; McDonald, 'Dry Bones', 59, 70. 'Bastaard' was a pejorative Dutch colonial term for a person of mixed Khoisan and European, or slave and European descent, while Korana were a mixed, though predominantly Khoisan, group which originated along the Orange River.

49 CA, Government House (hereafter GH), 1/48/669. *Complaints by the London Missionary Society of certain grievances sustained by their institutions at the Cape*, 4 July 1825; Szalay, M. 1995. *The San and the Colonisation of the Cape*. Köln: Rüdiger Köppe, 55; Macmillan, W.M. 1968. *The Cape Colour Question: A Historical Survey*. Cape Town: Balkema, 130; McDonald, 'Dry bones', 76.

when he asserted that the retention of San women and children 'ought never to take place without the greatest precaution, for the future treatment of these unfortunates, and prevention of the possibility of their merging into the class of slaves'. The approach taken by both Somerset and Stockenström was couched in humanitarian reasoning and was clearly reflected in the proclamation of 1817. Article 12, for example, stipulated that San orphans be apprenticed to 'respectable and humane inhabitants'. By being so placed, it was hoped that such children would be 'tamed' and become useful labourers. For the government it was acceptable for San children to be assimilated as 'Hottentot' labourers, but not as slaves.[50]

Forced transfer of San children to Boer society in the 1820s

There can be little doubt that the effectiveness of Somerset's 1817 proclamation would be severely compromised in a frontier region such as that which existed along the Cape's north-eastern border. It often happened that even when officials such as field-cornets were in a position to act against farmers implicated in bartering or kidnapping San children, they did little to stop them. Field-cornets themselves were farmers, sometimes slave-owners, and similarly bent on acquiring cheap labour. They had little motivation to implement the government's vision of a more humane and closely regulated system of San child labour in the interior. This ineffectiveness is apparent from Stockenström's re-issuing of key directives of the 1817 proclamation in December 1822. Entitled 'Instructions respecting the introducing, permitting, and apprenticing of Bosjesmen children in the District of Graaff-Reinet', these directives reveal much about the continued use of San child labour as well as its likeness to slavery. Article One stipulated that at the next *opgaaf*[51] in 1823, the name and age of each San child on the farmstead had to be provided, along with an explanation of how the child came to be in the colony. There was, however, an important caveat:

> Such of the Bosjesmens children who from long residence have mixed with the Hottentots, and have been considered as such, and who have as Hottentot children been apprenticed among the inhabitants, by any of the landdrosts, are not here included; in future, however, this mixing of these two descriptions of people shall not be permitted, but the registers of them be kept separate.[52]

Stockenström's 'Instructions' stipulated that should the 'good treatment' of children be doubted by any *landdrost*, the child should be 'placed under

---

50   HCPP, 202 of 1826-7, 17, 21.
51   An *opgaaf* involved the enumeration of farmers' assets for taxation.
52   HCPP, 202 of 1826-7, 21.

better care'. Although the new measures were well intentioned, their implementation was deeply flawed. Those children given up by their parents were to be presented before the *landdrost* or his deputy 'within a month after having been received' so that they could be legally indentured. This was meant to provide local authorities with an opportunity to determine whether children had been acquired with parental consent. In addition, it was stipulated that orphaned children captured by commandos were 'to be put out with respectable and humane inhabitants'. The problem with the scheme was that it depended on the goodwill and integrity of farmers. Captive children were not likely to dispute their new masters' claims before the *landdrost* of having acquired them legitimately. And by sanctioning the distribution of orphaned children, Stockenström's instructions created an incentive for commandos to kill San parents to claim their children. Another proviso was that if captured together, parents and children were 'not to be separated'. The inclusion of this point suggests that parents and children had been separated in the past. If so, this bears a striking similarity to slave experiences. It was only in the late 1820s and early 1830s that ameliorative legislation prevented the separation of parents and children at slave auctions. Article Ten of the 'Instructions' alluded to the growing number of San being forced to work for farmers, declaring that in the case of 'Bosjesmen' desirous of entering into contract work, such arrangements were to be 'considered equally binding as that entered into between the inhabitants and the Hottentots'. Farmers were warned that they would face a fine of 50 Rixdollars 'for every Bosjesmen wrongly detained'.[53]

The *opgaaf* of 1823 provides a sense of the number of San children living and working on colonial farms despite considerably understating reality. In Graaff-Reinet, the district most dependent on Khoisan labour, most involved in commando activity and administered by Stockenström, this was the first year that the number of San child labourers was formally counted. During 1823, 155 San children had been 'placed under the care and protection' of settlers in Graaff-Reinet. The number officially apprenticed stood at 49. These figures do not include those children acquired and apprenticed before 1823. In contrast, the report of the Graaff-Reinet sub-district of Cradock included all San children and adults designated 'Ingeboekte Bosjesmans' then residing with farmers, not only those acquired or apprenticed in 1823. The number of such San below the age of 16 stood at 437, while those older

---

[53]   HCPP, 202 of 1826-7, 21–22.

numbered 405. Some farmers in Cradock had as many as 20 San, both adults and children, in their service. Many more had between 10 and 15.[54]

Slip-shod record-keeping of the number of San children in settler employ favoured the interests of farmers. Commissioner Bigge, in his report on the Cape's 'Bushmen', noted that throughout the colony, wages were lowest in Graaff-Reinet. This, he said, was 'attributable to the facility with which the farmers [had] been able to procure the services of the Bushmen'. Stock farmers had a clear incentive to subvert government regulation of San child labour. The blurring of distinctions between San and 'Hottentot', which continued apace in the 1820s, facilitated such subversion. In 1824, Stockenström reported that in the seven years since the passage of the 1817 proclamation, only two farmers, J. Pyper and C. Jantzen, had been prosecuted for transgressing its provisions and that there had been no convictions before the circuit court. The prosecution of only two farmers amid numerous reports of the abduction of San children in missionary correspondence, government despatches and travel writing, highlights the difficulties the Cape government faced in imposing its will on frontier society.[55]

The reluctance of local officials to regulate the acquisition of San child labourers according to the letter of the law was reflected in a case which came to government attention in November 1826. Major Andrews, who commanded a military post on the north-eastern frontier, reported that two San men had complained about 'unprovoked aggression ... by the border farmers'. The men accused two farmers 'of having murdered some of their children, and forcibly carried off others of them into slavery'. Stuurman and Ackerman, the San men laying the complaint, informed Andrews that they had not bothered to take up the matter with the local field-cornet or his deputy, 'thinking that doing so would be useless'. Andrews noted that if true, this complaint went some way in accounting 'for the very great degree of dissatisfaction evinced by the farmers residing in this part of the frontier at the arrival of troops in their neighbourhood'. The military post gave the San a new avenue of complaint against farmers. This irked farmers who consistently opposed British interference in labour relations on the frontier.[56]

Subsequent investigation into the complaint reveals several noteworthy aspects of San experience with settler stock farmers on the frontier. Both Stuurman and Ackerman accused stock farmers Hans and Johannes van

---

[54]   CA, Imperial Books on South Africa (hereafter OPB), OPB 1/2, no. 12. *Employment of Bosjesmen, and Apprenticing of Children*, 143–44.
[55]   Theal, 'Report of J.T. Bigge', 315; CA, OPB 1/2, no. 12, 140.
[56]   CA, OPB 1/2, no. 15. *Papers relative to Acts of Aggression and Commandos against the Hottentots, and Capture of Bushmen Children*, 148–157.

Tonder of abducting their children.[57] Stuurman, who lived on the northern side of the Orange River beyond the official boundary of the colony, complained that in September 1826, Van Tonder came to his kraal and 'without saying a word to him … took away his youngest child, a boy about five years of age'. When Stuurman followed Van Tonder, he threatened to shoot him and so he turned back. The second complainant, Ackerman, from another kraal in the region, told of how around the same time a group of farmers and 'Hottentots' approached him asking for children. Ackerman explained to the group that there were only two children left in his kraal, with all the others having already been taken. He requested that the two remaining children be left with him as he was old and required their assistance. Hans van Tonder allegedly responded by assaulting Ackerman, beating him 'so severely that he was unable to stir for some days'. The group then, without his permission, took away his son aged 13. At some point later on they returned and took away the kraal's last child, his seven-year-old daughter. These two cases suggest that by the mid-1820s, San kraals on the north-eastern frontier were generally not able to prevent their children from being forcibly removed. Children were summarily abducted by farmers whenever they were in need of labourers, and not only during commando operations.[58]

During the investigation that followed Stuurman and Ackerman's complaints, it was discovered that the Van Tonders had 14 San in their service. There were six children, with four of the adults having been in their service since childhood. All 14 San gave testimony to the inquiry. None of them complained about the treatment they received, nor did they implicate the Van Tonders in child raiding. Andries, aged about 25, recounted how he had lived with Hans van Tonder since childhood. Explaining how he came to reside with Van Tonder, he stated:

> The Bushmen had stolen horses, and done other mischief. A commando went in pursuit of them and after the cattle. My master found me there. I had no parents living, and therefore willingly came with my master …[59]

The San servants testified that they found the Van Tonders agreeable and were happy to remain in their service. It is highly likely the Van Tonders intimidated their servants into giving favourable evidence. In the end, the Van Tonders were not prosecuted, but in order to ensure that no similar

---

57 Johannes van Tonder also appears as John van Tonder in the records. Both Hans and Johannes also appear initially with the surname Van Zender, but later on, following an investigation and the questioning of witnesses, they appear as Van Tonder.
58 See also Philip, *Researches*, vol. 2, 267; HCPP, 202 of 1826-7, 23; HCPP, 425 of 1837, 28.
59 CA, OPB 1/2, no. 15, 153.

complaints arose in future, the *landdrost* ordered that '[a]ll the Bushmen, women and children then be called in [to the court], and the contents of the proclamation of 8 August 1817 clearly explained to them, and the attention of the field cornet called to it'. What this indicates is that even when the colonial government sought to enforce the 1817 proclamation, farmers were easily able to circumvent it. The investigation provides one of the rare instances in which San 'voices' appear in the records of the period.[60]

Numerous observers noted that the San on the north-eastern frontier had been reduced to a deplorable condition by the 1820s. For example, George Thompson, a traveller and explorer, wrote in 1824 of the San on the north-eastern frontier:

> *The Bushmen on this frontier, whatever may have been the original condition of their progenitors, are now entirely destitute of cattle or property of any description, and now that the larger game have been generally destroyed, or driven out of the country by the guns of the Boors and Griquas, they are reduced to the most wretched shifts to obtain a precarious subsistence ...*[61]

It is not surprising that under such circumstances, a sizeable number of San children would have been orphaned or kidnapped as they were the most vulnerable victims of frontier turmoil. Some children only appeared in the colonial records as apprentices many years after they had first been acquired. In spite of flaws in the apprenticeship system, some farmers did heed the new regulations and sought to apprentice children that had been in their custody for several years. The 1823 *opgaaf* returns for Graaff-Reinet reveal that many of the children had been held for up to eight years already. With the average age of those children apprenticed in 1823 standing at eight, many had either been acquired while very young, possibly as infants, or their ages were deliberately understated to have them work for longer.[62]

The woeful state to which the San on the north-eastern frontier had been reduced by the 1820s drove many kraals to livestock raiding for survival. This in turn further provoked stock farmers' disdain and ire. Settlers wanted to clear the land of hindrances and dangers, while securing much needed labour. The removal of children from San society formed an important part of this wider agenda. San resistance only fanned the flames of settler aggression and provided frontier farmers with justification for acquiring San children as labourers. George Thompson reported that colonists

---

60   CA, OPB 1/2, no. 15, 148–57.
61   Thompson G. 1968. *Travels and Adventures in Southern Africa.* Cape Town: Van Riebeeck Society, parts 2, 4.
62   CA, 1/GR 15/71, *Register van de Aanbesteeding van Bosjesmans Kinderen in het District Graaff-Reinet.*

'maintained … that the Bushmen are a nation of robbers' and 'that they would live much more comfortable [sic] by becoming the herdsmen and household servants of the Christians'.[63] If captured alive and found suitable, adult San were no doubt incorporated as labourers. However, children were especially valued as they were the most malleable.[64]

Child abduction and genocide of the San

The removal of San children from their families formed an integral part of the destruction of the Cape's hunter-gathering communities. In commando raids, some children were killed while many were captured and raised as forced labourers on settler farmsteads. For stock farmers, the abduction of these children served two purposes. Firstly, it eliminated a future threat as San children might grow up to be raiders and resisters, and secondly, it provided a means for acquiring scarce labour resources. With ties to their families, culture and land severed, abducted children became entirely dependent on their masters. In this regard, the fate of San children on the Cape frontier during the early nineteenth century bears a striking similarity to that of Aboriginal children in colonial Australia, in particular Queensland. There too, indigenous children were not only caught up in the violence of the frontier, but forced removal from their communities formed 'an integral part of Aborigine's experiences of colonisation'. Child removal in both arenas destabilised indigenous society, diluted their social identities and undermined aboriginal claims to the land, contributing to rapid population decline.[65]

Two questions arise from this assessment. Firstly, to what extent did the forcible transfer of San children to Boer society contribute to the genocide of the San? And secondly, is it appropriate to refer to the status of these abducted children as slavery? Both questions invite controversy. That the fate of the Cape San peoples during the eighteenth and nineteenth centuries was genocide has only recently gained traction in academia, though detractors remain. One of the most important reasons for a lack of consensus is debate around the definition of genocide. A fundamental condition for an episode of mass violence to be accepted as genocide is proof

---

63   Thompson, *Travels and Adventures*, parts 2, 4.
64   For a discussion of the perceptions around the malleability of child labourers, see Mendes, A. 2009. 'Child slaves in the early north Atlantic trade in the fifteenth and sixteenth centuries', in *Children in Slavery Through the Ages*, eds G. Campbell, S. Miers & J.C. Miller. Athens: Ohio University Press.
65   Robinson, *Something like Slavery?*, 10; Hetherington, *Settlers, Servants and Slaves*, 3; Haebich, *Broken Circles*, 70.

of intent to eradicate a particular group 'in whole or in part'. This appears difficult to establish in the case of the San. As mentioned, settlers depended on indigenous labourers to fill the void created by a dearth of imported slaves on the frontier. It seems contradictory and self-defeating to suggest that settlers sought to eliminate those individuals upon whom they relied as labourers. This is where a greater recognition of the role played by the abduction of San child labourers and their incorporation into the settler frontier economy is able to shed light. Genocide entails more than just mass murder. The definition outlined in the United Nations Convention on the Prevention and Punishment of the Crime of Genocide (UNCG) of 1948 includes inflicting 'serious bodily or mental harm', as well as the introduction of 'measures intended to prevent births within the group' as genocide. The UNCG definition also includes the forcible transfer of children from the victim group as an act of genocide.[66]

Acts, other than murder, which are calculated to bring about the eradication of a particular group have been designated as cultural genocide by Van Krieken and others. This conceptual approach is highly applicable to settler colonial contexts. In the case of the San, the commandos did the work of crushing indigenous resistance and clearing the land for stock farming. Many thousands of San lost their lives in the resulting frontier warfare. Those who survived commando attacks were subject to forced assimilation as labourers. The threat posed by the San to European settlement in the Cape interior was eliminated by means of slaughter as well as the abduction of survivors. The majority of the survivors of commando attacks were children. Acknowledging the forcible transfer of San children into Boer society helps reconcile the apparent contradiction between the killing of San and stock farmer dependence on San labour, making the destruction of Cape San society more clearly genocidal. Cultural genocide proved the most effective means for facilitating indigenous integration into colonial society while avoiding their physical annihilation. Forced child removal played a fundamental role in this process. Writing about Australia, Van Krieken argues that '[t]he predominant aim of Indigenous child removals was the absorption or assimilation of the children … so that their unique cultural value and ethnic identities would disappear'.[67]

---

[66] Adhikari, *Anatomy*, 80–93; Moses A.D. 2005. 'Genocide and settler society in Australian history', in *Genocide and Settler Society: Frontier Violence and Stolen Indigenous Children in Australian History.* New York: Berghahn Books.

[67] Van Krieken, 'Rethinking cultural genocide', 125–26, 129. See also Mako S. 2012. 'Cultural genocide and key international instruments: framing the indigenous experience'. *International Journal on Minority and Group Rights,* 19, 176–77.

It is with this in mind that Orlando Patterson's conceptualisation of slavery as 'social death' becomes useful. Enslavement of parts of South Africa's indigenous peoples, including the San, is not widely acknowledged in South African historiography. That the Cape Colony had a distinct, imported, chattel slave class partly explains this. While San and Khoikhoi may have endured conditions on settler farms that were very similar to slavery, they were never formally labelled slaves. The evidence also suggests that life as farm labourers was at times worse for 'Hottentots' than it was for slaves. Not being owned by their masters and not having a market value, 'Hottentots' suffered even more cruel treatment than slaves. Nonetheless, legal ownership is not the sole criterion for defining slave status. Forcibly removed from their parents by farmers who ruthlessly exploited them as herders and domestic servants, coerced to perform these duties for which they received no compensation and often bound to their masters until adulthood, the experience of these children bore several markers of slavery. Just as with Aboriginal children in Queensland, 'this was the hidden side of the story of [the] extermination' of the San. And as with the experience of chattel slaves, social death was central to this story.[68]

Social death involves the loss of social vitality and with it, loss of identity. The extreme violence of commandos not only meant a high casualty rate for the San, but as the commandos facilitated European settlement, so the San's ability to subsist was undermined. For survivors, the result was forced estrangement from their communities, culture and land. Under these circumstances children, even when enslaved within their native land, suffered natal alienation. The rupturing of intergenerational connections destroyed their distinct culture and with it, the foundational relationship between San and the land. Along with their forced subjugation and natal alienation, the social death of San children was completed by their near absolute dependence on their masters.[69] They may not have been slaves in name, nor were they legally recognised as slaves, but as forced labourers, their childhood and adolescence bore striking similarities to the social death suffered by slaves.

The post-capture experience of San children growing up and working on settler farms is difficult to evoke. A dearth of source material obscures the detail and intricacies of their assimilation to servitude. The government's intention was that such children be subsumed under the 'Hottentot'

---

68 Wells J. 2000. 'The scandal of Rev. James Read and the taming of the London Missionary Society by 1820'. *South African Historical Journal*, 42, no. 1, 142–43; Haebich, *Broken Circles*, 79.

69 Card, 'Genocide and social death', 73; Patterson, *Slavery and Social Death*, 5–9.

category and this is by and large what happened. As children, they were particularly susceptible to internalising colonial ideas of race and negative stereotypes imposed on them. John Philip realised the crucial role that the apprenticeship of children played in ensuring settler society of the lasting subservience of 'Hottentots':

> As early impressions are the most abiding, and as the future character is formed in early life, the habits acquired during these ten years' bondage, must stick to the individual during life; and a very serious question arises out of these circumstances, namely, what are the habits the young Hottentots are likely to acquire during this servitude?[70]

Peruvian historian, Teresa Vergara, in exploring the experiences of Native American children growing up in colonial households in Lima, has emphasised how this experience facilitated their acculturation as a colonial underclass. Domesticated children became 'familiar with colonial principles such as obedience, recognition of authority, and acceptance of their subordinate role'. For similar reasons there was every likelihood that captured San children remained in the service of masters to whom they had been apprenticed after the expiry of their indenture. In a labour regime 'something like slavery' based on force and natal alienation, masters wielded immense power over child and adolescent apprentices under their patriarchal authority. Farmers would certainly have wanted to retain their services and may well have coerced them into staying.[71] Philip was of the opinion that child apprenticeship perpetuated 'the slavery of the parents and the whole family'.

San children, like Aboriginal workers in colonial Australia, were not 'slaves in the strict sense' of the term, 'but neither were they free'.[72] And while they were not legally bonded for life, many remained in the service of their masters well into adulthood. From the 1830s onwards, the fate of San children who were reaching adulthood became intertwined with that of the colony's 'Hottentots' and slaves. The abolition of slavery in 1838 meant that the former legal distinctions between 'Hottentots' and slaves were removed. Thereafter, 'Hottentots' and liberated slaves came to constitute a new, social conglomerate, increasingly referred to as 'coloured' in contemporary

---

[70] Philip, *Researches*, vol. 1, 183.
[71] Haebich, *Broken Circles*, 79; Vergara T.C. 2007. 'Growing up Indian: migration, labour and life in Lima, 1570–1640', in *Raising an Empire*, eds O.E. González & B. Premo, 76. For an analysis of a similar form of patriarchy in Namibia, see Sylvain, R. 2001. 'Bushmen, Boers and baaskap: patriarchy and paternalism on Afrikaner farms in the Omaheke region, Namibia'. *Journal of Southern African Studies*, 27, no. 4, 717–37.
[72] Robinson, *Something Like Slavery?*, 9.

parlance. Captive and indentured children followed a trajectory of cultural erasure from San to 'Hottentot' to coloured.

Rather than preventing the 'ancient custom' of kidnapping and bartering San children, the apprenticeship system introduced by Somerset and Stockenström afforded the practice a legal legitimacy manipulated in their favour by frontier farmers. The records of the Graaff-Reinet district reveal a clear lack of political will on the part of the Cape government to implement the regulations fully. This was true even of Stockenström himself. Farmers, often with the complicity of local officialdom, were easily able to conceal the means by which they had acquired San children, if necessary claiming to have taken them in as orphans who would otherwise have perished. Thereafter they could seek to indenture such children, at least until they became adults. The forcible transfer of San children to Boer society and their incorporation into the 'Hottentot' category during the early nineteenth century was crucial in bringing about the demise of the Cape San. Compared to the prominence afforded to the 'Bushman Wars' and the commandos of the late eighteenth century, it is a factor that has not received the attention it is due.

Chapter Four

'We Exterminated Them, and Dr. Philip Gave the Country': The Griqua People and the Elimination of San from South Africa's Transorangia Region[1]

Edward Cavanagh
University of Ottawa

Colonial frontiers are generally racialised in our scholarly appraisals of them, with 'white' appearing on one side and, depending on the kind of colonised population, a different skin colour on the other.[2] This has had a fundamental impact on the ways in which we have imagined such episodes of violence, some of which escalated into genocidal campaigns that took place along these frontiers.[3] This chapter, in its analysis of a southern African genocide, seeks to transcend this racialised tendency. Viewed in the *longue durée* no neat, colour-coded binary exists between native and newcomer in the history of the African subcontinent. On the contrary, layers of dispossession and disruption characterise the region's history.[4] By analysing social relations of production on the frontier, focusing specifically on the interaction between hunter-gatherers and commercial stock farmers, one is able to avoid reproducing the simplistic, colour-coded binary that often pervades histories of settler colonialism.

---

[1] My thanks to Jared McDonald, Mohamed Adhikari, Julian Brown and Clive Glaser for their helpful comments during the course of this research.

[2] Patrick Wolfe, decoding the 'mundane' racial discourses of selected settler colonial societies offers a sophisticated appraisal of how these 'colours' were imbued with meaning depending on the nature of the frontier. See, in particular, Wolfe P. 2001. 'Land, labor, and difference: elementary structures of race'. *American Historical Review*, 106, no. 3, 866–905. This framework has not yet been applied to southern African contexts.

[3] For discussion on genocide in settler colonial situations, see Moses A.D. 2000. 'An Antipodean genocide? The origins of the genocidal moment in the colonization of Australia'. *Journal of Genocide Research*, 2, no. 1, 89–106; Moses A.D. ed. 2004. *Genocide and Settler Society: Frontier Violence and Stolen Indigenous Children in Australian History*. New York: Berghahn Books; Kiernan B. 2007. *Blood and Soil: Genocide and Extermination in World History from Carthage to Darfur*. Yale: Yale University Press, 165–391; Moses A.D. ed. 2008. *Empire, Colony, Genocide: Conquest, Occupation and Subaltern Resistance in World History*. New York: Berghahn Books.

[4] See Cavanagh E. 2013. *Settler Colonialism and Land Rights in South Africa: Possession and Dispossession on the Orange River*. Basingstoke: Palgrave.

As historians sometimes underemphasise,[5] but archaeologists readily acknowledge, an aboriginal hunter-gatherer population referred to as San or Bushmen inhabited southern Africa for tens of thousands of years before human history there was drastically changed by a number of developments.[6] The first of these was the domestication of grazing animals. Archaeologists date the appearance of domesticates in southern Africa to between 1 240 and 2 180 years ago. Those people who became known as Khoikhoi were the first pastoralists to enter the region about 2 000 years ago when they migrated into the winter rainfall region of the south-western part of the subcontinent. Here they interacted extensively with the San. Thereafter the region's economy was split into hunter-gatherer and herding groups with significant interaction between the two.[7] The second important development was the gradual expansion of Bantu-speaking peoples southward from the north-east, inaugurating the Iron Age in southern Africa and bringing more complex systems of agro-pastoralism along with it. This expansion, which consisted of a number of migratory streams into the highveld and the eastern Cape, occurred over a thousand-year period beginning no earlier than 1 600 years ago.[8]

Then in 1652, during the latter stages of this migration, European colonialism began when the *Verenigde Oost-Indische Compagnie* (VOC) established a settlement at Table Bay. Within a few decades, VOC-sanctioned settlers moved beyond the arable south-western Cape into the

---

[5] For some recent exceptions, see Szalay M. 1995. *The San and the Colonization of the Cape, 1770–1879: Conflict, Incorporation, Acculturation*. Köln: Rüdiger Köppe Verlag; Penn N. 2005. *The Forgotten Frontier: Colonist and Khoisan on the Cape's Northern Frontier in the Eighteenth Century*. Athens: Ohio University Press; Adhikari M. 2010. *The Anatomy of a South African Genocide: The Extermination of the Cape San Peoples*. Cape Town: UCT Press.

[6] Modern humans have occupied southern Africa for perhaps 120 000 years, but opinions vary as to cultural continuity between hunter-gatherer communities over this time, or to put it more simply, when early Stone Age humans became San. For an introduction to these questions, see Mitchell P. 2002. *The Archaeology of Southern Africa*. Cambridge: Cambridge University Press, 71–160; Deacon H.J. & Deacon J. 1999. *Human Beginnings in South Africa: Uncovering the Secrets of the Stone Age*. Cape Town: David Philip, 48–106.

[7] Gifford-Gonzalez D. 2000. 'Animal disease challenges to the emergence of pastoralism in sub-Saharan Africa'. *African Archaeological Review*, 17, no. 3, 96, 104–05; Sadr K. 2008. 'Invisible herders? the archaeology of Khoekhoe pastoralists'. *Southern African Humanities*, 20, 179–203. It remains unclear whether Khoekhoe (alternative spelling for Khoikhoi) and San were physically distinct from each other, how the two groups interacted over the longer term, and whether anthropological data can be projected onto the prehistoric record with any confidence.

[8] See Hall S. 2010. 'Farming communities of the second millennium: internal frontiers, identity, continuity and change', in *The Cambridge History of South Africa*, vol. 1, *From Early Times to 1885*, eds Hamilton C., Mbenga B.K. & Ross R. Cambridge: Cambridge University Press, 112–67; see also Parkington J. & Hall S. 2010. 'The appearance of food production in southern Africa 1,000 to 2,000 years ago', *Cambridge History of South Africa*, 63–111.

interior to acquire land and practice stock farming. San communities who clung most doggedly onto their traditional hunter-gatherer ways were the most victimised groups on the frontier. Conflict intensified from the late eighteenth century onwards, when genocidal massacres by settler commandos cleared the way for a frontier of settlement, as Mohamed Adhikari has shown.[9] But these were not the only organised instances of retributive campaigns against the San. African peoples also participated in the eradication of the San, first explored in depth by George Stow in his posthumous publication, *Native Races in South Africa*, but subsequently downplayed in historical scholarship until recent years.[10]

It is certainly likely that pastoralism became a source of conflict in southern Africa from the moment domesticates were incorporated into the social relations of production. Tensions increased to unprecedented levels through the eighteenth century, as rural production commercialised and competition for resources on the frontier intensified. All stock-keeping communities on the frontier during this time—whether Bantu, Boer, Khoikhoi or hybrid groups of whatever description—faced the prospect of having their herds raided. Often individuals of mixed descent—those known as 'Bastaards' in colonial discourse—raided neighbouring communities to accumulate livestock. Stock raids were also carried out to secure food to replace waning herds of game. The San were commonly the perpetrators of such raids, in particular those who refused to labour for others, and saw no merit in adopting the new economies of pastoralism or sedentary agriculture. To them, animals existed to be hunted, not to be farmed or accumulated. This case study focuses on one such episode of genocidal conflict in the lands to the north of the middle Orange River generally referred to as Transorangia, and explores interaction between Griqua stock farmers and San hunter-gatherers during the first half of the nineteenth century.

Griqua state formation and stock farming in Transorangia

Though the Griqua people had ancient links to southern Africa, they were relative newcomers to Transorangia. Consisting mainly of displaced Khoikhoi and refugees from Cape colonial society, the Griqua had converged on the region during the late eighteenth century and were fragmented into

---

9   Adhikari, *Anatomy of a South African Genocide*, 36–59.

10   Stow G.W. 1905. *The Native Races of South Africa: A History of the Intrusion of the Hottentots and Bantu into the Hunting Grounds of the Bushmen, the Aborigines of the Country.* London: Swan Sonnenschein & Co.

a number of communities just north of the Orange River. According to historian P.J. van der Merwe, 'they had come to stay', on land which had been occupied by hunter-gatherers for tens of thousands of years and by the Korana, a Khoikhoi speaking people, who had been living there for several centuries. Increasingly, new settlers of both European and Bantu-speaking origin infiltrated the area from the early nineteenth century onwards, resulting in sporadic violence.[11]

The adoption of the name 'Griqua', adapted from Grigriqua or Chirigriqua, by Khoikhoi groups who had lived along the western Cape coastal belt, occurred in the early nineteenth century, roughly coincident with their ethnogenesis as a group. The Griqua consisted of a collection of diverse peoples. Initially the group included a large proportion of Bastaards, remnant Grigriqua groups, some Nama and Korana, a small number of San, as well as a few runaway slaves and renegades from Cape colonial society. Their communities soon also came to incorporate several Sotho and Tswana families.[12] What distinguished the Griqua from most others in the region was their innovative social and political organisation.[13] By exploiting geopolitical uncertainties in the region and making deft use of missionaries deployed there by the London Missionary Society (LMS), the Griqua succeeded in establishing powerful polities in Transorangia.

Griquatown was the original Griqua state. It was named Klaarwater before the community accepted the advice of the LMS's John Campbell in 1813 to adopt the name Griqua. Griquatown quickly transformed into a small

---

[11] Van der Merwe P.J. 1937. *Die Noordwaartse Beweging van die Boere voor die Groot Trek, 1770–1842.* Den Haag: W.P. van Stockum & Zoon, 262. Although dated, Van der Merwe's book remains a key text for this and other aspects of pre-Trek Cape history.

[12] In early 1845, the Cape government began a series of investigations into the state of the northern frontier. As a result, both Griqua chiefs Andries Waterboer and Adam KoK III received questionnaires from the colonial secretary. Kok's response presents one of the earliest and clearest statements of Griqua origins, and their place in the region alongside the Sotho and remaining Khoe-San peoples: 'My subjects are not all of one tribe, and consist of Grikwas, Bechuanas and Bushmen. Of these the lastmentioned were the original possessors of the country, and the Bechuanas consist chiefly of such persons as sought refuge amongst us from the wars of the interior. Some are, however, the subjects of Mosesh, and are subject to my laws only as long as they reside in my country. There are also some Korannas living in my territory under a subordinate Chief named Piet Witvoet. None of the other tribes are under a subordinate chief, but live immediately under my rule'. Adam Kok III to John Montagu, 18 April 1845, reproduced in Schoeman K. ed. 1996. *Griqua Records: The Philippolis Captaincy, 1825–1861.* Cape Town: Van Riebeeck Society, 93.

[13] For the early history of the Griquatown state, see Legassick M. 2010. *The Politics of a South African Frontier: The Griqua, the Sotho-Tswana, and the Missionaries, 1780–1840.* Basel: Basler Afrika Bibliographien, chs 4, 6, 8, 10–12. For Philippolis, see Ross R. 1976. *Adam Kok's Griquas: A Study in the Development of Stratification in South Africa.* Cambridge: Cambridge University Press, chs 3–6.

city-state, a place where Griqua government and missionary endeavour awkwardly coexisted, until 1825, when factional conflict erupted within the Griqua community. In response, LMS agent James Clarke, with the permission of LMS director Dr John Philip, allowed some of the dissenting Griquas to move east with their stock and settle in Philippolis, some 200 kilometres south-east of Griquatown.[14] There Adam Kok II established a polity as influential and powerful as Andries Waterboer's Griquatown. Both states became hubs of a thriving Griqua pastoral enterprise. Few rival communities could escape their dominance of the Transorangia region between the 1820s and the 1840s. This was especially true of the San.

Before the start of the nineteenth century and explosive growth of Griqua pastoralism, it was well nigh impossible for indigenous communities to engage in rural production on a commercial scale.[15] There were vast differences between traditional modes of production and more intensive patterns of production and accumulation favoured by settler farmers, and these could not easily be bridged. In addition, economic opportunities were quite restricted at the Cape. Only a small consumer base existed within the Cape itself, and that was a market completely dominated by settlers and the VOC. There were few opportunities for export. While many Khoikhoi groups enjoyed healthy trade with the company in the seventeenth century, by the early eighteenth century most in the western Cape were either coerced into trading on highly detrimental terms or had their stock confiscated, before being decimated by the smallpox epidemic of 1713.[16] While trade beyond the frontier was not unheard of before this, it comprised mostly modest transactions between indigenous groups and was done independently of the colonial market.[17]

---

[14] A solid understanding of the establishment of Philippolis may be gleaned from the documents in Schoeman K. ed. 2005. *The Griqua Mission at Philippolis, 1822–1837.* Pretoria: Protea Book House.

[15] Ross R. 1981. 'Capitalism, expansion and incorporation on the southern African frontier', in *The Frontier in History: North America and Southern Africa Compared*, eds H. Lamar & L. Thompson. New Haven: Yale University Press, 209–333; Penn N.G. 1986. 'Pastoralists and pastoralism in the northern Cape frontier zone during the eighteenth century', in *Prehistoric Pastoralism in Southern Africa: The South African Archaeological Society Goodwin Series*, vol. 5, eds M. Hall & A. Smith, 62–68.

[16] Elphick R. 1977. *Kraal and Castle: Khoikhoi and the Founding of White South Africa.* New Haven and London: Yale University Press, 90–192.

[17] Although, as Shula Marks points out, trade briefly prospered at the Cape before the arrival of Jan van Riebeeck, with increasing European immigration this trade gradually declined. Trade would only flourish again in the interior from the nineteenth century onwards, with the arrival of white, cash-bearing merchants and bible-bearing missionaries. See Marks, 'Khoisan resistance', 60–61; Beck R. 1989. 'Bibles and beads: missionaries as traders in southern Africa in the early nineteenth century'. *Journal of African History*, 30, no. 2, 211–25.

By the end of the eighteenth century, this situation started changing. Modest capital accumulation became a possibility, and tempting, to some outside of settler society. This can be attributed to two main developments. The first was the advance of white stock farmers known as trekboers into the Cape interior in pursuit of land for grazing, especially after the implementation of the loan farm policy in 1714. Trekboers, who bartered with indigenous people for cattle, and offered rewards or coerced them into becoming labourers, began to incorporate these producers into the colonial economy. Observing the changes occurring around them and wanting to take advantage of opportunities that arose, many indigenous pastoralists adopted the intensive farming techniques that allowed white stock farmers to maintain larger numbers of stock, and came to understand the potential benefits of producing for the colonial market.[18] The second development of importance was British annexation of the Cape Colony in 1806. British rule liberalised Cape society and economy in significant ways, including the passage of new labour ordinances. At the same time, missionaries from England and Scotland came in greater numbers to proselytise among indigenous peoples and instruct them in various arts of production and trading practices.[19] Most significantly, being part of the British Empire meant that the Cape was connected to new markets, and that new products and needs were introduced into Cape society. This combination of Boer frontier expansion and British annexation gave indigenous peoples an opportunity to participate more actively in the Cape colonial economy as free labourers, traders and producers. This had a significant influence on the social organisation of indigenous communities at the Cape.

The Griqua people emerged among the most successful of the frontier communities to adapt to the new situation, becoming the 'commercially oriented people' whom Ross describes in his 1976 book, *Adam Kok's Griquas*. 'In the early days of the community', he explains of the Griqua economy, 'its extent can best be defined by the measure of integration into the cash economy which stemmed from Cape Town'.[20] According to another historian of the Griqua, Martin Legassick, the secret to Griqua success lay in their versatility: 'Like the white frontier farmers, the Griqua were traders, hunters, herders, raiders rather than agriculturalists'.[21] Theirs was, indeed, a

---

[18] Penn, *Forgotten Frontier*, 41–48, 52–55, 108–12; Van der Merwe, *Noordwaartse Beweging*, 1–65.

[19] For the impact of 'Christian political economy' and English missionary experience, see Comaroff J & Comaroff J. 1997. *Of Revelation and Revolution: The Dynamics of Modernity on a South African Frontier*. Chicago: University of Chicago Press, 166–217.

[20] Ross, *Adam Kok's Griquas*, 70.

[21] Legassick, *Politics of a South African Frontier*, 246.

very mixed economy, fusing a variety of pursuits with pastoralism, the most lucrative of all. Courtesy of the fat-tailed sheep indigenous to the Cape, Griqua farmers were 'rising to opulence' in the 1810s. Griquatown was also home to several thousand cattle during this period.[22] Pastoralism reigned supreme from very early on in Griqua history.

Agriculture was also eventually adopted by the Griqua, a development not without political consequences, as Margaret Kinsman shows in her research on Griquatown.[23] Early on, she writes that many of the established pastoral elite often engaged in a significant degree of cultivation, but 'overall they regarded it as peripheral to their herding and trading activities, and the pastoral regime remained largely indifferent to agriculturalists' problems'.[24] The ascendance of Griqua captain Andries Waterboer threatened to change this. Waterboer was a staunch promoter of cultivation, a stance which distanced him from the 'pastoralist majority' at Griquatown. As Kinsman argues, this conflict between herding and horticulture was the fundamental cause of political discontent that spread through the Griqua community during the early 1820s, and which ultimately led to a split in the Griqua polity.[25]

When the breakaway faction of a few hundred Griqua loyal to Captain Adam Kok II left Griquatown for Philippolis in 1825, most did so with a desire to continue stock farming. It is fair to say that this was one of the main motivations behind their move. The rapid expansion of the pastoral economy at Philippolis confirms that Kok II's community considered it the most lucrative frontier pursuit. In 1831, John Melvill of the LMS and formerly of Griquatown, recorded a population and stock count for the settlement of Philippolis as follows:

> *At station, Griquas: 6 males, 10 females, 16 children; Bechuanas: 120*
> *Outposts, Griquas: 868; Bechuanas: 840*
> *Connected with station: total, 1860. The population of the station is rapidly increasing.*

---

22   Philip J. 1828. *Researches in South Africa: Illustrating the Civil, Moral, and Religious Condition of the Native Tribes*, vol. 2. London: James Duncan, 67; Orpen F.S. 1964. *Reminiscences of Life in South Africa from 1846 to the Present Day*. Cape Town: C. Struik, 116. See also Legassick, *Politics of a South African Frontier*, 87; British Parliamentary Papers (hereafter BPP), 50 of 1835. *Papers Relative to the Condition and Treatment of the Native Inhabitants of Southern Africa*, G. Thompson's evidence, 6 Sept 1824, 134. See also 31, 32, 33, 36, 38, 39.

23   Kinsman M. 1989. 'Populists and patriarchs: the transformation of the captaincy at Griquatown, 1804–22', in *Organisation and Economic Change: South African Studies*, vol. 5, ed. A. Mabin. Johannesburg: Ravan Press, 1–20.

24   Kinsman, 'Populists and patriarchs', 12.

25   See also Legassick, *Politics of a South African Frontier*, ch. 7 for further detail.

Cattle and implements, belonging to the Griquas: 362 horses; 4550 oxen, cows and calves; 14 200 sheep and goats; 45 wagons; 15 ploughs.
Belonging to the Bechuanas: 2 100 oxen, cows and calves; 1 200 sheep and goats.

By the early 1830s, as Melvill's returns show, Griqua families at Philippolis on average kept four times as much stock as Tswana families. The more enterprising Griqua stockowner was likely to own significantly larger herds than compatriots, along with a few horses and a wagon. Stock numbers tell one side of the story; geographical reach tells another. Melvill estimated the pastures 'in possession' of the Philippolis Griqua at a substantial '3,000 square miles' or just short of 2 000 000 acres.[26]

In Griquatown, despite Waterboer's efforts to make agriculture the primary economic activity, ecological realities undermined his vision. Transorangia was excellent sheep-grazing country, and without intensive irrigation, could never support large-scale crop farming. As Waterboer admitted to colonial secretary John Montagu in 1845: 'My people are partly a pastoral people being compelled thereto by the circumstances of the land, for there are very few fountains in the ward which can be used to promote agriculture'.[27] The situation was the same in Philippolis, where Adam Kok III's subjects attempted agriculture only on a small scale, while developing their more lucrative stock-farming enterprise. By the 1830s, a hardy breed of merino sheep with high-quality fleece began replacing the indigenous Cape variety across the southern African countryside.[28] The Griqua of Philippolis made the transition to this new breed fairly quickly. Happily Adam Kok III could report in 1845 that his subjects had 'commenced the breeding of wool sheep'.[29] This diversification of the pastoral economy gave Philippolis the edge over Griquatown and most other communities in the region, and resulted in significant prosperity for the polity as Robert Ross shows. To illustrate this growth, Ross quotes from Edward Solomon's 1852 report to the LMS in which he was clearly impressed with 'the improvement of their flocks'. Solomon claimed that:

---

[26] John Melvill's Returns, 18 January 1831, reproduced in Schoeman, *Griqua Mission*, 63.
[27] Cape Archives (hereafter CA), Government House (hereafter GH), 21/1, Waterboer to Colonial Secretary, 29 July 1845.
[28] Merino sheep were first brought to the Cape at the end of the eighteenth century, and the revolution in wool production that followed was similar to that which transpired across eastern Australia around the same time, and New Zealand shortly afterwards. See Thom H.B. 1936. *Die Geskiedenis van Skaapboerdery in Suid-Afrika*. Amsterdam: Swets & Zeilinger; McMichael P. 1984. *Settlers and the Agrarian Question: Capitalism in Colonial Australia*. Cambridge: Cambridge University Press, 54–75, 101–44; Belich J. 2009. *Replenishing the Earth: The Settler Revolution and the Rise of the Anglo-World, 1783–1939*. Oxford: Oxford University Press, 221–432.
[29] Adam Kok III to John Montagu, 18 April 1845, reproduced in Schoeman, *Griqua Records*, 93.

They have begun to appreciate the value of the merino sheep—many are now doing their utmost to get a flock and some have already flocks, varying from 300 to 1,500 in number. This year they have sent to market about 20,000lbs of wool, the produce of their own flocks.[30]

The Griqua discovered in these 'years of the sheep'[31] that a good annual clip was more valuable than a few elephant tusks, and far easier to produce than maize or wheat.

Pastoralism had swept across South Africa in an eventful millennium, before colonial capitalism prevailed. Sadly for indigenous producers, market-based pastoralism came to be completely dominated by Boers from the mid-nineteenth century onwards, but in the decades preceding this, the market was more open. The growth of the Cape Colony as a consumer market and Cape Town as an outlet for exports, combined with the extension of colonial frontiers in the early nineteenth century, led to more expansive rural production and greater levels of stock accumulation by some indigenous communities, including the Griqua. As Robert Ross has established, the Griqua benefited from this market for pastoral products, grazing their stock in the pastures of Transorangia, and keeping larger flocks of sheep than any other people in the region.[32] The Griqua's stock-keeping economy was not established on empty land, however. The San people had hunted and gathered on this land for many thousands of years, and the dangers they posed to the Griqua pastoral enterprise often brought them into conflict with these newcomers. This threat had to be neutralised for Griqua communities to prosper.

Griqua colonialism and the elimination of the San

For those San situated north of the middle Orange River during the seventeenth, and much of the eighteenth, centuries—between the Tswana and Sotho states to the north, and the expanding Cape Colony to the south-west—conflict with other groups was negligible, especially when compared to the late eighteenth and early nineteenth centuries. Korana pastoralists traversed the Transorangia region, but their interaction with the San, while occasionally frictional, did not boil over into all-out war. The late eighteenth and early nineteenth centuries were very different. Bantu-speaking communities such as the Tswana, a number of mixed-descent groups, and later trekboers, inflicted great damage on the San population

---

30 LMS Annual Report for 1852, quoted by Ross, *Adam Kok's Griquas*, 74.
31 This quote comes from the title of chapter 5 in Ross, *Adam Kok's Griquas*.
32 Ross, *Adam Kok's Griquas*, 66–80.

during this period. By the early 1810s, though the San were still reputedly 'very numerous' in Transorangia, they had suffered significant violence at the hands of invading pastoralists.[33] In the case of both Griquatown and Philippolis, the main periods of San–Griqua conflict occurred within the first decade or so of the establishment of each settlement. During these periods—1813–1825 for Griquatown, and 1826–1835 for Philippolis—the Griqua were decidedly exterminatory in their attitude towards the San. Afterwards, conflict was episodic as most San had been exterminated or expelled from the area. In both locales, the colonial archive suggests that San resistance was worn down within the space of a single generation, with numerous genocidal massacres.

Since the start of the nineteenth century, the intensity of settler violence directed at the San had alarmed the London Missionary Society, whose initial efforts were directed at their protection.[34] Yet, amid early annexations and vicious frontier wars, their fate concerned surprisingly few colonial officials. Andries Stockenström was an exception. In his capacity as *landdrost* (magistrate) of Graaff-Reinet, Stockenström attempted single-handedly to police slave-raiding and massacres on the northern frontier between the mid-1810s and early 1830s, which often put him at odds with the Griqua. He was troubled by the situation in Transorangia, and considered those San 'beyond the Orange River perhaps the most unfortunate beings under the sun'. Both at Griquatown and the nearby Tswana settlement at Latakoo, Stockenström reported 'a horrible animosity towards the Bosjesman, rendered still more frightful by an ancient prejudice, which considers the murder of Bosjesman, woman, or child, meritorious under any circumstances'.[35] As he would confide to a military superior in 1820:

For a long time back, as is known to Government, I have looked with a suspicious and watchful eye on the increasing tribe calling themselves Griquas, originally allowed to move from more inner parts of the Colony, under the care of a missionary, to the uninhabited tracts near the northern frontier, for the conveniency of a more extended pasturage ... being consequently scattered over an extent of country, the

33 See, for example, Kirby, P.R. ed. 1939–40. *The Diary of Dr. Andrew Smith, Director of the Expedition for Exploring Central Africa, 1834–1836*, vol. 2. Cape Town: Van Riebeeck Society, 285.

34 Schoeman K. 1993. 'Die Londense Sendinggenootskap en die San: die stasies Toornberg en Hepzibah, 1814–1818'. *South African Historical Journal*, 28, no. 1, 221–34; Schoeman, K. 1993. 'Die Londense Sendinggenootskap en die San: die stasies Ramah, Konnah en Philippolis, 1816–1828'. *South African Historical Journal*, 29, no. 1, 132–52.

35 BPP, 50 of 1835. Andries Stockenström to Lieutenant Colonel Bird, 13 Sept 1820, 131; also reproduced in Stockenström, A. 1964. *The Autobiography of the Late Sir Andries Stockenström, Sometime Lieutenant-Governor of the Eastern Province of the Colony of the Cape of Good Hope*. Cape Town: C. Struik, 1, 188.

greatest diameter of which I do not conceive to be less than 250 miles, formerly occupied by innumerable Bushmen kraals, which found in the immense flocks of game then covering the plains ample resources, of which they have been deprived by their inhuman oppressors, together with their country.[36]

Moreover, missionary attempts at protecting the San were failing miserably.

According to some reports, in the first few years after Klaarwater became Griquatown in 1813, violence against the San was rife. The influential Griqua renegade Barend Barends had little scruple subjecting San to forced labour, while driving others out of the area. According to Robert Moffat, who spent time in Griquatown in 1820 on his way to preach among the Tswana at nearby Kuruman, the appointment of Captain Andries Waterboer in 1819 changed the situation. Moffat testified before a commission of inquiry into the treatment of indigenous tribes that Waterboer 'has exerted himself to protect them and to cause them [San] to be treated with lenity and conciliation … The hostile feeling that formerly subsisted has considerably abated, and an amicable feeling has succeeded'.[37] Waterboer was said to be primarily of San descent, which might explain his compassion towards hunter-gatherers. The extent of this compassion should not, however, be overstated. For several years after his rise to the captaincy, Griqua commandos continued to be deployed against the San.

George Thompson, a merchant adventurer who travelled through Transorangia in 1823–1824, in contrast to Moffat, reported that the Griqua had acquired a number of rifles through trade, which gave the Griquas 'a decided advantage over the native tribes in their vicinity'. With this firepower, they rarely terrorised 'the Bechuana or Koranna tribes, with both of whom they lived in amity', but rather targeted the San: 'Towards the wretched Bushmen, I found them, in general, animated by the same spirit of animosity as the frontier boors, and Mr. Melvill's exertions to restrain this spirit, have doubtless increased his unpopularity'.[38] He continued:

In these deplorable wars the Bushmen are doubtless, in general, the aggressors, by their propensity to depredation. Yet, on the other hand, have they not some cause to regard both Boors and Griquas as intruders upon their ancient territories,—as tyrannical usurpers, who, by seizing their finest fountains, and destroying the wild game on which they were wont to subsist, have scarcely left them even the desolate wilderness for an habitation?[39]

---

36 BPP, 50 of 1835, Stockenström to Bird, 13 Sept 1820, 129–30.
37 BPP, 50 of 1835, evidence of Mr Moffat, 20 April 1824, 127.
38 Thompson G. 1827. *Travels and Adventures in Southern Africa*, vol. I. London: Henry Colburn, 152.
39 Thompson, *Travels and Adventures*, vol. 1, 155.

Thompson was well acquainted with the modus operandi of Griqua commandos, as indicated in his evidence before the 1824 commission of enquiry:

> The Bushmen ... are rarely attacked, unless to resent their thefts, which they sometimes commit for subsistence, upon the flocks and herds of the Griquas. Commandos are then sent out, the offenders are surprised and surrounded, when those who resist are destroyed, and the remainder, including the children, are made captives.[40]

The main example to which Thompson referred was the affray between Waterboer and a San leader, Huil (occasionally spelt Uil), which took place in June 1823. 'The unequal conflict commenced—poisoned arrows against powder and ball;—and it was not until eight of his followers had fallen, and he himself was mortally wounded, that Huil would permit his sons to surrender. Seventy men, women, and children, were found in the kraal, and carried prisoners to Griqua Town.'[41]

The fate of these prisoners is not clear, although we can assume that it was grim. It would not be until 50 years later, in testimony before the commission of enquiry into the Diamond Fields dispute of 1871, that an aging Griqua named Jan Pienaar recalled the same 'case of a Bushman named "Uil"', and offered further insight into this episode. Unsurprisingly, cattle were at the heart of this conflict. Uil's kraal was pursued, Pienaar explained:

> for stealing eighty head of cattle belonging to my grandfather. Uil was then residing on the left-hand side of Langeberg, and he and the men belonging to that kraal were all shot down by Waterboer, and the women and children taken to Griqua Town. Uil's kraal fought against Waterboer.[42]

That Pienaar recalled the incident so vividly suggests that it might have become part of Griqua folklore, though it certainly was not the only atrocity of its kind. At the same Diamond Fields enquiry, a passerby on his way through Griquatown some time in the 1820s testified to a similar incident. Waterboer arrived from a commando raid 'with nineteen Bushmen. He said the Bushman had committed a theft'.[43] Others were likely slain in this retributive expedition.

---

40   BPP, 50 of 1835, evidence of Mr G. Thompson, 6 September 1824, 134.
41   Thompson, *Travels and Adventures*, vol. 1, 153–4; see also BPP, 50 of 1835, 134.
42   CA, House of Assembly (hereafter, HA) 89. Annexure 24, 1872. *Evidence Taken at Bloemhof before the Commission appointed to investigate the Claims of the South African Republic, Captain N. Waterboer, Chief of West Griqualand, and certain other Native Chiefs, to portions of the Territory on the Vaal River, now known as the Diamond-fields*, evidence of Jan Pienaar, 16.
43   CA, HA 89. Annexure 24, 1872. *Evidence Taken at Bloemhof*, evidence of Etzard Johan Adolph Grimbeck Snr, 195.

From the mid-1820s, evidence of organised violence against the San around Griquatown fades from the historical record due to the effective eradication of the San from the area. On the other hand, at the more recently established Philippolis polity, conflict with the San was at its height during the ensuing decade. When Adam Kok II was given possession of the mission station at Philippolis by the LMS in 1825, it was on condition that he promise 'to protect the Bushmen against the aggressions of the Boers', and 'not to dispossess the Bushmen of such lands'.[44] That, at least, is how the society's director, Dr John Philip, recalled the transaction. Philip had mistakenly hoped that Adam Kok II's Griqua would promote peace in the region and help protect the San, thereby setting a wholesome example for other groups in conflict with hunter-gatherers.[45] He failed to appreciate that Griqua actions were more likely to be driven by their own interests than protection of the San. Herds of game were already dwindling in the Philippolis region before the Griqua arrived, and fast disappeared shortly afterwards.[46] And when Griqua graziers came with thousands of sheep, the San found in these flocks an alternative food source. Naturally, this brought the two groups into conflict.

Within a year of its handover to the Griqua, Philippolis had become a base from which a number of deadly commandos against the San were organised. By allowing the Griqua to move there, Philip had in effect signed the death warrant of San living in the area. Griqua Jan Pienaar's pithy summation of this episode in Philippolis' history was that 'Bushmen inhabited the country about Philippolis. We exterminated them, and Dr Philip gave the country'.[47] His synopsis stands in stark contrast to Philip's intentions.

---

44 Council for World Mission Archive (hereafter CWMA), London Missionary Society Incoming Correspondence (South Africa), 18B/4/a, John Philip to George Napier, 25 August 1842. Appendix B: 'The Tenure by which the Griqua hold the Lands of Philippolis'.

45 After coming across two separate groups of raiding Bergenaars and Koranas in 1825–26, each of whom were guilty of recently decimating Bushman kraals, Philip's main reprimand for such behaviour was for the offenders to go with Piet Sabat (or Sabba), a 'native' preacher, to meet with Adam Kok at Philippolis and 'unite with the Griquas', or otherwise 'to go ... to Griqua Town, where they would hear the gospel preached, and have the means of getting their children educated'. See Philip, *Researches* vol. 2, 334–41. A useful appraisal of Philip's programme between the 1820s and early 1840s, although dated and occasionally biased, remains Macmillan W.M. 1963. *Bantu, Boer, and Briton: The Making of the South African Native Problem*. Oxford: Clarendon Press, especially 52–70, 239–61.

46 When Andrew Smith encountered two Korana men near Philippolis in the mid-1830s, they explained to him that game had been scarce for decades. Kirby, *Diary of Andrew Smith*, vol. 1, 161. W.M. Macmillan, for all his astute reading of the Philip papers, had it wrong when he wrote that 'game abounded' in the region during this period. See Macmillan, *Bantu, Boer and Briton*, 243.

47 CA, HA 89. Annexure 24 of 1872. *Evidence Taken at Bloemhof*, evidence of Jan Pienaar, 20.

The diary of John Melvill, the Griquatown missionary who relocated to Philippolis in 1827, reveals how the settlement, like Griquatown, was transformed from a small mission station into a thriving Griqua settlement and how frequently retributive commando raids against San stock raiders were carried out. In his entry for 19 February 1827, he wrote of a Griqua commando that 'went out in pursuit of the Bushmen who stole the cattle on the 9th inst. and murdered the herdsman'. The bloody details of the commando were not fully relayed to Melvill, but he recalls them returning the morning of the following day, 'with eight Bushmen, including three boys, whom they took prisoners without firing a shot'. These captives received a series of vicious lashings.[48]

Just a few weeks later, Melvill reported a similar incident in which a Griqua commando 'went out against some Bushmen who had stolen three head of cattle and murdered the herdsman'. Two days later, on 17 March, one of the party gave him the following account:

> Having followed the footmarks of the Bushmen, they came upon the kraal, and found part of the meat, but the inhabitants had fled to a covert of thick reeds. They were followed and surrounded ... Some shots were then fired, and it appears one of the Bushmen was killed, upon which the only two that remained made a most determined resistance, talking and swearing in the Dutch language at the Griquas, until at last they were shot with two women and two children that were with them.[49]

Sliding into rhetoric of desperation, Melvill's lament over this particular event shows both the ruthlessness of Griqua commandos as well as how common the hunt for San raiders had become during this period:

> It is not to be wondered at that these people would not give themselves up, for the usual method pursued by such commandoes against them must leave them ignorant of such a thing as giving quarter. O, when will the time come to favour this wretched people?[50]

Things only got worse for the San of Transorangia, and their numbers fell away quickly. 'They occasionally steal the cattle of these their enemies it is true, but they have no alternative between that and literal starvation', explained Stockenström, who attributed the conflict between the San and others to incompatibility between the settler economy and the hunter-gatherer lifestyle. 'These people do not settle themselves near springs, make permanent residences, or cultivate land; they live in remote corners

---

48 John Melvill's diary, reproduced in Schoeman, *Griqua Mission*, 40–41 (hereafter *Melvill's Diary*).
49 *Melvill's Diary*, 44–45.
50 *Melvill's Diary*, 45.

and rocks, and remove as often as they expect to find a part of the country more full of game'.[51] Yet when game became scarce in the early nineteenth century, the San were invariably drawn into conflict with stock farmers whose sheep and cattle became a substitute for it.

Stockenström gave much thought to their predicament, and from the early 1820s developed a plan to ameliorate their condition. The solution, as he saw it, was to resurrect a policy tried without much success by Governor George Macartney back in 1798. This essentially entailed providing the San with colonial protection and stock, in the hope that they might settle down and become pastoralists.[52] Instead, for all its fine intent, Stockentröm's project failed, probably because of the irreparable damage inflicted upon San society by the time he implemented it. 'In consequence of the Landdrost's plan of giving cattle to the Bushmen', Melvill reported from Philippolis in the winter of 1827, '66 [San] men, women and children have arrived. It is remarkable that there is not one child to each family, there being only 17 to about 25 families'. He attributed this not to the violence systematically inflicted upon them by Griqua and other stock farmers, but to other causes: '... probably owing to several being in the service of the Farmers, though indeed the few children generally found among the Bushmen may also be accounted for from their hard life and insufficient subsistence, and from their sometimes practising infanticide'.[53] Unfortunately, by the end of the 1820s, the result was the same in Transorangia as it had earlier been in areas such as Beaufort West, Colesberg and Graaff-Reinet under Macartney. Most of the stock given to San were either lost to raiders or consumed out of necessity.

The Cape government was dismayed by developments in Transorangia, where Stockenström's reforms barely had an impact. The San were fast dying out in the region and their enslavement was still rife. Early in 1830 Stockenström, promoted to commissioner general by this time, received further instructions to investigate the situation.[54] When he arrived to conduct interviews in Philippolis, he heard from trekboers how Griqua often massacred large kraals of San. The Griqua, for their part, did not deny such claims, but contended that colonists often joined Griqua in their exterminatory raids. These allegations are recorded in the Philippolis annexure to Stockenström's 'Commission of Inquiry into Reports of

---

51   Stockenström, *The Autobiography of the Late Sir Andries Stockenström*, vol. 1, 226.
52   Adhikari, *Anatomy of a South African Genocide*, 62.
53   *Melvill's Diary*, 55.
54   For Stockenström's attempts to protect the San, and the tension between trekboers and Griqua, see Van der Merwe, *Noordwaartse Beweging*, esp. 205–322.

Cruelty against Native Tribes Beyond the Orange River, 1830', a harrowing catalogue of calculated mass killing.[55]

Perhaps nowhere are the genocidal actions and attitudes of Griqua towards San more potently expressed than in the testimony of trekboer Johannes Coetzee. According to him, 'a quiet and peaceable' San kraal was recently attacked by 'a party of Bastards under the [Griqua] Field Cornet Abel Pienaar ... without the least provocation'. Recalling a conversation with Willem Barend, a Griqua, about the event, Coetzee reported that he had:

> asked him why they act so cruelly towards the Bushmen, who had done no harm—he replied the Bushmen steal our Cattle, we are determined to exterminate them, so that our Cattle may graze unmolested day and night, and I asked him why they murdered the women and children, he said the children grow up to mischief and the women breed them.

Coetzee also related to the inquiry that just north of Philippolis near the Caledon River lay 'the bones of many hundreds' of San, 'remnants of a wandering tribe', murdered, he insisted, by Griqua.[56] Field-Cornet Schalk Burger was also interviewed during the inquiry. Deflecting an accusation that he had himself committed atrocities against San, Burger referred to a conversation he had with a Griqua man as proof that they were far more bloodthirsty than the Boers. 'One Evening a Commando of Griquas passed my location', he related. 'I took [one of them] aside to my tent and asked him upon what principle he intended to act. He said "I will destroy all the Bushmen I meet with".'[57] Just how many San this Griqua commando encountered on their journey is unknown.

The further north of Philippolis Stockenström travelled, the more people he encountered who were willing to testify to Philippolis Griqua killing San. Even a number of 'Korana chiefs' came forward, stating that 'the Griquas have long made up their minds to exterminate the Bushmen; for the Bushmen are a great plague to them and to us'. Another Korana man of importance named Gatoo recalled encountering Hendrick Hendricks out in the veld, where he 'gave a full account of the Destruction of the Bushmen kraal, he mentioned to me all the People who went on that Commando. He did not mention a Boor ... Nobody could tell why the kraal was destroyed'.[58] Further towards the Bushman station on the Caledon River, Stockenström met trekboer Herculus Jacobus Visser, who recalled another episode of

---

55 CA, Lieutenant-Governor (LG) 9.
56 CA, LG 9, evidence of Johannes Coetzee, 1 March 1830.
57 CA, LG 9, evidence of Schalk Burger, 1 March 1830.
58 CA, LG 9, evidence of Korana Chiefs, March–April 1830.

Griqua violence. 'On a Certain Sunday in January 1829', Visser claims to have encountered:

> *four Bushmen ... [belonging] to a kraal situated near du Pré's wagon ... as we were thus engaged a party of Griquas came and departed. When we had finished, I heard that the said Griquas took the four Bushmen with them; next morning the Griquas attacked and destroyed the Bushmen.*[59]

Two separate reports of Griqua violence dominated the hearing. Stockenström's summary of these accounts after the investigation of March of 1830 is most revealing:

> *I had discovered that a kraal of Bushmen living among the migratory Boers, daily fed by, and assisting with these people, being perfectly peaceable and, as the Boers say, without the slightest shadow of bad intention on their part, were attacked by a Commando of Griquas of Dam Kok's party, who killed fifteen, left two for dead badly wounded, and carried off the only survivors (three children), after offering them for sale to the farmers.*

> *The manner in which the women had been put to death is too awful to be here related. In another kraal fourteen were killed by a party of Griquas under the command of Kok's son-in-law, Hendrik Hendriks, and other outrages against the Bushmen were related, of which I have no proof.*[60]

The Griqua side of the story differs slightly and alleges, quite correctly, that trekboers played active roles in the elimination of the San too. Abel Kok, a Griqua, even went as far as to claim that the trekboers often sponsored their commandos against the San.[61] Hendrick Hendricks, for his part, confessed:

> *It is true that I went with a Commando against a kraal of Bushmen—they had stolen horses; but the Boors Sybiam [or Sybrand?], Bronkhorst, Thomas Botha, and Johannes Strydom went with us and fired on the Bushman as briskly as ourselves. Klaas Visser offered to purchase from us the Children which were saved; I told him that they were no slaves.*[62]

---

59   CA, LG 9, evidence of Herculus Jacobus Visser, March–April 1830.
60   Stockenström, *Autobiography*, vol. 1, 376.
61   CA, LG 9, evidence of Abel Kok, March–April 1830.
62   CA, LG 9, evidence of Hendrick Hendricks, 1 March 1830. On behalf of those accused, Burger denied the charge vehemently: 'I came across a Bushman kraal which had been destroyed by the Griquas who told me that said kraal had stolen their horses. I found fourteen dead bodies ... I can take my oath that I never heard and do not believe that any Boor ever went against the Bushmen with the Griquas, or applied for their assistance or supplied them with ammunition'.

'Whatever foundation there may be for these mutual charges', Stockenström concluded, 'it is clear that the greatest and most inveterate jealousy exists between the Colonists and Griquas, about the possession or occupation of that part of the Bushman country, into which both parties have of late migrated'.[63] But, as long as either of both parties were settled in Transorangia, sheep and oxen, not San, would roam the land.

Conclusion

Over the past 2000 years, hunter-gatherer society in southern Africa underwent significant change and upheaval due to a succession of migrations into the area by pastoralist and agro-pastoralist peoples. During this period, hunting and gathering remained as viable a way of life as ever, even though many San groups were displaced from their most favourable environments. It was, however, only after Europeans penetrated the Cape interior over the course of the eighteenth and nineteenth centuries, that hunter-gatherer society faced direct and sustained onslaught, amid intensifying competition for resources on the frontier. In the process San society was, for the most part, destroyed. While there is no denying that other indigenous groups were also seriously threatened by the new settler-dominated order, it was the San who experienced the most extreme forms of colonial violence, often culminating in exterminatory drives against them as the recent work of Mohamed Adhikari and other chapters in this book demonstrate.[64]

This chapter argues that the two main Griqua states also perpetrated genocide against the San in the Transorangian frontier zone during the first half of the nineteenth century. Taking advantage of the market created by the Cape Colony, and situating themselves along its northerly borders, the Griqua established an economy centred mainly on commercial sheep farming. In order to put their pastoral economy on a secure footing, Griqua felt the need to clear the land of its hunter-gatherers who preyed on their livestock. Many San viewed Griqua livestock—and, likewise, domesticates belonging to Korana, Sotho, Tswana, trekboers and others— as an alternative to game that was fast disappearing from the veld. Stock raiding thus became increasingly necessary for their survival. As a result,

---

63 Stockenström, *Autobiography*, vol. 1, 378.
64 Adhikari, *Anatomy of a South African Genocide*. See also the chapters by Nigel Penn, Jared McDonald and Robert Gordon in this collection.

in the early decades of the nineteenth century, the San in Griqualand were either violently driven off their ancestral lands or massacred.[65]

This conflict can be explained in terms of economic competition between hunter-gatherers and stock farmers. While communities of hunter-gatherer San had coexisted with pastoralist communities in varied and complex ways for the better part of two millennia, it was the introduction of pastoralist practices for surplus production that escalated the conflict to unprecedented levels. Commercial stock farming was a much larger and much more intensive enterprise than its subsistence equivalents, and as competition for water, grazing and access to land mounted, so did the intensity of conflict. It was in this context that stock-farming communities in the Cape interior resorted to eradicatory violence against hunter-gatherers. In the cases of both the Griquatown and Philippolis polities, exterminatory raids against San followed very soon after their establishment. The sad reality is that it took little more than a decade before hunter-gatherer communities in both areas were effectively wiped out. This provides an indication of both the efficiency of Griqua commandos and the vulnerability of San society by this time.

For over a century, some historians have presented the Griqua people as bloodthirsty murderers, the most savage community on the South African frontier.[66] Despite the findings presented in this chapter, this kind

---

[65] While this chapter highlights only the role played by Griqua in the destruction of San society in Transorangia, it is clear that many of the other pastoral groups played a part in the effective extermination of San in the region. There is clearly an ethical question at stake when writing about acts of genocide performed by people whose plight today is distressing. How do we reconcile our sympathy for their adversity with our need for scholarly objectivity? I maintain that it is important for scholars to identify genocide wherever, and in whatever form, it appears. The question is whether scholars should be passing moral judgement on them or not. As Raymond Evans puts it, one has to decide if one is 'catching a crook or writing a book'. I place myself in the latter category: I have presented a few genocidal moments of many in South African history, but have not done so to indict the Griqua, who have received a condemnatory appraisal by historians for over a hundred years. Evans R. 2008. '"Crime without a name": colonialism and the case for "indigenocide"', in *Empire, Colony, Genocide*, 138. For the Griqua people in South African historical tradition, see Cavanagh E. 2011. *The Griqua Past and the Limits of South African History*. Oxford: Peter Lang.

[66] This attitude is evident in the early twentieth century tomes of George McCall Theal, George Cory, Frank Cana and George Stow. The trope emerged again after the publication of Cobbing J. 1988. 'The *Mfecane* as alibi: thoughts on Dithakong and Mbolompo'. *Journal of African History*, 39, no. 3, 487–519; contributors to a collection in response to Cobbing's arguments—most memorably Elizabeth Eldredge and Jeff Peires—uncritically repeat negative appraisals of 'Griqua' raiders in the Dithakong conflict, rehashing Stockenström's observations about Griqua 'atrocities' and Mzilikazi's remark that Griqua were 'a pack of thieves, destitute of courage' in Hamilton C. ed. 1995. *The Mfecane Aftermath: Reconstructive Debates in Southern African History*. Johannesburg: Witwatersrand University Press; for further discussion on these developments in South African historiography, see Cavanagh, *Griqua Past*, 21–23, 97–98, 113–14.

of appraisal is unfair and outdated. It must be remembered that the Griqua were not the only parties guilty of exterminatory violence against the San. 'Bantu, Boer and Briton' all actively participated in sustained, violent campaigns against the San, and were responsible for the appropriation of their land and the destruction of their resource base, as Stow argued in his groundbreaking ethnographic study of the late nineteenth century.[67] To observe as much does not absolve the Griqua of blame, but it does disrupt simplistic, colour-coded assumptions that often inform studies of genocide in settler colonial contexts. While it is true that the perpetrators of colonial genocide in the nineteenth century southern African context were often white settlers, they were not necessarily so. Frontier conflicts, such as the one described in this chapter, are often more complex and multifaceted than the racially reductionist historical appraisals sometimes presented in the literature. This case study suggests a need to re-imagine conflicts of this nature.

---

[67] Stow, *Native Races of South Africa*. The quotation comes from the title of Macmillan's *Bantu, Boer and Briton.*

Chapter Five

Vogelfrei and Besitzlos, with no Concept of Property: Divergent Settler Responses to Bushmen and Damara in German South West Africa

Robert Gordon
University of Vermont

This chapter considers an interesting conundrum in German South West Africa (GSWA), a mainly pastoral settler colony that waged genocidal warfare on several indigenous groups in the early part of the twentieth century. While those foragers in the territory labelled San or Bushmen were the object of genocide or genocidal acts, another group of hunter-gatherers known as Damara thrived after the onset of colonialism to the extent that they have become the third largest ethnic group in present-day Namibia. How did settlers and the colonial administration come to believe that Bushmen were such a threat that the only way to deal with them was *Ausrottung* (extirpation) while Damara were believed to be generally valuable workers?

What makes this question even more intriguing is that in the period prior to colonisation and during the early years of German rule, Europeans' attitude towards Bushmen was one of guarded ambiguity, given their value as hunting guides. At that time there was, however, little ambiguity about how Damara should be treated. The reflections of William Chapman, a long-term inhabitant of Namibia and Angola, who followed his father, the famed explorer James Chapman, into the area in the 1870s, were typical:

> *The Bastards (a recent mulatto immigrant group from the Cape Colony) suffered much ... from the depredations of the Berg Damaras ... who continually raided the country, stealing cattle and even horses to slaughter ... instead of seeking employment ... In those days Mr W. Coates Palgrave (the Special Commissioner appointed by the Cape Colony) ... gave the order that those raiders (or thieves) were to be arrested and not to be shot ... whereas if captured what was to be done with them? There was no government, no prisons, and what was to be done with such vermin? ... The only way to stop this marauding was to hunt them and exterminate them as lions, tigers and wolves are exterminated.*[1]

---

[1]   Chapman W. 2010. *Reminiscences*, ed. N. Stassen. Pretoria: Protea, 105.

Such examples advocating the slaughter of Damaras can be multiplied many times over.[2]

While Bushmen too were subject to being hunted down, their ambiguous status is well captured in Rosenblad's anecdote about a Christmas Eve festivity involving the selfsame Chapman, 'a rather magnificent gentleman and quite sensitive about his dignity':

> The Bushman Dekopp (Thick-head) who had previously been in his service, knew his storage places and had succeeded in stealing a couple of bottles of brandy. It was soon noticed that Dekopp was drunk because he constantly turned to Chapman and pointed out that he was behaving very stupidly: if only he would listen to Dekopp's good advice the crossing would proceed like a dance.

> Chapman tried to look unconcerned but did not succeed at all. However respect must be upheld and therefore Reinhold (Trader Erikssen's brother) ordered Dekopp to go to bed, which naturally did not appeal to him. A Bushman in an intoxicated condition is impossible to handle, and in the end he had to be tied to a tree. There he stood, all the time shouting in Dutch: 'You are very stupid Chapman, you will not listen to good advice'.[3]

When it came to hunting, Bushmen were viewed as indispensable. Not only did they serve as invaluable guides, but they would also undertake menial camp chores and serve as messengers, all at minimal cost to the hunters, as they were apparently satisfied with meat and some tobacco. Swiss botanist, Hans Schinz, found them the most trustworthy and reliable of all the natives, working without pay, except for a few sticks of tobacco.[4] There are also numerous tales of their helping lost or stranded Boers who might otherwise have died in the Kalahari Desert.

In German South West Africa, genocide did not occur at the outset of colonisation in 1884, and when it did occur it was selective in its application. For Bushmen the horror came in the aftermath of the 1904–1907 wars, a defining period in Namibian history in so far as it led to the transformation of a relatively weak colonial state into a strong one. It was in this latter format, with its laws and bureaucrats and pretensions to scientific colonial administration, that the machinery for implementing genocide against 'bandits' and other forager groups known as Bushmen was put in place. It was as a *Musterstaat* (model state), as historian Juergen Zimmerer

---

2   See Brigitte Lau's exceptional essay critiquing Vedder's construction of the Damara. Lau B. 1995. '"Thank God the Germans came": Vedder and Namibian historiography', in *History and Historiography: Essays in Reprint*. Windhoek: Discourse/Msorp, 1–16.

3   Rosenblad E. 2007. *Adventures in South West Africa 1894–1898*. Windhoek: Namibian Scientific Society, 48.

4   Schinz H. 1891. *Deutsch-Suedwest-Afrika*. Leipzig: Schulzesche Hofbuchhandlung, 392.

felicitously calls it,[5] that much of the dirty work of genocide against the San was perpetrated. Horst Drechsler famously termed this period the 'peace of the graveyard'.[6] Yet for all the deathly silence of historians on this era, it was a time when many ghosts were abroad.[7]

Between 1907 and 1915, GSWA experienced an economic boom with the discovery of diamonds, expansion of the Tsumeb copper mines, development of roads and railways, a near tripling of farmland, mostly pastoral operations, under European occupation from 4.8 to 13.4 million hectares, and a doubling of the number of settlers to 13 962 as colonial settlement moved beyond the Herero heartland of central Namibia. This activity occurred within the context of German policy that emphasised the need for the colony to pay for itself, which fuelled a demand for cheap labour. But such a large part of the potential labour force had been killed in the preceding wars that there was a crippling shortage of workers. So desperate were settlers that larger employers were forced to recruit labourers from South Africa while efforts to obtain labour from other German colonies failed. The importation of Chinese and Indian labour was seriously considered.[8] Labour recruitment from Ovamboland, an area to the north of the Etosha Pan, became a major priority and nearly tripled from about 4 000 in 1908 to 11 764 by 1914.[9]

In addition, the colonial administration did its utmost to mobilise labour internally by way of draconian ordinances that stripped indigenes of access to land and livestock. Deprived of their traditional livelihood, it was assumed that they would be forced into the colonial economy. Another ordinance sought to control the movement of indigenes through pass laws. They were forced to wear brass tokens around their necks, a central register of natives was developed and work contracts were regulated. Settlers were given the right to engage in 'fatherly chastisement' of their workers. Lastly, and ominously for foragers, the pass laws stipulated that: 'Natives who are loitering, may be punished as vagrants, when they can show no means of

5   Zimmerer J. & Zeller J. eds. 2003. *Völkermord in Deutsch-Südwestafrika*. Berlin: Ch. Links Verlag, 36.
6   Drechsler H. 1980. *Let Us Die Fighting*. Berlin: Akademie-Verlag, 231–47.
7   Parts of my 2009 '"Hiding in full view": the forgotten Bushman genocides in Namibia'. *Genocide Studies & Prevention*, 4, no. 1, 29–58 are used here with the permission of the publisher, the University of Toronto Press.
8   Stals, E.L.P. 1978. *Kurt Streitwolf: Sy Werk in Suidwes-Afrika 1899–1914*. Johannesburg: Perskor, 102.
9   Stals, E.L.P. 1984. 'Duits Suidwes-Afrika na die groot opstande'. *Archives Yearbook for South African History*, 46, 43.

support'.[10] These regulations locked together in mutually supporting ways to force indigenes into the settler-controlled economy.

Not only was there significant expansion in pastoral settlement in this transformation from weak colonial rule to *Musterstaat*, but the location of these settlers was also important. One of the magnet areas was the north-eastern district of Grootfontein where a higher rainfall and ample springs made the area attractive to stock farmers. The extension of the railway line to the nearby Tsumeb copper mines with their ready market for meat further served to enhance the area for settlers and speculators. Of all the towns and districts in Namibia, Grootfontein grew most rapidly, with the number of European farms in the district expanding from 25 in 1904 to 173 in 1913. Outjo District lying adjacent to Grootfontein experienced similar expansion.[11] This land was not vacant but inhabited by Bushmen and Damara. If one assumes that police were stationed where indigenous resistance was at its most intense, then these two districts were clearly the epicentre of such conflict. In 1907, Grootfontein boasted the single largest contingent of some 82 policemen in the colony, while that dubious honour fell to Outjo in 1912.[12] Settlers were forced to make do with Bushman labour, no matter how unsatisfactory it was alleged to be. Already in 1908 police and military patrols were rounding up Bushmen and allocating them to farmers as labourers. Indeed, by 1912 most of the farm labour in Grootfontein was performed by Bushmen.

By 1910, the only significant security problems for settlers in the colony came from the Bondelswarts, a Nama-speaking group in the far south whose resistance was part of the nagging legacy of the 1904–1907 war, and from the Bushmen in the north and east. The murder of a few Ovambo and settlers by Bushmen led to an outcry in the press. Headlines reading 'Bushman Pestilence', 'Bushman Plague' and 'Bushman Danger' were common coinage at that time. Influential parties such as the Chamber of Mines and farmer organisations called on the government to act decisively against the Bushman threat. Especially alarming to the mining industry was a series of attacks on returning Ovambo contract workers that they feared would disrupt the labour supply. The press thundered that energetic disciplinary action was necessary, reinforcements and mobile police stations

---

10 Bley H. 1971. *South-West Africa Under German Rule, 1895–1914*. Evanston: Northwestern University Press, 170–73.

11 Gordon R.J. 1992. *The Bushman Myth and the Making of a Namibian Underclass*. Boulder: Westview, 201–02.

12 Rafalski H. 1930. *Vom Niemansland zum Ordnungstaat*. Berlin: Werseitz, 72.

were needed, and that captured Bushmen were to be sent to work on the diamond mines.

Governor Seitz opted for the strong-arm strategy of increasing the number and power of police and military units in the troubled area. He proclaimed inter alia that while patrolling in Bushman areas: 'Firearms are to be used in the slightest case of insubordination against officials. Also, when a felon is either caught in the act, or when being hunted down, and does not stop on command but tries to escape through flight'.[13] Given the broad interpretation of what constituted the 'slightest case of insubordination', their dubious linguistic capacity to communicate to Bushmen to stop 'on command', and that it was common knowledge that Bushmen fled at the sight of any patrol, this ordinance constituted, in effect, as later events were to show, a warrant for genocide. This *Verordnung* was crucial in providing legal underpinning for sustained, purposeful action by officials and settlers in carrying out a policy referred to in the settler press and administration as *Ausrottung*. The violence against Bushmen that followed was more than simply episodic massacres or pogroms. All the facilitative characteristics for genocide were present, namely, deep structural divisions, identifiable victim groups, a legitimating hate ideology, a breakdown of moral restraint, and what might be called audience obliviousness, or toleration by local, national and international communities.[14]

Booty capitalism

Marx called situations such as those prevailing in GSWA 'primitive accumulation', while Weber termed them 'booty' or adventure capitalism. This was a daring and predatory form of capitalism in which profit was made possible by direct force or domination. It was, said Weber, a largely unethical capitalism, inspired by the 'inner attitude of the adventurer, which laughs at all ethical limitations ... Absolute and conscious ruthlessness in acquisition has often stood in the closest connection with the strictest conformity to tradition'.[15] In this respect there were five aspects that drove the proclivity to violence, which in certain combinations can make for a lethal genocidal cocktail.

Firstly, neither Marx nor Weber, nor indeed most works on colonial genocide, take into account the severe gender imbalances that usually characterise frontier

---

13 National Archives of Namibia (hereafter NAN) ZBU 2043. Verordnung J. nr 26883/5391, 24 October 1911.
14 Fein H. 1993. *Genocide: A Sociological Perspective*. London: Sage.
15 Weber M. 1957. *The Protestant Ethic and the Spirit of Capitalism*. New York: Scribners, 121.

situations.[16] As historian David Courtwright demonstrates, where there are large concentrations of single males, violence in its various manifestations is endemic.[17] Immediately prior to the First World War, the gender balance in the settler community reached its most equitable ratio of one female for every five males.[18] Colonial writers often took pride in the violent ethos of the colony.[19] Violence was evident in both action and attitude. After a visit to Luderitzbucht, prospector Fred Cornell described the treatment of Herero and Nama prisoners:

> *I had seen something of this myself, and had heard more from ex-German soldiers themselves, who with extraordinary callousness used to show whole series of illustrated postcards, depicting wholesale executions and similar gruesome doings to death of these poor natives. One of these, that enjoyed great vogue at the time, showed a line of ten Hottentots dangling from a single gallows, and each and every German soldier in the photo was striking an attitude and smirking towards the camera in pleasurable anticipation of the fine figure he would cut when the photo was published. This, I repeat, was only one of many that enjoyed a big sale in German South-West for the delectation of admiring friends in the Fatherland. Absolutely no mercy was shown to these unfortunate creatures.*[20]

Such public acceptance of violent behaviour and active encouragement of treating indigenes as decidedly inferior, was an important aspect of creating and sustaining the local *Zeitgeist* (ethos) in which genocide could occur.

A second factor concerns sexual relations. Contemporary accounts estimate that as much as 90 per cent of all white males in the colony lived in concubinage with indigenous women. While this might have helped dampen disorder and violence, it was government policy, especially after 1904, to actively discourage inter-racial sexual relations. In GSWA, such relationships helped to precipitate violence between settlers and Bushmen. The first South African military magistrate in the Grootfontein district commented: 'It seems that the Bushmen have lost all faith in the white man's methods (of justice), more especially as their women were being constantly interfered with by both farmers and police'.[21] The Blue Book on

---

16   See, for example, Palmer A. 2000. *Colonial Genocide*. London: C. Hurst; Moses A.D. 2004. 'Genocide and settler society in Australian history', in *Genocide and Settler Society: Frontier Violence and Stolen Children in Australian History*, ed. A.D. Moses. New York: Berghahn Books; Zimmerer J. 2004. 'Colonialism and the Holocaust: towards an archaeology of genocide', in Moses, *Genocide and Settler Society*.
17   Courtwright D. 1996. *Violent Land: Single Men and Social Disorder from the Frontier to the Inner City*. Cambridge: Harvard University Press.
18   Walther D. 2002. *Creating Germans Abroad*. Athens: Ohio University Press, 58.
19   Ridley H. 1983. *Images of Colonial Rule*. New York: St Martins, 140–43.
20   Cornell F. 1921. *The Glamour of Prospecting*. London: Fisher-Unwin, 41.
21   NAN. ADM 13/26, 6 November 1915.

German treatment of indigenes concluded that, based on evidence from missionaries, German officials and statements by natives, '[t]he chief cause of all the trouble between Germans and Bushmen was that the Germans would persist in taking the Bushwomen from their husbands and using them as concubines'. It claimed that '[t]he whole district [of Grootfontein was] full of these German–Bushwomen cross-breeds'.[22] Not only were they a visible reminder of settler sexual predation, but also generated fears of Bushman retribution, which many settlers believed was best pre-empted by killing those Bushmen.

The third factor, the abuse of alcohol, is generally a good indicator of social disorder. Writing of the earlier colonial period, William Chapman reported that:

> [t]he drunkenness in those days was frightful … nearly every man one met was a drunkard if he could only get the liquor, and it was drink, drink, so long as it lasted and no eating, at least this was the case with a great many, and then the saddest part of it was that those who had wives usually ill-treated them during their inebriated state, and most of these men died premature deaths.[23]

Excessive alcohol consumption continued to be a striking feature of life in GSWA. By 1913, there was one licensed drinking establishment for every 78 Europeans, while Windhoek had approximately one tavern for every 41 settlers.[24] Estimates put beer consumption in the *Schutzgebiet* (protectorate) at 50 per cent higher than in Germany.[25] Discussing unsuccessful horticultural smallholders, Clara Brockmann suggested that many failed not only because of 'inactivity' and 'stubbornness', but also by 'playing the great gentleman' and 'drinking themselves to ruin by buying rounds of champagne'.[26] Alcohol numbed any sense of bourgeois decency they may have had. The breakdown of moral restraint in facilitating genocide is well known and excessive alcohol consumption is generally associated with such breakdowns.[27]

Fourthly, the socio-economic background of all these virile and boisterous settlers needs to be considered. This is important when one considers Weber's insight about the connection between adventure capitalism and its

---

22 Silvester J. & Gewald J. 2003. *Words Cannot be Found: German Colonial Rule in Namibia. An Annotated Reprint of the 1918 Blue Book*. Leiden: Brill, 235–45.
23 Chapman, *Reminscences*, 102.
24 Gordon R.J. 2003. 'Inside the Windhoek lager: liquor and lust in Namibia', in *Drugs, Labor and Colonial Expansion*, eds W. Jankowick & D. Bradburd. Tucson: University of Arizona Press, 117–34.
25 Walther, *Creating Germans*, 97.
26 Brockmann C. 1912. *Brief Eines Deutschen Mädchens aus Südwest*. Berlin: Mittler & Sohn, 171.
27 Hinton A. ed. 2002. *Genocide: An Anthropological Reader*. Malden: Malden, 14.

'closest connection with the strictest conformity to tradition'. Recalling his 1907 visit to the *Schutzgebiet*, the political economist Moritz Bonn observed that:

> [i]n South-West Africa, we have created a kind of manorial system with a European lord of the manor and an African serf ... you quickly drift into European problems ... but whatever you do on African soil; will always be merely 'semi-European.' The democracies you create are not a people, but merely a class, whose progress, existence and safety depends on the services of a subject race which they cannot amalgamate, but which they must rule. There lies ... the labour foundation of the African society.[28]

Most of the junior officials he encountered 'were scions of the Prussian nobility who had not learned much and who were suspicious of every kind of learning. They had come out to Africa because it offered them a chance of bossing on a scale no longer available even in darkest Pomerania'. Their legacy lives on in the form of the fake Rhenish castles and monuments that are still popular with tourists. Even the missionaries Bonn found disappointing: 'Their small-town minds had been trained in that docile obedience which was a distinctive feature of German Lutheranism; they did not dare to stand up for the rights of the natives or even for their own work'.[29] This mindset of arrogance combined with the notion of unquestioning acceptance of authority or the dictates of science helped facilitate the exercise of killing people defined as 'lesser'.

The fifth factor concerns the role of rumour in provoking settler apprehension.[30] Rumours are particularly apt to generate insecurity where the settlers are thinly spread—Namibia still has the distinction of having the second lowest population density in the world. The situation undoubtedly bred a remarkable paranoia which was widely recognised at the time. As one army commander advised his troops: 'The people out there will have some gruesome stories to tell you but only half of them are true'.[31] Indeed, Jan-Bart Gewald sees rumour as a major factor leading to the German–Herero War, and Elizabeth Hull reports that even General von Trotha, who bears the main responsibility for destroying 80 per cent of the Herero population, was susceptible to rumour. He refused to believe the magnitude of the

---

28 Bonn M. 1914. 'German colonial policy'. *United Empire*, 5, no. 2, 135. Details about this important but forgotten figure in the political economy of colonialism are to be found in Gordon, R.J. 2013. 'Moritz Bonn, Southern Africa and the critique of Colonialism'. *African Historical Review*, 45, no. 2, 1–30.
29 Bonn M. 1949. *Wandering Scholar*. New York: Day & Co., 135, 138.
30 Courtwright, *Violent Land*, 174.
31 NAN A214. 'Kriegstagebuch von Gunther Walbaum, 1914–1915'. Unpublished manuscript, 39. All translations are my own.

destruction he had wrought, fearing that the Herero would return to fight.[32] Paranoia infiltrates the business of living in subtle ways and can help fuel mass violence.

While colonial laws were draconian, their effectiveness was constantly doubted. Attempts at ensuring tighter regulation of indigenes through a plethora of rules and ordinances only served to exacerbate settler fears. The administration soon realised this: 'It will frequently be found that natives who are actually vagrants are in possession of registration badges, these are obtained from other natives or stolen. Care should therefore be taken that proper proof of employment is produced and that the native is in possession of his own registration badge'.[33]

The colonial wars in Namibia between 1903 and 1907 were subject to extensive and embarrassing international media scrutiny, and this influenced how settlers treated outsiders who might be critical of German colonial practices. Bonn, for example, found on his 1907 visit to the territory that officials and many settlers refused to assist him in his enquiries until he threatened to make public their refusal to help him.[34] It was also difficult for officials to send critical reports to Germany because, for reasons of economy, colonial civil servants, unlike their metropolitan counterparts, lacked tenure. To take a stand against abuses, or question or criticise superiors, was to risk losing their jobs.[35]

Ritual and righteousness: *Musterstaat* and *Rechtstaat*[36]

The situation in GSWA was rife with contradictions. Settlers hated the indigenes, yet depended on them. They disliked the government, but relied heavily on it. In such circumstances, there was a strong emphasis—some visitors felt an overemphasis—on ritual and ceremonialism. On a 1913 visit, South African anthropologist Winifred Hoernlé complained: 'It is awkward having anything to do with the Germans because rank counts so much and

---

[32] Gewald J-B. 1999. *Herero Heroes*. Athens: Ohio University Press, ch. 5; Hull I. 2003. 'Military culture and the production of "final solutions" in the colonies: the example of Wilhelminian Germany', in *The Specter of Genocide*, eds R. Gellately & B. Kiernan. New York: Cambridge University Press, 151.

[33] NAN, SWAA 2/14/2. Native affairs. Memoranda and reports, 1916. Paranoia about Bushmen has a long history in Namibia extending through to the current period. See Gordon, *Bushman Myth*, 209–20.

[34] Bonn, *Wandering Scholar*, 134, 138.

[35] Gann L. & Duignan P. 1977. *The Rulers of German Africa*. Stanford: Stanford University Press, 188.

[36] While *Musterstaat* means 'model state', *Rechtstaat* roughly translated means 'constitutional state'.

one can't get to the individual direct'.[37] Excessive formality can disguise many features including ignorance, and had two important consequences in GSWA. Firstly, it meant an excessive reliance on the letter of the law, and secondly that the words and works of academics and scholars usually carried an exaggerated authority. Both were crucial factors in the Bushman genocide.

Ritual plays a crucial role in both coping with uncertainty and insecurity on an individual level, and state formation on a collective level. While Bley is undoubtedly correct to note the emotional and political impact of ritual upon indigenes, the concern here is to observe their impact on colonists as well.[38] Often ignored, but crucial, were the day-to-day rituals. Indeed, this was where indigenes most commonly experienced the state. There was a veritable industry in Germany for socialising prospective settlers, ranging from *Handbucher für Auswanderungslustige* (Handbooks for Intending Immigrants) to special schools where 'proper' inter-racial etiquette featured prominently in the curriculum.[39] In GSWA, laws underwrote the subordination of indigenes in seemingly trivial acts of daily intercourse such as prohibiting indigenes from walking on sidewalks, forcing them to greet settlers respectfully, and forbidding them from making loud noises in public. Laws also reinforced racial stereotypes. Consider the *Väterliches Züchtigungsrecht*, the law of paternal chastisement, which allowed employers and officials to act *in loco parentis* and flog children without permission. This meshed well with the prevailing racist notion that Africans were like children who required strict discipline in order to become responsible adults. This notion gained further credence from the fact that in Germany, corporal punishment was only allowed in schools and the home.

Given the lack of personnel to enforce compliance with all these regulations, ritualised interaction between coloniser and colonised took on added significance. The colonial situation called forth exaggerated etiquette by both coloniser and colonised. According to Albert Memmi, the Tunisian-born existentialist philosopher, 'formalism is the cyst into which colonial society shuts itself and hardens, degrading its own life in order to save it'.[40] Memmi noted the profound ambivalence that permeated the colonial project. How could the coloniser look after his workers while

---

[37]   Hoernle A.W. 1987. *Trails in the Thirstland: The Anthropological Field Diaries of Winifred Hoernle*. eds P. Carstens, G. Klinghardt & M. West. Cape Town: Center for African Studies, UCT, 44.

[38]   Bley, *South-West Africa*, 63–65.

[39]   Walther, *Creating Germans*, 58.

[40]   Memmi A. 1967. *The Colonizer and the Colonized*. Boston: Beacon, 101.

periodically gunning down a crowd of the colonised? For the coloniser to think about the contradictions inherent in colonialism was to undermine it. The plethora of regulations and the theorising of scholars were mechanisms through which colonisers granted themselves moral absolution from the dirty work of 'taming' the country. Public ritual, which was meant to promote the image of a smoothly functioning social order, created the capacity for authoritarian self-delusion.

Settler colonialism entails not only the physical movement of people, but also a psychological element. Anxieties need to be allayed for settlers to become settled. Law is crucial in this operation, creating what Jurgen Habermas refers to as 'facticity'.[41] Settlers, while in a position of domination, suffered the unbearable powerlessness of 'waiting'[42] and sought to stabilise their situation with the validating use of law. Law contributed to the social construction of the settler world by creating images of social relationships as natural and fair because they were endowed with legality.

Emphasis on the instrumentality of legislation has diverted attention from the contradictions inherent in it. One needs to look not only at what the law says, but also what it does. In particular, the cultural and attendant moral meanings of legislation have been ignored. The 1907 Native Ordinances were important not only on an instrumental level, but also symbolically. For the first time the distinction between 'whites' and 'indigenes' was legally recognised and thus the issue of sovereignty was significant. Sovereignty was not so much about determining the law, as about who was exempt from it.[43] There were two types of exemption. The first allowed those with power to ignore the law and foist their will upon the less powerful. The second defined the vulnerable and less powerful as beyond the law, as *Vogelfrei*.[44] This is an obvious, if frequently overlooked aspect of Von Trotha's infamous 'Extermination Order' which begins by declaring of the Herero that 'you have ceased to be German subjects', putting them beyond the realm and protection of German law. This corresponded with the German jurisprudential notion of *Rechtstaat* that essentially made everyone subject to the same law, equal within the bounds of the state. According to the Native Ordinances, indigenes without labour contracts were without legal rights and could be punished as vagrants. It also validated the ability of settlers to

---

41 By facticity, Habermas refers to the decisionistic aspect of the law, its origination in the will of the sovereign, and that compliance with the law is externally motivated by the threat of sanctions. Habermas J. 1996. *Between Facts and Norms*. Cambridge: Polity, 129.
42 Crapanzano V. 1985. *Waiting: The Whites in South Africa*. New York: Doubleday.
43 Agamben G. 2005. *States of Exception*. Chicago: University of Chicago Press.
44 Roughly meaning both 'outlaw' and 'fair game'.

engage in private policing. The *Musterstaat* survived by franchising its legal use of violence to settlers.

Legality displaced legitimacy as the key concern in GSWA during its *Musterstaat* phase. In the *Schutzgebiet*, oppression took place not so much through terror per se as through the routinisation of terror in day-to-day interaction. Ignoring officialdom and do-it-yourself justice were common settler strategies on outlying farms.[45] This misguided settler sense of self-help was not seen as mistreatment, but justified as *Züchtigung* (discipline).

There was another level at which the *Rechtstaat* played a role. This concerns the quality of the formal judicial structure. In 1912, *Reichstag* member, Dr Müller, complained in the *Reichstag*:

> *Our civil and military administration of justice is simply indefensible … With regard to native justice and administration there exists an incredible uncertainty concerning the powers of the administrative authorities … One judge uses the German penal code without further ado … Another does not use the penal code at all. In short, our criminal proceedings leave the natives entirely without rights.*[46]

The courts were lenient when forced to take action against settlers for killing indigenes because homicides were invariably justified as 'accidental' or necessary for 'public safety'. In Namibia, concludes Harry Schwirck, 'a whole legal discourse and law itself enabled rather than restrained colonial abuse'.[47] Given this situation the question arises as to why only Bushmen were subject to genocidal acts in the era after the colonial wars of 1904–1907 had ended.

Science and the framing of Bushmen and Damara in the settler imagination

How did the labels 'Bushman' and 'Damara' come to be part of the discourse of domination, especially since these groups were seen as incompatible and perpetually at war with each other? Many early travellers, and especially missionaries, actively promulgated the view that Bushmen and particularly Damara were brutally killed and enserfed by pastoralist Herero and Nama peoples. Such perceptions made sense in terms of conventional nineteenth century unilineal evolutionary models. They moreover provided moral justification for the missionary presence in the territory as well as an

---

45   Mattenklodt W. 1931. *Fugitive in the Jungle*. Boston: Little Brown; Reiner O. 1924. *Achtzehn Jahre Farmer in Afrika*. Leipzig: Paul List Verlag.

46   Cited in Olivier M.J. 1961. 'Inboorlingbeleid en -Administrasie in die Mandaatgebied van Suidwes-Afrika'. DPhil dissertation, Stellenbosch University, 223.

47   Schwirck H.M. 1998. 'Violence, race and the law in German South West Africa 1884–1914'. PhD dissertation, Cornell University, 23, 121, 233.

argument in favour of colonisation. This thinking nonetheless flies in the face of empirical evidence. No less a personage than Darwin's cousin, Francis Galton, fell victim to this fallacy. In 1850 he mounted an expedition, partly scientific and exploratory, but mostly for hunting, to what is now Namibia. His narrative of this adventure won the Royal Geographical Society's gold medal. Galton was to build on these experiences to achieve fame as a polymath, making a name for himself in fields as diverse as statistics, anthropology and perhaps most ominously, eugenics. As an eminent Victorian, his views carried weight.

En route home, he reported his findings concerning the state of knowledge about the region in the *St Helena Gazette*. Using the latitude of Walvis Bay as reference, he claimed the following:

> *[To the south live] partly civilised Hottentots, called in the aggregate, the Namaguas. North of this line, live the Damaras and dispersed tribes of perfectly savage Hottentots; the Namaguas call these 'Saen' (or Bushmen)—look down on them with the greatest contempt and catch them. As they do the Damaras, for slaves. They are not so diminutive as the Bushmen, commonly so called, neither are they quite so low in the scale of humanity, though in every other respect they exactly resemble them.*

> *Again, living together with these Bushmen, and hunted down in the same way as they by both Damaras and Namaquas, are another and a very peculiar race called the Ghou Damup; they are blacks, speaking no other language than Hottentot, and who have retained no tradition whatever of their origin; they used to be despised and made slaves of, even by the Bushmen, but of quite late years community of misfortune has much equalised the two races, and they now intermarry.*

> *The Ghou Damup appear to be the aborigines of Damaraland ... Ages ago, I presume that the Bushmen entirely conquered them, so that they then lost their own language, and about 70 years ago the Damaras came like a swarm from their original home (some 10 days east of Cape Cross) and overran the whole country, driving both Bushmen and Ghou Damup together to the hills and other uninhabited places, where they now live together ...*[48]

Yet, soon after, when he in 1853 published his book *Tropical South Africa*, and certainly in his later publications, he yielded to the conventional wisdom of the metropole of regarding 'Bushmen' in the terms expressed by Prichard:

> *Writers on the history of mankind seem to be nearly agreed in considering the Bushmen or Bosjesmen of South Africa as the most degraded and miserable of all nations, and the lowest in the scale of humanity ... these people are so brutish, lazy,*

---

[48]   Francis Galton Papers. GB 0103. University College London Archives. Also available at http://www.ucl.ac.uk/library/special-coll/galton.shtml; *St Helena Gazette*, 31 January 1852.

and stupid, that the idea of reducing them to slavery has been abandoned ... It is no matter of surprise that those writers who search for approximations between mankind and the inferior orders of the creation, fix upon the Bushmen as their favourite theme.[49]

From the start, ethnographic observations were fashioned by metropolitan orthodoxy. That many Bushmen were actively engaged in copper mining and trade, for instance, was noted in such a way as to allow it to slide into intellectual insignificance.[50]

Reading early missionary and traveller accounts against the grain, it is clear that most communities were polyglot. It was not simply a question of serve, die or flee. As distinguished archaeologist Graham Clarke noted, relationships between foragers and indigenous pastoralists were highly flexible temporally and spatially, and encompassed a wide array of possibilities including the tolerative, symbiotic, parasitic, competitive and the disoperative, which was disadvantageous to one or more parties.[51]

Early travellers found that interspersed with, and often extending beyond ecological zones occupied by pastoralists, were people practising a hunting-and-gathering or fugitive type of existence, whom they arbitrarily categorised as Bushmen or Damara. In order to understand the dynamic of their existence, it is necessary to underline the critical importance of that volatile and complex environment. Drought and epidemics of various sorts would often force once proud pastoralists to grub for roots. There are also many reports of pastoralists later labelled by Europeans as Nama and Herero becoming 'Bushmen' and later reverting back to their previous lifestyle.[52] Similarly, foragers might be forced by drought to enter into subservient relations with pastoralists or agriculturalists. There was no linear trajectory from the one to the other. The distinction between foragers and pastoralists was a political one. Fluidity, competition and movement appear to have been the dominant characteristics of these communities.

While 'Bushmen' excited the colonial imagination, 'Damara' appear not to have attracted much attention, despite being touted as the 'mystery people' of Namibia—the mystery being how a Negroid people supposedly came to

---

49 Prichard J.C. 1851. *Researches into the Physical History of Mankind*, 1. London: Sherwood, Gilbert & Piper, 177–78.

50 Heintze B. 1972. 'Buschmaenner unter Ambo-aspekte ihrer gegenseitigen Beziehungen'. *Journal of the South West Africa Scientific Society*, 26, 47; Hahn C.H. 1985. *Diaries of a Missionary in Nama- and Damaraland 1837–1860*, ed. B. Lau. Windhoek.

51 Cited Wadley L. 1979. 'Big elephant shelter and its role in the Holocene prehistory of central South West Africa'. *Cimbebasia*, 3, no. 1, 1–76.

52 Lebzelter V. 1934. *Eingeborenenkulturen in Suedwest-und Suedafrika*, 2. Leipzig: Karl W. Hierseman, 184.

lose their language and speak Nama.[53] In part, this can be attributed to the established role of 'Bushmen' in the Western imagination stretching back to the colonisation of the Cape and their place in emergent theories of unilineal evolution. The entry for Bushmen in the authoritative *Deutsche Kolonial-Lexicon* published in 1920 is three times as long as that for Bergdama, while there are approximately 10 times as many entries for Bushmen as for Damara in N.J. van Warmelo's magisterial *Anthropology of Southern Africa in Periodicals to 1950*.[54] The *Deutsches Kolonial-Lexikon* summarised colonial knowledge about the Damara as a black *Urbevolkerung* (primal people), which had earlier been viewed as a dependent *Mischrasse* (mixed race), but later found to be 'undoubtedly' a 'pure' Negro race with distinctive cultural characteristics. Turn-of-the-century scholarship believed that they were part of the great migration from north Africa, but had been subjugated by the Hottentots and thus lost their language. The first European travellers distinguished between the Berg (mountain) Damaras and the (cattle) Damara. They called themselves *Haukoin* or in other spellings, /=*Nu-khoin* (black people), while the Nama called them *Chaudaman* (shitkaffers).[55] The *Lexicon* concluded: 'The Bergdama's intelligence is noteworthy and this characteristic in conjunction with their powerful body development make them valued by Whites as labourers and domestic servants'.[56] The 1912 census estimated that 19 600 Damaras were living among whites as compared to approximately 8 400 Bushmen.

Foundational discourse concerning Berg Damara was laid by early missionaries such as C.H. Hahn and C.G. Buttner, who claimed that they neither hunted nor herded, but lived merely on what fell into their hands.[57] They had no inclination to acquire wealth and stole livestock not to enrich themselves as the Herero did, but to slaughter, and this in Herero eyes was

---

[53]   Linguist Willi Haacke has recently argued that the Damara version of Khoekhoegowab, the preferred name for the Nama language, is older than that spoken by Nama. See Haacke W. 2000. *Linguistic Evidence in the Study of Origins: The Case of the Namibian Khoekhoe-speakers*. Inaugural lecture. Windhoek: University of Namibia. The mystery is clearly of European making.

[54]   Van Warmelo. N.J. 1977. *Anthropology of Southern Africa in Periodicals to 1950*. Johannesburg: Witwatersrand University Press.

[55]   Not because they were full of it, or as an insult, but because they left their faeces uncovered.

[56]   'Die intelligenz der B. ist beachtenswert, und all diese eigenschaften bewirkten im verein mit ihrer kräftigen körperlichen entwicklung, daß sie als arbeiterklasse und als hausbedienstete von den weißen sehr geschätzt werden', in *Deutsches Kolonial-Lexicon*, ed. H. Schnee. Downloaded from Archives, Deutsche Kolonial Gesellschaft, Frankfurt University at http://www.ub.bildarchiv-dkg.uni-frankfurt.de/Bildprojekt/Lexikon/lexikon.htm.

[57]   Buttner K. 1879. 'The Berg Damara'. *Cape Monthly Magazine*, 18, 285–94.

equivalent to murder. They were allegedly highly desirous of obtaining European clothing, and especially guns, and unlike Herero and Nama who had livestock to trade, they had to work for settlers to obtain these items. Theophilus Hahn, adventurer and academic, thought that while they were intellectually inferior to their neighbours, they had 'strength of character' and so were 'industrious, provident and made good servants'.[58] Similarly, Special Commissioner Palgrave praised them for their industrious habits, but found that because of their timid disposition, they allowed themselves 'to be hunted like hares without offering any resistance'.[59]

Although Nama-speaking, Damara tended to live in the more mountainous parts of Hereroland, where they practised a foraging, hunting and petty herding existence, mostly with goats. Later, as European knowledge increased, some writers distinguished several distinct subcultures including the Sand Damara who were to be found in the east on the fringes of the Kalahari, the Honey Damara who lived in the Otavi area, and the Berg Damara proper. The Damara, if early accounts are to be believed, were treated even worse than Bushmen. They were seen as of even lower status than the latter, who were at least valued as hunting guides. Like Bushmen, they practised a flexible production strategy, largely in areas unattractive to pastoralists such as the more mountainous and drier regions. Foraging was often supplemented by small herds of goats and the growing of cannabis. Their economy lent their settlements greater stability than those of Bushmen, and this was reflected in their more permanent hut construction.[60]

---

[58] Hahn C.H. 1878. 'Damaraland and the Berg Damaras'. *Cape Monthly Magazine*, 16, 217–30, 289–97.

[59] Anon. 1878. 'The Bluebook'. *Cape Monthly Magazine*, 16, 186.

[60] The usual social unit of the Damara in pre-colonial times was the band, consisting of between 10 and 30 people. Bands were highly flexible and mobile within a determined area. They were based on bilateral kinship with a distinct bias towards patrilineality and typically consisted of extended kinship groups. Each band normally had a single person regarded as the headman or groot-man, or *gei-khoib*, who had no formal powers but ruled by strength of personality and purse. Given the size of the band, there was no need for a complex division of labour. Among some bands, the *gei-khoib* was assisted in ritual activities by his senior wife and by a special assistant called a food-master, who was typically an experienced elderly man who would not only decide which plants were fit for human consumption, but would also serve as messenger between groups. A key to Damara flexibility was their system of bilateral kinship in which relatives were acknowledged through both the father's and the mother's line. This provided an extensive network of relatives from whom individuals could solicit help. According to Vedder, some Damara practised iron-working which they undertook for neighbouring pastoralists as well. Inskeep A. & Schladt M. 2003. *Heinrich Vedder's The Bergdama: An Annotated Translation of the German Original With Additional Ethnographic Material*. Cologne: Köppe.

Science, especially ethnology and anthropology, enjoyed much higher status in Germany than in other metropolitan countries. German ethnological associations had more members than in Great Britain, the United States and France combined.[61] Given the mandarinate nature of German academia, this in practise meant that academic and scientific pronouncements enjoyed much wider currency and authority than in other metropolitan centres. Even critics of colonialism such as Bonn conceded that German scientific colonialism, resplendent with its *Kolonial-Institut* and the emerging science of *Kolonialwissenschaft* (colonial science), was more advanced than its British or French equivalents.

These scholars were taken seriously from the very beginning of colonisation, especially within the settler establishment that placed a premium on scholarship and science. Dr Theophilus Hahn, son of a missionary and the first person to obtain a doctorate based on Namibian research, while readily dismissed as an unsavoury character, nevertheless had his scholarly pronouncements taken seriously. Until Hahn's publications, the term 'Bushman' was largely a lumpen category into which all those who failed to conform to colonial perceptions of pastoralist or agriculturalist categories were dumped. It did not denote an ethnic group, but a socio-political category. In a series of papers, Hahn argued that the gloss for the San should not be 'bandit', but 'original inhabitant', which fitted well with the emerging and increasingly popular theory that Bushmen were the original inhabitants of the country who were then dispossessed by the Khoikhoi and Herero.[62] This interpretation suited Hahn's political activities in Namibia at that time, providing useful justification for European conquest of Khoi and Herero territory. Most importantly, Hahn was seen as an authority by early German colonial officials and settlers as well as by Palgrave, the commissioner sent by the Cape Colony to assess the situation in Damaraland and Namaqualand. He made extensive use of Hahn's ethnographic notes to compile his reports. Hahn's views helped frame German colonial discourse on those labelled 'Bushmen' and thus settler reaction to them.[63]

Later, two other academics were to play a key role in shaping the discourse around what should be done to 'solve' the 'Bushman problem'. The immediate reference point for debate around the issue was Siegfried

---

[61] For further details, see Gordon R.J. 1998. 'The rise of the Bushman penis: Germans, genitalia and genocide'. *African Studies*, 27–54, 57.

[62] See, for example, Brace C.L. 1868. *The Races of the Old World: A Manual of Ethnology.* New York: Charles Scribner, 303.

[63] Gordon R. 2003. 'Collecting the gatherers', in *Worldly Provincials: Essays in the History of German Anthropology*, eds H.G. Penny & M. Bunzl. Ann Arbor: University of Michigan Press.

Passarge. His research was based on a sojourn of a few months in the Kalahari on an expedition led by Lord Lugard, and accompanied by a Dutch-speaking Bushman. Most of Passarge's information was derived from white traders or Bechuanas since he found it difficult to get information directly from Bushmen. As a race, Bushmen were on a closed development path, he claimed. They were incapable of adapting to agriculture or pastoralism. 'Nothing is more changeable, undependable, and unpredictable than the character of the Bushman; it combines within itself the greatest imaginable contrasts, virtues, and vices.'[64] He concluded that the only viable policy, if their territory were to be available for settlement, was to exterminate them: 'What can the civilized human manage to do with people who stand at the level of that sheep stealer? Jail and the correctional house would be a reward, and besides do not even exist in that country. *Does any possibility exist other than shooting them?*'[65] Passarge's efforts were enough to have him appointed to the inaugural chair of geography at the Hamburg Kolonial-Institut in 1908.

The Austrian geographer, Franz Seiner,[66] also participated in this discussion. He argued that adult male Bushmen were incorrigible and thus best deported from the area where captured. The way to turn Bushmen into reliable labourers was to start with the children and re-socialise them from an early age, while divorced from their traditional milieu and parents. Bushmen were in no danger of extermination by farmers, he argued, because they had a vast 'natural reserve' in the Kalahari. Seiner felt that by having women placed on settler farms, miscegenation with local black people would produce superior labourers. He suggested that all Bushmen north of Grootfontein were 'Bastard Buschmaenner' and thus not a primal race worthy of protection.

Seiner and Passarge were not isolated academic voices. On the contrary, consider the remarks made by Professor Leonard Schultze, later a renowned geographer-anthropologist who coined the term *Khoisan* that lumped 'Bushmen' and 'Khoi' (or Nama) together. Schultze undertook his research during the notorious Namibian wars of 1904–1907. The sample on which his famous classification is based was neither random nor large. It consisted mostly of prisoners in Keetmanshoop measured anatomically to classify them into anatomical types. Given what we know about naming practices

---

64 Passarge S. 1907. *Die Buschmänner der Kalahari*. Berlin: Reimer, 2.
65 Passarge, *Buschmaener*, 124, 132. Emphasis mine.
66 Seiner F. 1912. 'Die Buschmanngefahr in Deutsch-Südwestafrika'. *Deutsche Koloniale Zeitung*, 311–12; Seiner F. 1913 'Die Buschmannfrage im nördlichen Deutsch-Südwestafrika'. *Deutsche Kolonialzeitung*, 745–46.

and theories of the time, it seems likely that his subjects were impoverished Nama and thus his new term simply reinforced conventional dogma.[67] There was economic value in such conflation. In 1914 he inveighed:

If we consider the natives according to their value as cultural factors in the protectorate, then one race is immediately eliminated right away: The Bushmen. The Bushmen lack entirely the precondition of any cultural development; the drive to create something beyond everyday needs, to secure or permanently to improve systematically the conditions of existence, even the most primitive ones like the procurement of food. In the course of centuries he has come into contact with cultures of all levels; in conflict with them he has often enough had the knife put to his throat; tireless missionaries have attempted to save him from such struggle, to protect and to join him as the modest member to a civilized community; but the Bushman has always run away. He feels better out in the Sandveld behind a windscreen of thin leaf thorn-bush than in a solidly built house with a full pot and regular work—as long as he is free. Colonists cannot count on such people; they let them live as long as they don't do damage. But when they don't fulfil this requirement, they have been killed off like predatory game. The idea has been considered to preserve the Bushmen in reservations as the last remnants of the primordial past of the human race, just as elsewhere attempts are made to save endangered animal species. But we won't be able to afford the luxury of leaving fallow the required land areas and everything else which man requires for the maintenance of the species without inbreeding.[68]

While sweating at their uneconomical smallholdings in the Grootfontein district, many of these inexperienced and underfinanced settlers projected their wildest fantasies upon 'vagabond Bushmen' and in this their fantasies often dovetailed with those of academics. This is also seen in the numerous reports written by officers and officials that were published in quasi-academic journals. Most of the scholars, with the exception of Seiner, whose material and ideas were so eagerly read and used by officials and settlers, were not in Namibia during the period when the Bushman hunts were carried out. Seiner appears to have played a key role not only in stimulating this debate, but also in influencing official policy towards Bushmen. Indeed, a closer reading of the newspaper headlines which featured 'The Bushman Danger' or 'The Bushman Plague' all seem to be traceable back to Seiner's pen. Some felt his claims were exaggerated, so much so, that Seiner tried to sue Rudolf Kindt, editor of the *Landestag*, a local settler newspaper, for libel because the latter accused him of presenting reports laced with fantasy. Answering the libel charge, Kindt obtained sworn statements from Pater Bierfort, a Catholic missionary on the Kavango River, who pointed out Seiner's

---

[67] Schultze L. 1928. *Zur kenntnis des Körpers der Hottentotten und Buschmänner.* Jena: Fischer, 211.
[68] Schultze L. 1914. 'Südwestafrika'. *Das Deutsche Kolonialreich*, 2. Leipzig: Verlag des Bibliographischen Instituts, 295.

numerous elementary linguistic faux pas. Other witnesses testified to Seiner being '*übernervoes*' (overanxious): he was prone to taking exception to the most trivial matters, and once punished his *bambuse* (factotum) with 25 lashes. Bierfort, who served as Seiner's interpreter, called his article on the 'Bushman Danger' pure 'invention'.[69] Seiner left the country before the case was settled. This raises an intriguing question: were Seiner and Passarge's statements about Bushmen based on scientific observation, or were they generated from interactions with settlers? And having scholarly credibility, did they in turn reinforce settler fantasies and nightmares? This seems not only possible, but also likely.

It was not coincidental that both feral animals and Bushmen were likened to convicts as they were deemed to share the attribution of having no moral compunction about taking what is not theirs. Since the eighteenth century, the bourgeois social and moral order was based on the principle of private property, solidifying a line of argument drawing sustenance from Aristotle, Locke, Hegel and Marx. The nineteenth century consensus was well stated by Engels when he wrote that production is the 'transforming reaction of man on nature. The most that the animal can achieve is to *collect*, man *produces*, he prepares the means of life, in the widest sense of the words, which without him nature could not have produced'.[70] Since Bushmen were seen as hunters living off wild animals, they were regarded as 'unproductive', as starkly portrayed by Schulze. Hugo von Francois, brother to the first governor, wrote in his memoirs that the problem with Bushmen was that they did not distinguish between '*herrenlose*' (ownerless) animals, namely game, and livestock. 'Both Races, the Herero as well as the Boers, have thus undertaken distasteful police raids and shot down Bushmen like vermin using organized battue[71] and the value (of such hunts) is shown in the large number of people shot.'[72] Both scholarly and official discourses portrayed Bushmen as unproductive, lacking a sense of property and little better than wild animals.

The foremost early twentieth century Namibianist, Heinrich Vedder held that the key to understanding the extermination of Bushmen was their distinct concept of property. Bushmen felt they owned all the animals of the veld and extended this concept to the domestic animals of pastoralists

---

69 NAN. B53/12, Seiner v. Kindt, GW 556.
70 Cited in Ingold T. 2001. *The Perception of the Environment*. London: Routledge, 63.
71 Defined by the *Oxford English Dictionary* as 'The driving of game from cover (by beating the bushes, etc. in which they lodge) to a point where a number of sportsmen wait to shoot them'.
72 Von Francois H. 1895. *Nama und Damara in Deutsch-SüdwestAfrika*. Magdeburg: Verlag G. Baensch, 236. My translation.

they later encountered with catastrophic results. At the same time Bushmen were *besitzlos* (possessionless). Like other scholars, Vedder was interpreting Bushman property relations as simulacra of European property relations.[73] Similarly, Bushman territory in Namibia was defined as 'Nomansland' by Palgrave, a definition partially maintained under German colonialism, allowing the land to be usurped and reallocated by the state.[74] This resulted in the South West Africa Company in 1892 being awarded the so-called Damaraland Concession, a freehold of some 33 670 square kilometres, along with railway and mineral rights that included the rich Otavi and Tsumeb mineral deposits which had been exploited by Bushmen.[75]

The change in focus from hunting to livestock farming after the consolidation of the colonial state had momentous implications for Bushmen. Their reputation as inveterate hunters meant that whereas they had previously been valued for their hunting skills, this reputation was now seen as detrimental to colonial interests and was increasingly used to justify their extermination. Part of this justificatory stereotype was that they had no concept of property and could not distinguish between domesticated animals and game, an allegation that is contrary to all modern scholarly findings on Bushman indigenous knowledge. In Bushman society, property was understood as rights of entitlement or usage rather than in the settler sense of possessive property, where the individual has exclusive dispositional rights, which is integral to capitalism. Not only did Bushmen communities have complex group entitlement rights, but they also often practised deferred gratification in their consumption of natural resources. Their relationship to the environment was not simply one of exploitation in a narrow economic sense, but was also relational and symbolic in nature. They had an immediate return exchange system and practised demand

---

73 Vedder H. 1926. 'Ueber die vorgeschichte der voelkerschaften von Suedwestafrika'. *Journal of the South West African Scientific Society*, 1, 14.

74 As Vattel, the influential eighteenth century jurist, commented: 'It is asked whether a Nation may lawfully occupy any part of a vast territory in which are found only wandering tribes whose small numbers can not populate the whole territory … these tribes can not take to themselves more land than they have need of or can inhabit and cultivate. Their uncertain occupancy of these vast regions can not be held as a real and lawful taking of possession; and when the Nations of Europe, which are too confined at home, come upon lands which the savages have no special need of and are making no present and continuous use of, they may lawfully take possession of them and establish colonies in them.' Cited in Curtin P. 1971 *Imperialism*. New York: Vintage, 44–45. For a recent Australian illustration, see Keen I. 2010. 'The interpretation of Aboriginal "property" on the Australian colonial frontier', in *Indigenous Participation in Australian Economies*, ed. I. Keen. Canberra: ANU Press.

75 Voeltz R. 1988 *German Colonialism and the SWA Company*. Athens: Ohio University Press, 14.

sharing—not out of personal choice, but because their social organisation and value system required it.[76]

With the onset of colonisation, a sharp distinction between Bushmen and Damara occurred. While Damara were sometimes ranked lower than Bushmen by European scholars, they were seen as at least having a concept of property and aspirations to ownership, their more permanent huts usually cited as evidence. The supposed paedomorphic qualities of Bushmen, as opposed to the 'stocky, robust' physique of the Damara, was another reason advanced to explain why the former were less suited to the rigours of farm labour, further reducing their possibilities of being absorbed into the colonial economy or raised in the 'scale of civilisation'. Another distinction between Bushmen and Damara was that farmers believed that Bushmen had an inherent 'meat lust' and thus could not be trusted around livestock. They thus had to be 'tamed' by being force-fed maize meal. Damaras, on the other hand, being experienced 'garden boys', had no such pathology.[77] Scheulen in his study of stereotyping in German colonial literature notes that Bushmen were described as the gypsies of Africa. They were vagabonds with all the negative implications this carried in Germany. They were seen as a pure *Jägervolk* (hunting people) possessed of an unbound love of freedom. The Damara, on the other hand, were believed to be born servants, capable of continuous and challenging labour.[78] This was their passport to survival in the brutal colonial situation.

Pragmatically, Bushmen made for unreliable proletarians as they could more readily abscond if they did not want to perform menial farm work, whereas Damara did not have that option. Ecological considerations were important here. All the areas traditionally inhabited by Damara— the Erongo and Otavi Highlands, and areas of the Khomas Hochland— were places that were rapidly hemmed in by settler farms or bordered by uninhabitable desert. In addition, Damara raised small stock, especially goats. This meant that they had limited alternatives. Bushmen, on the other hand, could readily drop out of rural labour by reverting to hunting and gathering because European and black settlement had not yet fully encircled their territories. They had the vast Kalahari—waterless, but game rich and of marginal ranching utility—to which to flee.

Galton, as we have seen, made a crucial distinction between Bushmen and Saen. The Saen (now commonly referred to as Hei-//om), he felt,

---

[76] Barnard A. 2007. *Anthropology and the Bushman*. Oxford: Berg.
[77] This myth was evident among farmers when I did fieldwork in Namibia in the early 1980s.
[78] Scheulen P. 1998. *Die 'Eingeborenen' Deutsch-Südwestafrikas*. Köln: Rüdiger Köppe Verlag, 90–96.

were impoverished Nama and lived interspersed among Herero, while the Bushmen 'proper' lived out to the north-east in an area commonly called the Kaukauveld or Omaheke. This is an area best visualised as a long arc sweeping from Outjo and Ovamboland, through the Kavango, Grootfontein and Tsumeb districts, and down to Gobabis. Even today this is still where most Namibian Bushmen are to be found. There are sound ecological reasons why foraging should have remained a viable mode of subsistence in this area for so long. It was not suitable for pastoralism, either by commercial ranchers or subsistence-oriented cattle-raisers. While the region had a relatively high average rainfall, precipitation was extremely irregular. In addition, the high probability of contracting lung-sickness and the presence of a seasonally poisonous plant called 'gifblaar' (poison leaf, *Dichapetalum cymosum*) served to inhibit anything but temporary cattle grazing in the area. Most importantly, the area was too isolated from markets to be commercially exploitable. Nor should one overlook the significance of Bushman resistance to such encroachment. This did not, however, prevent the movement of European hunters and traders into the area. In the early twentieth century, it still attracted a few speculators who saw some potential in the area. Most quickly cut their losses and ran.

Interpreting the destruction of Bushman society in terms of resource competition appears attractive on the surface. Ecological pressure was certainly a significant factor. Not only did settlers move into Bushman territory after the war, but 1910 was a bad drought year with only 42 per cent of the average rainfall. That four out of the following five rainy seasons were also below average aggravated the situation. In addition, the 1907 proclamation of the Etosha Game Park, which encompassed prime Bushman territory north of Grootfontein, and 1908 proclamations outlawing hunting out of season or without a licence, added to the pressure. The problem with this line of argument is that it implies that genocide occurred covertly and over the longer term. Bushmen, farmers and officials occupied different ecological niches on the same terrain and thus were not in direct or immediate competition. Rather, as in other parts of the Kalahari, a symbiosis emerged and resource competition only became an issue much later. As far as the game laws went, it is obvious that police and soldiers were sparsely spread and had little chance of enforcing them.

Conclusion

Theories concerning colonial genocides and situations of brute 'booty capitalism' need to consider how factors such as ecology, social and demographic structures, economic conditions, conflicts and ideology became aligned in ways that generated mass violence. Of particular importance, especially in explaining variation, is the issue of how the imagination and fantasies of settlers were manipulated and tied to the colonial project. These shackling mechanisms were often embedded in other societal institutions. Of particular importance in this regard was the *Rechtstaat*.

In Namibia, most settlers came from a strong German 'tradition'. Indeed, if they had not been so tradition bound, they would probably have sought their fortunes in regions beyond German hegemony, as many, for example, did in North America. In settling settlers in GSWA, ceremonialism played an important role, particularly through the formality and rituals of the *Rechtstaat*, as confirmed by Elizabeth Hull's recent emphasis on the role of German military culture in the Namibian genocides—a culture she understands as a complex of habitual practices and basic assumptions imbricated in the German military's doctrines and administration.[79]

The *Rechtstaat* franchised coercive power to settlers while psychologically empowering and validating their oppressive behaviour. Rohrbach complained that 'the conviction has gained ground that without the formality of the law and the juristic atmosphere of our high Prussian-German officials, nobody can administer anything'. Nevertheless, such formality was a crucial factor in giving settlers the self-confidence that Rohrbach believed rendered them 'spiritually more effective than any average million of people at home'.[80] Operationally the *Rechtstaat* facilitated the attempt to create a pliable labour supply by removing key elements of the means of production belonging to indigenes, especially Herero and Nama, by confiscating their land and livestock and then tying them down to colonial employers through the permit system. Indigenes not on reservations or carrying a pass were defined as criminal and punished as vagrants. Bushmen by definition, then, were defined as vagrants and subject to punishment. For all the problems settlers claimed to have with Herero, Nama and even livestock-aspiring Damara, as workers, they could still be massaged into the colonial economy by manipulating their love and desire for livestock. While indigenes were by law prohibited from owning livestock, farmers allowed them informal ownership as a means of ensuring labour. According to the *Landestag*

---

79 Hull I.V. 2003 'Military culture and the production of "final solutions" in the colonies: the example of Wilhelminian Germany', in *The Specter of Genocide: Mass Murder in Historical Perspective*, eds R. Gellately & B. Kiernan, 141–62. New York: Cambridge University Press, 151.

80 Rohrbach P. 1915. *German World Policies*, trans. by E. von Mach. New York: Macmillan, 135.

(Legislative Council), indigenes informally owned about 25 per cent of all small stock in the territory and over 20 000 head of cattle.[81] Bushmen, believed to have no concept of property or wealth, could not be manipulated in this way, and this emphasised their 'worthlessness' in settler eyes. As foragers, they were not dependent on their colonial masters and could disengage from the colonial economy whenever they wanted. They could not be controlled or permanently integrated into the economy and thus were deemed to be of little economic value. Fuelled by plentiful tales about 'wild' Bushmen, a topic guaranteed to excite the imagination of even the more sober settlers, the fires of genocide were stoked. These tales facilitated settlers' tendency to project their worst fantasies and nightmares onto Bushmen, who served as convenient scapegoats to cover the incompetence of novice, under-funded farmers.

German society valued the opinions of scholars to a far higher degree than other Europeans, and academics played a key role in developing, underwriting and sustaining stereotypes of subject peoples. In GSWA, colonisers and scholars mutually reinforced each other's beliefs that indigenous peoples belonged to tribes or ethnic groups, and since those with power have a better chance of imposing their definitions and conceptions upon reality, indigenes created tribes and groups to function within the colonial framework. Underpinning the settler myth that various ethnic groups lived in bellicose isolation from each other was the notion that their forms of subsistence were mutually incompatible. This myth was most famously summarised by Vedder and drummed into countless Namibian schoolchildren (including myself) until recently: 'Where the cattle of the Herero trod, there was Hereroland and where the Nama hunter cast his eye, there was Namaland'.[82] Statements of this ilk exaggerate economic competition between indigenous groups. Given the precarious ecological situation, all the ethnic groups in the region were often forced to engage in a variety of subsistence strategies. Furthermore, subsistence strategies focusing on cattle, hunting and gathering, small-scale goat-raising and horticulture were not incompatible because the animals fed predominantly on different types of plants and grasses. For example, the standard myth that Herero cattle drove away Bushman game, and that Bushmen were thus forced to kill Herero cattle, and that this in turn led to Herero attacking Bushmen simply does not hold since cattle and game usually had different

81 Prein P. 1994. 'Guns and top hats: African resistance in German South West Africa, 1907–1915'. *Journal of Southern African Studies*, 20, 99–121.
82 Vedder H. 1937. *Die Voorgeskiedenis van Suidwes-Afrika*, trans. by H. Rooseboom. Windhoek: John Meinert, 205. My translation.

feeding regimes. Game went into marked decline with the introduction of firearms, not cattle.

The common threads tying together colonial discourses of settler and scholarly concerns are notions of production and property. In his popular Herero war novel, *Peter Moors Fahrt Nach Südwest Afrika*, the author Gustav Frenssen has one of his soldiers exclaim: 'These blacks deserved to be killed in the eyes of God and men; not because they murdered two hundred farmers and rose up against us in rebellion, but because they built no houses and dug no wells'.[83] The critical distinction between Bushmen and the other groups lies here. In the hierarchical typology developed by academics, Bushmen generally ranked lowest because it was alleged that they had no concept of property. It is not enough to recognise this hierarchy as being neo-Darwinian. Crucially one needs to consider the basis on which this hierarchy was constructed. According to many colonials, Bushmen were *Vogelfrei* precisely because they owned no property and did not have laws. Their alleged incapacity for work was also tied to notions of property. Most importantly, having no property meant that their territory was seen as *terra nullius* and thus available for the taking by settlers.[84]

---

[83]   Frenssen G. 1906. *Peter Moors Fahrt Nach Südwest Afrika: Ein Feldzugsbericht*. Berlin: G. Grote, 198.

[84]   This view is argued by many, perhaps most elegantly by Patrick Wolfe: 'Whatever settlers may say—and they generally have a lot to say—the primary motive for elimination is not race (or religion, ethnicity, grade of civilisation, etc.), but access to territory. Territoriality is settler colonialism's specific, irreducible element'. Wolfe P. 2006. 'Settler colonialism and the elimination of the native'. *Journal of Genocide Research*, 8, no. 4, 388.

Chapter Six

Why Racial Paternalism and not Genocide? The Case of the Ghanzi Bushmen of Bechuanaland

Mathias Guenther
Wilfrid Laurier University

Their needs were simple and the land they occupied was only a comparatively small stretch of territory. On the unfenced and largely undeveloped farms there was little need for labourers other than herds. Bushmen did the work capably enough for their requirements and each farmer would have several families of Bushmen resident on his land, intermittently working for him. Cash wages were unheard of and the employer–employee situation had much in common with the patron–client relationship between Bantu and Bushman. It was stable, and both sides recognized their duties and obligations. The farmer was not very much better off than his labourer as far as material comfort went, and the Bushmen were content to have enough to eat and get a regular ration of tobacco.[1]

The *modus vivendi* between Western pastoralists and indigenous hunter-gatherers described in the above passage is one of reciprocity and interdependence, in the form of paternalistic employment or servitude. Nowhere in the description do we detect any hint of mass violence, let alone genocide. The passage refers to the pattern of interaction between the early Ghanzi Boer settlers and indigenous Bushmen in the Bechuanaland Protectorate. Its author, the late George Silberbauer, had first-hand dealings with both pastoralist Afrikaner farmers and the hunter-gatherer Bushmen in his capacity as Ghanzi district commissioner in the early 1960s, a few years before the Bechuanaland Protectorate gained independence in 1966. This passage, from Silberbauer's survey of the protectorate's Bushman population,[2] specifically in the western Ghanzi district, offers a summation of what this chapter argues, namely, that instead of displacement and eradication, contact between Western pastoralists and hunter-gatherers may under certain circumstances have resulted in

---

[1] Silberbauer G. 1965. *Bushman Survey Report*. Gaberones: Bechuanaland Government, 116–17.
[2] Silberbauer's survey focused specifically on the /Gwi of what would later, largely at his recommendation, become the Central Kalahari Game Reserve. His report became the basis for a doctorate in social anthropology and an important monograph on the /Gwi. Silberbauer G. 1981. *Hunter and Habitat in the Central Kalahari Desert*. Cambridge: Cambridge University Press.

accommodation. In the case at hand, this took the form of racial paternalism, with bonds that were emotionally and morally charged. I will analyse the historical, ecological, economic and cultural circumstances that led to this accommodation in the Ghanzi region, as opposed to the rest of southern Africa where Western stock farmers were frequently bent on driving Bushmen off the land and even exterminating them.

Ghanzi veld: incursions into a 'howling wilderness'

The most significant topographical feature of the Ghanzi veld is a limestone ridge that runs diagonally across this stretch of the western Kalahari, from the south-west to the north-east. Its ecological significance lies in the water pans formed by depressions in the ridge which may yield water all year round, especially after good rains. There are, however, periods of drought that may last for years during which the pans dry out, and game and stock populations decline. Wild food plants (*veldkos*) and crops of maize and pumpkins fail. The Ghanzi veld is not well suited to ranching or crop growing as pans and water holes yield insufficient water. Pans need to be deepened and wells with wind-driven pumps installed for any degree of commercial farming to take place.

The subsistence pattern of hunting and gathering as practised by Bushmen[3] was, however, well suited to this environment and developed to a high level of efficiency over millennia. Their acutely honed foraging skills and small-scale, versatile social organisation allowed for a fairly secure existence notwithstanding the vagaries of their desert-like environment. Edible wild plants were seasonally available, and the pans along the limestone ridge attracted large numbers of game at certain times of the year. This provided the economic base for relatively complex band societies which, in the first half of the nineteenth century, may have consisted of as many as 200–300 members. The evidence also suggests the presence of centralised political leadership among some of the Ghanzi Bushman bands that allowed them to organise into multi-band polities that for two or three generations held their own against Oorlam and BaTawana marauders from

---

[3] The Bushmen of the Ghanzi area are of two main linguistic groups, the Naro (Nharo), the majority, and the =Au//eisi, who lived south and north of the farming block, respectively. There are, in addition, a number of other groupings, such as the /Gwi, //Gana and !Xhõ. Regarding the collective ethnonym, I use 'Bushman' in this article, even though 'San' has become the preferred term. Given the chapter's historical context, in which the people were known by no other name, 'Bushman' seems the appropriate term. See Guenther M. 1999. *Tricksters and Trancers: Bushman Religion and Society.* Bloomington: Indiana University Press, 10–11.

the west and north-east, respectively. Both groups of invaders claimed the region as a hunting preserve, which they soon over-exploited for antelope, ostrich and elephant,[4] as the market for hides, feathers and ivory experienced a boom in the second half of the nineteenth century.[5]

In 1851, the Swedish explorer Charles Andersson was the first European to set foot in the Ghanzi veld at Tunobis, today's Rietfontein, near the Botswana–Namibia border. Daunted by what he perceived to be a 'howling wilderness totally destitute of water',[6] Andersson abruptly returned to Walvis Bay, ending his voyage of exploration to Lake Ngami which lay to the east of the Ghanzi region. In the same year another European, the Canadian big-game hunter Frederick Green, did venture into the region, perhaps the first European to do so.[7] Others followed, and during the second half of the century, one after another, white hunters and traders travelled to the Ghanzi veld to hunt elephant and rhinoceros that were abundant around the waterholes of the Ghanzi ridge. Others, primarily explorers, also went through the region, on their way to Lake Ngami and Victoria Falls, to reconnoitre and map what was to become an important lateral route through southern Africa. From the 1870s, contingents of peripatetic Dorsland Trekkers in search of a new home started moving through the area on their way to South West Africa and Angola.[8]

---

[4] For example, in 1847 the Oorlam chief Amraal Lambert took 50 riders and 20 ox wagons from his capital Gobabis, which means Elephant Fountain, into the Ghanzi veld, netting about 6000 pounds of ivory. Lau B. 1987. *Namibia in Jonker Afrikaner's Time*. Windhoek: Namibian National Archives, 45.

[5] Wilmsen E. 1989. *Land Filled with Flies: A Political Economy of the Kalahari*. Chicago: University of Chicago Press, 91–129; Guenther M. 1993. '"Independent, fearless and rather bold": a historical narrative on the Ghanzi Bushmen of Botswana'. *Journal of the Namibian Scientific Society*, 44, 25–40; Guenther M. 1997. '"Lords of the desert land": politics and resistance of the Ghanzi Basarwa of the nineteenth century'. *Botswana Notes and Records*, 29, 121–41; Guenther M. 2002. 'Independence, resistance, accommodation, persistence: hunter-gatherers and agro-pastoralists in the Ghanzi veld, early 1880s to mid-1900s', in *Ethnicity, Hunter-Gatherers, and the 'Other'*, ed. S. Kent. Washington: Smithsonian Institution Press, 127–49.

[6] Andersson C. 1856. *Lake Ngami or Explorations and Discovery During Four Years of Wandering in the Wilds of South-Western Africa*. London: Hurst and Blackett, 374.

[7] Vedder H. 1934. *Das alte Südwestafrika*. Berlin: Martin Warneck, 361.

[8] The Dorsland trekkers were for the most part Transvaal farmers who trekked north, through the *dorsland* (thirstland), the term Afrikaners applied to the Kalahari, because they were dissatisfied with President Kruger's political and religious policies. They moved in a series of treks that ranged in size between 10 and 120 wagons throughout the 1870s and 1880s, settling for various lengths of time at places as far north as the Cunene River and beyond, in Angola. For a summary of the Dorslanders' peregrinations, see Tabler E. 1973. *Pioneers of South West Africa and Ngamiland: 1738–1880*. Cape Town: Balkema, 31–34. For accounts that focus on the Dorslanders' stay in the Ghanzi region, see Silberbauer, *Bushman Survey*, 114–15; Russell M. & Russell M. 1979. *Afrikaners of the Kalahari: White Minority in a Black State*. Cambridge: Cambridge University Press, 10–12, 32; Van Rooyen P.H. & Reiner P. *Gobabis Brief History of the Town*. Gobabis: Municiplaity of Gobabis, 15.

When, at the very end of the nineteenth century, the next group of trekboers, the subjects of this chapter, traversed the Ghanzi region, it was no longer a 'howling wilderness', but made more familiar by the reports of people who had ventured through it the previous 50 years. In 1895, three years prior to their long and arduous trek through the Dorstland, a small, advance party of settlers had gone to the Ghanzi veld under the leadership of Captain Fuller, and a contingent of 25 Bechuanaland Border Police. Their task was to survey farms to be allocated to settler families on the border of the BaTawana chiefdom. These settlers arrived in several groups, during 1898 and 1899, after a gruelling trek that took between three and seven months. They had opted to follow the longer but more widely travelled eastern route via Ngamiland, rather than the more direct western route through the Kalahari. The trekkers suffered great cattle losses as they had set out at the height of the dry season. They embarked on this arduous venture on the promise of being given farms by the Cape government that wanted to establish a settlement of Europeans, preferably Boers, in the Ghanzi region. The move was prompted by geo-political considerations, including the Cape government's desire to block German expansion eastward from South West Africa, to deter northward expansion of the Transvaal republic, and to pre-empt independent Boer incursions into the area.[9]

Forty-one 5 000 morgen (± 6.5 sq. km) farms were allocated, for which a farmer was required to pay a 'perpetual quit rent' of £5, which granted free-hold title to the lease and issued him with a certificate of occupation. Farms were located around pans and waterholes along the Ghanzi ridge, with empty stretches of land in between, and a hinterland seasonally rich in *veldkos* and game animals, allowing both San and settlers to subsist.

---

[9]   For details of the realpolitik behind this move, especially the motives of Cape prime minister Cecil Rhodes, see Sillery A. 1965. *Founding a Protectorate: A History of Bechuanland 1885–1895*. The Hague: Mouton & Co., 180–92; Sillery A. 1974. *Botswana: A Short Political History*. London: Methuen & Co., 104–06; Silberbauer, *Bushman Survey*, 114–26; Silberbauer, *Hunter and Habitat*, 11–16; Childers G. 1976. *Report on the Survey Investigation of the Ghanzi Farm Basarwa Situation*. Gaborone: Government Printer, 6–19; Russell M. 1976. 'Slaves or workers? Relations between Bushmen, Tswana, and Boers in the Kalahari'. *Journal of Southern African Studies*, 2, no.2, 185–88; Russell & Russell, *Afrikaners of the Kalahari*, 10–39; Maylam, P. 1980. *Rhodes, the Tswana, and the British: Colonialism, Collaboration, and Conflict in the Bechuanaland Protectorate 1885–1899*. Westport, Conn.: Greenwood Press, 147–48, 196–97; Guenther M. 1986. *The Nharo Bushmen of Botswana Tradition and Change*. Quellen zur Khoisan-Forschung, 3. Hamburg: Helmut Buske Verlag, 40–49; Ng'ong'ola C. 1997. 'Land rights for marginalized ethnic groups in Botswana, with special reference to the Basarwa'. *Journal of African Law*, 41, no.1, 1–26.

Bushmen had for millennia hunted and gathered in the region and some of the pans and waterholes that now sustained settler farms had previously been the nuclei of band territories. All but four of the original settler families were Afrikaners. Most of them were from that area of the northern Cape, which in 1895 had been annexed to the Cape Colony from British Bechuanaland. Prior to its incorporation into Bechuanaland in 1885, the territory had been within the Afrikaner geo-political sphere, and included the two small, short-lived Boer republics of Stellaland and Goshen.

The first generation: *trekboere* and veld Bushmen

Life was hard for the first generation of Ghanzilanders,[10] in a land constantly threatened by drought and other ecological calamities such as flooding, malaria and locust infestations. Outbreaks of rinderpest and foot-and-mouth epidemics in the Ghanzi region, in 1897 and 1934 respectively, decimated cattle herds, as well as antelope species and other ungulates. Farming was a haphazard economic enterprise for the early Ghanzi settlers. As one of their descendants explained to South African sociologists Margo and Martin Russell during their ethnographic study of the Ghanzi Afrikaners: 'We did not really farm. In those early days we lived by the gun and we lived off the veld. We had some cattle but few, very few'.[11] Tracking, trekking and trading their semi-feral, free-range beasts scattered widely over the unfenced veld, along with hunting for food, trophies and ivory, made for a lifestyle that was unsettled and restless. This was the lifestyle of the trekboer, of whom the Ghanzi settlers are descendants. The line of descent stretches back over a century, to trekboer ancestors eking out a precarious life in the wastes of Bushmanland and Namaqualand. Ghanziland was the trekboers' last frontier and for the first years and decades, settlement there was sporadic as people came and went, some staying on their farms, others moving on to Gobabis in the west and Molepolele in the south, or as far as Angola, to join up with Dorslanders who had been through Ghanzi 20 years earlier. Others went back south to the Cape, Transvaal or Orange Free State. Some of these moved back again to Ghanzi after a few years. It was not until the second and third generation

---

10   This is Silberbauer's designation for the pioneer Ghanzi settlers, as well as their descendants.
11   Russell, 'Slaves or workers?', 187.

that Ghanzilanders set down roots, as cattle farmers—*veeboere*—rather than as peripatetic *trekboere*.[12]

As such, the first generation of Ghanzilanders followed a lifestyle that was similar in a number of ways to that of indigenous Bushmen, especially with respect to their economies. Their precarious cattle economy was what the Russells refer to as a 'trekking economy'—'an amalgam of hunting, gathering, transhumance, erratic subsistence agriculture and exchange trading'.[13] It mirrored the foraging economy of the Ghanzi Bushmen in both its mobile, opportunistic, hand-to-mouth, loosely scheduled, haphazard style as well as its reliance on veld resources and the skills to exploit them. The effect of these similarities between the trekking economy of the Ghanzi Boers and the foraging economy of the Bushmen was to draw the two groups into each other's economic orbit, on a cooperative rather than a competitive footing. Because their relationship was symbiotic, interaction between the two groups became charged with mutual obligations.

The usefulness of the Bushmen had been apparent to the Ghanzilanders from the very start of their Kalahari venture in 1895. The Ghanzi region experienced an especially severe dry spell that year, necessitating a forced march through the Kalahari to the Cape, to get help to the drought-stricken settlers. This desperate measure forced the men to leave the women and children behind, in the care of Bushmen. When they returned two years later they found them in good health and spirits as 'the Bushmen had taken excellent care of the women and children'.[14] This incident, which is reported by George Silberbauer and has surfaced in my own Ghanzi fieldwork, is engraved in the collective memory of Boer descendants, as a debt they owe Bushmen, and which they honour 'by not refusing a Bushman's plea for food, shelter, or living place on their properties'.[15] It is symptomatic of

---

[12] These two Afrikaans terms, meaning 'stock farmer' and 'migrant farmer' respectively, are an established, almost iconic dichotomisation of the South African Boer farmer, harking back to eighteenth century Cape society. Historians of South Africa debate the degree to which they reflected reality on the ground. Some, like Mohamed Adhikari, use 'trekboer', more broadly, as ranchers who move around with their herds in transhumant fashion, often from a permanent base, usually a loan farm. See Adhikari M. 2010. *The Anatomy of a South African Genocide: The Extermination of the Cape San Peoples.* Cape Town: UCT Press, 29. Others, such as Susan Newton-King, see the trekboer as much more peripatetic; '"wandering men", the true nomads of the frontier, who moved with their stock from one temporary camp to another, making use of the interstitial spaces between registered farms and moving on when the water ran out or the pastures deteriorated'. See Newton-King S. 1999. *Masters and Servants on the Cape Eastern Frontier.* Cambridge: Cambridge University Press, 23–24. The Ghanzi variant of the trekboer is closer to Adhikari's characterisation.

[13] Russell & Russell, *Afrikaners of the Kalahari*, 17–18.

[14] Silberbauer, *Hunter and Habitat*, 12.

[15] Silberbauer, *Hunter and Habitat*, 12.

the cooperative and symbiotic relationship between the Ghanzi Boers and Bushmen and gives salience to their place in the Ghanzi Boers' perspective on the early days, which, for all their hardships, are viewed in positive terms. A Ghanzi farmer interviewed by the Russells explained that, 'We lived well. The world was a free place in those days. We had no worries'.[16] This nostalgic perspective drew Bushmen into their salutary purview of the past. In contrast to other regions of trekboer settlement in southern Africa, in the Ghanzi veld, the presence of Bushmen eased settlers' lives and mitigated the hardships they experienced, especially in the earlier period. The presence of an indigenous population of hunter-gatherers that was well adapted to the vagaries of the land and well disposed towards the cattle-herding settlers who had taken over their land held significant benefits. These consisted of subsistence and material resources and skills, as well as labour, on which Ghanzilanders became increasingly dependent.

Veldkos, of the kind foraged by Bushmen, was an important supplement to the early Ghanzi settlers' meagre staple of maize, precariously grown by means of small, low-yield crops or bartered in Ngamiland with the BaTawana for trekker manufactures such as carts and wagons, or specialised services such as blacksmithing and well digging. They either gathered veld plants themselves or employed Bushmen women to do so. Some of these foods became an integral part of the Ghanzi trekkers' diet, including the nutritious and tasty *morama* bean, the cherished *khutsu* desert truffle and coffee substitutes made from either shepherd's tree (*witgat*) roots or camelthorn tree seeds (*koffiepeel*). Because of its periodic superabundance, the *tsamma* veld plant was especially important to Ghanzilanders. After good rains, this wild melon would be found scattered over the ground by the ton, providing a copious supply of food as well as water, for both people and cattle.[17]

In addition to availing themselves of the Bushman's foods, the early Ghanzilanders also drew on their foraging skills, especially hunting. Bushmen frequently assisted the Boer farmers on their hunts, tracking, stalking and butchering animals in return for portions of the meat. They also provided certain specialised hunting services to Boer farmers, such as tracking leopards or lions that killed stock, and ridding farms of pests

---

16 Russell, 'Slaves or workers?', 187.
17 Anon. 1926. 'The great Ngami trek'. *The Round Table: The Commonwealth Journal of International Affairs*, 328; Russell & Russell, *Afrikaners of the Kalahari*, 19; Guenther M. 1996. 'From "lords of the desert" to "rubbish people": the colonial and contemporary state of the Nharo of Botswana', in *Miscast: Negotiating the Presence of the Bushmen*, ed. P. Skotnes. Cape Town: University of Cape Town Press, 226–27.

such as porcupines and springhares. Farmers hired Bushmen to track down dispersed cattle and gather bones to be ground down as a calcium supplement for cattle. The Boers dried antelope meat to make *biltong*, an important component of their diet, and they cured and tanned animal skins with the same tanning agent, elephant's root shavings, as Bushmen have done for centuries. They made donkey whips from giraffe skin, warm blankets from *mathlose* (bat-eared fox) skin, floor mats and furniture coverings from duiker skin, both softly cured. Wildebeest and rhinoceros hides provided the materials for saddles, halters and reins that were used primarily for donkeys, and occasionally oxen, as horses were scarce during the early days. In addition to *veldskoene*, boot-style shoes, the Ghanzi farmers made jackets, trousers and other items of clothing from tanned steenbok and hartebeest skins. Housing, too, was derived from the veld and patterned on the dwellings of the indigenous population. Wattle-and-daub dwellings with thatched roofs and cow dung floors known as *hartebeeshuise* were sometimes built for them by Bushmen. These structures were more common during the earlier period than the more permanent, dressed limestone houses preferred by Boers.[18]

To this day, when farmers reminisce about the early days they still tell of family members crowding together in the *hartebeeshuis* on rainy summer nights, or sleeping out in the open under a starlit sky and a *matlohse* blanket around an all-night fire during the dry winter. This kind of nostalgia provides much grist to Ghanzi Boer folklore, despite all the deprivations of life back then. While such memories derive first and foremost from a pioneering life in the Ghanzi veld, they in part also echo Afrikaners' collective 'nostalgic mythology of the "*lekker lewe*"'. Sheila Patterson, in her classic study, traces this aspect of Afrikaner mythology back to 'the farmer, the Boer, in the old Republics; a life when land was there for the taking, where the veld grass grew tall, where the fountains never failed and the game thundered in uncounted herds'.[19]

For the Ghanzilanders, the Bushmen are part of that Golden Age as well. They are integral to it and define much of its nostalgic overlay. This was different elsewhere, in the northern Cape or colonial German South West Africa, where the Bushmen, often 'killed and maimed burghers' cattle and

---

[18] Russell & Russell, *Afrikaners of the Kalahari*, 17–18; Guenther, *Nharo Bushmen*, 42–46. Another service, of an esoteric rather than practical kind, that some Bushmen provided Ghanzi Boers was to perform rain dances in times of drought. This is an arcane practice that some of the older Boer farmers still solicited from Bushmen when I did my field work there in the late 1960s.

[19] Patterson S. 1957. *The Last Trek: A Study of the Boer People and the Afrikaner Nation*. London: Routledge & Kegan Paul, 239.

sheep, murdered herders and mutilated their corpses'.[20] Actions of this sort, all of them reactions to relentless and aggressive, indeed genocidal, incursions into their land, earned them appellations such as 'vermin', the 'Bushman Plague' or 'Bushman pestilence'. Such imprecations are absent from Ghanzilanders' discourse about Bushmen. While the relationship of Ghanzilanders with Bushmen was not without tension, especially over periodic incidents of rustling, the Bushman practice of veld burning, and 'squabbles over Tsamma melons',[21] the incidence and intensity of conflict was by comparison very restrained. It was not enough to mar Ghanzilanders' appreciation of Bushmen with whom, throughout the first generation or two of settlement, they shared the land, its vagaries and challenges. They did so as a poor, isolated settler community which 'did not really farm, but lived by the gun and off the veld', themselves 'to some extent at least, hunters and gatherers'.[22] Bushmen were thus drawn into the lives, and the social and moral sphere, of the early Ghanzilanders. This association brought Bushmen a number of benefits, countering tensions that rose from competition for resources, on land that had been taken from them.

Topping the list of direct material benefits accruing to Bushmen from their association with settlers was the availability, all year round, of water. This was useful during the dry winter season, but critical during droughts that might last for years, and when pans and natural wells dried out. Bushmen depended on settlers for water as their farms included most of the water pans as well as water holes. A skill the Bushmen could not match was the Boers' ability to sink and prop wells as deep as 30 metres using dynamite to blast through limestone layers. Sporadic or seasonal visits to farmers' water sources by veld Bushmen tended to become more and more regular over time, especially after Bushmen performed the occasional

20   Giliomee H. 2003. *The Afrikaners: Biography of a People*. Charlotteville: University of Virginia Press, 62. See also Guenther M. 1980. 'From "brutal savages" to "harmless people": notes on the changing western image of the Bushmen'. *Paideuma*, 26, 126–29; Gordon R. 1992. *The Bushman Myth: The Making of a Namibian Underclass*. Boulder: Westview Press, 57–68; Gordon, R. 2009. 'Hiding in full view: the "forgotten" Bushman genocides of Namibia'. *Genocide Studies and Prevention*, 4, no. 1, 34; Adhikari, *Anatomy of a South African Genocide*.
21   Russell, 'Slaves or workers?', 189. Fire ecology was used by hunter-gatherers to replenish the veld. Boers did not see matters in this way, deeming it instead highly destructive of grazing, as well as dangerous, because changes in wind direction could cause wildfires that could burn down cattle kraals and farmers' houses. See Guenther, *Nharo Bushmen*, 101–03.
22   Russell, 'Slaves or workers?', 187.

service for farmers in return for food and clothing, as well as medicine when needed.[23]

While they did draw on resources made available by Boers, Bushmen who resided and worked on settler farms continued to forage. Others living beyond the farming zone turned to farms sporadically, such as during milking season or in periods of severe drought, to seek water, food and shelter with farm-associated kin, or kin of kin, namesakes or friends, thereby activating a widely cast, complex network of social relationships. The main reason farm Bushmen could continue foraging was that there were not all that many farms on the Ghanzi block in the early decades. Another reason was that the unfenced Ghanzi farms were spread far apart, leaving large stretches of veld in between on which farm Bushmen were able to hunt and gather. It was not until well into the second half of the twentieth century that farms incorporated much of the surrounding veld, reducing the range accessible to foragers considerably.[24]

Another major benefit Bushmen gained from the Boer presence was political rather than economic in that it afforded them protection from marauders who had encroached on the Ghanziveld for generations. Oorlam raiders had come from Gobabis in the west, and from the latter half of the nineteenth century BaTawana of Ngamiland had raided from the northeast. While for the first half of the nineteenth century BaTawana attacks had been effectively resisted by some of the Ghanzi Bushman groups, especially the =Au//eisi, raids had become more persistent and intense throughout the latter half of the century and were still occurring by the time Captain Fuller and the advance settler party arrived in 1895. In anticipation of possible attacks from BaTawana, and possibly Bushmen, Fuller and his party set up a defensive laager with their wagons. No attacks were launched by the BaTawana. As for the Bushmen, instead of attacking them, 'they appear[ed] very well disposed towards white people'. As Fuller reported:

> *in fact, we have been followed by about 30 or 40 of them since we have entered the country and they do not seem to be inclined to leave us, now that we are encamped. I believe their principal reason for wishing to be near us is that we may protect them from Segkome's people, who [sic] they accuse of taking their women and children, the skins, feathers etc. they hunt for and often killing men in addition. It is said that parties of the Lake people come down occasionally purposely to get slaves etc. from amongst the Bushmen.*[25]

---

23 Guenther, *Nharo Bushmen*, 98–111; Anon., 'Great Ngami trek', 326; Russell & Russell, *Afrikaners of the Kalahari*, 19.

24 Anon., 'Great Ngami trek', 330; Childers, *Report*, 16–17; Russell, 'Slaves or workers?', 186–87; Guenther *Nharo Bushmen*, 42–44.

25 Russell, 'Slaves or workers?', 185.

The ruthlessness and severity of BaTawana raids in the northern Ghanzi region in the last four decades of the nineteenth century were such that the historian Barry Morton refers to this period as a 'general reign of terror'.[26] BaTawana depredations on the Bushmen of Ghanzi was doubtless a factor in the compliant attitude of Ghanzi Bushmen towards European settlers who took over their land and replaced its antelope with herds of cattle.[27]

In sum, throughout the first two or three decades after settling in Ghanziland, the relationship between Boer and Bushman was very much one of cooperation and interdependence, and indeed, of symbiosis. Both parties benefited from their association with each another. For Boers the benefits were the availability of survival-enhancing veld skills, foods, tools and techniques, along with sporadic labour service. Bushmen's foraging life style remained intact throughout these early decades due to the low impact of the settlers' farming practices on the veld and its autochthonous inhabitants. The benefits for Bushmen were protection, a reliable, year-round supply of water, meat, tobacco and certain implements. Through sharing the deprivations and challenges of a taxing lifestyle mutual dependencies emerged, and social and emotional bonds were established between Boer and Bushman.

The second generation: *veeboere* and farm Bushmen

Bonds of interdependence between the Boers and Bushmen of Ghanzi stabilised in tandem with the expansion of the cattle component of the trekboer economy. In the process, Bushmen became more and more settled on farms and acculturated to a labouring way of life which tied them more closely to farmers than in the previous generation. This started 10 to 20 years after their arrival, and was in place on most of the Ghanzi farms as the second generation of Ghanzilanders took over farms from their fathers. It did not happen on all farms as some Ghanzilanders retained their trekboer economy into the second, or even third, generation. And for the Ghanziland

---

26   Morton B. 1994. 'Servitude, slave trading and slavery in the Kalahari', in *Slavery in South Africa: Captive Labour on the Dutch Frontier*, eds E. Eldridge & F. Morton. Boulder: Westview Press, 228.

27   Gadilobae M.N. 1985. 'Serfdom (bolata) in the Nata Area 1926–1960'. *Botswana Notes and Records*, 17, 26–28; Morton, 'Servitude, slave trading and slavery', 214–50; Guenther M. 1989. *Bushman Folktales Oral Traditions of the Nharo of Botswana and the /Xam of the Cape*. Stuttgart: Franz Steiner Verlag Wiesbaden, 152–55; Guenther, 'Lords of the desert land', 129–34; Guenther, 'Independence, resistance', 136–46.

farming community as a whole the trekboer economy remained a cultural backdrop until at least the mid-twentieth century.[28]

The Ghanzi Boer cattle enterprise started out on a haphazard footing. Herds were small and stagnant, ranging from a few head to between 30 or 40 'in good times'.[29] Cattle numbers were especially low in the first 10 years as their herds had been decimated by the trek through the Kalahari. Though replenishing their herds through natural increase was slow, they augmented the process by bartering cattle with African pastoralists, primarily BaTawana in neighbouring Ngamiland, 300 kilometres to the north-east. Beasts were allowed to roam freely over unfenced land and even calved out in the veld. Apart from disease and drought, lions were a constant threat, and African wild dogs took an unrelenting toll on herds. Cattle on occasion also fell victim to rustlers, mostly veld Bushmen during times of drought. Scattered over a large area, cattle would have to be tracked down and rounded up every so often. This was an arduous exercise that might take days to complete as herdsmen had to cover scores of miles, as often as not, on donkey back. It was also a hazardous business as the beasts, having 'roamed wild for years, were as cunning and fierce as buffaloes'.[30] Cattle round-ups generally occurred in calving season, in order to brand calves. It frequently happened that farmers claimed calves belonging to neighbours, as cattle from unfenced farms mingled freely. The haphazardness of cattle branding in Ghanzi generally meant that 'the first man to get his brand on a calf, ... owned it'.[31] Another reason for tracking and rounding up cattle was to take them to market, usually the abattoir in Lobatse. This, for the first decades of settlement, happened rarely as it was both arduous and potentially unprofitable. The 400-mile trek south in relays from one pan to the next, took four to six weeks. Many cattle perished on the way from thirst or predators, and those that got through lost up to 100 pounds in weight.[32]

In some ways, the cattle management of the Ghanzi *veeboer* could be compared to those of his African counterparts. As in so many African pastoral economies, cattle were valued less for their meat or market value and more for their measure of a man and providing 'the proper social foundation underpinning family and community life'.[33] Cattle were thus

---

[28] Russell & Russell, *Afrikaners of the Kalahari*, 27–39; Guenther, 'From "lords of the desert" to "rubbish people"', 25–26.
[29] Russell & Russell, *Afrikaners of the Kalahari*, 21.
[30] Silberbauer, *Bushman Survey*, 116.
[31] Russell & Russell, *Afrikaners of the Kalahari*, 29.
[32] Silberbauer, *Bushman Survey*, 116–19; Childers, *Report*, 8–9; Russell & Russell, *Afrikaners of the Kalahari*, 21–31, 39; Guenther, *Nharo Bushmen*, 135–36.
[33] Russell & Russell, *Afrikaners of the Kalahari*, 17.

rarely slaughtered. Instead, meat was obtained largely from goats as well as hunting. A Ghanzi Boer's cattle were prized possessions and integral to his standing in his community. Ghanzi farmers spent much time talking about their *beeste*, expansively and volubly, making use of an extensive cattle vocabulary which included not only the names of breeds, but descriptions of markings, colour, posture, age, horn shapes and other features.[34]

Another Ghanzi Boer practice comparable to African peers was that of lending cattle to dependants. The latter, known as *bywoners*, lived on the farm, usually helping to look after the cattle. Even though they were landless and of low status, *bywoners* as often as not were hardly any less poor than many a landowner on whose farm they squatted. They would sometimes be lent a few head of cattle by the farmer and, in addition to being allowed to use milk from the cows, was given leave by the farmer to start his own herd from some of the offspring. As remarked by historian Fred Morton, this practice, which was common in pioneer Boer society, resembled the Tswana loan cattle pattern of *mafisa*. Also, like the Tswana practice of *tshwaiso*, the early Ghanzilanders gave their children a beast when they were born, which over the course of their maturation into adulthood, would expand into the nucleus of their own start-up herd.[35]

In short, what the Ghanzilanders practised in the early decades was what Silberbauer refers to as a 'primitive' cattle economy. Its traits were incipiently capitalist in that it was characterised by small herds used mainly for subsistence, unfenced grazing lands, rudimentary cattle management techniques, loosely defined ownership of stock, isolation from markets, as well as vulnerability to predators, drought and disease. Moreover, the use of cattle for social rather than economic ends, along with a detailed semantic and aesthetic elaboration, gave the Ghanzilanders' cattle economy strong resonance with what Melville Herskovits referred to as the African 'cattle complex'.[36]

Regarding the capital and labour component of the Ghanzilanders' cattle operations, one again finds parallels with African patterns. One of its characteristics, according to the economic anthropologist Harold Schneider, was a relatively low need for capital and labour. Free-range grazing on unfenced land, and trekking rather than trucking cattle to market,

---

[34] Russell & Russell, *Afrikaners of the Kalahari*, 17.
[35] Morton F. 1994. 'Slavery in South Africa', in *Slavery in South Africa: Captive Labour on the Dutch Frontier*, eds E. Eldridge & F. Morton. Boulder: Westview Press, 263; Russell & Russell, *Afrikaners of the Kalahari*, 17.
[36] Silberbauer, *Bushman Survey*, 118; Herskovits M. 1926. 'The cattle complex in East Africa'. *American Anthropologist*, 28, 230–72.

required little capital outlay. Labour requirements of the first generation of Ghanzilanders were met primarily by their own sons and by *bywoners*. Bushman labour was used primarily for small stock herding, especially of the large number of goats found on most farms. Work with cattle consisted primarily of tracking, rounding up and droving a farmer's scattered, semi-feral beasts. It was only when the Ghanzi farmers developed a creaming industry in the 1930s that the need for Bushman labour intensified and changed from casual service to a more permanent form.[37]

In keeping with the rudimentary nature of the Ghanzi pastoral economy, the remuneration of Bushman labourers was in kind rather than cash. It was only around the middle of the twentieth century that cash wages started being paid. Before that, labourers received food rations, cast-off clothing, medicines and occasionally stock, usually goats. Cattle was given only rarely, and only to the most trusted and long-serving Bushman labourers. The farmer's motivation here derived as much from the heart as from the head: to increase the Bushman herder's vigilance and to inculcate in him a sense of responsibility for the herd, in which he now had a vested interest.

It is worth noting that as a form of remuneration, rations tended to reinforce personal and paternalistic socio-economic bonds between the early Ghanzi Boers and their Bushman labourers. This was less likely to happen when remuneration was in the form of a cash wage. As Georg Simmel suggests in his classic treatise on money, cash wages promote rational calculation in human relations, and when introduced into a *gemeinschaft*-type society, is likely to weaken bonds based on kinship or loyalty, paving the way to a *gesellschaft*-type society.[38] The latter is based not on kinship or patron–client relationships and their inherent personal ties, but on impersonal, contractual and socially divisive employer–employee relations. A progressive depersonalisation of their relationship is precisely what came

---

[37] Schneider H. 1981. *The Africans: An Ethnological Account*. Englewood Cliffs, NJ: Prentice Hall, 62–64; Silberbauer, *Bushman Survey*, 118–22; Russell & Russell, *Afrikaners of the Kalahari*, 79–88; Guenther, *Nharo Bushmen*, 130–40.

[38] *Gemeinschaft* and *gesellschaft* are the two basic, polar types of human associations according to the turn-of-the-century German sociologist Ferdinand Tönnies, who coined the terms. While the former is based on family and kinship ties, altruism, ascribed status and moral consensus, the latter is characterised by extra-family ties, self-interest contractual relationships, achieved status and a low degree of shared mores. Tönnies F. 1912. *Community and Civil Society*, trans. by ed. M. Hollis & J. Harris. Cambridge: Cambridge University Press.

to pass between later generations of Ghanzi farmers and Bushman labourers when cash replaced payment in kind.[39]

What had started out as a tenuous attachment of farm-associated Bushmen to a farm and the *baas* (master) that owned it, became more and more fixed. Sporadic or seasonal appearances on the farm by Bushmen, along with their families, for occasional labour became more regular or even permanent. In the process, the farmer came increasingly to rely on Bushman labour. More and more of the regular tasks of running a farm, both around the Boer's residence and out at the cattle posts, were performed with, or by, Bushmen. These chores included watering and milking cattle, herding goats and sheep, ploughing, repairs and maintenance to wagons, houses and equipment, and later on, from the 1960s, the building of fences.

While Bushman labour had initially not been essential to running the farm, subsequent generations of Ghanzi farmers increasingly came to rely on it. As farmers became more dependent on Bushman labour, their tolerance for labourers' low-effort levels and limited work skills, and especially their not infrequent leaves of absence to go hunting and gathering, or to visit kin at other farms or in the veld, became more strained. The labour problems Ghanzi farmers experienced with Bushman workers became increasingly irksome. Economic pressures on the farmer increased when, in addition to rations, cash wages were expected by workers. And in the 1970s, the government introduced a minimum wage, putting further strain on the Ghanzi Boer's finances, as well as on his relationship with Bushman labourers.[40]

All of these factors from the late 1960s onwards, resulted in a progressive loosening of the close social and economic bond between Ghanzi farmers and Bushmen. In the process, Bushmen progressively gravitated from the centre of the Ghanzilanders' social and moral community to its margins. This was very much to the farm Bushmen's detriment, as under- and unemployment translated into poverty, hunger, sickness and destitution.[41]

---

[39]   Simmel G. 1978. *The Philosophy of Money*, trans. by T. Bottomore & D. Frisby. Boston: Routledge & Kegan Paul; Coser L.A. 1977. *Masters of Sociological Thought: Ideas in Historical and Social Context*. New York: Harcourt Brace Jovanovich, 193–94; Peterson N. 1991. 'Introduction: cash, commoditisation and changing foragers', in *Cash, Commoditisation and Changing Foragers*, eds N. Peterson & T. Matsuyama. Osaka: National Museum of Ethnology, 3; Russell & Russell, *Afrikaners of the Kalahari*, 85.

[40]   Silberbauer, *Bushman Survey*, 120–26; Guenther M. 1977. 'Bushman hunters as farm labourers'. *Canadian Journal of African Studies*, 11, 195–203; Guenther, *Nharo Bushmen*, 133–35; Russell & Russell, *Afrikaners of the Kalahari*, 87–88.

[41]   Guenther M. 1976. 'From hunters to squatters: social and cultural change among the Ghanzi farm Bushmen', in *Kalahari Hunter-Gatherers*, eds R.B. Lee & I. De Vore. Cambridge: Harvard University Press; Guenther, *The Nharo Bushmen*, 50–67.

Paternalism and clientage on the Ghanzi farms

Starting with the first generation of Ghanzilanders and subsequently for two or three generations, each farmer had living on his farm a core group of Bushman labourers, along with their families and dependents. They all remained with him permanently and they relied on him for their material needs. They lived in a small settlement of grass huts usually a few hundred metres from the farmer's house, or far away at cattle posts. After the farmer's death and the take-over of the farm by one of his sons, the Bushman labourers, their families and descendants frequently stayed on, so that the master–labourer relationship became generationally fixed. After two or three generations, it was customary for a farmer to refer to such labourers as 'his' Bushmen and continued to 'look after' them the same way his father and grandfather had done. Three generations later the descendants of the original Ghanzi settlers, as opposed to recent arrivals, continued to regard such 'looking after the Bushmen' as their duty, even when they no longer had much need for Bushman labour after the modernisation of their ranching operations from the middle of the twentieth century onwards. Food continued to be provided to Bushmen even when they were too old or too sick to work. Those fed by the farmer included all of the family members of the Bushman worker and other unemployed hangers-on, putting strain on the farmer's resources. A day or two of work time might be lost whenever a farmer drove a sick Bushman to the doctor or to the Ghanzi clinic. And when one died, he would drive the corpse, along with mourners on his truck, to the farm's burial site because 'he was old, he had been with me for a long time'.[42]

After decades and generations of stable economic and social interaction, the relationship between the Boer farmer and the Bushmen in his employ became personal and emotionally charged. According to the Russels, the two knew each other with an 'intimacy that comes from prolonged acquaintance'.[43] The Bushmen knew, and were keenly interested in, the affairs of 'their' Boer farmer, as well as his wife, children and extended family. They knew their names and personality traits, and much time was spent talking about the employer's family affairs. As *die oude baas* (the old master), the Boer farmer also entered Bushman folklore, featuring either in gossip, memorates and tall tales, or trickster stories in which the *baas* appears as the foil or dupe of the trickster protagonist, usually the baas's trusted, yet wily Bushman farmhand. The Bushmen, likewise, were a

---

42   Russell & Russell, *Afrikaners of the Kalahari*, 86.
43   Russell & Russell, *Afrikaners of the Kalahari*, 86.

favoured topic of conversation for Ghanzi farmers who, as noted by the Russells in their ethnography on the Ghanzilanders, knew each one of 'their' Bushmen 'as carefully delineated individuals, whose names, parents, birthplaces, biographies, quirks and foibles' were well recognised:

> *If you say to a group of Afrikaners, 'A Bushman told me', they will interrupt to ask, 'Which Bushman?' and will then amongst themselves piece together, on the basis of your poorly observed information ('Did he wear a red woollen hat? Was he tattooed between the eyebrows? Was he with his yellow-skinned wife?) who your informant was. 'That must have been Tshali from Buitswango. I wonder what he was doing on your side?*[44]

Many of the Ghanzilanders were fluent in either Naro or =Au//ei, or both, having learnt the language(s) in childhood, perhaps from a Bushman nanny, or from playmates. It was not unusual for a special bond to be forged between Boer and Bushman playmates that lasted into adulthood.[45]

Sexual relations were another way in which Boer–Bushman intimacy was manifested. Such liaisons were more frequent during the earlier period than among later generations of Ghanzilanders. 'In the old days, we all did it' was the somewhat wistful comment of an old Ghanzi Boer to the Russells.[46] It was invariably Boer men who took sexual liberties with San women and some of the early Boers kept Bushman concubines. A small number also married Bushman women and had children with them, and were ostracised as a result. Disapprobation was extended also to young Afrikaner men whose sexual adventures with San girls resulted in pregnancy. The main reason this was strongly condemned was that Boer mores required an acknowledgment of paternity as well as a degree of parental responsibility. In the Afrikaner value system this would draw Bushmen into the Boer kin group and community, which the Ghanzi Afrikaner community had great difficulty accepting.[47]

For all the intimacy and emotional attachment in Boer–Bushman relations, there also existed a rigidly defined, racially cast, social boundary between them that Afrikaners observed from the start. This acted as a distancing mechanism, as delineated in sociologist Pierre van den Berghe's classic analysis of how status boundaries are maintained between subordinates and dominants in systems of stratification. The distancing component notwithstanding, this mechanism allows for intimacy between

---

44   Russell & Russell, *Afrikaners of the Kalahari*, 86–87.
45   Guenther, *Bushman Folktales*, 124–41; Guenther, *Tricksters and Trancers*, 103; Russell & Russell, *Afrikaners of the Kalahari*, 92.
46   Russell & Russell, *Afrikaners of the Kalahari*, 89.
47   Russell & Russell, *Afrikaners of the Kalahari*, 88–91.

different groups whose members live together in stable social relationships. Through a series of status differences, a framework is created within which intimacy can play itself out without threatening the dominant group's integrity or the participating individuals' status. It is analogous to a stern but loving parent setting boundaries for children within which interactions can unfold smoothly and predictably and with a measure of amicability.[48]

While loving, the stern father of the patriarchal mould would also at times punish his transgressing child. Ghanzi Boer farmers in the early period likewise at times meted out corporal punishment to Bushman workers.[49] The early Ghanzilanders considered it fair to do so, albeit only if warranted, and with due measure of restraint.[50] If physical punishment was meted out arbitrarily and with excessive brutality, Boer mores were seriously contravened and Boer farmers who acted in this fashion were subject to moral censure. While there were brutal farmers in each generation of Ghanzilanders, who were talked about censoriously by Boer and Bushman alike, they represented isolated cases. An abusive farmer would soon find that did he not have any Bushman labourers left, as they would vote with their feet, a typical tactic in traditional Bushman society.

What all of these traits amount to is paternalism in its classic manifestation. It is the social template by which Ghanzi Boer–Bushman relationships operated during the first two generations. Intimacy blended with sternness, closeness with remoteness, inclusion with exclusion. Paternalism pervaded economic relations between Boer and Bushman in Ghanzi and explains their personal relationships, the system's morality, its lack of economic rationality, and its preference for rations over cash for remuneration.

Paternalism also defined the basic structure of labour relations between Bushmen and Boer farmers in Ghanzi and explains why this was not an employee–employer relationship, but one of clientage. As such, it resembled patterns of clientage found among other pastoralists in the region, most notably Tswana practices of *botlhanka* or *malata*, which has also been described as serfdom, even slavery. The variant of the nearby BaKgalagadi, which was more personal and benign than that of the BaTawana and

---

[48]   Van den Berghe P. 1960. 'Distance mechanisms of stratification'. *Sociology and Social Research*, 44, 155–64; Russell & Russell, *Afrikaners of the Kalahari*, 86.

[49]   The practice ceased soon after independence, in part because it could readily lead to an assault charge being laid at a police station, a court fine or even imprisonment by the district commissioner.

[50]   Ghanzi oral history features one of the early Ghanzi Boer farmers as reading what he deemed a suitable scriptural passage to the Bushman while he was being flogged in the presence of other farm Bushmen as a moral lesson to all and sundry. This he did to demonstrate that his punishment was not arbitrary, but in line with God's commands.

BaNgwato (BaMangwato) further east, was the pattern with which the Ghanzi Bushmen were most familiar. This was especially true of the Naro, of whom approximately 600 were linked to Bantu-speaking villagers on those terms. *Botlhanka* was a hereditary form of servitude. There was no labour contract and payment was in kind not cash. Labour was performed sporadically, with clients frequently absenting themselves from work to attend to their own affairs at their own settlements some distance from the patron's compound, or at remote cattle posts. Apart from rendering labour, clients were also expected to provide tribute to patrons, mostly in the form of proceeds from the hunt. They had no control over land, no property rights, their legal status was equivalent to that of minors and, like them, they were subject to punishment by patrons. Bushman clients, however, had a right to leave abusive patrons, to seek protection from, and offer servitude, to another patron.[51]

The reason for similarities between Ghanzi Boer and African patterns of clientship, as well as with those of the Tswana cattle practices of *mafisa* and *tshwaiso*, was not due to acculturation or imitation of African practices on the part of Ghanzi farmers. Instead, correlations in the clientage and stock-keeping patterns of these two pastoral societies stem from similarities in the circumstances they both faced when they entered the Ghanzi veld, an arid environment that made cattle herding difficult. A key part of that environment was indigenous hunter-gatherers, who hunted game that competed for grazing with settlers' cattle, and who gathered food plants that were utilised by both settlers and their beasts. A modus vivendi had to be found by the herders that allowed their beasts to survive in the Kalahari, and for them to get along with its indigenous inhabitants. The patron–client relationship that developed between settlers and the indigenous desert dwellers was a mode of production that was as adaptive as it was efficient.

---

51 That 'the employer–employee situation had much in common with the patron–client relationship between Bantu and Bushmen' was first noted by George Silberbauer, in the context of his *Bushman survey*, 65. It is the premise also of the Russells' extensive analysis of the economic and social relationship between the Ghanzi Boers and the farm Bushmen. See Russell, 'Slaves or workers?'; Russell & Russell, *Afrikaners of the Kalahari*, 81–94. There is a sizable literature on what the historian Barry Morton refers to as 'botlhanka studies'. See Morton, 'Servitude, slave trading and slavery', 217–19. It started with the investigations and reports into the matter in the 1920s and 1930s by the colonial government and the London Missionary Society, see Tagart, E.S.B. 1935. *Report on Conditions Existing among the Masarwa in the Bamangwato Reserve of the Bechuanaland Protectorate and Certain other Matters Appertaining to the Native Living Therein.* Pretoria: Government Printer; London Missionary Society. 1935. *The Masarwa (Bushmen): Report of an Inquiry by the South African District Committee of the London Missionary Society.* Alice: Lovedale Press; Joyce, J.W. 1938. *Report on the Masarwa in the Bamangwato Reserve, Bechuanaland.* League of Nations Publications, C112, M98,VIB., Slavery, Annex 6, 57–76.

'Their circumstances as cattle keepers', argues Margo Russell, 'have led into similar solutions to the problem of coexistence with these hunter-gatherers ... and a lifestyle which had as much in common with African as with European social organization.'[52] The development of an employer–employee relationship based on Bantu-style clientage is one of the most significant manifestations of what the Russells refer to as the 'Africanisation' of the Ghanzi Afrikaners, and use this as the basic framework for their analysis of Ghanzi Boer society. In addition to managing their cattle in the style of African pastoralists, Ghanzilanders drew elements of Africanness from another ethno-cultural source, namely, Bushman society. What Russell refers to as their 'trekking economy'—'by the gun and off the veld'[53]—resonated and interlinked with the Bushmen's foraging mode of production, as did such aspects of their lifestyle as wearing antelope-skin clothing, living in *hartebeeshuise* and sleeping under *mathlose* blankets under the open sky.[54]

The brand of racial paternalism, blended with symbiotic cooperation, which developed in Ghanzi in early Bechuanaland challenges historical, archaeological and anthropological conventional wisdom about the irreconcilability of settler-herders, especially Western ones, and indigenous hunter-gatherer Bushmen.[55] The South African colonial historian and settler apologist Donald Moodie's assertion that 'they [Bushman hunters] were then, as they still are, the scourge of every people possessing cattle'[56] is premised on this notion, as is that of his contemporary George McCall Theal, that 'it was impossible for pastoral white men and savage Bushmen who

---

52 Russell, 'Slaves or workers?', 179.
53 Russell, 'Slaves or workers?', 187.
54 Russell & Russell, *Afrikaners of the Kalahari*,15–20, 42–50, 113–19, 131.
55 The conventional wisdom here is based on a substantial body of literature. Two general works that draw on and summarise much of this literature, and that trace the perceived systemic, structurally ingrained irreconcilability between foragers and farmers ranging from ecological adaptation to world view and religion are Berman, M. 2000. *Wandering God: A Study in Nomadic Spirituality*. Alabany, N.Y.: State University of New York Press; and Brody, H. 2000. *The Other Side of Eden Hunters, Farmers and the Shaping of the World*. Vancouver: Douglas & McIntyre. I have recently suggested, in the context of Khoisan pre- and ethno-history, that this position needs to be modified, in view of the structural resilience of San society. See Guenther M. 2010. 'Sharing among the San, today, yesterday and in the past', in *The Principle of Sharing Segregation and Construction of Social Identities at the Transition from Foraging to Farming*, ed. M. Benz. Berlin: Ex Oriente, 105–36. A related issue is Miklos Szalay's critique of Rüdiger Schott's notion on the supposed *akkulturationsunfähigkeit* (inability of being acculturated) of the Cape Bushmen that stems from structural incompatibility with colonising Boer pastoralists. See Schott R. 1955. 'Die Buschmänner in Südafrika: Eine Studie über Schwierigkeiten der Akkulturation'. *Sociologus*, 5; Szalay M. 1983. *Ethnologie und Geschichte Zur Grundlegung einer ethnologischen Geschichtsschreibung Mit Beispielen aus der Geschichte der Khoi-San in Südafrika*. Berlin: Dietrich Reimer Verlag, 263–70.
56 Quoted in Smith A., Malherbe C., Guenther M. & Berens P. 2000. *The Bushmen of Southern Africa: A Foraging Society in Transition*. Cape Town: David Philip, 32.

neither cultivated the ground nor owned domestic cattle of any kind to live side by side in amity and peace'.[57] This was, in fact, possible in Ghanziland, where pastoral settlers and hunter-gatherers accommodated themselves to each other's lifeways through a mutual process of acculturation that Africanised the one, and to a degree 'Afrikanerised' the other.

The Ghanzilanders were thus a far cry from land-hungry, market-oriented Western ranchers, the kind found in other regions of southern Africa and the world. In these situations, practices of land tenure and farm management such as 'exclusive usage, fixed boundaries, registration of title deeds, alienability and permanent settlement',[58] provided the ingredients for serious conflict with indigenous hunter-gatherers. When stock farming became more commercialised, herd sizes increased and with this the need for grazing land. The pressure on hunter-gatherer indigenes increased accordingly, leading all too often to radical efforts to displace or eradicate them. In the Cape Colony, this generated 'battles between burghers and Bushmen as merciless as those fought … on any frontier',[59] culminating, as recently argued by Mohamed Adhikari, in genocide.[60]

No such battles ensued in the Ghanzi veld, where Western pastoralists who had settled the land were largely subsistence pastoralists, herding precariously small herds on arid, isolated stretches, far from market outlets. They exploited the land's resources through hunting and gathering which provided them with an indispensable source of food. Indigenous Bushmen assisted them with both of these tasks and in the process economic, social and emotional bonds developed between the two that precluded systemic conflict, let alone genocide, despite strict social barriers being maintained. Instead, what developed was a pattern of clientage blending benign concern and emotional closeness with stern aloofness and sharply delineated status differences. Paternalism, characterised by Van den Berghe as being of a 'racialist, stern and rugged' form,[61] had been bequeathed to the Ghanzilanders by their trekboer ancestors in the colonial Cape. Its harsh and punitive edge was softened while still stern and rugged in many ways, and based on an underlying 'premise of inequality'. Ghanzi Afrikaner

---

57   Theal G.M. 1911. 'Introduction', in *Specimens of Bushman Folklore*, comp. W.H.I. Bleek & L. Lloyd. London: George Allen & Company, Ltd, xxxi.

58   Adhikari, *Anatomy of a South African Genocide*, 19, with reference to eighteenth and nineteenth century Cape trekboers.

59   Giliomee, *Afrikaners*, 62.

60   Adhikari, *Anatomy of a South African Genocide*; Adhikari M. 2010. '"A total extinction confidently hoped for": the destruction of Cape San society under Dutch colonial rule'. *Journal of Genocide Research*, 12, 19–44.

61   Van den Berghe, *South Africa*, 21.

paternalism, however, included cooperation, interdependence, and social and emotional closeness.[62]

The humanitarian factor

We cannot understand why the racial paternalism that developed in Ghanzi assumed the benign cast it did without also considering humanitarian influences of the time. European pastoral settlers in the Ghanzi area of southern Africa had their run-in with indigenous hunter-gatherers at a time and place where genocidal actions would not have been tolerated. Adding Bechuanaland to the British Empire in 1885 and the Bechuanaland Protectorate to the north 10 years later, were imperialist actions based not only on the usual pragmatic considerations around trade, territorial expansion, balance of power, military strategy and the like. In addition, they also contained a not insignificant dose of humanitarianism. Indeed, some colonial historians see the Bechuanaland case as an instance of 'humanitarian imperialism'.[63] This is explained in large measure by the pervasive influence on the establishment and early administration of the colony by missionaries such as Robert and John Moffat, Charles William Willoughby and John Mackenzie. The last mentioned, who was appointed British Bechuanaland's first resident deputy commissioner in 1894, stands as the embodiment par excellence of the 'missionary imperialist'. Notwithstanding his grandiose objective of bringing about a 'great dominion' under the British crown that stretched from the Molopo to the Zambezi—and that he dubbed 'Austral Africa'—Mackenzie was also 'emphatic in presenting himself as a truly "humane" imperialist'.[64] John Moffat, another LMS missionary-administrator, served as Bechuanland Protectorate's first assistant commissioner.[65]

---

[62] As shown by the Hungarian ethnohistorian Miklós Szalay, a patron–client pattern of social and economic interaction between Boers and Bushmen was also found in some regions of the northern Cape in the first quarter of the nineteenth century. Szalay contrasts its benignly paternalistic, 'socially symbiotic' aspects with the coercive, oppressive and punitive nature of the relationship in the latter quarters of the century. This was when patron–client relationships, which Szalay deems inherently humane, were transformed into a master–servant relationship. See Szalay, *Ethnologie und Geschichte*, 241–49, 252.

[63] Sillery A. 1971. *John Mackenzie of Bechuanaland, 1835–1899: A Study in Humanitarian Imperialism*. Leiden: A.A. Balkema; Dachs A.J. 1972. 'Missionary imperialism: the case of Bechuanaland'. *Journal of African History*, 13, 647–68; Comaroff J. & Comaroff J. 1986. 'Christianity and colonialism in South Africa'. *American Ethnologist*, 13, 7–10, 17; Zins H. 1997. 'The international context of the creation of the Bechuanaland Protectorate in 1885'. *PULA Botswana Journal of African Studies*, 11, 54–62.

[64] Comaroff & Comaroff, 'Christianity and colonialism', 10.

[65] Sillery, *Founding a Protectorate*, 39–40, 54–56, 99–102.

The LMS's watchfulness over imperialist visions and colonial actions in early colonial Bechuanaland, and over the policies of Tswana chiefs and 'kings', especially the influential Khama III, included within its purview the welfare of the territory's Bushman population, especially those 'Basarwa' individuals and families subservient to the Tswana elite. While inconsistent and half-hearted in the first three or four decades of colonial rule, this humanitarian concern became abiding and focussed in the 1930s, after Tshekedi Khama, Khama III's successor, initiated an LMS investigation into the nature of the Basarwa's servitude. This investigation was triggered by a similar initiative the colonial government had undertaken two years earlier headed by Edward Tagart, a former colonial Secretary for Native Affairs in neighbouring Northern Rhodesia. The Tagart Report was a response to concerns of reform-minded individuals both within and outside the protectorate, after the condition of its Bushman population had received international attention. These liberal, reform-minded sensitivities were aroused by the League of Nations' investigations into slavery in the 1920s. The key questions framing both investigations were whether the territory's Bushmen were enslaved, and whether their status was in blatant violation not only of the laws of the protectorate and its metropole, but also of international law. Both investigations dispelled any notion that Bushmen were enslaved by their Tswana overlords and concluded instead that they were enserfed in a benign patron–client relationship. As such, they were not in need of emancipation the reports concluded, and no action was required by the colonial government. Its response was to issue two general proclamations, one affirming the abolition of slavery in the territory, and the other on the protection of labourers in general. In 1938, a third investigation was launched by the colonial government at the behest of the League of Nations, which was presented with a report on its findings. One of its outcomes was the establishment of a short-lived settlement scheme in the eastern Kalahari where Bushmen received agricultural training.[66]

With international attention on Bechuanaland's Bushmen and their possible enslavement by the Tswana majority, colonial administrators

---

[66] On the influence of the LMS on Khama III and other chiefs, see Du Plessis J. 1911. *A History of Christian Missions in South Africa*. London: Longmans, Green & Co., 154–64; Schapera I. 1958. 'Christianity and the Tswana'. *Journal of the Anthropological Institute of Great Britain and Ireland*, 88, 6; Tlou T. 1969. 'Khama III—great reformer, "king" and innovator'. *Botswana Notes and Records*, 2. For discussions of these three initiatives, see Russell, 'Slaves or workers?', 181–85; Hermans J. 1977. 'Official policy towards the Bushmen of Botswana: a review, part I'. *Botswana Notes and Records*, 9, 55–67; Gadilobae. 'Serfdom (*bolata*)', 27–29; Barnard A. 1992. *Hunters and Herders of Southern Africa. Cambridge*. Cambridge: Cambridge University Press, 119–20.

were all the more vigilant about human rights abuses that might have been perpetrated against them. Genocidal practices in the protectorate, even in its remote regions such as the Ghanzi district, would not have gone unnoticed by colonial authorities and would not have been tolerated.

Conclusion

Yet, genocide against Bushmen did occur in southern Africa at the time, for instance in Bushmanland in the northern Cape from the 1850s through to the 1880s, notwithstanding humanitarian initiatives in the Cape Colony earlier in the century. Closer in time and space, in neighbouring German South West Africa, we find genocidal violence targeted at Bushmen, though genocides perpetrated against the Herero and Nama people are more widely known.[67]

Despite its inclusion in the Bechuanaland Protectorate and humanitarian attention it received, the Ghanzi veld was one of the most remote and isolated regions of the territory. A few decades before white settlers' arrival, it had been referred to as a 'howling wilderness', a 'dreadful and distant place' and a *'nullius terra* ... [sic] occupied only by roving Bushmen'.[68] It was not until 1922 that a magistracy was established in the district, with roads and communication links opened up subsequently. As for missionary contact, this did not occur until 1965 when a Dutch Reformed Church mission station was established at D'kar village. For the first two or three decades of settlement, Ghanzilanders were isolated from the outside world, their nearest connections being Gobabis to the west, and Ngamiland to the east, both hundreds of miles and several days of travel time away. Far removed from the *pax Britannica* enjoyed in the wider territory and missionaries' humanitarian watchfulness, assaults and atrocities against indigenous hunter-gatherers could have been perpetrated by early European pastoralists. Mass violence and genocide could have reared its head here as well, as it did elsewhere in the subcontinent. Indeed, dire predictions to this effect were expressed by the German geographer, Siegfried Passarge, when he visited and surveyed parts of the region during 1897–1898. In his musings

---

67 Van den Berghe, *South* Africa, 20–37; Adhikari, *Anatomy of a South African Genocide*, 74–75; Gewald J. 1996. *Toward Redemption: A Socio-Political History of the Herero of Namibia Between 1890 and 1923.* Leiden: School of Asian, African and Amerindian Studies; Adhikari M. 2008. '"Streams of blood and streams of money": new perspectives on the annihilation of the Herero and Nama peoples of Namibia, 1904–1908'. *Kronos,* 34, no. 1, 303–20; Gordon R. 2009. 'Hiding in full view: the "forgotten" Bushman genocides of Namibia'. *Genocidal Studies and Prevention,* 4, no. 1, 29–57.

68 Sillery, *Botswana,* 104–5.

about impending Boer settlement in the Ghanzi veld, Passarge expressed the fear that the Bushmen, given their predilection for cattle theft, might here well suffer the same 'war of extermination' (*Vernichtungskrieg*) as their compatriots in the Cape colony a century before.[69]

Yet, they did not. Instead of eradication, the nature of Boer–Bushman contact in this region was one of accommodation and while social boundaries were rigid, the relationship between the two groups, for the first two or three generations, was one of economic symbiosis and social interdependence and familiarity, albeit in a paternalistic framework. This form of clientage was the product of a sterner and more punitive variant practised by their Cape trekboer ancestors who brought murder and mayhem, and eventual annihilation to Bushmen in the regions they occupied. This did not happen in the Ghanzi veld because paternalism here developed an intensely personal flavour, of easy familiarity, intimacy and an abiding interest in one another's lives and affairs. The context for all this was one of set social boundaries that determined limits to familiarity and intimacy, and provided the social and moral space for close social interaction. There was no room for genocide, and while humanitarian currents contributed to its suppression, they were not a determining factor.

---

[69] Passarge, S. 1907. *Die Buschmänner der Kalahari*. Berlin: Dietrich Reimer Verlag, 123.

Chapter Seven

The Destruction of Hunter-Gatherer Societies on the Pastoralist Frontier: The Cape and Australia Compared

Nigel Penn
University of Cape Town

Both the Cape and Australia were once the home of hunter-gatherer societies. At the Cape, hunter-gatherer societies were almost completely destroyed by colonial pastoralist farmers during the eighteenth and nineteenth centuries. In Australia, the colonies of white settlement were also spear-headed by pastoralist farmers who advanced at the expense of hunter-gatherers. Though members of Australian hunter-gatherer societies survived into the twentieth century, they did so largely as labourers within the pastoral economy, in barren reserves, or on land deemed undesirable for pastoral production. One estimate is that from a pre-contact population of about one million, the Aboriginal people had been reduced to 31 000 by 1911, an attrition rate of 97 per cent.[1]

One of the most obvious features of the dispossession and destruction of these hunter gatherer societies across two continents is the high level of violence evident in both. In the Australian case, a full-scale debate rages in the historical literature as to whether or not it may justly be described as genocide.[2] In the South African case, the impact of frontier violence was even more devastating in that it led to the almost total disappearance of the Cape San as a distinct people by the end of the nineteenth century. Confronted by evidence of such extirpationist fury, it is essential to ask why it was that these frontiers were so violent. An integral part of my response is

---

[1] Evans R. 2004. '"Pigmentia": racial fears and white Australia', in *Genocide and Settler Society: Frontier Violence and Stolen Indigenous Children in Australian History*, ed. A. Moses. New York: Berghahn Books, 107.

[2] See, for instance, the chapters in Moses, *Genocide and Settler Society*; Moses A. ed. 2008. *Empire, Colony, Genocide: Conquest, Occupation, and Subaltern Resistance in World History*. New York: Berghahn Books; Wolfe P. 2006. 'Settler colonialism and the elimination of the native'. *Journal of Genocide Research*, 8, no. 4, 387–409; Barta T. 2008. '"They appear actually to vanish from the face of the earth". Aborigines and the European project in Australia Felix'. *Journal of Genocide Research*, 10, no. 4, 519–39. In addition, see Boyce J. 2008. *Van Diemen's Land*. Melbourne: Black Inc., 261–317; Taylor R. 2013. 'Genocide, extinction and Aboriginal self-determination in Tasmanian historiography'. *History Compass*, 11, no. 6, 405–18.

to determine in what ways the Australian and Cape frontiers were similar, and different. It is the intention of this chapter to initiate such a comparison in the hope that it may illuminate some of the darker reaches of the colonial back-country.

It is important to note that there is a great imbalance in the historical literature dealing with this topic. While a great deal of material exists on the settler–Aboriginal frontier in Australia, there is very little on the settler–San frontier in South Africa. In Australia, the historical debate about the treatment of Aborigines is an integral part of that nation's 'History Wars', the outcome of which is crucial to defining Australian identity.[3] What makes the debate of more than academic interest is the continued existence, in the Australian population, of a significant Aboriginal presence. In South Africa, however, there is virtually no interest in, or debate about, the fate of the indigenous San. As an almost obliterated people, they have little presence in South African popular consciousness and the historical literature is correspondingly miniscule.[4] Apart from a handful of Khomani San on the borders of the Kalahari desert, the only San societies in South Africa today originated in Angola or Namibia and served as trackers in the South African Defence Force during its 1980s offensives in those countries. Given this imbalance, this chapter will have more to say about the Cape frontier and will not attempt an exhaustive review of the vast literature on the Australian frontier.

The frontier between white settler pastoralists and hunter-gatherers in the Cape opened in about 1700, in the Tulbagh area of the south-western Cape, and closed in about 1890, as the last San of Bushmanland perished through murder, starvation or imprisonment. In Australia, settlement began shortly after 1788 in New South Wales and 1803 in Van Diemen's Land. Though

---

3   See Attwood B. 2005. *Telling The Truth About Aboriginal History*. Crows Nest: Allen & Unwin; Attwood B. & Foster S.G. 2003. *Frontier Conflict: The Australian Experience*. Canberra: National Museum of Australia; Connor J. 2002. *The Australian Frontier Wars: 1788–1838*. Sydney: University of New South Wales Press; Manne R. ed. 2003. *Whitewash: On Keith Windschuttle's Fabrication of Aboriginal History*. Melbourne: Black Inc.; Windschuttle K. 2002. *The Fabrication of Aboriginal History: Volume 1, Van Diemen's Land 1803–1947*. Sydney Macleay Press.

4   For the Cape San, see Penn N. 2005. *The Forgotten Frontier: Colonist and Khoisan on the Cape's Northern Frontier in the 18th Century*. Cape Town: Double Storey Books; Penn N. 2013. 'The British and the "Bushmen": the massacre of the Cape San, 1795 to 1828'. *Journal of Genocide Research*, 15, no. 2, 183–200; Newton-King S. 1999. *Masters and Servants on the Cape Eastern Frontier*. Cambridge: Cambridge University Press; Adhikari M. 2010. *The Anatomy of a South African Genocide: The Extermination of the Cape San Peoples*. Cape Town: UCT Press; Skotnes P. ed. 1996. *Miscast: Negotiating the Presence of the Bushmen*. Cape Town: University of Cape Town Press. For the Drakensberg San, see Wright J. 1971. *Bushman Raiders of the Drakensberg, 1840–1870: A Study of Their Conflict With Stock-keeping Peoples in Natal*. Pietermaritzburg: University of Natal Press.

Van Diemen's Land Aborigines were removed from the island in the 1830s, Aboriginal societies continue to exist in the back-country of the Australian mainland, though not as hunter-gatherers. These survivors have not, however, gone unscathed, and many Aboriginal groups and languages had completely disappeared by the end of the nineteenth century.

Since both Australia and the Cape were under British authority, it is tempting to look for a common denominator in British policy towards the indigenous hunter-gatherer societies. The Cape case is very different to Australia, for the British only became colonial masters in 1795, and then only for a brief period, that is, until 1803. Between 1803 and early 1806, the Cape was ruled by a Dutch government, the Batavian Republic, before the British returned. Thereafter, it is true, British influence was a common feature on both sides of the southern Indian Ocean. The pre-1795 period, however, is absolutely crucial in explaining the fate of the Cape's hunter-gatherers.

Pastoralists and hunter-gatherers at the Cape

It is not just the period of VOC (*Verenigde Oostindische Compagnie*, or Dutch East India Company) rule from 1652–1795 that is significant here. From about 2 000BP pastoral societies, entered the Cape and interacted with its indigenous hunter-gatherer societies. These pastoralists, who had once been hunter-gatherers themselves, were known as the Khoikhoi. Between c.2 000BP and 1652 the Khoikhoi, while maintaining a semi-nomadic existence, occupied those areas of the Cape that were suitable for pastoralism, leaving the more arid and mountainous regions to the San. The well-watered summer rainfall areas of the north-east and eastern regions were occupied by agro-pastoralist Bantu-speakers who had entered southern Africa not long after the Khoikhoi.[5] What these early interactions reveal is that, in the pre-colonial era, relations between pastoralists and hunter-gatherers were not characterised by genocidal fury. In most areas suitable for pastoralism, hunter-gatherers were displaced. There is also sufficient evidence to indicate that, over a period of about 1 500 years, Khoikhoi–San interactions included amity as well as enmity, peaceful exchanges as well as warfare, and personal relationships that included inter-marriage and the provision of labour services. These relationships might have been unequal, but the San remained a formidable presence who could not be vanquished by pre-colonial pastoralists equipped with simple weapons and lacking

---

5   See Parkington J. 1984. 'Soaqua and Bushmen: hunters and robbers', in *Past and Present in Hunter Gatherer Studies*, ed. C. Schrire. Orlando: Academic Press.

horses. Though these pastoralists probably regarded themselves as superior to hunter-gatherers, they did not have the ability to eradicate them even if they had wanted to. Fifteen hundred years of interaction had proved, however, that the southern African landscape was big enough to support both pre-colonial lifestyles simultaneously.[6]

This equilibrium was destroyed by the arrival of European settlers at the Cape in 1652. Initially, white settlement was restricted to the well-watered winter rainfall areas of the south-western Cape and those who became farmers were predominantly concerned with producing wheat and wine. The colony's, and company's, meat requirements were largely met by encouraging the Khoikhoi to part with their livestock—by force, fraud or unequal exchange. By 1700, however, as the colony expanded into the interior, more and more colonists themselves turned to pastoral production. This new class of stock-farmer, or trekboer, adopted a semi-nomadic lifestyle similar to that of the Khoikhoi, from whom they obtained land, livestock and labour. The aggressive expansion of these white pastoralists soon brought them into contact with the San, and from 1700 onwards, with only intermittent breaks in fighting, trekboers were engaged in a struggle with both Khoikhoi and San resisters, who sometimes made common cause against this foe. In general the Khoikhoi, being skilled pastoralists, were absorbed into the economy of the trekboers as labourers. The San, on the other hand, seemed unwilling to become subjugated shepherds and fought to preserve their ancient and preferred hunter-gatherer existence.

At its heart, the struggle was essentially over scarce environmental resources that were needed by both pastoralists and hunter-gatherers—land, water, grazing and animals.[7] But the struggle was also about the collision of two world views. Hunter-gatherers belonged to a culture

---

[6] For interactions between the pre-colonial Khoikoi and San, see Elphick R. 1985. *Khoikhoi and the Founding of White South Africa.* Johannesburg: Raven Press; Barnard A. 1992. *Hunters and Herders of Southern Africa: A Comparative Ethnography of the Khoisan Peoples.* Cambridge: Cambridge University Press; Smith A.B. 1986. 'Competition, conflict and clientship: Khoi and San relationships in the Western Cape', in *Prehistoric Pastoralism in Southern Africa: The South African Archaeological Society Goodwin Series,* vol. 5, eds M. Hall & A.B. Smith. For evidence from Botswana and the Kalahari, see Denbow J. 1984. 'Prehistoric herders and foragers of the Kalahari: the evidence for 15,000 years of interaction', and Gordon R.J. 1984. 'The !Kung in the Kalahari exchange: an ethno historical perspective', in *Past and Present in Hunter-Gatherer Studies,* ed. C. Shrire. Orlando, Florida: Academic Press; Wilmsen E. 1989. *Land Filled with Flies.* Chicago: University of Chicago Press.

[7] For the dynamics of pastoralist production in the frontier zone, see Penn N. 1986. 'Pastoralists and pastoralism in the Northen Cape frontier zone during the eighteenth century', in *Prehistoric Pastoralism in Southern Africa: The S.A. Archaeological Society Goodwin Series,* eds M. Hall & A.B. Smith. Cape Town: South African Archaeological Society, 5.

where there was no private property, where food was shared and land was a group, rather than an individual, possession. Colonists, on the other hand, believed in accumulating private wealth through the increase of livestock, private ownership of land and a monopolisation of resources. The religious system of the San was also far more closely bound to the landscape, and the animals that lived on it, than was the religious system of the colonists, whose Calvinistic beliefs encouraged them to divide men into the damned or the elect, and who believed that earthly prosperity was a token of God's approval.[8]

The fighting that occurred between the trekboers and the San reached a peak of intensity in the 1770s and continued with unabated ferocity until the British government succeeded in negotiating a peace between the warring parties in 1798. This frontier of violence extended from Namaqualand in the north-western Cape, along the interior escarpment of the Roggeveld and Nieuweveld mountains, to the Sneeuberg in the east. Beyond this point lay the Xhosa. Here the colonial frontier was one between settler pastoralists and Nguni agro-pastoralists. However violent this eastern frontier became, it is doubtful whether the colonists ever envisaged the complete annihilation of this powerful and populous society. The San, however, were different.

The attitude of Dutch colonists towards the San is best reflected in their deeds and not in their words for there are very few documents which contain direct statements concerning their thoughts about the San as a people. They referred to the San most commonly as 'Bushmen', or 'Bushmen-Hottentots'. We may assume that the San were regarded as being even more primitive than the 'Hottentots', or Khoikhoi, who were already seen as being a 'widely accepted symbol of irredeemable savagery and the very depths of human degradation'.[9] San would be hunted down by groups of armed and mounted colonists, together with their Khoikhoi or mixed-race (Bastaard) servants. These groups were known as commandos and were ostensibly engaged in retaliatory attacks against fleeing robbers. In fact, commandos often ranged deep into San territory and attacked whichever San groups they might find. It became common practice for commandos to take no male captives, as it was believed they would eventually run away again. Women and children

---

8   For the San's belief system, see Lewis-Williams J.D. & Pearce D. 2004. *San Spirituality: Roots, Expressions & Social Consequences*. Cape Town: Double Storey.

9   On the image of the Khoikhoi, see Smith V.W. 1992. '"The most wretched of the human race": the iconography of the Khoikhoin (Hottentots), 1500–1800'. *History and Anthropology*, 5, nos. 3–4, 285–330; and Penn N. 2011. 'Written culture and the Cape Khoikhoi: from travel writing to Kolb's "Full Description"', in *Written Culture in a Colonial Context: Africa and the Americas, 1500–1900*, eds A. Delmas & N. Penn. Cape Town: UCT Press.

under the age of 12 were, however, taken as captive since, being perceived as more malleable than men, they were forced into servitude. This merciless hostility toward the San was also prompted by the San waging an effective guerrilla war against trekboers. San targeted livestock, which they preferred to kill rather than keep, and vulnerable Khoikhoi or slave shepherds, who were often killed with great cruelty. The San were thus perceived as a type of vermin, such as jackals—a predator, or '*schepsel*' (creature) to be removed from the veld in order to protect their flocks and herds.[10]

For their part, the San realised that the trekboers were destroying the game upon which they depended. Hunting was important not only for economic reasons, as the San religious system was deeply intertwined with the spiritual forces associated with animals, particularly the eland. It was the eland too, that the trekboers especially valued as a source of biltong, or dried meat. Rather than eat their own livestock, the Boers shot game in great quantities as commandos often doubled their function and hunted both humans and animals. As intrusive pastoralists monopolised water points and consumed grazing, game also became harder to find and the San either had to stand and fight, or retreat. Beyond a certain point, however, retreat was impossible as it would have taken them either into even more inhospitable territory or into land already occupied by agro-pastoralist groups such as the Tswana to the north, or the Xhosa to the east. It was the very marginality of the Cape interior's environment that made the struggle so desperate. Seasonal fluctuations in resources, and droughts, also necessitated the movement of both humans and animals between regions of winter and summer rainfall. These cycles of transhumance were vital, and if such movement was ever impeded by, for instance, a *trekboer* claiming exclusive ownership over a section of the land, the consequences were fatal.

Despite documented losses of hundreds of people per year—and undocumented losses that were undoubtedly substantial—the San were not defeated by the commandos. There were periods during the 1780s and 1790s when the colonial frontier was in retreat. Though human losses among trekboers were negligible, livestock losses were considerable. Poisoned arrows may not have been a match for muskets and horses, but the San were adept at driving flocks and herds into remote areas where they could be destroyed, and eaten, at leisure.

A feature of the fighting on the northern Cape frontier zone, and one which links it to the frontier zones of Australia, is that a high proportion of fatalities

---

10 Penn N. 1996. '"Fated to perish": the destruction of the Cape San', in *Miscast: Negotiating the Presence of the Bushmen*, ed. P. Skotnes. Cape Town: UCT Press.

inflicted on the San were the result of massacres. Recent study on massacres has stressed that massacres are usually perpetrated against people who are regarded as being 'other' by the perpetrators. Those who are massacred are usually seen as a threat or an obstacle to the killers and although they are perceived as being of less worth, even at times as sub-human, they are also feared. Fear of the other, in fact, drives the urge to exterminate them. Massacres are usually distinguished from battles in that the victims of a massacre are often killed while in a position of relative powerlessness with regard to their murderers. They have either been surprised or disarmed, have surrendered or been entrapped, have been outnumbered or out-armed. Because massacre is so much like murder, perpetrators of massacres are often secretive about their actions and reluctant to provide details of the killings. Massacres frequently take place at night or at dawn, in locations far removed from the eyes of moral authority. Masses do not need to have been killed for it to be a massacre. One authority estimates that a minimum of six people killed in one operation constitutes a massacre.[11] A great many small massacres can add up to genocide.[12]

A close examination of the nature of commando action against the San confirms the impression that the great majority of San were killed in massacres. The typical mode of operation was for a commando to sneak up on a group of sleeping San at night and quietly encircle them. At first light the commando members would then fire their muskets at the sleeping figures, killing the men and, if they pleased, taking some women and children captive. Those who tried to escape were hunted down by commando members on horseback. For the most part, such massacres were on a small scale. But there were exceptions. During the General Commando of 1774 in the northern Cape, the participants of its three constituent forces recorded that they had killed 503 San and taken 239 captive. A breakdown of these figures reveals that they were the result of attacking a number of separate kraals where the smallest group consisted of six people and the largest of 30. In 1792, commandos in the Nieuweveld killed over 500 San in a series of actions with 300 alone dying in one kraal. Such large concentrations of San were exceptional, however, and

---

11 Ryan L. 2012. 'Untangling Aboriginal resistance and the settler punitive expedition: the Hawkesbury River frontier in New South Wales, Australia, 1794–1810'. Unpublished paper presented at the Violence and Honour in Settler Colonial Societies Conference, University of Cape Town, December 2012 cites Clark I.D. 1995. *Scars in the Landscape: A Register of Massacre Sites in Western Victoria*. Canberra: Australian Institute of Aboriginal and Torres Strait Islander Studies, 7.

12 This is a point made by Barbara Mann in 'Fractal massacres in the Old Northwest: the destruction of the Miami people'. Unpublished paper, Violence and Honour Conference, University of Cape Town, 2012.

the great majority of massacres were on a much smaller scale. What is also noteworthy of these actions is that there were virtually no colonial casualties, evidence again that these were massacres and not battles.

Despite the low number of colonial casualties, both sides in the frontier war were suffering and as the eighteenth century drew to an end, it was not obvious that the forces of European colonisation would prevail. The VOC was bankrupt and quite unable to enforce its authority in the frontier zone or protect its subjects. The continuous war against the San in the north was matched by defeats at the hands of the Xhosa in the east. In these insecure circumstances, certain frontier farmers rebelled against the government while their over-exploited Khoikhoi servants deserted to the enemy. It was thus in many ways fortuitous for the Cape's settlers that it was conquered by the British in 1795, for without the arrival of a powerful military force the colony may well have experienced a prolonged crisis of authority.[13]

The British clearly were not responsible for the violent character of the Cape's frontier. They inherited this situation from the VOC which had long since handed responsibility for maintaining law and order on the frontier to commandos whose composition and leadership was wholly civilian. Apart from confirming the appointment of local strong men as *veldwagtmeesters* (field sergeants) or *veldkorporaals* (field corporals), the company's major function was to supply commandos with gunpowder and shot. Occasional letters of admonition were despatched to distant *veldwagtmeesters* urging them to kill only as many San as was deemed necessary, but these were balanced by other missives which urged more strenuous efforts in pursuing and overcoming 'bushmen' robbers. At the *landdrosts* (magistracies) of Stellenbosch and Graaff-Reinet, evidence was sometimes received, and colonists tried, for brutal treatment of Khoikhoi servants or slaves, but it was nobody's business to investigate what was being done to San in a time of war. The closest *landdrosts* got to learning about the savage fighting on the frontier were the irregular and unrevealing reports, sent by *veldwagtmeesters*, of official commandos undertaken. These listed the date, the number of hours ridden between places, the name of the vicinity, and how many San had been shot dead or taken prisoner. They might also have included the number of sheep stolen or destroyed, the number of commando members present and the quantities of ammunition requested. It would thus be true to say that for both VOC authorities and frontier settlers, the struggle against the San was seen as a military and not a moral problem.

---

[13] For the first British occupation of the Cape, see Boucher M. & Penn N. 1992. *Britain at the Cape, 1795–1803.* Johannesburg: Brenthurst Press.

The new British government at the Cape could not afford to act in such a heartless manner. Philanthropic and humanitarian interests had already been exerting considerable moral pressure in Britain to bring an end to the slave trade, and public opinion in Britain would hardly have tolerated the continuation of a war of extermination against the indigenous inhabitants of a new British possession—at least not until a thorough attempt had been made to resolve matters peacefully.[14] It was official British policy, unlike the VOC, to encourage missionary activity at the Cape as the propagation of Christianity was seen as being integral to the advance of civilisation. Thus it was that British authorities at the Cape felt constrained to act within the broad parameters of the discourses of humanitarianism even though, in other respects, the regime was closer to a form of despotism, whose principal objective was to hold and maintain power.

One of the priorities of the British was to establish peace on the colony's borders. On the eastern frontier, this meant defusing the burgher rebellion, which it did by cutting off supplies of ammunition to these colonists; pacifying discontented Khoikhoi servants, which it did by promising reforms; and forcing a truce with the Xhosa, which it did by sending troops to the frontier. In the north, peace with the San was to be achieved by encouraging farmers to give the San gifts of sheep. This initiative, interestingly, came not from humanitarian British officials, but from a Roggeveld *veldwagtmeester* named Floris Visser who had become a convert to evangelical Christianity shortly before the British arrived. By itself, Visser's proposal to pacify the San by kindness would have come to nothing. It was only when the British government at the Cape decided to put its weight behind the idea that it was implemented. Missionaries of the London Missionary Society (LMS) were encouraged to preach the gospel to the San of Bushmanland while simultaneously acting as the distributors of the livestock which frontier farmers were to donate to the San. Governor Macartney announced a clearly defined northern boundary to the colony, which the VOC had never done, and the region beyond it, Bushmanland, to be set aside as a reserve for San.[15]

Most of these ideas were based on an extensive report of the Cape interior compiled by Macartney's secretary, John Barrow. Barrow had witnessed, at first hand, a Boer commando attacking a group of San, and the experience had convinced him that San were innocent victims of cruel aggression.

---

14 For the nature of British imperialism at this time, see Bayly C.A. 1989. *Imperial Meridian: The British Empire and the World 1780–1830*. London: Blackwell.

15 Penn N. 2007. '"Civilising" the San: the first mission to the Cape San, 1791–1806', in *Claim to the Country: The Archive of Wilhelm Bleek and Lucy Lloyd*, ed. P. Skotnes. Jacana: Cape Town.

For Barrow, it was the San who merited British protection and the Boers who were the inhuman and uncultivated savages. This does not mean that he idealised the San and their way of life. Barrow was no admirer of the hunter-gatherer lifestyle for he sought, instead, to wean them from their predatory ways and have them become pastoralists. It was for this reason that the San were to be given gifts of sheep and allowed the exclusive use of Bushmanland. And it was for this reason that missionary instructors were to be encouraged to educate the San so that, in addition to the precepts of Christianity, they would be taught the dignity of labour and be inculcated with the desire to obtain goods and commodities.[16]

This, then, was an attempt to 'civilise' the San out of their hunter-gatherer way of life. It failed, for a variety of reasons. In the first place, the San had no intention of becoming pastoralists and abandoning their 'way of life perfected'. In the second place, it is doubtful whether, even with the best will in the world, they could have become pastoralists in the harsh environment of the northern Cape's Bushmanland. Bushmanland is a drought-prone, summer rainfall area and unless the San adopted transhumance strategies and moved into winter rainfall areas controlled by colonists, they would not have survived. Thirdly, the LMS mission to the San, at Sak River in Bushmanland, proved to be a failure as the San had no desire to remain for days in the same spot being lectured to in Dutch, English or Latin. Their good behaviour lasted only as long as the missionaries' supplies of meat and tobacco. Once these were finished, the San went off hunting. Finally, the entire experiment of 'civilising' the San depended on the colonists staying out of Bushmanland. This they did not do. It was impossible to police the frontier and to prevent hunting parties of colonists from entering Bushmanland. It was equally impossible to prevent colonial pastoralists driving their own livestock into Bushmanland during the summer to pasture there. In fact, now that peace prevailed, it was easier for them to do so than it had ever been before. In exchange for a few sheep and a handful of tobacco, the San allowed the colonists behind their lines and soon experienced rapid alienation of water holes, accelerated destruction of game, and degradation of the veld over which eland had once grazed. Peace, for the San, meant defeat.[17]

---

16   Penn N. 1993. 'Mapping the Cape: John Barrow and the First British Occupation of the Cape, 1795–1803'. *Pretexts*, 4, no. 2, 20–43. For an unsympathetic account of Barrow's mission, see Pratt M.L. 1985. '"Scratches on the face of the country": or what Mr. Barrow saw in the land of the Bushmen', in *'Race', Writing and Difference*, ed. H.L. Gates. Chicago: Chicago University Press.

17   Penn, *Forgotten Frontier*, 221–67.

The departure of the British in 1803 did nothing to help matters, for the Batavian government showed no inclination to enforce what it saw as British frontier policy and was, moreover, markedly hostile towards missionaries. And when Britain re-conquered the Cape in 1806, there was no mention of restoring to Bushmanland its status as a San sanctuary. From 1806 onwards, the Cape government's interest in the San was decidedly muted. It had become evident to the British that the greatest threat to peaceful control of the Cape came from the eastern frontier, where clashes between Boer farmers and Xhosa were constantly in danger of escalating into war. With government attention almost entirely on frontier security in the east, the less threatening, and economically less important, northern frontier was largely forgotten.

Another reason for government neglect of the San was that they did not constitute a significant portion of the colony's labour force, whereas the Khoikhoi did. The abolition of the slave trade throughout the British Empire in 1807 had provoked the British into an urgent re-examination of the status of the Khoikhoi, who now loomed even larger as a source of labour. The Caledon Code of 1809 confirmed the status of the Khoikhoi as a labour force bonded to their masters and restricted to a specific place of residence. But it also gave the Khoikhoi greater protection under the law against the cruelty of their masters. The Cape government sought to ensure that the law's protection would extend to the remote districts by instituting travelling courts of circuit, to which Khoikhoi could bring their complaints and plead for justice. The awkward status of the Khoikhoi, neither slave nor free, attracted a great deal of missionary and humanitarian attention, particularly since it was the Khoikhoi, and not the San, who were flocking to mission stations. Champions of Khoikhoi rights, such as Dr John Philip of the LMS, campaigned hard to repeal the Caledon Code, arguing that the Khoikhoi should be free to sell their labour in an open market. This campaign was crowned with success in 1828 when Ordinance 50 removed all legal restraints from Khoikhoi. There was, however, no similar legislation passed to protect the San.[18]

While the efficacy of the Caledon Code, the courts of circuit and even Ordinance 50 may be a matter for debate, it is quite clear that, so far as the

---

[18]   For the debate about these reforms and their effectiveness, see Dooling W. 2005. 'The origins and aftermath of the Cape Colony's "Hottentot Code" of 1809'; and Penn N. 2005. 'The Onderbokkeveld ear atrocity', *Kronos*, 31, 50–61. Malherbe V.C. 1978. 'Diversification and mobility of Khoikhoi labour in the eastern districts of the Cape Colony prior to the labour law of 1 November 1809'. Master's dissertation, University of Cape Town; Elphick R. & Malherbe V.C. 1989. 'The Khoisan to 1828', in *The Shaping of South African Society, 1652–1840*, eds R. Elphick & H. Giliomee. Cape Town: Longmans. See also Penn, 'The British and the "Bushmen"'.

San were concerned, the reforms meant little. Most of the San lived outside colonial boundaries and hence outside of the law. Some of the magistrates on circuit did, however, include reports on the conditions of hunter-gatherers in the frontier districts, if they happened to come across any. This information was added to by a report made by Colonel Collins, who toured the frontier districts on behalf of the government during 1809 and 1810. The picture painted by these reports was one of desperate poverty, of people eking out an existence on drought-ravaged plains by scratching for bulbs and roots. It was also noted that the cycle of robbery and retaliatory commando raids continued.[19]

In an attempt to contain this violence, the Cape government ordered *landdrosts* to submit returns on commando activities. How often were commandos despatched? For what reasons were they despatched? How many San were killed or taken captive? *Landdrosts* were reminded that a commando could only be authorised in response to robbery or attack, and that deadly force could only be used if the offenders tried to resist capture. According to *landdrosts*, official casualty figures were low. But official commandos were not the only ones to ride against the San. Dr John Philip of the LMS believed that colonists were guilty of committing atrocities against the San far worse than those which had been perpetrated under the rule of the VOC. Philip published what he knew about atrocities against the San and indeed, against the Khoikhoi, in his *Researches in South Africa* in 1828.[20] Although Philip exaggerated the extent of the massacres that were taking place in the 1820s and these were not the worst years in the history of San massacres, there was little cause for complacency. Despite its good intentions, the British government was powerless to prevent the destruction of San society and it does not appear as though any settlers were ever brought to trial for atrocities committed against the San.

An interesting feature of enquiries into the treatment of San provoked by Philip's allegations was that they brought to light the large, and increasing, use of San captive labour in the trekboer economy. A mere 258 San child captives were officially recorded in government records between 1776 to 1803. In 1823, the Bigge-Colebrooke Commission recorded 1 071 San children in service to settlers in the district of Graaff-Reinet alone.

---

19   Collins' report is contained in Moodie D. ed. 1838, 1842, reprint 1960, 1966. *The Record: Or a Series of Official Papers Relative to the Condition and Treatment of the Native Tribes of South Africa.* Balkema: Cape Town.

20   Philip J. 1828. *Researches in South Africa; Illustrating the Civil, Moral, and Religious Condition of the Native Tribes.* Two vols. London: James Duncan. See also Penn 'The British and the "Bushmen"'.

Given the likely under-reporting of San captives in the eighteenth century, this suggests a massive increase in the use of San labour and a decrease in the murder rate of adults. In the Cradock district, for instance, Bigge reported that there were 825 San children and 862 adult San in service. Significantly, both of these districts were in the north-eastern Cape and in 1823 were in an area of rapid colonial expansion.[21] In the 1820s, 48 000 square miles of territory in this region were added to the colony at the expense of the San. Also, farmers were desperate to find a source of cheap labour, given the abolition of the slave trade in 1807 and that Khoikhoi labourers were now protected by contracts, as required by the Caledon Code. The British government was anxious that increased use of San labour did not expose the colony to charges of trading in San slaves and implemented laws to ensure that only willing labourers or genuine San orphans, entered service. The effectiveness of these laws is questionable. It was only in 1828 that Khoikhoi were granted legal equality, but no provision was made for San. Captive San were counted as Khoikhoi within a few years of captivity and, in theory, therefore under the protection of Ordinance 50. While their increased utility as labourers may have saved San in certain areas of the colony from being massacred, and while they may have survived as individuals, this does not mean that they were not victims of genocide. Assimilation and absorption into colonial society, argue Adhikari, Wolfe, Moses and others, was part of the genocidal process, for it succeeded in destroying their cultural identity and way of life.[22] We may note a similarly high incidence of the use of Aboriginal child labour in Australia, particularly in Queensland in the nineteenth century.[23]

Those San beyond the proclaimed boundaries of the colony were removed from any form of government protection and thus vulnerable to the unrestricted violence of the expanding and lawless colonial frontier. As the frontier expanded unofficially across the Orange River, the LMS between

---

21   The Bigge-Colebrooke Report may be found in House of Commons Parliamentary Papers (HCPP), 1835 (50). 'Papers relative to the condition and treatment of the native inhabitants of southern Africa within the colony of the Cape of Good Hope, or beyond the frontier of that colony. Part 1. Hottentots, and Bosjesmen; Caffres; Griquas'. Ordered by the House of Commons to be printed, 18 March 1835.

22   See Szalay M. 1995. *The San and the Colonization of the Cape, 1770–1879: Conflict, Incorporation, Acculturation*. Koln: Rudiger Koppe Verlag, for an account of the absorption of San captives into the colonial labour force. Adhikari, *Anatomy of a South African Genocide*, 90; Moses A.D. 2008. 'Empire, colony, genocide: keywords and the philiosophy of history', and Wolfe P. 2008. 'Structure and event: settler colonialism, time, and the question of genocide', in Moses, *Empire, Colony, Genocide*.

23   Robinson S. 2008. *Something Like Slavery? Queensland's Aboriginal Child Workers, 1842–1945*. Melbourne: Australian Scholarly.

1814 and 1833 attempted to create areas of refuge for San around mission stations. These missions failed, for much the same reasons that the Sak River station had failed: the San did not want to become a sedentary people and they had no desire to become Christians. Since the missions were usually situated around a spring or permanent water source, pastoralists resented the occupancy of such places by San. Colonists complained that the stations were havens for robbers, and were openly hostile toward the occupants and their instructors. Once the game around missions had been shot out, San moved away. It was obvious that they preferred to take their chances beyond the fragile protection of the missions' boundaries, rather than endure a regime of religious and agricultural instruction.[24]

The failure of the missions signalled the end for the San. They had lost their only protector. Truth to tell, there was no way that their hunter-gatherer lifestyle could have survived at the mission stations, but certain individuals might have survived had they embraced agriculture. However ineffective the LMS had proved to be in sheltering the San, they had at least recognised that without some form of intervention the San would be destroyed by the advance of the frontier. The colonial government was not prepared to intervene and had no obligation to concern itself with matters beyond its borders. Much of the northern Cape, Bushmanland included, lay outside of the colony until 1848, when the boundary was officially advanced to the Orange River. In the north-east, trekboers and Bastaards had already crossed the river in the eighteenth century into Transorangia. Before 1834 the Griqua were left to govern themselves, but after that date the number of trekboers in the region grew dramatically as a result of the Great Trek. The fate of the San in the new Boer republic that would shortly emerge in Transorangia, was largely beyond British control.

By the time that the Cape's borders encompassed Bushmanland in the mid-nineteenth century, San societies of that region were already on the verge of extinction. When Louis Anthing, the magistrate of the new magisterial district of Kenhardt, brought it to the attention of his superiors that the San were being systematically massacred by commando groups

---

24 McDonald J. 2007. '"When shall these dry bones live?": interactions between the London Missionary Society and the San along the Cape's northeastern frontier, 1790–1833'. MA dissertation, University of Cape Town; Schoeman K. 1993. 'Die Londense Sendinggenootskap en die San: die stasies Toornberg en Hephzibah, 1814–1818'. *South African Historical Journal*, 28, 221–34; Schoeman K. 'Die London Sendinggenootskap en die San: die stasies Ramah, Konnah en Philippolis, 1816–1828'. *South African Historical Journal*, 29, 132–52; Schoeman K. 1994. 'Die London Sendinggenootskap en die San: die stasies Boesmanskool en die einde van die sending, 1828–1833'. *South African Historical Journal*, 30, 85–97.

consisting of both white and Bastaard pastoralists, his complaints fell on deaf ears. Anthing pointed out that if the San were guilty of stock theft it was because they were starving, and that sheep had replaced game as the principal herbivores of Bushmanland.[25] It is more than likely that the increased pastoral presence in Bushmanland was driven by the boom in the Cape's merino wool market, which made the farming of marginal land more attractive. As previously marginal land was bought up, land prices rose, and those who could not afford land, mostly poor whites and Bastaards, moved to 'unallocated' crown land in Bushmanland.

Embarrassed by Anthing's revelations, but unwilling to spend money on either policing or administering justice in this remote region, the Cape government transferred Anthing to another district and later suspended his pay. Those San who were not killed outright by commandos were arrested as stock thieves and the men placed in prison gangs to work on the Cape's roads, mountain passes and harbour breakwaters. The women were placed in domestic service and the children into servitude with farmers as orphans or 'destitute children'. Many San were doubtless involved in the Korana wars, which flared up along the Orange River in the 1870s.[26] They too, after the defeat of this rebellion against colonial rule, either died in arms or perished in hard labour. It was from the ranks of captive San at the Cape's breakwater prison that Dr Wilhelm Bleek and his sister-in-law, Lucy Lloyd, interviewed San informants about their culture and language. Thanks to them we know what little we do about the /Xam's unique, and now extinct, consciousness.[27]

We may conclude, from this brief account of the Cape San, that the governments of the day, whether Dutch or British, largely gave frontier pastoralists a free hand to deal with hunter-gatherer resistance as they saw fit. This laissez-faire approach should not hide the fact that, by the nineteenth century, the consequences of such inactivity were clear: the San would become extinct. The colonial authorities may have consoled themselves with the thought that it was not a people who would disappear, but a mode of subsistence, an anachronistic, unproductive, primitive way of life, namely, hunter-gathering. The San were fated to perish, in the words of South African historian Theal, because they could not adapt to modernity.

---

[25] For Anthing, see Findlay D. 1977. 'The San of the Cape thirstland and L. Anthing's "special mission"'. BA honours thesis, University of Cape Town.

[26] For the Korana wars, see Strauss T. 1979. *War Along the Orange: The Korana and the Northern Border Wars of 1868–69 and 1878–79*. Cape Town: Centre for African Studies.

[27] For the W. Bleek and L. Lloyd archive, see Skotnes P. 2007. *Claim to the Country*; Bank A. 2006. *Bushmen in a Victorian World: The Remarkable Story of the Bleek-Lloyd Collection of Bushman Folklore*. Double Storey: Cape Town.

Pastoralists and hunter-gatherers in Australia

It is a precisely similar attitude that has been identified by certain Australian historians as characterising the British government's attitudes towards Australian Aborigines. Indeed, historians such as Patrick Wolfe and Dirk Moses argue that such an attitude was not confined to Australia, but typical of a number of colonial societies. More fundamentally, Moses argues, it was not so much governmental impotence that caused the near annihilation of Australian Aborigines, but what he terms the genocidal nature of settler colonialism. This is an insight he shares with Wolfe, who argues that settler colonialism was, by nature, genocidal or 'eliminationist', in that it inevitably worked towards removing indigenous people from the land if they were surplus to labour requirements. More fundamentally, genocide was, in a way, 'structural' to settler colonialism. Although settler colonialism did not always actively seek to exterminate indigenes, it did not really care what happened to them once they had been dispossessed of their land. For Moses, colonial genocide did not have to be an active or deliberate policy of extermination. It occurred when the deep structures of settler colonisation were allowed to proceed unhindered. If colonial settlement in Australia entailed the almost total destruction of Aboriginal life, and if colonial government failed to prevent this, then it was genocidal.[28]

It is not the intention of this chapter to decide whether these insights are applicable to all varieties of colonial settlement, but it is self-evident that settler colonialism could only triumph or enter its eliminationist phase where or when it was able to impose its will absolutely. Where indigenous people could not be entirely removed from the land, such as in New Zealand and South Africa, or as Wolfe points out, where their labour was indispensable, as in parts of South Africa, settler colonialism stopped short of genocide. As other essays in this book illustrate, settler colonialism was most effective, or most likely to succeed, against hunter-gatherer societies since these societies were usually smaller and weaker than their rivals. Being semi-nomadic, they were most likely to move out of a contested area if the threat to their existence became too great. Thus trekboers could destroy the San, but they could not brush aside populous and politically powerful agro-pastoralist groups such as the Xhosa and Zulu. Of all the societies in southern Africa, it was the San who were most vulnerable to settler colonialism. In a recent book, Mohamed Adhikari has convincingly tested the applicability of the term 'genocide' to the fate of the San and it is not my intention to re-cross

---

28   Moses A.D. 'Genocide and settler society in Australian history', in *Genocide and Settler Society*, ed. A.D. Moses, 3–48.

this terrain here.[29] More modestly, this chapter seeks to point to similarities and differences between the treatment of the San and Aborigines by both settlers and their governments in southern Africa and Australia.

The first point of similarity is that both San and Aborigines were hunter-gatherers, and their colonial enemies pastoralists. The Aborigines had been hunter-gatherers for at least 50 000 years before the British arrived in Australia and had many attitudes towards the land and its creatures that were similar to the San.[30] They had not, however, ever had to share their world with pre-colonial pastoralists, and would have had no precedents to prepare them for the invasion of their land by strange new animals and the people who owned them. The idea that certain animals were owned, or domesticated, and could not be hunted without dire consequences, was one that the San had presumably learnt over a lengthy period of time, whereas the Aborigines had to learn that lesson within one or two generations. All things considered, it is remarkable that Aborigines learnt to become colonial stock-men so quickly after this first contact.

The colonising British were starting a pristine colonial frontier. They had not inherited a pre-existing, violent frontier. The settler–indigene frontier began with them. It is, in some ways, easier to make assumptions about British attitudes towards the Aborigines than about Dutch attitudes towards the San. The Dutch settlers of the seventeenth, eighteenth and nineteenth century Cape did not leave behind many memoirs, journals or even letters revelatory of their attitudes towards the indigenous people of the Cape. The further from Cape Town a settler was, the greater the chances of that settler being illiterate. Nor was such a person likely, even if literate, to write a detailed account of any murders or massacres that they might have learnt about or participated in. The great majority of travel narratives dealing with the Cape interior in the eighteenth or nineteenth centuries were written by foreign visitors. Those Dutch visitors who did write were, with few exceptions, VOC officials whose narratives described the Cape as part of the wider world of the VOC's East Indian Empire, and their accounts tended to dwell on the more sophisticated societies of the East. The Cape was significant only in relation to this world, and if the Dutch settlement around Cape Town was sometimes described, there was virtually nothing to be said about the wild inhabitants of the remote African frontier.

---

29   Adhikari, *Anatomy of a South African Genocide.*
30   For the Aboriginal world view, see Flood J. 1994. *Archaeology of the Dreamtime: The Story of Prehistoric Australia and its People.* Sydney: Allen & Unwin.

The British, on the other hand, came to Australia with a considerable amount of intellectual baggage pertaining to supposedly primitive people. There had been a lengthy British encounter with native Americans in North America, while Cook's voyages of exploration in the Pacific had given analysts of human society a great deal of material for contemplation. Marshall and Williams have argued that, by the time the First Fleet reached Botany Bay, the British had effectively been cured of their belief that either Pacific Islanders or Australian Aborigines were noble savages and that they were quite happy to acknowledge the superiority of British culture and British achievements. The learned and well-travelled leaders of the First Fleet would also have been familiar with the ideas of Adam Smith, popularised by other thinkers of the Scottish Enlightenment, that there was a basic division of humanity into four categories based on their mode of subsistence: hunting, pastoralism, agriculture and commerce. Implicit in this theory was that the first stage of development was a primitive one, and that the last stage represented a higher level of human society. Also implicit in this hierarchy of value, as Moses points out, was the assumption, based on John Locke's argument, that since hunter-gatherers did not cultivate the land, they did not rightfully own it, and that Australia was thus *terra nullius*. We may thus safely conclude that neither the commanders of the new convict colony, nor their charges, believed Aboriginal society to be superior to that of the British.[31]

An interesting point of comparison here is that the Dutch had never acted as though the Cape was devoid of indigenous occupants who had no right to the land and that it was, therefore, *terra nullius*. They took care to destroy Khoikhoi land rights through the usual quasi-legal methods of lopsided treaties, unfair purchase or blatant conquest. On occasion, the trekboers even claimed to be defending Khoikhoi pastoralists against San hunter-robbers. Naturally, the price for such protection was the loss of Khoikhoi independence. The San, however, were regarded, like the Aborigines, as having no claim to the country. What these two peoples had in common was that they were hunter-gatherers and the European perception was that, as such, they were not properly using, or improving, the land.

The dynamics of pastoral production both drove colonial expansion and provided the rationale for the commando system—an institution that protected the trekboer's livestock while it ensured the procurement of both land and labour. Initially, self-sufficiency and meat production for a limited

---

31   Marshall P.J & Williams G. 1982. *The Great Map of Mankind: British Perceptions of the World in the Age of Enlightenment*. London: Harvard University Press, 134–51, 214; Moses, 'Genocide', 13.

market were the only incentives for Cape trekboers. By the early nineteenth century, however, wool production had become a factor and the introduction of merino sheep drove the trekboers further into environmentally marginal territory in search of profits, much to the detriment of the San. It would seem as though wool was the motivation for settler pastoralism almost from the start in Australia and it is possible to correlate the growing demand for wool with surges in the invasion of Aboriginal land. It is also possible, to some extent, to chart the increasing use of San or Aboriginal labour in pastoral production against shortages in other forms of labour, such as Khoikhoi or slaves at the Cape and convicts and free settlers in Australia. Once the land had been won and there was work to be done, hunter-gatherer labour no longer seemed so unsuitable.[32]

All of this was far into the future when the First Fleet arrived in Botany Bay in 1788. Initially, there seems to have been a remarkable degree of restraint and forbearance on the part of Governor Philip and his men towards instances of Aboriginal aggression and resistance. This restraint, Clendinnen argues, was the result of the British officers having internalised the Enlightenment discourse of the noble savage, that humans in a state of simple primitivism were naturally virtuous.[33] One may argue, of course, that it was the Aborigines who showed remarkable restraint to the invasion of their land. There are even those who argue that British friendliness was a mask which concealed their true intention—which was to infect the Aborigines with small pox.[34] Whatever the truth, relations between Aborigines and the settlers deteriorated irrevocably due to the expansion of white settlement which, once again, was spear-headed by pastoralist farmers who, unlike their rulers, had probably never internalised the discourse of noble savagery. As happened at the Cape, once the frontier moved beyond the area under the direct scrutiny of government officials, the settlers dealt with hunter-gatherer opponents as they saw fit.

---

[32]   Ryan L. 2012. '"No right to the land": the role of the wool industry in the destruction of Aboriginal societies in Tasmania, 1817–32 and Victoria, 1835–51 compared'. Unpublished paper delivered at the Violence and Honour Conference, University of Cape Town, December 2012. See also McMichael P. 1984. *Settlers and the Agrarian Question: Capitalism in Colonial Australia.* Cambridge: Cambridge University Press, for an argument that suggests that early pastoral production in Australia relied on free or convict labour and not Aboriginal labour—a preference that initially made Aborigines seem surplus to settler requirements.

[33]   Clendinnen I. 2001. *Dancing With Strangers.* Melbourne: Text, 23.

[34]   This is the argument of Jan Kociumbas in Kociumbas J. 2004.'Genocide and modernity in colonial Australia', in *Genocide and Settler Society*, 77–102. See also Finzsch N. 2008. '"Extirpate or remove that vermine": genocide, biological warfare, and settler imperialism in the eighteenth and early nineteenth century'. *Journal of Genocide Research*, 10, no. 2, 215–32.

One should not, however, exaggerate the degree of paternal care or solicitude exerted by British officials on behalf of Aborigines. Lyndall Ryan has shown that in the very first frontier zone between settlers and Aborigines in Australia, that of the Hawkesbury River in New South Wales between 1794 and 1810, British troops were active in mounting punitive expeditions against Aborigines who were resisting the encroachment of British settlers. These settlers, who were engaged in both agriculture and pastoralism, were vital to the colony's attempts to feed itself and could not be allowed to fail. Under the pretext of conducting reprisals, the New South Wales Corp took part in a series of massacres against the Bediagal Aborigines that succeeded in annihilating them as a people within about five years. Ryan goes on to argue that 'massacre in the form of the punitive expedition was the most common strategy deployed by the British invaders to kill numbers of aborigines in one operation and thus demoralise and terrorise the survivors into submission'.[35] Tellingly, Ryan has also noted that the colonisation of Van Diemen's Land began with a massacre of Aboriginal people in 1804, at Risdon Creek, by British military units.[36]

It is the use of massacre as a means of dealing with Aboriginal resistance that most closely links the trekboer–San frontier of the Cape to several pastoralist–Aboriginal frontier zones of Australia. Just as in the Cape, the principal intention of retaliatory commandos was to eradicate and terrorise the hunter-gatherer resisters, similarly in Australia, the perpetrators of massacres were often secretive or evasive about the circumstances under which they had killed resisters. If one accepts a definition of massacre as involving as few as six victims, then the number of massacres against Aborigines becomes almost impossible to compute. The attention of revisionist Australian frontier historians have recently swung from large massacres, such as those at Myall Creek and Waterloo Creek, to smaller atrocities such as the ones Lyndall Ryan documents.[37] She estimates that in Tasmania the Aboriginal population plummeted from 1 200 in 1826 to fewer than 250 in 1832, and in Victoria from about 10 000 in 1835 to 1 907 in 1853 as a result of armed, punitive expeditions.[38] These were both pastoral frontiers, but as the Hawkesbury material shows, if hunter-gatherers threatened agriculturalists, they were dealt with equally harshly.

---

[35] Ryan L. Forthcoming. 'Untangling Aboriginal resistance and the settler punitive expedition: the Hawkesbury River frontier in New South Wales, Australia, 1794–1810'. *Journal of Genocide Research*.

[36] Ryan L. 2012. *Tasmanian Aborigines: A History since 1803*. Sydney: Allen & Unwin, 43–57.

[37] Attwood B. & Foster S.G. 2003. 'Introduction', in *Frontier Conflict: The Australian Experience*, eds B. Attwood & S.G. Foster. Canberra: National Museum of Australia, 5.

[38] Ryan, 'Untangling Aboriginal resistance'.

It should be pointed out that the attempt by white settlers to extirpate Aborigines was neither instantaneous nor universal. Similarly, at the Cape, relations between hunter-gatherers and invasive pastoralists differed from region to region and depended on the availability, or abundance, of environmental resources at a particular time. In areas of rich resources and few settlers, a short period of peaceful cooperation might occur, such as happened around Bathurst in New South Wales between 1815 and 1821, and Van Diemen's Land before 1820.[39] It is true that there was an unfortunate massacre of Tasmanian Aborigines at Risdon Creek, near present-day Hobart, by a party of soldiers, convicts and settlers in 1804, soon after the initial British invasion occurred. This event indicated that Aboriginal life was held to be cheap, but it did not necessarily signal that the extermination of Aborigines would become customary.[40] Once resources began to dwindle and Aborigines began to be forced off the land, conflict escalated. This is what happened in Van Diemen's Land in the 1820s as free settlers followed convict pastoralists into Aboriginal land and used violence to evict indigenous people. As the Aborigines fought back, Lieutenant-Governor Sorell realised the colony had a war on its hands and threw the weight of the government behind settlers. His successor, George Arthur, took this war to the limit.[41]

Arthur's actions are a source of debate among Australian historians. There are some who see him as a humane and decent man, sympathetic to the plight of the Aborigines and appalled at the prospect of their extinction. Others see him as having presided over the eradication of the Van Diemen's Land Aborigines, not having done enough to curb settler violence against them, and devising a scheme that effectively ensured their extinction. Arthur's dilemma was that he felt he could not leave the settlers vulnerable to attack and that he therefore had to render the Aborigines harmless. War having failed, like Macartney at the Cape, he tried peace. His solution was to get the Aborigines to agree to being exiled to Flinder's Island off the coast of Van Diemen's Land. In this project he was assisted by the humanitarian efforts of George Robinson, whose 'friendly mission' to the Aborigines convinced them to go into exile so as to be safe from attack. Unfortunately,

---

[39] Connor J. 2002. *The Australian Frontier Wars 1788–1838*. Sydney: University of New South Wales Press, chs 4, 6.

[40] Ryan L. 2012. *Tasmanian Aborigines: A History since 1803*. Sydney: Allen & Unwin, 49–57. Ryan's account suggests that the early years of British settlement in Tasmania were indicative of the horrors to come.

[41] For the war between settlers and Aborigines in Van Diemen's Land, see Reynolds H. 1995. *Fate of a Free People*. Ringwood, Victoria: Penguin; Reynolds H. 2012. *A History of Tasmania*. Melbourne: Cambridge University Press, 5–87; Boyce J. 2008. *Van Diemen's Land*. Melbourne: Black Inc.; 1–209; Ryan, *Tasmanian Aborigines*, 1–272; Pybus C. 1992. *Community of Thieves*. Melbourne: Minerva Australia.

on Flinders Island the Aborigines were expected to don Western clothes, adopt Western manners and receive Christian instruction.[42]

There are parallels with Barrow and Macartney's plans to isolate the San in a Bushmanland reserve serviced by missionaries. The Cape plan failed because Bushmanland could not be isolated from the colony. The Flinder's Island experiment suggests it could not be isolated from colonial diseases and that for hunter-gatherer societies to survive they needed to be able to practice a hunter-gatherer lifestyle. Ultimately neither the plains of Bushmanland nor Flinders Island allowed for the perpetuation of seasonal mobility in the pursuit of natural resources. The pastoral frontier had choked the hunter-gatherers' breathing space.

The activities of Arthur and Robinson, though ultimately disastrous, remind us that humanitarian interventions were attempted in Australia as well as in South Africa. Colonial officials were responsive to humanitarian concerns expressed by British policy makers, and Philip's tireless campaign for South Africa's indigenous people, in both Britain and the Cape, reminds us how important missionary and humanitarian networks were in recording unpalatable truths and forcing governments into action.[43]

Faced with information reaching it from both the Cape and Australia concerning indigenous people, the British government convened a Select Committee on Aborigines in British Settlements to hear evidence concerning the treatment of indigenes empire wide. It met in 1836 and delivered its report in 1837.[44] It is here that the frontier histories of Australia and South Africa intersected for the first time. The select committee's report was potentially a document of great significance, since it seemed to promise that in the future there would be more active government intervention in the mistreatment of aboriginal inhabitants of Britain's colonies. In retrospect, however, it seems as though the report was the high-water mark of liberal humanitarianism and not the beginning of a new era of colonial protection of aboriginal rights. Although the report contained many noble sentiments, the men expressing these sentiments ultimately could not stop the killing.

---

[42]   For recent debates about Robinson and his 'friendly mission', see Johnston A. & Rolls M. 2008. *Reading Robinson: Companion Essays to Friendly Mission.* Hobart: Quintus.

[43]   For the growing literature on this theme, see Lambert D. & Lester A. eds. 2006. *Colonial Lives Across The British Empire: Imperial Careering in the Long Nineteenth Century.* Cambridge: Cambridge University Press. Lester A. 2005. 'Humanitarians and white settlers in the nineteenth century', in *Missions and Empire: The Oxford History of the British Empire Companion Series,* ed. N. Etherington. Oxford: Oxford University Press, 64–85; Elbourne E. 2008. 'Between Van Diemen's Land and the Cape Colony', in *Reading Robinson,* eds A. Johnston & M. Rolls, 77–94.

[44]   BPP VII.425. 1837. *Report of the Select Committee on Aborigines (British Settlements). Imperial Blue Book,* facsimile reprint. Cape Town: Struik.

In the sections which deal with South Africa, there are surprisingly few pages devoted to the San. Most of the evidence heard was concerned with the colony's relations with Xhosa on the eastern frontier. Those parts which do deal with the San record suggestions that land should be put aside for them and that they should be protected, but nothing was done to enforce these suggestions. It is as though their lack of 'system of order of government' and wandering lifestyle made it impossible to deal with them and thus help them. One gains the impression that by 1837, the San had become too insignificant to matter and that, notwithstanding Dr Philip's concerns, they would be left to their fate unless they suddenly organised themselves into a distinct polity. The implication is that the hunter-gatherer lifestyle was not worth defending, and that the San had only themselves to blame if they did not come to an accommodation with their economically more productive foes.[45]

In Australia, it was hardly the case that Aborigines comprised an insignificant part of the population, and they could not therefore be ignored to the same extent as the San. The committee noted that in New South Wales the rights of Aborigines had never been considered, that they were in a degraded state, and that not enough had been done to civilise them. Indeed, in comparison to South Africa, the level of missionary activity was meagre.[46] It was pointed out that while the laws provided for the punishment of colonists who had committed acts of transgression against the natives, there had not been 'a single instance in which such redress [had] been afforded'. Events in Van Diemen's Land were noted with concern, and in 1837 there were already fears that the removal of the Aborigines had not been a success and that they were on the brink of extinction.[47]

Despite the moral weight of the select committee's report and its urging that those in power adopt 'conciliatory policies' towards Aborigines, the report did little to turn back the tide of settler advance. One exception to this was the firm action taken by Sir George Gipps, the governor of New South Wales, in 1838 when he insisted that seven of those colonists who had been guilty of massacring a group of Aborigines at Myall Creek should be hanged. This was one of the few occasions when capital punishment was inflicted on white settlers for crimes against Aborigines. Significantly, all seven of the executed were, or had been, convicts, making it easier for

---

[45]   *Select Committee on Aborigines*, 1553–1556; Penn, 'The British and the "Bushmen"'.

[46]   The LMS missionary in Australia who played a similar role to Philip at the Cape in drawing attention to atrocities against Aborigines was Lancelot Threlkeld. See Johnston A. 2004. 'A blister on the imperial antipodes: Lancelot Edward Threlkeld in Polynesia and Australia', in *Colonial Lives*, eds D. Lambert & A. Lester, 58–87.

[47]   *Select Committee on Aborigines*, 487–88, 682–84.

the government to pose as liberal defender of natives against criminal murderers. Free settlers who killed Aborigines, on the other hand, were deemed to have acted in self-defence. The hangings nonetheless provoked such an outcry among settlers that the government would think twice before using such punishments again. Out on the frontier, meanwhile, 'official and unofficial action against the Aborigines was renewed'.[48] In the words of Atwood and Foster, the humanitarians' impact was quite limited for several reasons: 'an inherent conflict between the goal of colonising a new country and the rights of indigenous people; the determined pressure from colonists that nothing should get in the way of economic progress; and the practical limits on colonial governments, however high minded, to enforce their policies in remote regions'.[49] Exactly the same could be said of the Cape. Later generations of humanitarian protectors and publicists in Australia succeeded in troubling the conscience of the settlers about their treatment of the Aborigines, but they did not change the course of Aboriginal history.[50]

Conclusion

Throughout the rest of the century, Aborigines would continue to be murdered and massacred or displaced from their land, largely out of sight of the official eye. Significantly, however, the Australian Aborigines were never entirely destroyed, as the Cape San were. Why? The answer is probably not to be found in a comparison of the character of settler frontiersmen. That Dutch or Bastaard pastoralists were simply more savage than the descendants of British or Irish convicts and free men cannot be proven. On the other hand, British humanitarianism, however ineffective it might have been, was more of a deterrent to massacre, in the long run, than Dutch negligence. British humanitarianism, though a latecomer to the Cape, was apparent in Australia from the outset of colonial expansion. But it is more likely that the sheer physical size of Australia and the relative homogeneity of its indigenous inhabitants allowed the Aborigines to survive. If they retreated, the chances are that they retreated into an area large enough to provide them with resources for their survival or dry enough to keep pastoralists out. If they fell back on to another indigenous society, it would be one of fellow hunter-gatherers, possibly one with which they had established reciprocal relationships, and not a hostile, indigenous pastoralist or agro-

---

48 Kociumbas J. 1992. *The Oxford History of Australia: Possessions, 1770–1860*. Melbourne, Oxford University Press, 203.
49 Attwood & Foster, *Frontier Conflict*, 6.
50 Reynolds H. 1998. *This Whispering in Our Heart*. St Leonards, Australia: Allan & Unwin.

pastoralist group. Despite the frequently attested occurrence of inter-group fighting among Aboriginal Australians, their ability to destroy each other was limited by their weaponry and we may assume that inter-group feuds were sometimes put aside in the face of a greater threat. Bushmanland, vast though it was, could not, as we have seen, sustain a society of hunter-gatherers once they were encircled by hostile pastoralists or, to the north, desert conditions. But the varied ecosystems of Australia provided niches where pastoralists could not prosper, but hunter-gatherers could survive.

A further reason for the survival of greater numbers of Aborigines than San may be that Europeans in Australia only truly gained the upper hand in combat in the 1860s, when firearm technology improved and they were supported by native police forces. Before this, settlers were simply unable to sweep the land clear of Aborigines and in certain regions had, perforce, to co-exist with them. The claim that improved firearms made a great difference may be exaggerated since horses and muskets had proved to be deadly enough in the eighteenth century Cape. But the addition of skilled native trackers, familiar with the land and customs of the people they were hunting, must have helped the process of colonial conquest. The Cape settlers had always had Khoikhoi members in their commandos who knew the land and the San very well. In Australia, improved weaponry and native police came together with deadly effect in the Native Mounted Police of Queensland, making that unit the 'singularly most destructive unit' in the state.[51]

It is also important to note that many Aborigines survived because, eventually, they were allowed to enter the settler economy as shepherds, drovers, labourers, trackers, guides or even policemen. This was a process that was facilitated by the demise of convict labour as a source of settler labour and the perception that the Aborigines could provide a cheap, acceptable substitute. Once within the colonial labour force, the Aborigines were described as being very adaptable.[52] This adaptability appears to be in marked contrast to the Cape San, who either refused to adapt or were not allowed to adapt. In fact, this lack of adaptability was more evident in the eighteenth century than in the nineteenth century. It may be that initially Cape colonial pastoralists were unwilling to employ male San as labourers because of the

---

[51] Evans R. 2003. 'Across the Queensland frontier', in *Frontier Conflict*, eds B. Attwood & S. Foster, 73. See also Evans R. 2007. *A History of Queensland*. Cambridge: Cambridge University Press, 51–140; Richards J. 2008. *The Secret War: A True History of Queensland's Native Police*. St Lucia: University of Queensland Press.

[52] See Henry Reynold's extensive documentation of this process in Reynolds H. 1981. *The Other Side of the Frontier: Aboriginal Resistance to the European Invasion of Australia*. Ringwood, Victoria: Penguin; Reynolds H. 1990. *Black Pioneers: How Aboriginal and Islander People Helped to Build Australia*. Ringwood, Victoria.

bitter legacy of the war without mercy waged throughout the eighteenth century.[53] It may be that Australian settlers were more flexible, not having had an extra century of frontier war with which to contend. But the San cannot have been intrinsically less adaptable to a pastoralist lifestyle than Aborigines. After all, the Khoikhoi had once been hunter-gatherers and the San had had almost 2 000 years of interaction with pastoralists by 1830, compared to the 40 or 50 years of Aborigines. In periods of peace, there is ample evidence that San made good servants if they were treated well, and that they were not immune to the attractions of commodities like tobacco, guns, brandy and steel knives. The large numbers of San in the labour force of Graaff-Reinet farmers by the 1820s is testimony to San labour being desirable in certain circumstances.

The real reason for the failure of the Cape San to survive as a distinct labouring class within the Cape settler economy was that their numbers, never great to begin with, were probably already too depleted by 1800 for them to reproduce themselves. Many males had been killed. Captive San women and children were absorbed into the trekboer's Khoikhoi, slave and Bastaard labour force, groups that would soon lose their particularities in the emerging colonial category of 'coloured' and their various languages in the hybrid tongue of Afrikaans. Irreparable damage had already been inflicted on the hunter-gatherer economy by the time that Barrow and Macartney's peace proposals left the San vulnerable to the enticement of gifts. Seeing the San lay down their weapons, the pastoralists saw no reason not to press home their advantage. Peace did not last for long, and when the San picked up their weapons again, the enemy was among them. During the last half of the nineteenth century, in the arid backveld of Bushmanland, the last of the /Xam were extinguished. Some stories, engraved rocks and a largely unrecorded history are all they left behind.[54]

Comparing the differing fates of the Cape San and the Australian Aborigines, it is evident that they were both victims of settler genocide. Revisionist Australian historians have long known this to be true of Aborigines. South African historians have only recently come to know this about the San. It is to be hoped that this short and sketchy essay will encourage an awareness that the histories of Australia and the Cape have more similarities than differences and that their frontier zones, peoples and historians are a rewarding field for comparative study.

---

[53] This is a point I have made in Penn, 'Fated to perish', 91.
[54] See Skotnes P. *Claim to the Country*; Bank A. 2006. *Bushmen in a Victorian World: The Remarkable Story of the Bleek-Lloyd Collection of Bushman Folklore*. Cape Town: Double Storey.

Chapter Eight

'No Right to the Land': The Role of the Wool Industry in the Destruction of Aboriginal Societies in Tasmania (1817–1832) and Victoria (1835–1851) Compared

Lyndall Ryan
University of Newcastle

The pastoral invaders of the British colonies of Van Diemen's Land, which changed its name to Tasmania in 1856, and the Port Phillip District, renamed Victoria in 1851, have recently been described by historian James Belich as forerunners to the white settler revolution that transformed the hunting grounds of Australia's indigenous peoples into a vast sheepwalk for the production of raw wool for the textile mills of northern England. Indeed, by 1851 these sheep farming districts supplied 50 per cent of Britain's demand for raw wool and were a critical part of the global economy. In both cases the revolution was achieved at the expense of the indigenous hunter-gatherer owners, who had effectively been eradicated within 15 years of the settlers' arrival. Yet, of the two colonies, only Van Diemen's Land bears the 'indelible stain' of genocide. How is it then, that the Port Phillip District has largely escaped similar opprobrium?[1]

A cursory glance at the ways some Australian historians have considered the fates of the Tasmanian and Victorian Aborigines reveals a deep unease about the question of genocide. Henry Reynolds, the leading historian of Aboriginal resistance, is not convinced that what happened to the Tasmanian Aborigines should be regarded as genocide, yet James Boyce, a recent historian of colonial Tasmania, vigorously contends that it was. Leading historians of Victorian Aborigines, Michael Cannon and Richard Broome, have each conceded that their virtual disappearance could

---

[1]   Belich J. 2009. *Replenishing the Earth: The Settler Revolution and of the Rise of the Anglo World 1783–1939.* Oxford: Oxford University Press, 183; Hughes R. 1988. *The Fatal Shore: A History of the Transportation of Convicts to Australia 1787–1868.* London: Pan Books, 414–24; Cocker M. 1988. *Rivers of Blood, Rivers of Gold: Europe's Conflict With Tribal People.* London: Jonathan Cape, 138; Curthoys A. 2008: 'Genocide in Tasmania: the history of an idea', in *Empire, Colony, Genocide: Conquest, Occupation and Subaltern Resistance in World History,* ed. A.D. Moses. New York: Berghahn Books.

be considered genocide, but that it was from the 'best of intentions' and certainly 'unintended'.[2]

Reynolds, for example, is not convinced that the Van Diemen's Land government had a clear intent to destroy the Tasmanian Aborigines, although Boyce is certain that it did. Cannon and Broome however can find no evidence that the authorities in the Port Phillip District had the necessary intent to destroy the Victorian Aborigines. But they do believe that the Van Diemen's Land government did commit genocide and point to several important differences between the two colonies to make their case for 'unintended genocide' in the Port Phillip District. First, Van Diemen's Land is an island of 26 000 square miles and physically quite different from the Port Phillip District, which is nearly 37 000 square miles in area and part of the Australian mainland. They argue that the island's limited capacity to support an expanding pastoral industry produced a particular set of circumstances that led to the virtual disappearance of the Tasmanian Aborigines within 15 years. By contrast, they consider the Port Phillip District's much greater capacity for sheep grazing to have had a lesser impact on the Victorian Aborigines and that other factors, such as increased inter-clan warfare and inadvertently introduced diseases, played a vital role in their virtual disappearance over a similar time frame. However, Alan Shaw, another historian of the Port Phillip District, is less convinced by the argument about inter-clan warfare.[3]

Historians Malcolm Levy and Lloyd Robson have offered a class-based explanation. Van Diemen's Land, they argue, was the receptacle for large numbers of transported male British felons known as convicts, who were deployed as shepherds for pastoral settlers. Convicts abducted Tasmanian Aboriginal women for sexual purposes, thus generating violent conflict with Aboriginal men. By contrast, as Broome points out, the Port Phillip District was a settler colony with a free labour force which would have led to 'some amelioration of hard-line frontier attitudes' compared to that of Van Diemen's Land.[4]

---

2   Reynolds H. 2001. *An Indelible Stain? The Question of Genocide in Australia's History.* Ringwood, Vic: Penguin, 49–66; Boyce J. 2008. *Van Diemen's Land.* Melbourne: Black Inc., 261–318; Cannon M. 1990. *Who Killed the Kooris?* Melbourne: William Heinemann, 263; Broome R. 2005. *Aboriginal Victorians: A History since 1800.* Sydney: Allen & Unwin, 92. See Reynolds, *An Indelible Stain,* 13–33, for his analysis of the UN Genocide Convention.

3   Blainey G. 1980. *A Land Half Won.* Melbourne: Macmillan, 75; Broome, *Aboriginal Victorians,* xxiii; Cannon, *Who Killed the Kooris?,* 263; Shaw A. 2003. *A History of the Port Phillip District: Victoria before Separation.* Melbourne: Melbourne University Press, 139–42.

4   Broome, *Aboriginal Victorians,* xxii; Levy M. 1953. *Governor George Arthur: A Colonial Benevolent Despot.* Melbourne: Georgian House, 5–6; Robson L. 1983. *A History of Tasmania,* vol. 1. Melbourne: Oxford University Press, 214–15.

Others, including historian Clive Turnbull, offer a political explanation. Van Diemen's Land, Turnbull argues, was a penal colony managed by an authoritarian governor, George Arthur, who declared martial law against the Tasmanian Aborigines and deployed large numbers of soldiers and police to forcibly remove them from their homelands and banish them to an island in Bass Strait, where they were expected to die out. By contrast, as Broome points out, the Port Phillip District was a free settler colony administered by a benign governor, Charles La Trobe, who established Aboriginal missions and an Aboriginal Protectorate to shield Victorian Aborigines from the awful fate that befell their counterparts in Van Diemen's Land.[5]

Still others such as archaeologist Rhys Jones have invoked an explanation based on the science of human evolution. According to Jones, Tasmanian Aborigines, by virtue of 10000 years of isolation on an island, were already on the road to extinction before the British arrived in 1803, while historian Judy Campbell argues that the Victorian Aborigines were in dramatic population decline from the impact of exotic diseases well before the pastoral settlers arrived in the Port Phillip District in 1836. In these racialised explanations, both groups are held responsible for the destruction of their societies.[6]

Taken together, the explanations appear to exonerate the settlers in the Port Phillip District from the charge of genocide. Even so, they offer some important clues that could help explain the virtual extinction of both indigenous groups within a similar period of time. They do, however, overlook the key factor which characterised both colonies in the respective 15-year periods, namely, the pastoral industry. Sheep farming, known in Australia as the wool industry, was by far the most important component of the pastoral industry in these two colonies. Stock farming not only drove both economies, but underpinned every facet of pastoral settlers' social and political behaviour, including the unquestioned belief that they had the right to displace indigenous peoples from their homelands. This vital factor alone, along with the fact that settler massacres of Aborigines took place in both colonies, would suggest that a comparative investigation of the role played by pastoral settlers in the virtual disappearance of the Tasmanian and Victorian Aborigines over similar time frames could yield important

---

[5] Turnbull C. 1965. *Black War: The Extermination of the Tasmanian Aborigines*. Melbourne: Lansdowne Press, ix; Broome, *Aboriginal Victorians*, xxii.

[6] Jones R. 1977. 'The Tasmanian Paradox', in *Stone Tools as Cultural Markers: Change, Evolution and Complexity*, ed. R. Wright. Canberra: Australian Institute of Aboriginal Studies, 189–204; Campbell J. 2002. *Invisible Invaders: Smallpox and Other Diseases in Aboriginal Australia 1780–1880*. Melbourne: Melbourne University Press, 136–62; Broome, *Aboriginal Victorians*, 10.

new insights into how it happened, and inform our understanding of the genocidal nature of these cases.[7]

The wool industry in Australia has largely been romanticised, even by the most trenchant of Australia's economic historians such as Stephen Roberts, Brian Fitzpatrick, Ronald Hartwell and Geoffrey Blainey, largely on account of its dominant position in the Australian economy in the nineteenth century and, indeed, for most of the twentieth. They tend to overlook the industry's brutal impact on indigenous peoples because the period during which most of them conducted their research was dominated by the convenient belief that indigenous peoples had simply 'faded away' in the wake of pastoral expansion. Roberts acknowledges that many pastoralists forcibly wrestled the land from its indigenous owners, but that this was a consequence of the government's failure to do its job of removing them beforehand. Blainey also concedes that the explosive expansion of the wool industry played a key role in the rapid population decline of the Tasmanian and Victorian Aborigines, but asserts that inadvertently introduced disease was a more significant factor.[8]

They all, however, agree that the wool industry emerged in the Australian colonies from four interlinked factors. The first requirement was to breed sheep that were well suited to the relatively low rainfall grasslands of eastern Australia. Experiments in Spanish merino sheep breeding conducted by Elizabeth and John Macarthur in New South Wales between 1806 and 1817 developed a strain of merino very well adapted to Australian conditions. The wool was rarely of superfine quality and from the outset, quantity rather than quality was the key to the industry's economic success. Second was the demand for capital to fund the purchase of sheep. After 1817, loans were available from the Bank of New South Wales. The third prerequisite was for cheap land and labour which were readily available in the Australian colonies. The final factor was the decision by the British government in 1822 to drop the duty on Australian wool to one-sixth the rate of that on German wool, thus assuring the industry's future.[9]

---

[7] Mitchell J. 2009. '"The galling yoke of slavery": race and separation in colonial Port Phillip'. *Journal of Australian Studies*, 33, no. 2, 127–28.

[8] Roberts S.H. 1939. *The Squatting Age in Australia 1835–1847*. Melbourne: Melbourne University Press, 87, 89; Fitzpatrick B. 1951. *British Imperialism and Australia 1783–1833*. London: George Allen & Unwin; Hartwell, R.M. 1954. *Economic Development of Van Diemen's Land 1823–1850*. Melbourne: Melbourne University Press; Blainey, *Land Half Won*, 75.

[9] Broome R. 1982. *The Aboriginal Australians*. Sydney: Allen & Unwin, 37; Johns L. & Ville S. 2012. 'Banking records, business and networks in colonial Sydney, 1817–24'. *Australian Economic History Review*, 52, no. 2, 167–90.

Thus, from the outset, as with the sugar industry in the West Indies which defined the British imperial economy in the eighteenth century, the pastoral industry in the Australian colonies in the first half of the nineteenth century was heavily subsidised by free land, cheap labour and low import duties to Britain. It is not surprising then that from 1817 to 1851, the wool industry became the economic lynchpin of the Australian colonies and the only export commodity that really mattered. But it also sounded the death knell for indigenous peoples in Van Diemen's Land and the Port Phillip District.

The destruction of Tasmanian Aboriginal society

In 1800, there were nine known Aboriginal nations in Van Diemen's Land with an estimated population of between 6000 and 8000 people. The best known were the Big River and Oyster Bay nations whose homelands were located in eastern Van Diemen's Land. The two nations consisted of at least four or five patrilineal clans led by a warrior chief, such as Petelega and Montpeliater, whose responsibilities included the conduct of political and social relationships with adjoining clans and nations. Being hunter-gatherers, they usually camped in extended family groups of about 20 people in multiple bark shelters and made seasonal migrations between the east coast and hinterland in search of game such as kangaroo, emu and a wide variety of birds, as well as fish, sea mammals and shell fish. They also gathered a wide variety of vegetable foods including yams, wild fruits and berries. Clans would periodically meet up with neighbouring clans and nations to exchange gifts of ochre and women, and perform ceremonies to maintain their ancestral connection to the land. As they travelled through their homelands and those of other clans and nations, they would use different names for themselves to denote whether they were visitors or claimed the land as part of their territory. On the grasslands they used firestick farming to attract kangaroos and emus, constructed bark canoes to dive for shellfish, used digging sticks to forage for small animals such as echidnas, and made wooden spears and clubs, known as waddies, to kill larger animals such as kangaroos and emus. After the first British colonists arrived in 1803, they quickly acquired European dogs which were trained to hunt kangaroo, and were used as items of gift and exchange. There is now general agreement that at the time of the British invasion in 1803, the population of the Big River and Oyster Bay nations was increasing.[10]

---

[10] Ryan L. 2012. *Tasmanian Aborigines: A History since 1803*. Sydney: Allen & Unwin, 1–42.

The Tasmanian wool industry took off in 1817 when the island, then a dependency of the British colony of New South Wales, had been partly occupied for 14 years by 2000 British settlers. With limited capital and outnumbered by more than two to one by the Tasmanian Aborigines, settlers initially avoided the hunting grounds of the Big River and Oyster Bay nations and clustered in the small towns of Hobart in the south and Launceston in the north, where they practised subsistence agriculture and engaged in maritime pursuits. However, the shortage of white women led to intermittent raids on Aboriginal camps for women and children. At the same time, a creole community of Aboriginal women from the North East nation and British sealers was beginning to emerge on the Bass Strait islands which retained seasonal relations with their Aboriginal kin through the exchange of kangaroo meat and skins for seal meat and skins as well as mutton bird meat and feathers. By 1817, a modus vivendi appears to have developed between the three communities, even though it was characterised by intermittent violence.[11]

At that point, Van Diemen's Land became the solution for two of the major problems facing the British government at the end of the Napoleonic wars, namely, the dramatic increase in crime in Britain's burgeoning industrial cities, and the demand by army officers for adequate recompense for their war service. The British government sought to resolve both problems by opening up Van Diemen's Land to the officers and their families to graze large flocks of sheep that would be tended by transported felons. Though creative, the solution singly failed to acknowledge that the Tasmanian Aborigines were the legal owners of Van Diemen's Land. Further, as political scientist Charles Rowley has pointed out, by relying upon a rapidly increasing convict labour force, the new economy had no demand for Aboriginal labour beyond the convicts' use of the sexual services of Aboriginal women. In trying to solve a major social problem at home by developing a pastoral economy in a distant colony, the British government created conditions that would lead to the virtual disappearance of the Tasmanian Aborigines within 15 years.[12]

Van Diemen's Land became a separate colony from New South Wales in 1825, by which time the settler population on the island had increased to 14512. They occupied more than half a million acres of the homelands of the Big River and Oyster Bay Aboriginal nations located on the 123-mile stretch of open

---

[11]   For the estimate of the colonial population in October 1816, see Vamplew W. ed. 1987. *Australian Historical Statistics*. Sydney: Fairfax, Syme Weldon & Associates, 25. See also Ryan, *Tasmanian Aborigines*, 58–73.

[12]   Ryan, *Tasmanian Aborigines*, 74–75; Rowley C.D. 1970. *The Destruction of Aboriginal Society*. Canberra: Australian National University Press, 35.

plain between Hobart and Launceston. This fertile area, hemmed in by rugged mountain ranges, was quickly renamed the Settled Districts. The new settlers stocked their 500-acre land grants with more than 182000 sheep and 35000 head of cattle, tended by about 3000 convicts. By 1831, when the population reached 30000 and there were 680000 sheep and 68000 head of cattle in the Settled Districts, all the best pastoral land in the colony had been taken up. Unable to find new land suited to sheep and cattle farming, the wealthier settlers consolidated their holdings to become what has generally been referred to as the '20000-acre gentry'. By then too, martial law was in force and the colony's governor, George Arthur, had recently completed a military operation to drive the Oyster Bay and Big River nations from the Settled Districts. Seven years later, when virtually all the remaining Tasmanian Aborigines had been forcibly removed from their homelands to an island prison in the Bass Strait, the number of sheep in the colony exceeded one million. Settlers were in open triumph that Van Diemen's Land was at last 'native free'. How then did this happen so quickly?[13]

Resistance by the Big River and Oyster Bay nations to the sudden arrival of settlers and sheep on their hunting grounds was immediate and violent. This is not surprising, for they believed that the settlers had broken important protocols over visiting rights to their homelands and the gifting and exchange of Aboriginal women and dogs. Some chiefs, such as Petelega and Montpeliater, at first tried to drive off the sheep which competed with kangaroos for grass. Then they robbed shepherds of flour, tea and sugar, as compensation for the loss of their hunting grounds. Finally, when the shepherds tried to abduct Aboriginal women for sexual purposes, the chiefs had no hesitation in seeking retribution and by the end of 1826, they were believed to have killed about 40 of them. In one case, the government arrested four Oyster Bay men on charges of murder. However, by virtue of their alleged savage state they were not permitted to give evidence in court in their defence and were hanged as a deterrent to further bloodshed. By then it was estimated that 1200–1500 Oyster Bay and Big River people remained in the Settled Districts, with another 500 Aborigines on the rest of the island.[14]

13 Vamplew, *Australian Historical Statistics*, 25, 115; Scott P. 1965. 'Land settlement', in *Atlas of Tasmania*, ed. J.L. Davies. Hobart: Lands and Surveys Department, 43; Ryan, *Tasmanian Aborigines*, 74–75; Boyce, *Van Diemen's Land*, 308.
14 Ryan, *Tasmanian Aborigines*, 143; Mackaness G. ed. 1965. *Henry Melville: History of Van Diemen's Land From the Year 1824 to 1835, Inclusive During the Administration of Governor Arthur.* Sydney: Horwitz-Grahame, 56–59; *Hobart Town Gazette*, 20 September 1826. For the estimate of 1200–1500, see *Hobart Town Gazette*, 11 February 1826. The estimate of 500 is based on my own research.

At that point, Arthur changed tactics. With increased policing resources at his disposal, he empowered magistrates to track down Aboriginal suspects in the Settled Districts and if they resisted arrest, to shoot at them. The policy shift led newspaper editor Andrew Bent to call for the removal of all Aborigines from the island to prevent them from being exterminated. The forced removal of indigenous people from their homelands had long been in practice across the British Empire. In Jamaica, for example, indigenous peoples had been forcibly removed from their homeland in 1796 to make way for sugar plantations. Similarities between the sugar and wool industries, both integral to the British imperial economy, were undoubtedly noted by some settlers in Van Diemen's Land and possibly by Governor Arthur, who had previously served in the West Indies. Both industries required large expanses of land, cheap labour and a ready export market to be profitable. Many groups of indigenous peoples in the Caribbean in the eighteenth century, such as the Caribs on the island of St Vincent in 1772, had been forcibly removed from their homelands to make way for sugar plantations, so it is not surprising that Bent called for the forcible relocation of the Tasmanian Aborigines to an island in the Bass Strait.[15]

Bent may have invoked a humanitarian discourse to save the Tasmanian Aborigines from extinction, but it was imbued with the Anglophone belief that by virtue of their alleged savage state, they had no inherent rights to their homelands. Governor Arthur, however, believed that as British subjects, Tasmanian Aborigines did have such rights, but articulated them as part of a broader humanitarian agenda which required them to relinquish their savage state, convert to Christianity, learn a trade and join colonial society. His mission therefore was to negotiate with the chiefs of the Big River and Oyster Bay nations to surrender their homelands in the Settled Districts in exchange for a reserve in the island's north-east. Here he envisaged them being converted to Christianity and learning useful trades. The process of humanitarian salvage could, however, not begin until they surrendered.[16]

To hasten their surrender, Arthur deployed the military and police forces at his disposal to carry out search and destroy operations against the Big River and Oyster Bay nations. In the 18 months between November

---

[15] British Parliamentary Papers (BPP), 19 of 1831. No. 259. *Van Diemen's Land. Copies of all Correspondence Between Lieutenant-Governor Arthur and His Majesty's Secretary of State for the Colonies, on the Subject of the Military Operations Lately Carried on Against the Aboriginal Inhabitants of Van Diemen's Land.* London: House of Commons, 20–21; *Colonial Times*, 20 November 1826; Gott R. 2011. *Britain's Empire: Resistance, Repression and Revolt.* London: Verso, 115–18.

[16] *Colonial Times*, 1 December 1826; Ryan, *Tasmanian Aborigines*, 78, 101; BPP, 19 of 1831, 24–26; Mackaness, *History of Van Diemen's Land*, 75–76.

1826 and April 1828, the forces appear to have killed an estimated 400 Big River and Oyster Bay Aborigines, with at least 250 succumbing in 15 known incidents of massacre. In seeking a military solution to the problem, Arthur dramatically escalated the Black War to a level never before seen in the Australian colonies. But the Oyster Bay and Big River chiefs had no intention of surrendering, let alone ceding their homelands to pastoralists. They continued their seasonal migration through the Settled Districts, to hunt kangaroo and fulfil their ceremonial obligations, meet their relatives from nearby nations and conduct warfare with others, as if nothing had changed. When two of their women were abducted and killed near Oatlands in October 1828, however, rather than killing the shepherd perpetrators in reprisal, as they usually did, they for the first time killed three white women.[17]

Enraged at their audacity, Arthur immediately proclaimed martial law. He declared the Big River and Oyster Bay people as 'open enemies of the state', dramatically increased military and police patrols and empowered them to kill any Aborigine on sight. Even though an estimated 200 Big River and Oyster Bay people were killed in the following 16 months, from the settlers' point of view, the tactic appeared to fail because the Aborigines responded by killing more than 60 shepherds and stockmen. With the settlers in high panic, Arthur further escalated the war. In September 1830, he called on them to join a combined force of soldiers and police in a military operation known as the Black Line. Comprising more than 2000 people, it stretched across the Settled Districts for more than 100 miles. Its sole purpose was to drive the Oyster Bay and Big River peoples out of the Settled Districts and force their surrender. This time Arthur was more confident of success.[18]

Although nearly all of the 200 or so surviving Oyster Bay and Big River Aborigines in the Settled Districts managed to slip through the Black Line, many of them were killed in the immediate aftermath and most of the rest, fewer than 70 in all, finally surrendered by the end of the following year. Only then could Arthur finally revoke martial law and declare that the settlers were in unfettered possession of the Settled Districts. By the end of 1832, only 15 years after the pastoralists had arrived in the colony, fewer than 300 Tasmanian Aborigines remained on the entire island. Over the next two years, most were rounded up and forcibly removed to an open

---

[17] Ryan L. 2008. 'List of multiple killings of Aborigines in Tasmania: 1804–1835', in *Online Encyclopaedia of Mass Violence*, ed. J. Semelin. Paris: http://www.massviolence.org/List-of-multiple-killings-of-Aborigines-in-Tasmania-1804; BPP, 19 of 1831, 4–7; Ryan, *Tasmanian Aborigines*, 103–04.
[18] BPP, 19 of 1831, 27–30, 64–70; Ryan, *Tasmanian Aborigines*, 104–21.

prison on Flinders Island in the Bass Strait where for the next 15 years they battled to survive respiratory diseases such as influenza and tuberculosis until a mere 44 survivors were allowed to return home to Tasmania in 1847.[19]

The official narrative of the Black War was constructed from despatches between Governor Arthur and the Colonial Office in London. They present a story of Tasmanian Aboriginal insurgency that prevented the pastoral settlers from carrying out their legitimate business of grazing sheep. Later accounts of the war, however, reveal that some settlers operated in concert with police and military forces to form roving parties that tracked down Aborigine camps and attacked them while asleep. Rather than playing the role of innocent bystanders in a war largely conducted by government forces, some settlers were clearly active participants in the fighting, and sometimes acted on their own initiative to perpetrate massacres against Aborigines. This is not at all surprising. As leading scholar of massacre Jacques Semelin points out, new colonial settlements that required extensive land for major economic enterprises such as sheep farming, often resulted in the massacre of its indigenous owners.[20]

Semelin regards the act of massacre not as an aberration, but as intentional. On colonial frontiers, massacre was usually a well-planned response to a particular act of perceived aggression, such as the killing of a settler or stock keeper, by indigenous people, even though the original aggression was by the settlers themselves. Massacres were meant either to intimidate indigenous peoples into subjection, or to eliminate them entirely. Semelin also considers the act of massacre not to have been carried out by colonists who felt in control of the situation, but rather by ones who lived in fear of the alleged aggressors and believed that by engaging in massacre, they would regain the upper hand. The act of massacre was thus usually an expression of weakness. For this reason it was usually carried out in secret, making it very difficult for the perpetrators to be identified in the immediate aftermath. However, witnesses and perpetrators sometimes spoke out long after the event, when fears of prosecution and persecution by perpetrators had passed.[21]

---

19   Ryan, *Tasmanian Aborigines*, 176–97, 219–52.
20   For the official account of the Black War, see BPP, 19 of 1831; See Bonwick J. 1870. *The Last of the Tasmanians or the Black War in Van Diemen's Land*. London: Sampson Low, Son & Marston; Fenton J. 1884. *A History of Tasmania from Its Discovery in 1642 to the Present Time*. Hobart: J. Walch & Sons. See also Ryan L. 2010. '"Hard evidence": the debate about massacre in the Black War in Tasmania', in *Passionate Histories: Myth, Memory and Indigenous Australia*, eds F. Peters-Little, A. Curthoys & J. Docker. Canberra: ANU Press, 39–50; Semelin J. 2007. *Purify and Destroy: The Political Uses of Massacre and Genocide*. London: Hurst & Company, 366–83.
21   Semelin, *Purify and Destroy*, 366–83.

More recent consideration of the subject by Philip G. Dwyer and myself indicates that on colonial frontiers, the pre-conditions for the massacre of indigenous peoples across the globe were remarkably consistent, namely:

> *the alleged destruction of valuable property and/or the alleged killing of a colonist coupled with the over-riding belief that the indigenous people [had] no right to the land. In these cases, massacre [was] a well-planned reprisal, usually in the form of an armed dawn attack on a camp of sleeping men, women and children.*[22]

We also found that the perpetrators usually knew their victims and had lived in close proximity to them for a period of time. Further, because the killing of innocents was morally reprehensible, massacres were usually disguised and reported to authorities as a military engagement such as a 'battle', or by using code words, such as 'collision', 'rencontre', 'clash' and 'dispersal'. Finally, along with Semelin, we established that massacres could be initiated both from above, for example by military commanders, or from below by settlers. We concluded that massacres such as these, when carried out in a consistent pattern over a substantive period of time, constituted genocidal intent.[23]

By using the consensus of Australian historians that a minimum number of six undefended people killed in one incident on the Australian colonial frontier constitutes a massacre, and employing Semelin's typology of massacre to investigate such incidents, it is possible to estimate the minimum number of massacres that were perpetrated against Tasmanian Aborigines between 1823 and 1834, and to identify their location. Based on an earlier study of settler massacres in the colony, I have identified 37 confirmed instances of massacre of Tasmanian Aborigines in this period. Most of them took place at night at Aboriginal camps in the hills and mountains on the borders of the Settled Districts and were carried out by roving parties that consisted of at least five armed men on foot, and sometimes up to 20 or more. These detachments usually comprised up to five soldiers, two field policemen, several shepherds and stock keepers, and sometimes a settler and an Aboriginal guide. Most of the perpetrators were armed with Brown Bess muskets that were supplied to British regiments in Van Diemen's Land, as well as cutlasses, swords and pistols. However, in a rare case of a daytime massacre near the Meander River west of Launceston, a swivel gun was used by an overseer to kill 19 Aborigines. Most incidents of massacre appear to have been triggered by an alleged Aboriginal killing of a shepherd or stock-

---

22 Dwyer P. & Ryan L. eds. 2012. *Theatres of Violence: Massacre, Mass Killing and Atrocity Throughout History.* New York: Berghahn Books, xvi.
23 Dwyer & Ryan, *Theatres of Violence*, xii–xiii, xix.

keeper. However, during the three-year period of martial law, opportunity massacres also took place, such as in September 1829 when settler John Batman and his party ambushed an Aboriginal camp at dawn and killed at least 17 Aborigines.[24]

The greatest number of undefended Aborigines estimated to have been killed in a single operation is about 40 and took place in a dawn raid on a campsite of Oyster Bay people near Campbell Town in April 1827. Another account records a small group of stock keepers and soldiers of the 40th Regiment killing about 100 Aborigines in five separate incidents over a five-week period in June and July 1827. The most important cluster of massacres, 15 of them, took place over the two-year period from November 1826 to October 1828, before the declaration of martial law. Both the timing and intensity of these massacres suggest that Governor Arthur may deliberately have tried to use them to force the quick surrender of the Oyster Bay and Big River nations. Indeed, my research indicates that more Aborigines were killed in this than any other comparable period. At least 400 Aborigines and 60 settlers were killed with an Aborigine/settler death ratio of more than 6.7:1, the highest during the entire Black War.[25]

Most reports of mass killings were either vigorously denied at the time or presented as a battle between a small detachment of lightly armed soldiers and a large group of male Aborigines armed with spears and clubs. In these cases, it was reported that some Aborigines were killed in self-defence. However, in at least one case, the Campbell Town massacre in April 1827, stories began to circulate not long after the 'battle' that it was in fact a massacre carried out on an undefended camp of the Oyster Bay people at daybreak in reprisal for the killing of two shepherds. Even so, further details of the incident did not appear until 2002, in a posthumously published memoir of one of the perpetrators in which he admitted that 'two score were killed'.[26]

---

24   For the minimum number killed to constitute massacre, see Windschuttle K. 2000. 'The myths of frontier massacres, part II: the fabrication of the Aboriginal death toll'. *Quadrant*, October, 18; Kiernan B. 2001. 'Australia's Aboriginal genocide'. *Yale Journal of Human Rights*, I, no. 1, 52; Ryan L. 2008. 'Massacres in the Black War in Tasmania 1823–34: a case study of the Meander River region, June 1827'. *Journal of Genocide Research*, 10, no. 4, 482; Ryan, 'List of multiple killings', 14; Plomley N.J.B. ed. 2008. *Friendly Mission: The Tasmanian Journals and Papers of George Augustus Robinson 1829–1834*. Hobart: Quintus, 231; Tasmanian Archive and Heritage Office, Colonial Secretary's Office,1/320: Batman to Anstey, 7 September 1829.

25   Ryan L. 2006. 'Massacre in Tasmania? How do we know?'. *Australia and New Zealand Law and History eJournal*, 6, available at http://www.anzlhsejournal.auckland.ac.nz/ pdfs_2006/ Paper_6_Ryan.pdf; Ryan, 'Massacres in the Black War in Tasmania', 479–99; Ryan, *Tasmanian Aborigines*, 143.

26   *Colonial Times*, 4 May 1827; Ryan, 'Massacre in Tasmania', 37.

Overall, the statistics reveal that between November 1823 and August 1834, the Van Diemen's Land government authorised the killing of more than 870 Tasmanian Aborigines of whom about 400, or nearly 50 per cent, were killed in massacres. This high loss of life appears to have brought about their final surrender and deportation. In the same period, 200 settlers were killed, producing an Aboriginal/settler death ratio of over 4:1. How then do these events and statistics compare with those of the Port Phillip District?

The destruction of Aboriginal societies in the Port Phillip District

As pointed out earlier, the land available for sheep grazing in Van Diemen's Land was limited and as early as 1827, settlers were looking across the Bass Strait to the Australian mainland for additional sheepwalks. The British government, cognisant of the dreadful impact of the wool industry on the Tasmanian Aborigines, was wary of establishing new colonies in Australia without strict provisions to protect the indigenous inhabitants. Undaunted, the Van Diemen's Land settlers brazenly took the law into their own hands. In 1834 the Henty brothers, one of the wealthiest pastoral families in Van Diemen's Land, secretly established a settlement at present day Portland on the southwest coast of the Port Phillip District and began grazing several thousand sheep there. They were followed a year later by John Batman acting as emissary for a cluster of Van Diemen's Land settlers who called themselves the Port Phillip Association. His brief was to contact the Kulin Aboriginal nation at the site of present-day Melbourne and another group at Indented Head at the entrance to Port Phillip Bay and negotiate the purchase of 600 000 acres of their homeland with hundreds of blankets, steel blades, mirrors, as well as beads and the promise of an annual tribute of rice, flour and sugar. Batman then sealed the deal with a treaty of purchase.[27]

Outraged by these audacious acts, the governor of New South Wales, Richard Bourke, who held jurisdiction over the Port Phillip District, immediately declared Batman's treaty null and void and the Henty Brothers as unlawful occupiers. But the damage had been done. Six months later, Bourke and the British government were forced to acknowledge that the pastoral invasion of the Port Phillip District from Van Diemen's Land could not be stopped. By the end of 1836, Bourke had opened the district to pastoral settlement and appointed a magistrate at the fledging settlement at

---

[27] Mc Combie T. 1858. *History of the Colony of Victoria From its Settlement to the Death of Sir Charles Hotham*. London: Chapman and Hall, 19, 23; Broome, *Aboriginal Victorians*, xxiii; Shaw, *History of the Port Phillip District*, 46–47.

Melbourne to oversee the lease of vast acres of Crown land for sheep grazing. In 1839, the pastoralists' triumph was sealed when Charles La Trobe was appointed superintendent of the district.[28]

The population of Aborigines in the Port Phillip District in 1836 is generally estimated to have been between 10 000 and 15 000. They were believed to have been the remnants of an original population of about 60 000 that had been ravaged by major smallpox epidemics in 1788 and 1830. Like their counterparts in Van Diemen's Land, they were also a hunter-gatherer people, originally comprising at least 30 nations in four distinct language groups. According to Broome, they had lived in the region for at least 1 600 generations and asserted affiliations to the land through their ancestry. Unlike their counterparts in Van Diemen's Land, who undertook regular seasonal migrations in search of food and to maintain ceremonial obligations with adjoining clans, Victorian Aborigines rarely left their homelands, because the land offered richer resources and they possessed more sophisticated technologies such as boomerangs, wooden axes, spears and fish traps to hunt for food, and were assisted by native dogs known as dingos. According to Broome, they operated in patrilineal clans as large as 300 to 500 people, which were led by warriors such as Billibellary, otherwise known as Jika-Jika, a Kulin chief who was one of the signatories to the Batman treaty. The clans usually 'interacted and intermarried with adjoining groups, but were at enmity with those further afield, who were feared as possible enemies and sorcerers'. Broome explains that 'warfare existed with such distant groups, and even with neighbours, after disputes arose over women, trade or ritual transgressions. However, there were traditional mechanisms for containing levels of violence, especially with neighbouring clans.'[29]

According to Broome, Billibellary's clan was part of a cluster of five others, which shared a common dialect and were loosely coalesced as the Woiwurrung clans, comprising about 1 500–2 500 people and were part of the loose confederation of similarly sized cultural-language groups known as the Kulin nation. Several other distinctive confederations have also been identified. These include the Kurnai nation in Gippsland, who do not appear to have been affected by the earlier epidemics and with an estimated population of 2 500 in 1836, and several clans of the Gunditjmara in the Western District also comprising at least 2 500 people. However, historian Jan Critchett estimates that in 1836 there were about 8 000 Aborigines in

---

28   Shaw, *History of the Port Phillip District*, 51, 66.
29   Broome, *Aboriginal Victorians*, xxi, 9.

the Western District alone, suggesting that Broome's Aboriginal population estimates for the entire Port Phillip District are rather low. [30]

Unlike Van Diemen's Land, where only 30 per cent of the land was suitable for grazing sheep, at least 60 per cent of the Port Phillip District was extremely well suited to the wool industry. As Broome points out, the 'grasslands lay for hundreds of kilometres to the west and north of Melbourne, into which squatters and their sheep made rapid forays', as fast as any expansion in the nineteenth century. Between 1836 and 1851, the settler population increased from 224 to 77 345 and the number of sheep skyrocketed from 3 000 to 6 000 000. Thus from the outset, the pastoral invasion of the Port Phillip District was more dramatic and more widespread than in Van Diemen's Land.[31]

Upon their arrival in the Port Phillip District, stock farmers encountered important differences in access to land and labour compared to their peers in Van Diemen's Land. First is that the land grant system of fewer than 1 000 acres per settler in Van Diemen's Land had been replaced by long-term pastoral leases of tracts of land of between 10 000 and 50 000 acres, much better suited for grazing large flocks of sheep. These stock farmers became known as squatters, because they did not own the land, even though they behaved as if they did. Second, although squatters from Van Diemen's Land spearheaded the pastoral expansion into the Port Phillip District, they were soon joined by stock farmers from New South Wales and by immigrants from Britain. The squatters arriving in the Port Phillip District were thus more experienced, better resourced and better prepared for the vicissitudes of sheep farming and for dealing with Aboriginal resistance than in Van Diemen's Land.[32]

Thirdly, the squatters were more likely to employ free labourers rather than convicts as stockmen and shepherds, and were thus relatively free of government interference. However, many 'free' stockmen were former convicts from Van Diemen's Land with considerable experience in dealing with insurgent Tasmanian Aborigines. For instance, James Gumm, John Batman's overseer, was a former convict known to have been involved in the massacre of Tasmanian Aborigines in September 1829. Even so, squatters experienced a severe labour shortage and Broome suggests that it led to some Victorian Aborigines being employed in the pastoral economy and thus

---

30   Broome, *Aboriginal Victorians*, xxi; Critchett J. 1990. *A 'Distant Field of Murder': Western District Frontiers 1834–1848*. Melbourne: Melbourne University Press, 38, 45, 85.

31   Broome, *Aboriginal Victorians*, xxiii; Vamplew, *Australian Historical Statistics*, 26; Critchett, *Distant Field of Murder*, 45.

32   Shaw, *History of the Port Phillip District*, 87–88.

being 'somewhat more valued as labourers'. There is, nonetheless, no clear evidence of this occurring until after their dispossession. Other squatters overcame the labour shortage by employing mounted stockmen to muster the sheep rather than large numbers of shepherds on foot. The stockmen also carried more firearms which appear to have been of the same calibre as those in use in Van Diemen's Land, namely, muzzle-loading, smooth bore rifles with gun powder pan and percussion cap ignition systems. Being mounted afforded them better protection from Aboriginal attack and offered greater opportunity to initiate offensives against Aboriginal camps.[33]

In summary, the pastoral invasion of the Port Phillip District was as rapid as any phase of the white settler revolution of the nineteenth century. It was carried out by experienced sheep farmers, who stocked their pastoral leases with enormous numbers of sheep, and were assisted by mounted stockmen who were adept at protecting their masters' property from Aboriginal resistance. In the face of this concerted onslaught, it would appear that Victorian Aborigines in the major pastoral regions of the Port Phillip District stood little chance of retaining their homelands.

The British government, however, fresh from its triumph of abolishing slavery in the British Empire in 1834, was determined that the awful fate that befell the Tasmanian Aborigines would not be repeated in the Port Phillip District. But the measures it devised to prevent this from happening were contradictory in intent and effect. It firmly believed, for example, that its humanitarian mission was not to acknowledge Aboriginal rights to the 'possession of the soil' nor to prevent their dispossession, but to prevent it from happening violently. To this end, it established the Aboriginal Protectorate with a chief protector and four assistant protectors to contact and conciliate Victorian Aborigines and induce them to leave their homelands voluntarily and seek protection at nearby reserves and mission stations. But it also established a variety of mounted police units to protect the squatters from Aboriginal attack. As historian Jessie Mitchell points out, in this dynamic tableau of colliding interests, the humanitarian impulse lost out to the demands of squatters and in 1849 the protectorate, along with the mission stations, were closed down.[34]

By 1853, the Victorian Aboriginal population had plummeted from a minimum estimate of 10 000 in 1836 to 1 907, a decline of more than 80 per cent. Broome estimates that '1,500–2,000 died violently at white *and*

---

33   Bonwick, *Last of the Tasmanians*, 99; Broome, *Aboriginal Victorians*, xxii, xxiv.
34   Shaw, *History of the Port Phillip District*, 116, 143; Ryan, *Tasmanian Aborigines*, 116; Mitchell, 'Galling yoke of slavery', 127–28.

black hands' and that 'perhaps a further 1,000 to 1,500 died of natural causes', leaving '4,000–5,000 who fell to diseases, disruption of food supplies and the impact of cultural dislocation. This was exacerbated by a dramatic decline in the birth-rate'. He believes that the outcome was unintended and that it was 'not dissimilar to genocide'. Is this a fair assessment?[35]

Unlike Van Diemen's Land, where a coherent narrative of Aboriginal dispossession appeared in British Parliamentary Papers while it was taking place, no similar narrative exists for the Port Phillip District. This can be partly explained by the forces of law and order usually arriving in a region long after the settlers had secured the land. The most coherent accounts of Victorian Aboriginal dispossession can be found in histories of two of the three major pastoral regions—the Western District and Gippsland. Jan Critchett, historian of Aboriginal–settler relations in the Western District, conservatively estimates that in 1834, the Aboriginal population was about 8000 and that by 1841, had fallen to 3500. The first magistrate servicing the region did not arrive until August 1840, by which time there were 41 pastoral runs on the Wannon River alone and a year later, more than 1200 in the Western District as a whole. Critchett is in no doubt that settlers took the law into their own hands and considers the settler hunting party, the equivalent of the roving party of Van Diemen's Land, as the most common strategy used to kill Victorian Aborigines. In support of her claim, she cites the diary of settler Anna Maria Baxter, who lived in the Dunmore region of the Western District in the mid-1840s. Baxter reports that between June 1845 and April 1847, at least 13 hunting parties were organised by settlers around Dunmore and Yambuck. Another settler in the Western District, Samuel Carter, admitted that 'the squatters often formed parties to shoot down the blacks, as it was a fight for life in many cases'. Critchett also notes that some settlers failed to report incidents where Aborigines were killed, that only five white men from the Western District were tried for shooting Aborigines, and that only one of them was found guilty on a lesser charge and sentenced to two months in gaol. She reports that more than 350 Aborigines in the region were shot and poisoned before 1850 and concludes that 'Aborigines and pastoralists were in close contact right across' the Western District and that by 1848, nearly 15 years after the settlers first

---

[35] Broome, *Aboriginal Victorians*, 91–92. Emphasis in the original.

arrived in the region, Aboriginal dispossession was complete. But, as we shall see, her numbers considerably underestimate the level of violence.[36]

In 1995, geographer Ian D. Clark compiled the first register of settler massacre sites in Western Victoria, covering the period 1803–1859. He was the first scholar in Australia to define a massacre as the 'unnecessary, indiscriminate killing of human beings, as in barbarous warfare or persecution, or for revenge or plunder' and closely matches Semelin's conception of massacres as tending to take place in secret, with perpetrators observing a code of silence to protect their identities. Given a legal system that prevented Aboriginal witnesses from presenting evidence in court, most perpetrators escaped conviction. When Broome analysed Clark's data in 2003, he found that 430 Aborigines had been killed overall, 80 more than Critchett's estimate. Of these, 262 had been killed in 32 mass killings of five or more, and the rest in 55 small-scale incidents. These astonishing statistics were the first indication that massacres could have accounted for more than half of the Aborigines killed in the region. However, as will be demonstrated, these figures also underestimate the violence. [37]

Gippsland, the homeland of the Kurnai nation, was opened up to pastoral settlement in 1840 and by 1846, about 1 000 settlers and more than 100 000 head of cattle were in the region. Even so, the first Commissioner of Crown Lands and mounted border police did not arrive in the region until 1844. Historians of the region have found it far more difficult to obtain evidence of serious conflict between Aborigines and settlers because of the code of silence that surrounded most of these incidents. Peter Gardner, for example, has wrestled with the 'absence of authentic primary evidence' and for many decades worked hard to uncover new sources. He comes to the grim estimate that out of an original population of at least 1 800 and probably closer to 3 000, no fewer than 800 Kurnai were killed in the period 1839–1850. He alleges that settlers usually sought mass revenge for the Aboriginal killing of a single settler or animal, and that they usually planned their operations carefully and went to great lengths to carry them out in secret. Massacres usually occurred at places where Aborigines could be ambushed or trapped, such as at waterholes, or on peninsulas and islands in river estuaries, or

---

36   Critchett, *Distant Field of Murder*, 12, 59–61, 85, 88, 124; Shaw, *History of the Port Phillip District*, 88; Critchett J. 2003. 'Encounters in the Western District', in *Frontier Conflict: the Australian Experience*, eds B. Attwood & S.G. Foster. Canberra: National Museum of Australia, 56–58.

37   Clark I.D. 1995. *Scars in the Landscape: A Register of Massacre Sites in Western Victoria 1803–1859*. Canberra: Australian Institute of Aboriginal and Torres Strait Islander Studies, 2–9; Broome R. 2003. 'The statistics of frontier conflict', in *Frontier Conflict*, eds B. Attwood & S. Foster, 94.

in ravines. Aboriginal survivors and settler witnesses only spoke out long after the event for fear of retaliation by perpetrators. The most horrifying set of massacres in the region took place at Warrigal Creek in July 1843. Organised by Angus McMillan and carried out by a posse of 20 horsemen dubbed the Highland Brigade, they slaughtered, over a period of five days, an estimated 150 Kurnai located in at least three campsites. Gardner found that the conspiracy of silence around this dreadful incident still permeated the region 150 years later.[38]

The Murray District, which still awaits a historical survey, was opened to squatters in 1837, yet the first magistrate did not arrive until 1841 and by 1844, it contained at least 3 000 settlers and half a million sheep. It seems that in each pastoral region, the forces of law and order arrived after the worst violence in the dispossession of Aborigines was over. However, at least two mission stations were established in the Western District between 1836 and 1839. The missionaries' letters and reports, along with those from the chief protector and four sub-protectors attached to the Aboriginal Protectorate which began operations in 1839, provide glimpses of violent conflict between Aborigines and squatters for possession of the land. Taken together with settler accounts and press reports, they indicate that the strategy of settler massacre was a critical factor in Victorian Aborigines' rapid population decline across all pastoral regions. Massacres were initially perpetrated by squatters and their stockmen, and later by mounted police units. It is not surprising then that by 1853 most of the surviving 1 903 Victorian Aborigines were clustered on surviving mission stations across the major pastoral regions.

In an earlier paper, I deployed Semelin's typology of massacre to interrogate a wide array of published sources on the Port Phillip District for instances of massacre in an attempt to construct a chronology of massacre incidents in three of its five pastoral regions for the period 1836 to 1851. The information was consolidated to produce a tally of known incidents of massacre overall. From the assembled data, 68 known massacres, each involving six or more Aborigine deaths, were identified. There was an average of more than four massacres per year, and an estimated 1 169 Aborigines killed. This tally comprises more than 11 per cent of Broome's estimated Aboriginal population of 10 000 in the Port Phillip District in 1836. It does not include Aborigines killed in incidents in which fewer than

---

38   Broome, *Aboriginal Victorians*, 20; Blainey G. 2006. *A History of Victoria*. Cambridge: Cambridge University Press, 33; Gardner P.D. 2001. *Gippsland Massacres: The Destruction of the Kurnai Tribes 1800–1860*. Ensay: self-published, 50–55, 95, 101.

six victims lost their lives. Nor does it include an estimate of the number of Aborigines killed in other regions in the Port Phillip District, or evidence of settler massacres found in other sources. Even so, the tally does suggest that settler massacres were responsible for more than half of the Aboriginal deaths in Broome's estimate of 1500 to 2000 deaths in the entire Port Phillip District, which includes small-scale killings and deaths from inter-tribal violence. An Aboriginal–settler death ratio of 25:1 is reached when compared with reported Aboriginal killings of 80 settlers.[39]

A deeper analysis of the data enabled key characteristics of settler massacres of Victorian Aborigines on the Port Phillip frontier to emerge. First is that they were widespread across the three pastoral regions. There were 40 incidents of massacre in the Western District, with the loss of 619 Aboriginal lives; 12 in the Murray District, with an estimated loss of 160 lives; and 16 massacres in Gippsland, with the loss of 390 lives. These statistics lend support to the conclusion by Critchett that the Western District experienced the highest level of violence between Aborigines and settlers and that her original estimate of 350 Aboriginal casualties is very low indeed. Most massacres took place between 1838 and 1843, when an estimated 940 Aborigines were killed in 45 known incidents across the three pastoral regions. In this period, there was an average of nine massacres per year, or one every two to three months with an average of more than 18 Aborigines killed in each incident. Thirty massacres were recorded in the Western District, eight in the Murray District and seven in Gippsland. Of these massacres, 15 were in reprisal for the killing of male colonists for which 397 Aborigines were slaughtered. There were 17 other massacres in reprisal for the appropriation of livestock and other property in which 301 Aborigines were killed. In addition, 13 pre-emptive strikes in which 142 Aborigines lost their lives, including four cases of poisoning, were perpetrated. As Clark points out, this violence occurred during the period in which stock farmer penetration of Aboriginal land was at its height, and when the drought and economic depression of 1843 caused wool prices to crash. The large number of massacres in this period suggests that they had an immediate and devastating impact on the Aboriginal population across the three regions.[40]

Second is that three causes of these massacres—alleged Aboriginal killing of a settler, alleged Aboriginal attack on livestock or property, and

---

[39]   Ryan L. 2010. 'Settler massacres on the Port Phillip frontier, 1836–1851'. *Journal of Australian Studies*, 34, no. 3, 263.

[40]   Ryan, 'Settler massacres', 263–64, 267–68; Critchett, *Distant Field of Murder*, 61; Clark, *Scars in the Landscape*, 9.

pre-emptive strikes by settlers—match the causes for massacre in Van
Diemen's Land. Third, is that four types of massacre were identified. The
most prevalent was reprisal attacks conducted by a hunting party specially
formed to exact revenge for the loss of sheep or the killing of a squatter or
his employee. The second most common type was the daylight ambush or
entrapment organised by shepherds. Most of these incidents took place when
the forces of law and order such as mounted police, native police or officers
of the Aboriginal Protectorate were not present. Such episodes are usually
the most difficult to detect. The third most prevalent was the poisoning
of Aborigines by station cooks. The fourth was the military-style massacre
carried out by mounted police, including native police detachments, in
revenge for the alleged killing of squatters or their employees. While in
at least two cases, major massacres were perpetrated in reprisal for the
alleged Aboriginal abduction of white women, in neither case could such an
abduction be proven. Rather, they indicate that the gross sexual imbalance
in the settler population, which was about 80 per cent male, rendered
Aboriginal women vulnerable to abduction and made the settlers overly
protective of the few white women. The data confirms that squatters and
their stockmen were the major instigators and perpetrators of massacre.
Mounted and Native Police, however, also played a key role.[41]

Of the four categories of evidence for massacre that were identified,
only two—reports by officers of the Aboriginal Protectorate at the time of
the incident, and evidence from squatters and Aboriginal survivors long
after the event—could be considered reliable unless corroborated by other
evidence. Further interrogation of the evidence suggests that contemporary
settler accounts of alleged 'clashes' and 'pitched battles' with large mobs of
Aboriginal men had little basis in fact. Rather, as in Van Diemen's Land,
the evidence suggests that these accounts were often fabricated to cover up
squatters' well-planned attacks on undefended Aboriginal camps in which
Aboriginal men, women and children were killed.[42]

Comparative statistical analysis

Let us first consider the raw statistics of Aboriginal dispossession. During
the Black War in Van Diemen's Land, 878 Tasmanian Aborigines were
killed in the Settled Districts, with the loss of 201 settler lives, producing an
Aboriginal/settler death ratio of 4.4:1. In the Port Phillip District between

---

41 Clark, *Scars in the Landscape*, 46–47; Gardner, *Gippsland Massacres*, 69–72; Ryan, 'Settler massacres', 265–66, 270; Critchett, *Distant Field of Murder*, 32.
42 Ryan, 'Settler massacres', 270.

1836 and 1851, however, an estimated 2000 Aborigines and 80 settlers were killed, resulting in an Aboriginal/settler death ratio of 25:1. It would appear that at least 50 per cent of the Tasmanian Aboriginal population in the Settled Districts were killed outright between 1823 and 1834. This is an astonishingly high proportion. By contrast only about 20 per cent of the Victorian Aboriginal population were killed in the Port Phillip District between 1836 and 1851. The discrepancy is explained by all-out war being conducted against the Tasmanian Aborigines, the statistics clearly showing its dreadful impact.

Statistics relating specifically to the massacre of indigenous people in each colony confirm the above findings. In Van Diemen's Land, 37 cases of massacre were recorded in the 15-year period between 1819 and 1834, while in the Port Phillip District 68 instances of massacre were recorded over a similar period between 1836 and 1851. From these statistics it is estimated that of the 878 Tasmanian Aborigines recorded killed, nearly 50 per cent lost their lives in massacres. Further, each colony appears to have experienced a distinct period of concentrated massacre. In Van Diemen's Land, for example, at least 15 massacres took place in the period 1826 to 1828, resulting in at least 260 casualties. This was precisely when the settler population was increasing rapidly and occupying Aboriginal land. In the Port Phillip District, 43 massacres took place in the period 1838 to 1843, with the loss of 940 Aboriginal lives. In this period, nearly 10 per cent of the estimated total Aboriginal population was killed.

However, of the 2000 Victorian Aborigines estimated to have been killed, it appears that more than 50 per cent lost their lives in massacres. The statistics also reveal that the average number of Aborigines killed in massacres in Van Diemen's Land was 11, and the greatest number killed in one incident is estimated at 40. In the Port Phillip District, the average number of Aborigines killed was 17, and the greatest number killed in one incident took place at Warrigal Creek in Gippsland, where 150 Kurnai were slaughtered. The higher numbers killed in massacres in the Port Phillip District would suggest that more successful strategies were devised to dispose of larger groups of Aborigines.

In considering settler deaths, the difference between 208 in Van Diemen's Land and 80 in the Port Phillip District can largely be explained by the fact that in Van Diemen's Land most casualties were among the large convict labour force of shepherds and hut keepers. Few of them had access to horses or carried effective defensive weaponry. Most were killed between November 1826 and December 1831. In the Port Phillip District, most settler victims were also shepherds and hutkeepers who were former convicts and very few were squatters, overseers and mounted stockmen. Unlike Van Diemen's Land, however, most of them carried defensive weapons and had access to horses. At least half were killed between 1836 and 1844. Of these, at least seven were killed in the only known massacre of Victorian settlers at Benalla in the Murray District in April 1838. There is no evidence of an Aboriginal massacre of settlers in Van Diemen's Land. Overall, most of the settlers in both colonies were killed in ones and twos.[43]

In Van Diemen's Land, there is very little evidence to suggest that many Tasmanian Aborigines died from exotic diseases until they surrendered to government agents and were taken to deportation camps. At this point they appear to have readily succumbed to respiratory diseases which quickly reduced their numbers. In the Port Phillip District, however, many Victorian Aborigines already had smallpox scars when settlers arrived in 1836, indicating that the Aboriginal population had already been decimated by the epidemics of 1788 and 1830. They, however, had no immunity to influenza, measles, venereal disease and tuberculosis, which ravaged the Aboriginal population in the following decade. In some cases, Victorian Aborigines appear to have become susceptible to these diseases after they had been violently dispossessed and had sought refuge on mission stations and reserves. Critchett notes that the birth rate in the Western District remained high until 1841, when many Aborigines succumbed to sickness. In the same year, in the Loddon Valley Aboriginal Protectorate, venereal disease was first noted in nine out of every 10 Aboriginal women. This evidence would suggest that these women were exposed to disease in the aftermath of dispossession.[44]

Inter-clan warfare was reported in Van Diemen's Land, and from a close reading of the journals of government agent George Robinson, who captured the Aboriginal survivors of the Black War, I recorded 30 Aboriginal lives that were lost in this way. This category, however, comprises less than three per cent of the overall number killed. In the Port Phillip District, however, according to Beverley Blaskett, who has scoured the available sources, inter-clan warfare accounted for 200 Aboriginal deaths, comprising 10 per cent of the overall number killed in the period 1836 to 1850. She considers the higher percentage due to the Victorian Aborigines' widespread practice of sorcery and tribal battles, although as Alan Shaw points out, before the British invasion of Australia, 'the Aboriginal population had remained

[43]   Shaw, *History of the Port Phillip District*, 114; Critchett, *Distant Field of Murder*, 32.
[44]   Ryan, *Tasmanian Aborigines*, 151–59; Blainey, *History of Victoria*, 31; Critchett, *Distant Field of Murder*, 38.

stable for generations while tribal "battles" were going on'.[45] Rather, it would appear that the pastoral invaders forced many Victorian Aborigines into the homelands of other clans, which undoubtedly increased inter-clan disputes over land and the exchange of women.

Conclusion

As this chapter has demonstrated, by taking a comparative statistical approach to the impact of massacre on the indigenous peoples in Van Diemen's Land and the Port Phillip District, several findings produce new insights into the genocidal nature of these two cases. First is that about 50 per cent of each Aboriginal group were killed over roughly similar 15-year periods, and roughly half appear to have lost their lives in massacres. This astonishing finding indicates that the strategy of massacre played a more significant role in rapid indigenous population decline in each colony than has previously been thought. In each case, it seems clear that the widespread use of massacre could constitute genocidal intent. Secondly, the massacres in both colonies were perpetrated by settlers as well as by soldiers and police. Indeed, it would appear that in the Port Phillip District, settlers used the pre-emptive strike and mass poisoning with considerable success. Third is that three times the number of settlers lost their lives in Van Diemen's Land than in the Port Phillip District, suggesting that stock farmers expanding into the latter colony were better prepared for dealing with Aboriginal resistance. Fourth is that exotic disease only made deep inroads into Tasmanian Aboriginal society in the aftermath of dispossession. However, its impact on Victorian Aborigines had been present from the outset. Similarly, inter-clan warfare also appears to have had a greater impact among Victorian Aborigines. Finally, and perhaps most importantly, Victorian Aborigines may have been forcibly dispossessed of their homelands, but unlike their counterparts in Van Diemen's Land, survivors were not banished to an island in the Bass Strait. Rather, many sought refuge on mission stations near their homelands, while others sought work as labourers on squatting runs.

It is the absence of two critical factors in the case of the Port Phillip District—a declaration of martial law and the banishment of Aboriginal survivors—that appears to have absolved the colony of the opprobrium of genocide in much

---

[45] Ryan, *Tasmanian Aborigines*, 144; Blaskett, B. 1990. 'The level of violence: Europeans and Aborigines in Port Phillip, 1835–1850', in *Through White Eyes*, eds S. Janson & S. Macintyre. North Sydney: Allen & Unwin Australia, 77–100; Shaw, *History of the Port Phillip District*, 142.

writing about its history. According to the UNCG definition, intent to destroy a designated social group is necessary for determining genocide. However, as this chapter has demonstrated, the systematic killing and concentrated period of massacre inflicted on Victorian Aborigines appears to demonstrate clear intent to destroy the entire population. In this regard, the Port Phillip District readily meets this definition of genocide.

Does this conclusion suggest that the rapid occupation of the homelands of hunter-gatherer peoples by stock farmers with large numbers of sheep and cattle always leads to genocide, or were the pastoral invasions of Van Diemen's Land and the Port Phillip District special cases? While genocide appears to have been the norm, there is important evidence from other parts of Australia to support the view that genocide was not an inevitable outcome of commercial stock farmers invading hunter-gatherer territories. When stock farmers arrived in the Northern Territory, for example, they were known to have perpetrated massacres of Aborigines, but more as acts of pacification than extermination because they needed their labour. As historian Ann McGrath points out, by the first decades of the twentieth century, the cattle industry was entirely dependent on Aboriginal labour and that following the passage of the Northern Territory Land Rights Act 1976, some Aboriginal groups made successful claims for ownership of cattle stations located on their homelands and on which they had worked for several generations.[46]

This example alone would support Charles Rowley's argument referred to at the beginning of this chapter, that the ready availability of cheap convict labour in the sheep industry in Van Diemen's Land precluded the need for Aboriginal labour and thus their survival. The employment of experienced white stockmen in the sheep and cattle industries in the Port Phillip District produced a similar outcome for Victorian Aborigines. As the historical experience of stock farming in Australia has shown, relations between stock farmers and hunter-gatherers were always violent at the outset because stock farmers considered themselves as having prior right to hunter-gatherer homelands. However, if their labour was required, hunter-gatherers had a better chance of survival. If this is the case, then the genocides of the Tasmanian and Victorian Aborigines stand as a stark reminder of the political and economic power of stock farmers in nineteenth century Australia to determine the fate of hunter-gatherer peoples whose homelands they invaded.

---

[46]   McGrath, A. 1987. *'Born in the Cattle': Aborigines in Cattle Country*. North Sydney: Allen & Unwin Australia, viii–x, 162–63.

Chapter Nine

Indigenous Dispossession and Pastoral Employment in Western Australia during the Nineteenth Century: Implications for Understanding Colonial Forms of Genocide

Ann Curthoys
University of Sydney

There is no chance, in Western Australia, of circumstances arising such as those which, in the eastern provinces, led to the sad episodes which have darkened their history ... We have wanted the services of the blacks. This has proved the salvation of the latter. It has been our interest to win them from savagery, to teach them to relish some of the simplest necessities and luxuries of civilisation and to give us their labour in exchange for them.

West Australian, 13 April 1888

A common view among scholars is that in settler societies, settlers seize the land but are less interested in exploiting the labour of indigenous hunter-gatherers, importing their main sources of labour from elsewhere—convict, indentured, slave, free. For some, the argument follows that it is this desire for indigenous peoples' land but not their labour that leads settler societies to be genocidal.[1] What happens, then, when the labour of indigenous hunter-gatherers *is* valued and becomes not merely useful, but essential? How is our understanding of settler colonialism, and of its relation to genocide, affected? This chapter investigates the connections between dispossession, genocide and the exploitation of indigenous labour in settler colonial contexts through a study of the specific case of the British colony of Western Australia in the nineteenth century. It compares the impact of pastoralism and pearling on the destruction of Western Australian Aboriginal society and considers how these two examples of Aboriginal employment affect our understanding of the relationship between settler colonialism and genocide.

---

[1] For recent examples, see Wolfe P. 2008. 'Structure and event: settler colonialism, time, and the question of genocide', in *Empire, Colony, Genocide: Conquest, Occupation, and Subaltern Resistance in World History*, ed. A. Moses. New York: Berghahn Books, 103; Wolfe P. 2006. 'Settler colonialism and the elimination of the native'. *Journal of Genocide Research*, 8, no. 4, 403–04.

The existence of competing definitions of genocide plagues many debates. This chapter uses a definition taken from Raphael Lemkin's foundational *Axis Rule in Occupied Europe*, written in 1944:

> Genocide has two phases: one, destruction of the national pattern of the oppressed group; the other, the imposition of the national pattern of the oppressor. This imposition, in turn, may be made [either] upon the oppressed population which is allowed to remain, or upon the territory alone, after removal of the population and the colonization of the area by the oppressor's own nationals.[2]

As a number of scholars have noted, this definition of genocide sounds remarkably like a definition of settler colonialism itself.[3] Lemkin here makes clear that genocide involves a process of displacement of one group by another, but the displaced group may either be removed altogether, or it may remain as an oppressed minority whose social structure and group identity, what he calls 'national pattern', has been destroyed. In *Axis Rule in Occupied Europe*, Lemkin is keen to note that genocide may take many forms, of which only one is mass killing. These other forms, he writes, involve considerations that may be cultural, political, social, legal, intellectual, spiritual, economic, biological, physiological, religious and moral.[4] Here I want to focus on one of these—the economic. There are two aspects. One is that a group may, potentially or actually, destroy another if it fatally undermines the economic foundations of the latter's peoplehood, its group existence. The other is that economic exploitation may itself become a means of effecting genocide. Slavery, for example, can destroy the relationship between parents and children, families and community, connections with land, cultural practices and religious belief, and in so doing be a means of group destruction.[5]

Does the need for indigenous peoples' labour mitigate the tendency to dispossession and genocide? Jean-Paul Sartre asked a similar question in 1967 in relation to Algeria in his notable essay, 'On genocide'.[6] Written

---

2   Lemkin R. 1944. *Axis Rule in Occupied Europe: Laws of Occupation, Analysis of Government, Proposals for Redress*. New York: Columbia University Press, 79–80.

3   See Docker J. 2008. 'Are settler-colonies inherently genocidal? Re-reading Lemkin', in *Empire, Colony, Genocide: Conquest, Occupation, and Subaltern Resistance in World History*, ed. A.D. Moses. New York: Berghahn Books, 83.

4   Lemkin, *Axis Rule in Occupied Europe*, ch. 9. For an extended evocation of this chapter, see Curthoys, A. & Docker, J. 2001. 'Introduction—genocide: definitions, questions, settler-colonies'. *Aboriginal History*, 25, 5–11.

5   See Lemkin R. 1951. 'Revised outline for genocide cases', two-page manuscript in Lemkin Papers, New York Public Library, Box 8, folder 11, printed and discussed in Docker, 'Are settler-colonies inherently genocidal?', 88.

6   Sartre J.P. 1967. 'On genocide'. Available at http://www.brussellstribunal.org/ GenocideSartre.htm.

in the context of the Russell Tribunal investigating the American war in Vietnam, which asked whether there were acts by American forces 'which can legally be called acts of genocide', Sartre's essay linked genocide and colonisation much as Lemkin had done over 20 years earlier. In the course of the argument, Sartre describes the actions of French colonial troops in Algeria as 'genocidal in character' since they aimed at the destruction of part of the population in order to terrorise the remainder and to 'wrench apart the indigenous society'.[7] The French desire to destroy and replace indigenous Algerian society was, however, significantly inhibited by the reliance on Algerian labour. In Sartre's words, 'their value as virtually free labour protects them to a certain extent from genocide'. The result of the French settler reliance on Algerian labour meant, Sartre contends, that the French could not continue the wholesale massacre of Algerians, of the kind that had happened at Sétif in 1945, without ruining the settler economy itself.[8]

In 1981 Leo Kuper, a scholar of African colonialism, took up the questions Sartre had asked in his book, *Genocide: Its Political Use in the Twentieth Century*. He agreed with Sartre that any tendency towards genocide is restrained when the labour of subject peoples is required. 'The corollary', he wrote, 'would be that the impulse to genocide will be given freer rein where there are no material advantages to be derived from restraint, as in the genocides against hunting and gathering peoples.'[9] Kuper's assumption that settlers would gain little or no advantage from hunting and gathering peoples, other than their land, anticipates more recent discussion of the nature of settler colonialism. In his well-known essay characterising settler colonialism as a structure not an event, involving a 'logic of elimination', Patrick Wolfe acknowledges the existence of Aboriginal employment in the northern cattle industry, but sees it as marginal to the 'dominant pattern' of Australian settler colonialism in the south-east, which he regards as settler colonialism in its 'pure or theoretical form'.[10]

Mohamed Adhikari's discussion of the genocide of the San peoples of southern Africa in his book, *The Anatomy of a South African Genocide*, considers the question of employment by colonisers of hunter-gatherers in

---

7   Sartre, 'On genocide', 62–63.
8   Sartre, 'On genocide', 352. For a more detailed discussion of Sartre's essay, see Curthoys, A. & Docker J. 2008. 'Defining genocide', in *The Historiography of Genocide*, ed. D. Stone. London: Palgrave, 23–26.
9   Kuper L. 1982. *Genocide: Its Political Use in the Twentieth Century*. New Haven: Yale University Press, 46.
10   Wolfe P. 2001. 'Land, labor and difference: elementary structures of race'. *The American Historical Review*, 106, no. 3, 871.

some depth. He points out that in the violent processes of the colonisation of southern Africa, the stock-farming trekboers conducted a major campaign, involving military and vigilante raids, to take San land and put down San resistance.[11] They drew San women into their households as servants, and raised San children to become farm labourers in a system of child slavery that was institutionalised in the late eighteenth and early nineteenth centuries into a system of apprenticeship.[12] Captured San, who were mainly women and children but could include some men, were, writes Adhikari, 'slaves in every sense except that they could not be sold openly'.[13] Under British rule in the nineteenth century, when settlers had already taken much San land and destroyed most of San society, settlers employed surviving San on the north-eastern frontier and thus drew them into the lower orders of colonial society.[14] Adhikari summarises these processes as extinguishing San society through 'encroachment on their land, enforced labour incorporation and periodic massacre'. The incorporated—that is, employed—San became part of colonial society as 'Hottentots'; their descendants, some of whom are reclaiming San or Khoisan identity, are part of South African society today.[15] Adhikari contests Miklos Szalay's argument that because the San were sought as labour and were accordingly absorbed into colonial society, what happened to them cannot be regarded as genocide.[16] He points out that the desire for San land was far greater than for San labour, many more San being killed than taken prisoner and employed, and that since the employment of women and children 'contributed directly to the violent dissolution of San society' it was part of, rather than a counter to, the genocide of the San.[17]

With these debates in mind, this chapter sets out to explore the relationship between genocidal and employment processes in colonial situations by considering the case of Western Australia in the nineteenth century. So far, historical debate on genocide in the Australian colonies has focused on other Australian colonies, notably Van Diemen's Land

---

11 Adhikari M. 2010. *The Anatomy of a South African Genocide: The Extermination of the Cape San Peoples*. Athens: Ohio University Press, 31.
12 Adhikari, *Anatomy of a South African Genocide*, 47.
13 Adhikari, *Anatomy of a South African Genocide*, 48.
14 Adhikari, *Anatomy of a South African Genocide*, 70.
15 Adhikari, *Anatomy of a South African Genocide*, 77.
16 Szalay M. 1995. *The San and the Colonization of the Cape 1770–1879: Conflict, Incorporation, Acculturation*. Cologne: Rüdiger Köppe Verlag.
17 Adhikari, *Anatomy of a South African Genocide*, 85.

(Tasmania) and Queensland, or on the continent as a whole.[18] What discussion there has been on genocide in Western Australia has focused on the question of child removal, rather than on the issues of dispossession, displacement and replacement that concern me here.[19] Western Australia, however, deserves separate close attention by genocide scholars, partly because of the unusual sparseness of British settlement over a very large territory, and partly because the British government retained direct control there for longer than in the other Australian colonies. Britain granted the colony responsible government quite late, in 1890, considerably later than to its other Australian colonies, which had gained new self-governing constitutions in the 1850s. This longer period of direct British rule enables us to scrutinise the changing imperial-settler dynamic in Aboriginal policy in the second half of the nineteenth century. So significant, furthermore, are the differences between the six Australian colonies that it is worth studying them separately. Scholarly arguments over whether dispossession involved genocide may produce conclusions pertinent to one colony, but not to the others.

Managing Aboriginal labour

From the colony's beginnings in 1829, British authorities and settlers wanted to employ Aboriginal people as labourers. [20] They brought with them some British indentured labourers of their own, but these were too few to serve the colony's labour needs, and free labour migration to the colony remained low for decades. Unlike the colonies to the east—New South Wales and Van Diemen's Land—there was for the first 21 years no convict transportation and hence no available convict labour. The official and settler need for labour, however, sat alongside an overwhelming desire to secure the future of the colony, which meant that the first priority for both government and settlers was not so much Aboriginal employment as preventing Aboriginal attacks.

---

18   See these two essay collections edited by A.D. Moses: Moses A.D. 2004. *Genocide and Settler Society: Frontier Violence and Stolen Indigenous Children in Australian History*. New York: Berghahn Books, and Moses A.D. 2008. *Empire, Colony, Genocide: Conquest, Occupation, and Subaltern Resistance in World History*. New York: Berghahn Books. See also Reynolds H. 2001. *An Indelible Stain: The Question of Genocide in Australia's History*. Sydney: Allen & Unwin. Reynolds mentions Western Australia only briefly, mainly in relation to the rebellion of the 1890s, now popularly known as Jandamarra's War.

19   See Haebich A. 2004. '"Clearing the wheat belt": erasing the indigenous presence in the southwest of Western Australia', in *Genocide and Settler Society*, A.D. Moses, 267–89. While Haebich focuses on child removal and the policy of absorption, she also discusses other forms of removing indigenous people and identity.

20   Hetherington P. 2002. *Settlers, Servants and Slaves: Aboriginal and European Children in the Nineteenth Century in Western Australia*. Perth: University of Western Australia Press, 101.

As agricultural settlement gradually spread outward during the 1830s from the initial settlement in Perth, on the Swan River, there were violent clashes between settlers, troopers and Aboriginal people, notably at Pinjarra in 1834, in which the governor himself was involved. The interest in converting indigenous people from violent antagonists into a useful labour force remained, however, and indeed intensified under the governorship of John Hutt from 1839 to 1846. Influenced by a new spirit of protectionism in the Colonial Office, prompted in part by the British parliament's 1837 Aborigines Report, Hutt attempted a system of governance aimed at protection, Christianisation and education.[21] He hoped to draw Aboriginal people into the colonial economy as workers, both to help the settlers and to 'civilise' the Aborigines.[22] Within two years, Hutt could report that employment of Aboriginal people as servants and farm labourers was common.[23] The distinctive feature of educational activity in Western Australia in these early years was, Pen Hetherington suggests, its emphasis on training Aboriginal people for work as labourers and servants, so that children worked for most of the day and then took lessons.[24] Hutt also sought to control and minimise frontier violence through a more determined application of the rule of law, meaning that Aborigines and settlers who attacked each other were both to be tried in court and if found guilty, imprisoned. As part of this policy, Hutt in 1840 formally established Rottnest Island, off the coast of Perth, as a prison and reformatory for Aboriginal offenders. The two aims of British colonial policy in this period—the imparting of 'civilisation' and insistence on the rule of law—coincided at Rottnest, where in the views of Hutt and his supporters, incarceration could have beneficial effects. As Mark Finnane and John McGuire suggest, its establishment 'signified a faith in the power of institutions to bring civilization to the subject peoples of the Empire'.[25]

Yet the continued expansion of settlement worked against the policies of Hutt and the Colonial Office. Aboriginal populations in the 'settled' areas rapidly declined as a result of violent conflict, loss of land and sources of food, and the impact of introduced diseases so that by the late 1840s, Aboriginal

---

21 Great Britain. Parliament. House of Commons. Select Committee on Aborigines (British Settlements) Report of the Parliamentary Select Committee on Aboriginal Tribes, (British settlements): reprinted with comments by the Aborigines Protection Society. London: Published for the Society by William Ball, 1837.
22 Hunter A. 2012. *A Different Kind of 'Subject': Colonial Law in Aboriginal–European Relations in Nineteenth Century Western Australia 1829–1861*. Melbourne: Australian Scholarly Publishing, ch. 9.
23 Hetherington, *Settlers, Servants and Slaves*, 116.
24 Hetherington, *Settlers, Servants and Slaves*, 118.
25 Finnane M. & McGuire J. 2001, 'The uses of punishment and exile: Aborigines in colonial Australia'. *Punishment and Society*, 3, no. 2, 286.

labour was becoming scarce. Their need for labour becoming desperate, the settlers in 1847 began importing Chinese indentured labour from Singapore, though the numbers were small.[26] In an attempt to increase the supply of Aboriginal labour, Governor Fitzgerald, who governed from 1848 to 1855, closed the Rottnest Island jail in 1849 and employed the prisoners in road building.[27] Aboriginal numbers were, however, still insufficient to meet the colony's growing labour needs. So great was the demand for labour that in 1850, just as the colonists in Van Diemen's Land were increasingly opposing convict transportation and those in New South Wales were campaigning for it not to be reintroduced, settlers in Western Australia supported its introduction. Still a Crown colony under direct British control, managed by a governor and his officials, and with a weak appointed and advisory Legislative Council, the liberal, radical and anti-pastoralist politics of the eastern colonies that so strongly opposed transportation were scarcely in evidence, and the labour demands of government and farmers held sway.

With the advent of convict labour from 1850, the need for Aboriginal labour declined for a time, and with it, attention to Aboriginal schooling and training.[28] When convict labour became available for work on the roads, Rottnest Island again became an Aboriginal gaol, reopening in 1855.[29] Where there had been some element of a civilising project on the island in its first phase under Governor Hutt, now it was just a prison.[30] During the convict era, settler society dispossessed one Aboriginal group after another as settlement continued slowly to spread, with wheat farming to the east of Perth in the 1850s and sheep farming in the Pilbara to the north in the 1860s. In each district, conflict between settlers and Aboriginal peoples erupted as the latter sought to maintain their homelands. Conflict could be triggered in a variety of ways, such as settler mistreatment of Aboriginal women, or Aboriginal attacks on livestock. Stock killing had a dual purpose, being prompted in part by hunger, as traditional food sources were undermined, and in part by a desire to drive the stockholders away altogether, and was a common form of frontier resistance around the continent. As the attacks

[26] Altogether about 1 000 male Chinese indentured labourers were imported in the 50 years between 1847 and 1897, an average of 20 per year. See Atkinson, A. 1991. 'Chinese labour and capital in Western Australia, 1847–1947'. PhD dissertation, Murdoch University, 21. By 1848, a census listed 541 Aboriginal people as employed, in a colony in which the total population was only 4 622. Green, N. 1984. *Broken Spears: Aboriginals and Europeans in the Southwest of Australia.* Perth: Focus Education Services, 143.
[27] Hasluck P. 1970. *Black Australians: A Survey of Native Policy in Western Australia, 1829–1897.* Melbourne: Melbourne University Press, 83.
[28] Hetherington, *Settlers, Servants and Slaves*, 126.
[29] Hasluck, *Black Australians*, 83.
[30] Hasluck, *Black Australians*, 84.

on stock and settlers intensified, settler attitudes hardened, and police responded with punitive expeditions, a deliberate over-reaction designed to break Aboriginal resistance and quell any future attacks.[31]

The colonial government established an administrative system to contain Aboriginal resistance in this huge, scarcely settled colony. It appointed Government Residents to the newly settled districts. Far from the seat of government in Perth, these Residents had the power to appoint Justices of the Peace, preside over Petty and Quarter sessions, and generally attempt to maintain law and order.[32] The task of police was to arrest any suspected Aboriginal offender and bring those charged, chained together, along with witnesses, to the nearest centre for sentencing and punishment. Justices of the Peace could pass sentences on Aboriginal people charged with a crime. In times of major disturbance, the Resident could swear in special constables to arrest Aboriginal people on suspicion of having committed a crime, a practice that could lead to government authorisation of settler violence against Aboriginal resisters.[33]

Pearling and pastoralism

With the end of convict transportation in 1868 and the rapid growth of pastoralism and extractive industries such as mining and pearling in the newly settled northern districts, the demand for Aboriginal labour rapidly grew until it became essential. It was especially vital to the growing pearling industry. From its beginnings in 1867 off the Pilbara coast in the north-west, the pearling industry quickly took off, using Aboriginal divers. As Kay Forrest explains, while there were many Aboriginal people working on the pastoral stations, pearling was more labour intensive, needing a constant supply of new workers, especially given high death rates among divers.[34] Aboriginal labour in the pearling industry in its early years was both forced and ill treated. Pearlers often tricked many divers into believing they would be working in their own country when in fact they took them hundreds of miles away.[35] Pearlers were sometimes also pastoralists, able to take Aboriginal men, women and children from their pastoral stations

---

[31] See Forrest K. 1996. *The Challenge and the Chance: The Colonisation and Settlement of North West Australia 1861–1914.* Carlisle, WA: Hesperian Press, 58–60.

[32] Mann W. 1994. 'Sagacious seers and honourable men: pearling, Aboriginal labour and representations of Australian colonialism', in *Papers in Labour History*, 14, ed. J. Bailey, 57–74, esp. 59.

[33] Hasluck, *Black Australians*, 110–11.

[34] Forrest, *The Challenge*, 165.

[35] Forrest, *The Challenge*, 78ff.

and encourage or force them to work in pearling. When the pearling season ended, Aboriginal people could be employed on the stations. Frontier violence, labour exploitation and intense use of imprisonment could be intertwined, as occurred at Flying Foam Passage, in the pearling district on the North West coast, in 1868. The Yaburara people killed a police constable and two associates while rescuing a relative arrested and chained for stealing food in 1868. In response, the Government Resident, also a major pearling employer, organised a revenge attack using two parties of special constables, each led by a prominent local settler; the reprisal escalated into a massacre, killing up to 60 Yaburara.[36]

Stories circulated of forced labour and the physical abuse of labourers in pearling. In an attempt to control the industry, the colonial government under Governor Weld (1869–1875) passed a series of Acts, in 1871, 1873 and 1875, prohibiting kidnapping, or 'blackbirding', and the employment of women.[37] Some pearlers sought Malay labour in an attempt to avoid the 1871 legislation, and a few hundred workers from a range of Malay-speaking places to Australia's north did arrive from this time, reaching a peak in 1875 when pearlers introduced almost 800. Mistreatment of these workers led the Dutch administration in Batavia to regulate the trade, ending it abruptly the following year.[38] The government introduced a more stringent Act controlling Aboriginal labour in 1880, restricting the age of divers, reducing the legal diving depth, and requiring pearlers to return workers to their own country after six months' work. So great was the hostility of the pearlers to this legislation that Governor Robinson hastily amended it, allowing deeper diving depths and enabling the hiring of Aboriginal workers as domestic labourers in the off-season, rather than returning them to their country.[39] With their working conditions thus unprotected, Aboriginal labour remained essential to the industry for some years, the numbers employed reaching between 600 and 700 in 1886.[40] That proved, however, to be the peak year for reliance on Aboriginal labour. In the late 1880s, pearlers

---

[36] Mann, 'Sagacious seers', 60–61; Shepherd B. 2009. 'Pearling', in *Historical Encyclopedia of Western Australia*, eds J. Gregory & J. Gothard. Perth: University of Western Australia Press, 669; Forrest, *The Challenge*, 58–63; Hunt S.J. 1978. '"The Gribble Affair": a study of Aboriginal–European labour relations in North-West Australia during the 1880s'. Honours thesis, Murdoch University.

[37] Forrest, *The Challenge*, 80.

[38] McCarthy M. 1994. 'Before Broome'. *Great Circle*, 16, no. 2, 76–89. Available at http://search.informit.com.au.ezproxy1.library.usyd.edu.au/fullText;dn=950808138;res=APAFT, accessed 21 November 2012. See also Moore, R. 1994. 'The management of the Western Australian pearling industry, 1860 to the 1930s'. *Great Circle*, 16, no. 2, 127.

[39] Hunt, 'Gribble affair', 10–11.

[40] Hasluck, *Black Australians*, 31.

turned to importing a range of Asian, including Japanese, divers skilled in the dress diving techniques that were replacing swimming diving, though maintaining Aboriginal labour for deck duties.[41] Attempts by a succession of governors to prevent the abuse of Aboriginal labour were consistently undermined by the local power of pearlers, the interconnections between pearlers and magistrates, and the very long distances between the pearling sites and the seat of government in Perth.[42]

While the story of the use of Aboriginal labour in pearling is an especially brutal one, Aboriginal labour came to be used for pastoral purposes for a much longer period. After a series of explorations in the 1870s in search of new stock-farming opportunities, millions of hectares of pastoral land in the northern districts were opened for settlement in the 1880s. This period saw both the expansion of wool growing and the emergence of a cattle industry, with parties of overlanders driving cattle long distances from Queensland to stock the Kimberley pastoral stations. The growing northern economy now depended on Aboriginal labour.[43] Unlike pearling, there was no legislation specifically governing the employment of Aboriginal workers in the pastoral industry. The only source of regulation was through the Masters and Servants Acts governing both European and Aboriginal workers alike. The settlers did everything they could to force Aboriginal people to work and whipping or beating them for absconding from work was common.[44]

Whether under duress or not, large numbers of Aboriginal people were quickly drawn into pastoral work. On the sheep stations, Aboriginal women worked as shepherds and wool classers, while the men sheared the sheep, and managed the horses and drays used to transport the wool. On cattle stations, Aboriginal people worked in a wide variety of occupations from stockriders to station hands. Whereas pearling often involved the separation of individuals from their clan and country, this was less often the case in pastoralism, where it was to the settlers' advantage to keep

---

[41] Bach J. 1961. 'The political economy of pearlshelling'. *Economic History Review*, new series, 14, no. 1, 109.

[42] Western Australian numbered Acts: Aborigines, Employment in Pearling Act 1871 (34 Vict. No. 14); Pearl Shell Fishery Regulation Act 1873 (37 Vict. No. 11); Pearl Shell Fishery Regulation Act 1875 (39 Vict. No. 13). See Western Australian Legislative Council (hereafter WALC). *Votes and Proceedings* (hereafter V&P), 1881, A15, for Pearl Shell Fishery Regulations under 39 Vict. No. 13, 5; Hunt, S.J. 1986. *Spinifex and Hessian: Women's Lives in North West Australia, 1860–1900*. Perth: University of Western Australia Press, 103; Mann, 'Sagacious seers', 59.

[43] Forrest, *The Challenge*, 104.

[44] Green N. 1981. 'Aborigines and white settlers', in *A New History of Western Australia*, ed. C.T. Stannage. Perth: University of Western Australia Press, 108.

whole families and communities on their own land. Families lived on the stations, working for food and clothing rather than wages, making them extraordinarily cheap for the employer.[45] As pastoralists and Aboriginal workers got used to one another, some mutually beneficial work patterns evolved. The seasonal nature of pastoral work provided a space for some forms of Aboriginal cultural and physical survival. By moving between pastoral work in the on-season and hunting and gathering, or, as time went on, visiting mission stations and reserves in the off-season, Aboriginal stock workers and their families could maintain aspects of social and spiritual life even while working for pastoralists. To this extent, the coming of white settlement neither fully displaced nor replaced the indigenous people, though their world had changed dramatically, and they had lost most of their autonomy and control over their lives.

Above all, Aboriginal people now found themselves under constant police surveillance, a reminder that they now had new masters. The primary aim of this police presence was not to protect Aboriginal people from the extensive violence and abuse they were suffering at this time, but to prevent Aboriginal attacks on settlers and their stock. When the northern settlers complained of a wave of stock theft in 1882, Governor Robinson sent an investigator, Robert Fairbairn, Government Resident at Busselton in the south. To the settlers' chagrin, Fairbairn reported that the settlers themselves were to blame, since they allocated shepherding duties to unsupervised women, who turned a blind eye when their male relatives engaged in sheep stealing. He also pointed out that with native foods scarce, many Aboriginal people outside the pastoral stations were hungry, and that furthermore, many Aboriginal attacks were prompted by the white men's misuse of Aboriginal women.[46] The result of the inquiry was an increase in the presence of magistrates and police in the northern districts. This led, however, not to the greater protection of Aborigines, but rather to an increase in their harsh punishment. A number of gaols were built in the north, the largest at Roebourne in 1886, at times holding hundreds of prisoners.[47]

Police had the task of rounding up Aboriginal people for crimes such as killing stock or absconding from work, often forcing them to walk long distances to the nearest magistrate or gaol.[48] They often chained together

---

45   Forrest, *The Challenge*, 126.

46   National Archives of Great Britain, Records of the Colonial Office, Western Australia, Original Correspondence, Secretary of State, Despatches (hereafter CO), 18/197, 16 August 1882, R. Fairbairn to Governor Robinson.

47   Finnane & McGuire, 'The uses of punishment and exile', 286.

48   Hunt, *Spinifex and Hessian*, 12–30; see also Mann, 'Sagacious seers', 57–74.

those they had arrested, sometimes at the neck, a practice that was criticised by many but stubbornly maintained for decades.[49] When they came before a magistrate, Aboriginal stock-killers and absconders were dealt with harshly. The punishment for not working was severe, ranging from physical beatings to gaol sentences, in the early years to Rottnest Island, or later, as more gaols were built, closer to home. The magistrate in the Murchison and Gascoyne districts, Charles Foss, was especially draconian, one newspaper describing his approach as one of 'transporting the whole of the native inhabitants to Rottnest'.[50] Thus, the emphasis on arrest and imprisonment that had long characterised the Western Australian frontier was now essential to its labour regime and specifically to the task of forcing Aboriginal people to work for settlers.

Many observers were to comment in the next few decades that the practice of enforced labour meant that Aboriginal people were virtual slaves on their own land. Governor Robinson agreed in a dispatch to the Secretary of State in 1881 that recent government-commissioned reports had disclosed 'a state of things little short of slavery'.[51] When Frederick Napier Broome arrived as the new governor in June 1883, just as high levels of Aboriginal employment in the expanding pastoral industry in the north were taking off, he recognised the need for an overhaul of Aboriginal policy. In addition to clear evidence of abuse of indigenous labourers in the pastoral and pearling industries, he had a report from the Colonial Surgeon that the conditions for Aboriginal prisoners at Rottnest were appalling, leading to many deaths from influenza.[52] It was clear that the long-standing policy of arrest and imprisonment was proving to be a humanitarian disaster. Yet the problem facing Broome was that it would not be easy to have appropriate legislation passed in a council where the elected members were generally opposed to any idea of Aboriginal rights or protection. Since 1870, Western Australia had had a part-nominated, part-elected Legislative Council, in which pastoral interests were prominent, and Broome sought to work with, rather than against it as a prelude to the introduction of responsible government, which by this time was clearly on the horizon.

---

49   Lydon J. 2012. *The Flash of Recognition: Photography and the Emergence of Indigenous Rights*. Sydney: NewSouth, 38–55.

50   Forrest, *The Challenge*, 142.

51   WALC, Parliamentary Papers (hereafter PP), 1881, no. 13, 5. *Correspondence Relating to the Question of Police Protection to Settlers in Outlying Districts, Promulgation of Pearl Shell Fishery Regulations and Protection of the Aboriginal Natives*. Printed copy of Governor William C.F. Robinson to Sec. of State, 9 March 1881, no. 45.

52   *The Inquirer and Commercial News*, 27 June and 4 July 1883; WALC, PP, no. A11. *Report by the Colonial Surgeon on the Condition of the Sick Native Prisoners at Rottnest Prison*, 3 August 1883.

In the council's view, it was the settlers, and not the Aboriginal people, who deserved greater protection. When Broome introduced an Aboriginal Native Offenders Bill in August 1883 in an attempt to lessen the summary powers of magistrates to arrest and sentence Aboriginal offenders, he encountered a divided and largely hostile council.[53] In response, he appointed a committee, composed largely of pastoralists, to inquire into the treatment of Aboriginal people. The committee proved somewhat sympathetic to the idea of increased government control over the hiring of Aboriginal labour.[54] A year later, it recommended the establishment of an Aboriginal Protection Board and a system of local protectors. The committee's report noted that 'fifty years of settlement by Europeans has had the effect in the "Home District" of causing the gradual disappearance of the native race. We fear that this will continue ...' The report expressed a hope that this would not be the case in future, and that some means could yet be found to 'maintain, on the soil owned and trodden by their forefathers, the descendants of the Aboriginals of Australia'.[55]

Action on these recommendations, however, was forestalled by several crises engulfing the colony, one of which became known as 'the Gribble affair', in which the exploitation of Aboriginal labour was a key feature. When John Gribble took up his position as Church of England missionary in the Gascoyne in the northern districts in September 1885, he was shocked by what he saw.[56] He witnessed, he later wrote in his journal, prisoners in chains, young women treated as personal property and a highly coercive system of labour contract.[57] He began to speak out about these abuses and in response, impassioned meetings of settlers in Carnarvon denounced him. In January 1886, they circulated a petition to have him removed.

---

[53]   WALC, Parliamentary Debates (hereafter PD), Perth: Government Printer, 1883, 13 August, 207–17, especially 209.

[54]   Green N. 1998. 'From princes to paupers: the struggle for control of Aborigines in Western Australia 1887–1898'. *Early Days*, 11, pt. 4, 448. For announcement of Broome's intention to appoint an enquiry, see WALC, PP, no. 21, 1884. *Correspondence between the Excellency the Governor and the Right Honourable the Secretary of State for the Colonies.* Printed copy of Broome to Derby, 30 August 1883, no. 65, 8–9.

[55]   WALC, V&P, 1884. *Report of a Commission appointed by his Excellency the Governor to Inquire into the Treatment of Aboriginal Native Prisoners of the Crown in this Colony: And Also into Certain Other Matters Relative to Aboriginal Natives.* Perth: Government Printer, 9. Available at http://www.nla.gov.au/apps/cdview/?pi=nla.aus-vn1057351-5x-s9-e, accessed 21 January 2013.

[56]   See Hunt S.J. 1987. 'The Gribble affair: a study in colonial politics', appendix to J.B. Gribble, [1886] *Dark Deeds in a Sunny Land.* Perth: University of Western Australia Press, first published in Reece, B. & Stannage, T. eds. 1984. *Colonial Politics in European-Aboriginal Relations in Western Australian History.* Perth: University of Western Australia Press. See also Reynolds, R. 1998. *This Whispering in Our Hearts.* Sydney: Allen & Unwin, ch. 7.

[57]   Green, 'From princes to paupers', 448.

Gribble counter-attacked by publishing his diary, detailing the abuses, in two Perth newspapers, one the liberal *Inquirer* and the other the conservative *West Australian*.[58] His reports provoked such a storm that the Church of England's Mission Committee, anxious about the isolation of the church from the community and the loss of wealthy patrons, who were supporting the building of a cathedral in Perth, turned against him and later closed the mission. Not a man to take a step backwards, Gribble then wrote to the Aborigines Protection Society in London informing them of what he had observed, and published his diary as a slim booklet, *Dark Deeds in a Sunny Land*, plus two long articles in the Melbourne *Daily Telegraph*.[59] His reports of extensive abuses aroused angry public debate, with many settlers, members of the Legislative Council and newspapers in Western Australia denying them outright. The honour of the colony, they said, one after another, was at stake. They were furious that Gribble had, as one MLC put it, 'traduced and maligned the settlers of Western Australia in the eyes of the world'.[60]

Gribble's claims, however, deeply concerned Broome, since some other reports he and his predecessor had received over the years supported them. In particular, David Carley, a resident in the area, had reported to the resident magistrate in Roebourne and others his observation of continued acts of cruelty in the pearling industry.[61] Now Gribble was insisting that the abuses were not confined to pearling, but involved pastoralism as well. Broome, who by this time had made close friendships with many of the northern pastoralists, instituted a survey of resident magistrates in the colony to investigate the veracity of Gribble's claims. To his consternation, one Government Resident, Colonel Angelo at Roebourne, described the employment of Aboriginal labour in the district as 'a disguised but unquestionable system of slavery'.[62] In addition, a pastoralist, David Forrest, wrote to Broome describing both the kidnapping of young

---

58   Hunt, 'Gribble affair', 65–66.

59   Gribble, *Dark Deeds in a Sunny Land*; Hunt, 'Gribble affair', 65–66; Reynolds, *This Whispering*, 152. Gribble, however, was to be punished for daring to criticise the treatment of Aboriginal people, not only in the colony, but outside it as well. When the *West Australian* in August 1886 accused Gribble of being 'a lying canting humbug', he brought a libel suit against the editors. The case, heard in May and June the following year, was a sensation, but Gribble lost the case, and left Western Australia forever. See Hunt, 'Gribble affair', 67–72.

60   Charles Crowther, speech in debate in Legislative Council on 1 September 1886, reported in the *West Australian*, 3 September 1886, 3.

61   Reynolds, *This Whispering*, 162–73.

62   State Records Office of Western Australia (hereafter SROWA), Acc. 391. Governors' confidential dispatches, Colonel Angelo to Broome, 10 April 1886. Quoted by Green, 'From princes to paupers', 449. See also Reynolds, 'This whispering', 159–73.

Aboriginal men to work on the pearling luggers and the system of forced labour on pastoral stations.[63] Broome was also receiving inquiries from the Colonial Office in London, itself pressed on the issue by the London-based Aborigines Protection Society.[64] Gribble's claims were being well publicised internationally—the *New York Times*, for example, carried a story headed 'Slavery in Western Australia' on 19 September 1886.

In response to Colonial Office pressures, Broome at last acted on the recommendations of the Committee of Inquiry he had instigated two years earlier, and introduced an Aborigines Protection Bill. It enabled the establishment of the Aborigines Protection Board and a new system of protectors, along the lines proposed by the committee, and furthermore dealt with the vexed question of labour contracts. After expressing considerable opposition and watering down its provisions as they related to protection of Aboriginal labour, the Legislative Council, perhaps conscious of Colonial Office pressure, passed the bill.[65] Yet 'protection' seems hardly the correct description, as the new Act in fact promised a regime of closer surveillance of Aboriginal people than ever before. It provided for a system of contracts between pastoral employers and their Aboriginal workers over the age of 14, and provided that only written contracts would have any force or validity. Contracts did not involve wage payment, but were to stipulate the supply of food, clothing, blankets and medical assistance. There were also provisions for a system of apprenticing Aboriginal children, a system which historian Pen Hetherington has described as 'a system of slavery that removed parents' control over their children and placed it in the hands of the pastoralists'.[66]

Before the new system envisaged in the Act could be put in place, reports of abuses continued to reach the governor. In December 1886, Robert Fairbairn was back in Roebourne undertaking yet another inquiry, this time interviewing Aboriginal informants as well as settlers. A man named Weribine told him of the cruelties of Sam McKay as a pearling master. McKay was also a pastoralist, professing to employ four hundred men on Mundabullangana, a huge sheep station, with a reputation for

63 SROWA, Colonial Secretary's Records, 3230/86, D. Forrest to Broome, 31 July 1886, quoted by Green, 'From princes to paupers', 449.

64 Reynolds, *This Whispering*, 170.

65 Legislative Council of Western Australia. 1886. Parliamentary debates, 19 and 30 August, reported in *The West Australian*, 21 August 1886 and 1 September 1886. For further discussion of the relationship between Aboriginal policy matters and the granting of responsible government to Western Australia, see Curthoys A. & Martens J. 2013. 'Serious collisions: settlers, indigenous people, and imperial policy in Western Australia and Natal'. *Journal of Australian Colonial History*, 15.

66 Hetherington, *Settlers, Servants, Slaves*, 155.

extremely harsh treatment of Aboriginal workers.[67] Kay Forrest describes as one example of settler–Aboriginal relations at this time the case of the Bresnahans, pastoralist owners of Ashburton Downs in the Pilbara. The Bresnahan brothers, she writes, 'took a hard stand against the Aboriginals. They rounded them up, forced them to work and flogged them for disobedience and absconding ... in their stock camps they had no blankets and rode naked ... [they] suppressed any trouble with brutality and contempt'.[68]

The treatment of Aboriginal people had by this time become such a live issue that it affected the framing of the new Western Australian constitution that would usher in responsible government. Anxious not to hand control of Aboriginal policy to settlers, the Colonial Office adopted Broome's suggestion that Britain keep control of the recently created Aborigines Protection Board to itself, via the governor, rather than handing it over to the new local legislature. Accordingly, the constitution, which came into effect in 1890, specified in a clause known as Section 70 that the board would be funded by an annual grant of £5000 which was to convert to one per cent of the colony's annual revenue when it exceeded £500000.[69] Leading settler politicians such as John Forrest did not want this kind of imperial oversight of Aboriginal affairs, and regarded Section 70 as a vote of no confidence in their ability to govern responsibly, and a slur on the honour of the colony. They reluctantly agreed to the clause, however, so that they could obtain responsible government, perhaps hoping to have it removed later—which they did in 1897. When Broome's term as governor ended and William Robinson returned for his third term in October 1890, the latter encountered a new situation. Now his powers as governor were far outweighed by those of the elected legislature, which was profoundly anti-Aboriginal.

The newly responsible settler government might have expected Aboriginal questions to subside, after the intense conflicts over labour management and general treatment that had prevailed in the 1870s and 1880s. It could, perhaps, leave the question to the Aborigines Protection Board, for which it was not responsible. It was not, however, to be. Conflicts between pastoralists and Aborigines in the Kimberley area, which had been evident from the mid-1880s, intensified as pastoral expansion continued

---

67 Forrest, *The Challenge*, 197; Hunt, 'Gribble affair', 91–92.
68 Forrest, *The Challenge*, 204.
69 WALC, PP, 1889. *Correspondence Respecting the Proposed Introduction of Responsible Government in Western Australia*, 36. Copy of Broome to Knutsford, 28 May 1888. Here it was called Section 52. It became Section 58 in a later draft and Section 70 in the Act.

and farmers consolidated their hold on the land. Attacks on stock increased, conflicts over the seizure of women escalated, and the police presence in the area was expanded.[70] The colonial government, now headed by John Forrest, responded with a massive police operation, and in reaction to press calls for harsher treatment of Aboriginal offenders, reintroduced in 1892 legislation sanctioning flogging of Aboriginal people, which Broome had abolished in 1883.[71] As Mark Finnane and John McGuire show, the use of corporal punishment at a time when it was generally rejected as inhumane and not formally practised or sanctioned in other Australian colonies, was a direct response to heightened Aboriginal resistance.[72] In the far north, the Banuba, led by Ellemarra, a stockman and one time police tracker, stepped up their attacks on white settlers and their property. Ellemarra's nephew, Jandamarra, for some years worked with the police, but made a dramatic defection in 1894, leading an attack on police that resulted in large scale revenge attacks and a manhunt that lasted two and a half years. Violent conflict between Aboriginal people and police continued in the Kimberley area until the 1920s. The historian of these events, Howard Pederson, estimates that between 1883 and 1926 about 40 Europeans and hundreds of Aboriginal people were killed 'on the unrecorded battlefields of the Kimberley region'.[73]

The exploitation of Aboriginal labour continued after the colony of Western Australia became a state within the new Australian nation in 1901. With the population growing fast under the impact of increased migration from other colonies and Britain as gold rushes stimulated the local economy, the political complexion of the parliament began to change. To the consternation of pastoralists in the north, middle-class liberals and working class trade unionists combined forces in the Legislative Assembly to establish, in 1904, a Royal Commission to Enquire into and Report upon the Administration of the Aborigines Department and the Condition of the Natives. As Anna Haebich argues, there was a mixture of motives here, with trade unionists wishing to protect white labour, some humanitarians shocked at the mistreatment of Aboriginal workers on pastoral stations and liberals seeking to displace the conservative establishment.[74] The inquiry became known as the Roth Royal Commission after its chair, Walter

---

[70]   Forrest, *The Challenge*, 204–05.
[71]   Forrest, *The Challenge*, 208.
[72]   Finnane & McGuire, 'The uses of punishment and exile', 284–85.
[73]   Pederson H. 2009. 'Frontier violence, Kimberley', in *Historical Encyclopedia*, eds J. Gregory & J. Gothard, 394–95.
[74]   Haebich A. 1988. *For their Own Good: Aborigines and Government in the Southwest of Western Australia, 1900–1940*. Perth: University of Western Australia Press, 71.

Roth, whom the new state government brought in from Queensland as an outsider and because of his experience in Aboriginal administration. His report found that the kind of abuses of which Gribble had complained in 1885 were still very much in evidence. Roth was highly critical of coercive and unfair labour practices and the role of the police in enforcing them, and recommended both a minimum wage for Aboriginal workers and major police reform.[75] Debates over frontier violence and the treatment of Aboriginal workers continued well into the twentieth century.

Western Australia: A case of genocide?

In pondering the effects of the employment of hunter-gatherer peoples on the genocidal processes involved in settler colonialism, one is inevitably drawn into the long-running debate over whether the labour system in Western Australia was a form of, or resembled, slavery. This debate began in the 1870s with the settlement of the north and the growing use of Aboriginal labour in the pearling and pastoral industries, and as noted above, colonial officials thought it to be either a form of slavery or something very like it. As we have seen, Governor Robinson in 1881 said his investigation of claims of forced labour and abuse had disclosed 'a state of things little short of slavery'.[76] Five years later, the charge of slavery was central to the Reverend Gribble's indictment of the forced labour and treatment of Aboriginal people in Western Australia. In his history of the Native Police, published in 1890, English journalist and traveller Arthur Vogan had represented the pastoral industry across the north of the country, including Western Australia, as dependent on slavery. The treatment of both adults and children as workers was similar, he wrote, to that evoked by Harriet Beecher Stowe in her famous novel, *Uncle Tom's Cabin*.[77] The charge of slavery, and more generally of forced labour and abuse, was important in the investigations of the 1905 Roth Commission.[78]

---

[75] Haebich, *For their Own Good*, 71, 77.

[76] WALC, PP, 1881, no. 13, 5. *Correspondence Relating to the Question of Police Protection to Settlers in Outlying Districts, Promulgation of Pearl Shell Fishery Regulations and Protection of the Aboriginal Natives.* Copy of Governor William C.F. Robinson to Sec. of State, 9 March 1881, no. 45.

[77] Vogan A. 2011. *The Black Police: A Story of Modern Australia.* London: British Library Historical Print Editions, 219. See the discussion of this text in Evans R. 1999. 'Kings in brass crescents: defining Aboriginal labour patterns in colonial Queensland', in his essay collection, *Fighting Words: Writing about Race.* Brisbane: University of Queensland Press, originally published as a chapter in Saunders, K. ed. 1983. *Indentured Labour in the British Empire, 1834–1920.* London: Croom Helm, 181. See also Holland A. 1995. 'Feminism, colonialism and Aboriginal workers: an anti-slavery crusade', *Labour History*, 69, 52–64.

[78] Haebich, *For their Own Good*, 71, 77.

The issue of slavery in Western Australia and the Northern Territory gained new purchase in the 1920s and 1930s in the context of the League of Nations, in which Australian feminist campaigners were active, hoping to use external pressure to bring about change in Australia's Aboriginal policies.[79] Women's organisations took these claims to the British Commonwealth League, and in the early 1930s some newspapers, notably the *Manchester Guardian*, took up the cause. The charges of slavery related especially to the sexual abuse of Aboriginal women and girls.[80] In 1932, anthropologist Ralph Piddington drew attention to the situation after two years of fieldwork in Western Australia, and in this the humanitarian campaigner Mary Bennett supported him the following year.[81]

In recent times, historians have again considered the charge of slavery in relation to Australia, particularly Queensland and Western Australia. Feminist historians Fiona Paisley, Alison Holland, and Marilyn Lake have taken up the story of the feminist anti-slavery campaigns of the middle decades of the twentieth century.[82] In a major essay published in 1983, Raymond Evans argued that the condition of Aboriginal workers on cattle stations in Queensland was indeed a form of slavery.[83] Shirleene Robinson's study of Aboriginal child workers in Queensland also describes their situation, to quote the title of her book, as 'something like slavery'. 'If slavery is seen to exist when an employer holds a grossly exaggerated degree of power and domination over an employee', she concludes, 'then there can be no doubt that Aboriginal children occupied positions that were analogous to a slave'.[84] Other historians have resisted the description of the labour system as one of slavery. Henry Reynolds does not describe the system of labour relations in northern Australia in the nineteenth century as one of slavery, though he does stress the prevalence of recruitment by force, the belief by many pastoralists that they owned their workers, the separation of children from their parents and the overall brutality of the system.[85]

---

79 Holland, 'Feminism, colonialism and Aboriginal workers', 62; Paisley F. 2000. *Loving Protection? Australian Feminism and Aboriginal Women's Rights 1919–1939*. Melbourne: Melbourne University Press, 112–13.

80 Paisley, *Loving Protection?*, 113.

81 Paisley, *Loving Protection?*, 31, 58; Gray G. 2007. *A Cautious Silence: The Politics of Australian Anthropology*. Canberra: Aboriginal Studies Press, 102–08.

82 Paisley, *Loving Protection?*; Holland, 'Feminism, colonialism and Aboriginal workers'; and Lake M. 1993. 'Colonised and colonising: the white Australian feminist subject'. *Women's History Review*, 2, no. 3, 377–86.

83 Evans, 'Kings in brass crescents', 180–200.

84 Robinson S. 2008. *Something Like Slavery? Queensland's Aboriginal Child Workers, 1842–1945*, Melbourne: Australian Scholarly Publishing, 264.

85 Reynolds H. 1990. *With the White People: The Crucial Role of Aborigines in the Exploration and Development of Australia*. Ringwood: Penguin, see esp. 216–17.

Writing of the Northern Territory for a later period, Ann McGrath in her book, *Born in the Cattle*, also opposes the notion that the system was one of slavery. While describing the prevailing harsh labour relations, she also emphasises the ways in which Aboriginal workers could use the situation to their own advantage, primarily through being able to move between periods of work and times when they were free to visit family, conduct ceremonies and maintain connections with country.[86]

It is interesting that a number of historians have concluded that the system of labour relations was 'akin to slavery' or 'something like slavery', just as colonial administrators did at the time. Thalia Anthony offers an alternative characterisation, suggesting that 'the pastoralists' jurisdiction [over Aboriginal people] represented a repository of feudal power'.[87] As she goes on to explain, the term 'feudal' best encapsulates the relation between the landed and the landless, controlled by the landowner, and in which the landless are answerable to the landed proprietor rather than the state, which largely complies with decentralised power in the hands of pastoralists. She also suggests that the system was much harsher in its early decades than later, thus accounting for some of the disagreements among historians. For the purposes of this essay, the question to be considered is not so much whether the system is best described as slavery or feudalism or something else—suffice it to say it was forced labour conducted often under very harsh conditions—as one of how this system of labour relations modified the process of dispossession and its corollary, genocide. In Kuper's terms, was the 'impulse to genocide' given the free reign he suggests is typical of the colonisation of hunter-gatherer societies, or was it significantly restrained by the need to maintain the labour supply?

The case of Western Australia suggests that the use of indigenous labour can have various effects; it neither *necessarily* prevents nor contributes to genocidal processes. It depends how the labour is recruited and treated, and what connections to traditional land and family it permits. The case of pearling, for example, seems much closer than pastoralism does to the story of the San as outlined by Mohamed Adhikari. In pearling, we see many of the practices Adhikari describes—kidnapping, a focus on child labour, moving people away from their clans and country, brutality and death. Pearling

---

[86] McGrath A. 1987. *Born in the Cattle: Aborigines in Cattle Country*. Sydney: Allen & Unwin, 147.

[87] Anthony T. 2007. 'Criminal justice and transgression on northern Australian cattle stations', in *Transgressions: Critical Australian Indigenous Histories*, eds I. McFarlane & M. Hannah. Canberra: ANU Press, 35; Antony T. 2004. 'Labour relations on northern cattle stations: feudal exploitation and accommodation'. *The Drawing Board: An Australian Review of Public Affairs*, 4, no. 3, 117–36.

helped destroy certain groups and their relation to country. The Flying Foam Massacre and its aftermath, for example, meant the near-destruction of a group, the Jaburara, which produced the rock art on Murujuga, now one of the most famous rock art collections in the world. Thus in pearling we witness two of the key elements of genocide as outlined by Lemkin: the destruction of emotional and family ties, including the taking of children, and the loss of cultural knowledge of value to humanity as a whole.[88]

When we turn to pastoralism, however, the story is a little different. Pastoralism relied on a powerful mix of dispossession and forced labour. Mary Bennett, a leader of the interwar feminist campaign for Aboriginal rights mentioned above, analysed this connection insightfully in her influential book, *The Australian Aboriginal as a Human Being* (1930), in her submissions to a Royal Commission on Aboriginal treatment in 1934, and in letters to newspapers. As Alison Holland points out, Bennett argues that the deprivation of Aboriginal people's hunting grounds forced them to accept unequal labour contracts on the settlers' terms,[89] and she supported the argument of the British government's East Africa Commission that forced labour could be prevented if native peoples had secure possession of their land.[90] Decades later, Raymond Evans offered a similar argument in his 1983 essay, when he said the excessive force and compulsion used by employers of Aboriginal labour in Queensland 'was grounded, literally, on the incomers' "greed of country" and the massive displacement or annihilation of that country's inhabitants which occurred as a result'.[91]

Nevertheless, pastoralism relied much less than pearling on practices such as kidnapping and separation of individuals from their kin. In pastoralism, the people were not so much driven off their lands, though some were, as forced to live upon it in a manner that undermined their sovereignty and autonomy. Pastoral employment involved forced labour and significant amounts of ill treatment, but it did not generally involve the same systematic separation of workers from their families and tribal groups. The seasonal nature of pastoral work also provided a space for some forms of cultural and physical survival. In the words of Mary Ann Jebb, writing of the Kimberley in a later period, although the pastoral system forced serious changes in social relations, it also 'encouraged Aboriginal people to live on or near their

---

[88] See Curthoys A. & Docker, J. 2008. 'Defining genocide', in *The Historiography of Genocide*, ed. D. Stone. Houndmills: Palgrave Macmillan, 10–13.
[89] Holland, 'Feminism, colonialism and Aboriginal workers', 57.
[90] Bennett M.M. 1930. *The Australian Aboriginal as a Human Being*. London: Alston Rivers Ltd, 137, quoted in Holland, 'Feminism, colonialism and Aboriginal workers', 59.
[91] Evans, 'Kings in brass crescents', 184.

own land, and supported a range of cultural continuities'.[92] It was a system that people could survive with some elements of culture and group life, if not intact, at least recognisable, valued and able to be transmitted to future generations.

To this extent, the British colonisation of Western Australia did not fully displace nor replace indigenous people. In the intensively settled agricultural and urban areas in the south-west of the huge colony, they suffered the substantial population decline and social destruction seen elsewhere on the continent. In the north, where their labour was valued and non-indigenous settlement sparse, the project of displacing and replacing them was far more complex. The task for the historian is to describe and explain this particular history in a way that captures both its genocidal character and the countervailing processes that made this particular genocidal situation both tragic and incomplete.

---

[92]   Jebb M.A. 2002. *Blood, Sweat and Welfare: A History of White Bosses and Aboriginal Pastoral Workers*. Perth: University of Western Australia Press, 297.

Chapter Ten

'A Fierce and Irresistible Cavalry': Pastoralists, Homesteaders and Hunters on the American Plains Frontier[1]

Tony Barta
La Trobe University

I have heard that you want to settle us on a reservation near the mountains. I don't want to settle. I want to roam over the prairies. There I feel free and happy, but when we settle down we grow pale and die ... These soldiers cut down my timber; they kill my buffalo; and when I see that, my heart feels like bursting ... Has the white man become a child that he should recklessly kill and not eat? When the red men slay game, they do so that they may live and not starve.

Satanta, Chief of the Kiowas, 1874[2]

They are the greatest grasslands in the world.[3] We all know them, in legend at least. If there is one place where the encounter between indigenous hunters and immigrant pastoralists has played out in popular consciousness round the world, it is on the Great Plains of the American West. The theatre could not have been grander. Once they crossed the Mississippi, the white men were confronted by teeming hordes of buffalo and small bands of Native Americans whose lives were sustained by them. Within decades, the buffalo were gone and the pastoralists, the cattle kings, reigned unchallenged. The Kiowa, and other peoples of the plains, did have to settle, defeated, on reservations. In battle it was the mounted soldiers of the United States who prevailed, backed by superior firepower, numbers and manufactured resources. The cattle drovers and not the Native Americans now roamed the prairies. Even before all the West was won by white settlers, indigenous survivors had to accept food handouts and teach their families merely to exist where they could no longer live. Those who did not grow pale and die, learned a new way of being: precarious survival in an alienated world.

[1] My thanks to Mohamed Adhikari, John Cashmere, Sid Harring, Jeff Ostler and John Salmond for most generous assistance in the research and writing of this chapter.
[2] Brown D. 2009. *Bury My Heart at Wounded Knee*. New York: Sterling, 273; first published New York: Holt, Rinehart & Winston, 1970.
[3] Flannery T. 2001. *The Eternal Frontier: An Ecological History of North America and Its Peoples*. Melbourne: Text, 226.

The conquering horse soldiers after the Civil War had a grim job to complete. But they came late to the fray. In the British parliament a century earlier, Edmund Burke invoked a 'fierce and irresistible cavalry'—less martial, more permanent and more damaging. They were the enterprising citizens of the original American colonies who were clamouring for more land. The government in London had good reasons for keeping control of a more compact territory and avoiding conflict with the other established North American power, France, to deny the expansionist drive. There would be no new grants of land. This 'hoarding of a royal wilderness' was hopeless, Burke declaimed:

> *If you stopped your grants, what would be the consequence? The people would occupy without grants. They have already so occupied in many places. You cannot station garrisons in every part of these deserts. If you drive the people from one place, they will carry on their annual tillage and remove with their flocks and herds to another. Many of the people in the back settlements are already little attached to particular situations. Already they have topped the Appalachian Mountains. From thence they behold before them an immense plain, one vast, rich, level meadow: a square of five hundred miles. Over this they would wander without a possibility of restraint; they would change their manners with their habits of life; would soon forget a government by which they were disowned; would become hordes of English Tartars; and, pouring down upon your unfortified frontiers a fierce and irresistible cavalry, become masters of your governors and your counsellors, your collectors and comptrollers, and of all the slaves that adhered to them. Such would, and, in no long time, must be, the effect of attempting to forbid as a crime, and to suppress as an evil, the command and blessing of Providence, "Increase and multiply." Such would be the happy result of an endeavour to keep as a lair of wild beasts that earth which God, by an express charter, has given to the children of men.*[4]

Everywhere in the world colonised by British settlers, land reserved for the indigenous owners was regarded as no better than an unproductive lair of wild beasts. Always, by God's express charter, it must be ceded to those who would increase and multiply. Even those newcomers who did not behave as hordes of English Tartars, who thought they were simply pasturing their livestock, had no doubt about their right to make better use of the land. There are reasons to consider this tidal movement of humans and animals onto the Great Plains as a genocidal one, destroying whole peoples as it destroyed the sustaining staples of their lives. But was it the pastoralists who

---

[4] Edmund Burke, a parliamentary activist as much as a theorist, had much to say on American politics. This speech, moving his resolutions for conciliation with the colonies, delivered on 22 March 1775, is available online at http://www.gutenberg.org/files/15198/15198-h/15198-h.htm. See Burke E. 1837. *The Works of the Right Honourable Edmund Burke*, vol II. London: John C. Nimmo, 132. The passage is quoted by Frederick Jackson Turner in his famous 1893 essay, 'The frontier in American history'.

brought destruction to Native American nations, many themselves newly settled on lands that had belonged to others, or was it the much larger horde of Euro-Americans who followed them? What impelled settlers intent on making a new west of farms with fences, to supersede the grazing era of open commons on the range? If we focus on one sector of the frontier, the area north of Texas officially named 'Indian Territory' to receive the forced removals from the east, the answers will become clear.

Ideology, dispossession, destruction

That North America was colonised by settlers who defined status by property had consequences that were disastrous for indigenous peoples. It is not too much to say—and many would say it, centuries before the word was invented—that genocide occurred because of the English passion for property. Ben Kiernan has retold the story in a larger context, linking agriculture to genocide through the ages.[5] It was tilling the soil that for Locke and his followers justified the dispossession of those who added no labour to the ground they had inherited.[6] Enclosing it with fences demonstrated responsibility and the right to all produce. Purposeful grazing was also invoked. 'When the English first arrived in New England', writes Jill Lepore, 'they found the land to be "spacious and void", a place where the Indians "do but run over the grass, as do the foxes and wild beasts"'. Lepore cites several other observations of the same kind, most influentially those of John Winthrop and Thomas More. Winthrop argued that New England was a *vacuum domicilium*, without evidence of true Indian ownership, 'for they inclose no ground, neither have cattell to maintayne it, but remove their dwellings as they have occasion'.[7] Nomads could expect no mercy from More's Utopians: 'They consider it a most just cause for war when a people which does not use its soil but keeps it idle and waste nevertheless forbids

---

5   Kiernan B. 2007. *Blood and Soil: A World History of Genocide and Extermination from Sparta to Dafur*. New Haven and London: Yale University Press; Cave A. 2008. 'Genocide in the Americas', in *The Historiography of Genocide*, ed. D. Stone. Houndsmills: Palgrave Macmillan, 273–295, provides a compact guide.

6   Locke J. 1984. *Two Treatises on Civil Government*. London: Routledge, first published London: Awnsham Churchill, 1689; Michael McDonnell and Dirk Moses note Locke's injunction to kill savages that threatened a just seizure of their lands and its influence on the originator of genocide studies in 2005. See 'Raphael Lemkin as historian of genocide in the Americas'. *Journal of Genocide Research*, 7, no. 4, 501–29; Arneil B. 1996. *John Locke and America: The Defence of English Colonialism*. Oxford: Clarendon Press.

7   Lepore J. 1998. *The Name of War: King Philip's War and the Origins of American Identity*. New York: Random House, 276. That Native Americans did indeed move their dwellings, and themselves colonised the lands of others, played no small role in the territorial claims and removals later to embroil them.

the use and possession of it to others who by the rule of nature ought to be maintained by it'.[8] Here is the nub of conflict. The Native Americans had always lived with the land as a part of nature. For the colonisers, nature belonged to whoever had the labour, capital and force to appropriate it.

Ronald Wright devotes a chapter to showing that Native Americans were not only hunters and gatherers. He titles it, after Ralph Lane's report to Hakluyt, 'Very well peopled and towned'. The first European visitors to North America knew that land was systematically worked and that agriculture supported impressive cities. Cartier described Stadacona (later Quebec) and Hochelanga (later Montreal) as fortified with a grid plan of houses around a central square. Their inhabitants numbered in the thousands. By 1600 they were gone. To the south, De Soto saw even larger centres of civilisation, supported by great fields of corn. Indigenous settlements with their maize economies were everywhere in possession of the eastern coast before the Europeans planted their colonies. And, as children are taught in schools across the United States, the first settlers would all have been extinguished had Native Americans not rescued them.[9]

The First Americans were repaid not only with relentless ideological hostility and suspicion. They were actively eradicated through violence and introduced diseases to which they had no immunity. Already subject to their own illnesses and hardships, a more catastrophic depopulation arrived with virgin soil epidemics brought by colonists. Russell Thornton takes care not to make infection deliberate, or uniformly disastrous. The Cherokee, notably, were able to recover from a loss as great as 50 per cent so that over the eighteenth century their decrease was less than 25 per cent. Critical were the different ways populations suffered social and economic disorganisation following an epidemic.[10]

A colonial foothold, and indeed capitalist enterprise, might not necessarily involve conflict with indigenous owners of the land. The Dutch hoped to demonstrate that on Manhattan Island. But expansion into hunting lands did.[11] De Tocqueville, who noted that the French were well regarded because they had traded without appropriating land, observed the second wave of

---

8   Lepore, *Name of War*, 77.
9   Wright R. 2008. *What is America?* Melbourne: Text, 46–60.
10   Thornton R. 2000. 'Population history of native North Americans', in *A Population History of North America*, eds M.R. Haines & R.H. Steckel. New York: Cambridge University Press, 13–22. Thornton estimates that there were more than seven million native North Americans at the start of colonisation, with a nadir of about 375 000 in 1900. Perdue and Green, using the 1890 census, estimate the figure to be about 250 000. Perdue T. & Green M. 2010. *North American Indians*. New York: Oxford University Press, 16.
11   Merwick D. 2006. *The Shame and the Sorrow: Dutch-Amerindian Encounters in New Netherland*. Philadelphia: University of Pennsylvania Press.

dispossession, east of the Mississippi, and testified to its dark realities. Most of the natives around the towns were drunk, often lying in the road, and settlers were not disposed to offer aid; 'one could read on their lips this half-expressed thought: "What is the life of an Indian?"'

> *The Americans of the United States do not let their dogs hunt the Indians as do the Spaniards of Mexico, but at bottom it is the same pitiless feeling which here, as everywhere, animates the European race. This world belongs to us, they tell themselves every day: the Indian race is destined for final destruction which one cannot prevent and which it is not desirable to delay. Heaven has not made them to become civilized: it is necessary that they die. Besides I do not at all want to get mixed up in it. I will limit myself to providing everything that will hasten their ruin. In time I will have their lands and be innocent of their death.*[12]

The 26-year-old De Tocqueville encountered his first derelict, dispossessed Indian in upstate New York, and pursued questions of their future when he travelled by riverboat towards the South. The great issue was Jackson's clearing of the famously civilised native peoples from the eastern states into a newly proclaimed 'Indian Territory' where they were to be guaranteed perpetual safety from European greed for land. He met one experienced frontiersman who was optimistic about the Indians, much too optimistic given the restless and ruthless land hunger pressing on them. This was a Mr Houston who had been governor of Tennessee but then withdrew, after family troubles, it was said, to live among the Creeks and marry the daughter of a chief. Houston arrived on a white charger to catch the boat to New Orleans. De Tocqueville was impressed: 'everything about him indicates physical and moral energy'. He could not then know, nor could Sam Houston, that he was to be the founding hero of Texas. He did not, however, convince the shrewd young Frenchman that Congress was acting in the Indians' best interests, or that the vast tract could be kept free from squatter incursion. 'The United States have bound themselves by the most solemn oaths never to sell the lands contained within those limits,' insisted Houston, 'and never in any form to allow the introduction of a white population there.'

What De Tocqueville witnessed, with continuing scepticism about the future, was the result of the first great push out of the original colonies. Though Andrew Jackson, among the early presidents, bears the opprobrium for the removal of the Cherokee along the Trail of Tears, the policy had been

---

[12] De Tocqueville A. 1959. *Journey to America*, trans. by G. Lawrence, ed. J.P. Mayer. New Haven and London: Yale University Press, 198-99. For persistence of the attitudes recorded by De Tocqueville, and problems of recognising genocidal intention, see Ostler J. 2008. 'The question of genocide in US history', in *Genocide, 2*, ed. A. Jones. London: Sage, 115–26.

incubating in colonial times and reached an unstoppable crescendo in the very first years of the United States. Thomas Jefferson, the iconic founding father, believed that all men were created equal, and equally that the less progressive humans, while they remained savages, must cede their ground to the more civilised. And woe to those who resisted progress by taking up arms: recalcitrant native peoples would face extermination. If the Seneca and the Cherokee failed to cease their attacks and remove themselves to the other side of the Mississippi, 'we should never cease pursuing them with war while one remained on the face of the earth'.[13]

The positive message Jefferson developed, even before independence, was that Indians needed to become farmers. When they embraced European rural productivity, they would be allowed to join his ideal Commonwealth of independent freeholders. The choice, as he saw it, was scarcely voluntary. It was their only hope of survival. Significantly, he enjoined pastoralism as well as agriculture. His *Notes on Virginia* observed that hunting and gathering could barely sustain a viable population. 'No wonder, then, if they multiply less than we do. Where food is regularly supplied, a single farm will show more of cattle, than a whole country of forests can of buffaloes.'[14] As president, he pursued the theme at every opportunity. His first Annual Message to Congress in 1801 proclaimed that the very opposite of genocide was happening as Indians gave up 'the precarious resources of hunting and fishing; and that already we are able to announce, that instead of the constant diminution of their numbers, produced by their wars and their wants, some of them begin to experience an increase in population'. In an address directly to Native American representatives, he reiterated: 'We shall, with great pleasure, see your people become disposed to cultivate the earth, to raise herds of the useful animals, and to spin and weave, for their food and clothing. ... These resources are certain; they will never disappoint you: while those of hunting may fail, and expose your women and children to the miseries of hunger and cold'.[15]

Pastoralism did not drive the land speculation with which Thomas Jefferson, George Washington, Patrick Henry and other founding fathers pushed out the western frontier. Land in urgent demand was for plantation agriculture, not grazing. It was the voracious tobacco plant that exhausted

---

[13]   Kiernan, *Blood and Soil*, 319–20 quotes letters written by Jefferson on 5 and 13 August 1776.

[14]   Koch A. & Peden W. eds. 1944. *The Life and Selected Writings of Thomas Jefferson*. New York: Random House, 212.

[15]   Jefferson T. 'Address to brothers and friends of the Miamis, Powtewatamies and Weeauks, Washington, 7 January 1802', in Koch and Peden, *Life and Writings*, 333.

even the best soil within four years: the weed that became a crop burst the bounds of the colonies. Then, with the sudden prospect of a much greater American republic opened up by the Louisiana Purchase, Jefferson led the charge for removing the successfully civilised Indians from the original United States to the newly acquired territory beyond the Mississippi. There would be only a short reprieve. By doubling the nation's size, he ensured an eventual transcontinental replication of his ideal homogeneity.

The pastoral frontier

The reason we should look afresh at Frederick Jackson Turner is not 'the Turner thesis', too often restricted to the frontier's ideological influence on a much-vaunted 'American exceptionalism'. It is for his realism about large-scale historical relations being worked through by people on the ground, thousands of people 'taking up' what they considered 'new' ground. Turner quoted the key passage from Burke for its specific relevance and for its boost to his larger thesis—the extraordinary compression of world history in the conquest of a continent:[16]

> *The United States lies like a huge page in the history of society. Line by line as we read this continental page from West to East we find the record of social evolution. It begins with the Indian and the hunter; it goes on to tell of the disintegration of savagery by the entrance of the trader, the pathfinder of civilization; we read the annals of the pastoral stage in ranch life; the exploitation of the soil by the raising of unrotated crops of corn and wheat in sparsely settled farming communities; the intensive culture of the denser farm settlement; and finally the manufacturing organization with city and factory system. This page is familiar to the student of census statistics, but how little of it has been used by our historians. Particularly in eastern States this page is a palimpsest. What is now a manufacturing State was in an earlier decade an area of intensive farming. Earlier yet it had been a wheat area, and still earlier the 'range' had attracted the cattle herder.*

---

[16] The following passages of Turner's 1893 thesis are from the 1921 edition now available online at http://xroads.virginia.edu/~HYPER/TURNER/. This availability fits with the ways the essay has served the purposes of many generations, and was indeed revised, sometimes almost to the point of *antithesis*, by Turner himself. The case is forcefully made in Limerick P. 2000. 'Turnerians all: the dream of a helpful history in an intelligible world', in her book *Something in the Soil: Legacies and Reckonings in the New West*. New York: Norton, 141–65, and in the introduction to her alternative history, 1987. *The Legacy of Conquest: the Unbroken Past of the American West*. New York: Norton. For recent stimulating theses on colonial appropriations, see Belich J. 2009. *Replenishing the Earth: The Settler Revolution and the Rise of the Anglo-world, 1783–1939*. Oxford: Oxford University Press; Weaver J.C. 2003. *The Great Land Rush and the Making of the Modern World, 1650–1900*. Montreal: McGill-Queen's University Press. On usurping land for cattle, see especially the section on Argentina, 11–17.

Turner emphasised a critical difference between French penetration of Native American lands and English appropriation of them:

> *French colonization was dominated by its trading frontier; English colonization by its farming frontier. There was an antagonism between the two frontiers as between the two nations. Said Duquesne to the Iroquois, 'Are you ignorant of the difference between the king of England and the king of France? Go see the forts that our king has established and you will see that you can still hunt under their very walls. They have been placed for your advantage in places which you frequent. The English, on the contrary, are no sooner in possession of a place than the game is driven away. The forest falls before them as they advance, and the soil is laid bare so that you can scarce find the wherewithal to erect a shelter for the night.'*

Rapid progress from buffalo trails to trading routes, turnpikes and railroads marked the foundation of the nation. The pastoral industry would expand with the road and rail network, but it already had an advantage:

> *Travelers of the eighteenth century found the 'cowpens' among the canebrakes and peavine pastures of the South, and the 'cow drivers' took their droves to Charleston, Philadelphia, and New York. Travelers at the close of the War of 1812 met droves of more than a thousand cattle and swine from the interior of Ohio going to Pennsylvania to fatten for the Philadelphia market. The ranges of the Great Plains, with ranch and cowboy and nomadic life, are things of yesterday and of today. The experience of the Carolina cowpens guided the ranchers of Texas. One element favoring the rapid extension of the rancher's frontier is the fact that in a remote country lacking transportation facilities the product must be in small bulk, or must be able to transport itself, and the cattle raiser could easily drive his product to market.*

Turner recognised that the restless agrarian advance in one sense meant ruin for the Native American way of life. Where grazing was mixed with agriculture, it did not take long for towns to develop. When the pioneering farmers found they could sell up at a profit, they were able to deploy their labour and new capital further to the west. The drive west demanded land, whether public land already assumed by the United States, or land declared off limits to settlers because it was reserved for Native Americans by treaty. Many were not the original owners; the Indians were more likely a troublesome nation already displaced from the north and east. This was the case in the large tract of plains country between Kansas and Texas designated 'Indian Territory'. The indigenous and displaced native peoples mortgaged their survival to a series of solemn agreements and treaties negotiated with the US government.

How long would the greatest sanctuary withstand the acquisitive advance? Migration figures from east to west are hard to come by, but the scale of population movement staggered all observers. After squatters broke out along the Ohio, ideas of halting the advance at the Mississippi seemed fanciful. By 1820, it was carrying the produce of a vast region of new agriculture stretching from north to south along the river system. The battle between North and South over extending slavery temporarily halted the extension of the Union. When it ended, the Civil War brought Native American peoples a disastrous redoubling of immigrant pressure. Some had sided with the South, and Congress immediately inflicted an irreversible reprisal.

The Homestead Act was a benign-looking piece of legislation passed almost unanimously by both houses of Congress once the slaveholding states were excluded. Signed into law by the frontier-bred President Lincoln in 1862, it enabled anyone who had not taken up arms against the US government to apply for a grant of 160 acres of newly opened land. The homesteader had to live on the land and improve it by building a dwelling and growing crops. Then, after five years, title would be transferred. The land rush was not immediate, but gathered pace over time. In the next 70 years, more than 270 million acres, over 10 per cent of US lands, would pass into the hands of settlers as railroads linked what had been communally held Indian territory to the newly industrialising economy. Union victory ignited an explosion of wealth and wealth seeking that powered the final push to continental conquest. The population of Kansas more than tripled, from 107 000 to 364 000 in the decade 1860–1870; Nebraska boomed from 28 000 to 123 000.[17]

The cattlemen fought against the Homestead Act. They did not want the open range divided up and sold off. Before long they found ways round it and learned that the farmer and the cowman could be friends. The growers of wheat and corn produced a surplus for fattening stock. As population increased, so did the demand for beef. Investment in grazing became highly profitable during the Civil War and the expansionist years that followed. It would not have been surprising if the main casualties were again the Native Americans removed to Indian Territory.

Cattle did not necessarily bring ruin to Indians. When the 'Five Civilized Tribes' (Cherokee, Chickasaw, Choctaw, Creek and Seminole) were uprooted and resettled, they brought large herds with them. The herds grew larger on the open range and the California gold rush created a demand for beef. At the outbreak of the Civil War in 1861, 'the Cherokee Nation alone had nearly a quarter-million head of cattle. Unfortunately, the havoc of the war and the depredations of cattle thieves resulted in an estimated loss of

---

17   Turner, *The Frontier in American History*, ch. IV 'The Middle West'.

three hundred thousand head among the Five Nations by 1865'.[18] But then came a remarkable age of prosperity before the inevitable greedy pressure on successful Indian ranchers. In the 20 years following the Civil War, the drives north from Texas to Kansas crossed Indian Territory with profit to all. On the Chisholm Trail and the Western Trail, the cowboys grazed their herds and sometimes paid their tolls. Most successful were the Osages. They had advantages of geography and nature, especially the bluestem grass on which cattle fattened rapidly and wintered well. 'Thus by an accident of location between supply and market as well as exceptional grass, the Osages were in the forefront of the developing western cattle industry.'[19]

Everything about the new cattle industry was big, bigger than Texas. But there the expansion was more dramatic. Already in 1860 there was a tally of 3 786 433 cattle in Texas. The earlier war with Mexico (1846–1848) had opened up more of the apparently limitless prairie and trails north opened the market. Before refrigeration, also pioneered in Texas, meat could not be shipped by sea. It could more reliably be supplied fresh to the Chicago slaughterhouses by droving. In 1882, good steers brought five and one-half cents a pound on the Chicago market, the highest price ever paid in the United States. The boom lasted until 1885 when a severe winter, followed by a drought, forced many to sell their animals. There were then some 7.5 million head of cattle on the Great Plains and one tally claimed a total of 5 201 132 cattle had been driven over all the trails from 1866 to 1884. [20]

Joseph G. McCoy described himself as 'the pioneer western cattle shipper' and none could doubt he knew his business.[21] In 1874, he divulged some of his trade secrets to the wider public. Direct from 'the real McCoy', we can still learn about the ideal qualities of grasses, about shorthorns and longhorns, the origin of the term 'maverick' for unbranded beasts, and the 'very complete' stock laws of south western Texas, where the largest livestock owners in the United States, 'owning from twenty-five to seventy-five

---

[18]   Oklahoma Historical Society, *Encyclopedia of Oklahoma History & Culture*. Online edition available at http://digital.library.okstate.edu/encyclopedia/entries/C/CA077.html. For divisions in Indian Territory brought about by the Civil War, the effects of reconstruction and the railroads, see Debo A. 1970. *A History of the Indians of the United States*. Norman: University of Oklahoma Press, chs 9–10.

[19]   Burns L.F. 2004. *A History of the Osage People*. Tuscaloosa and London: University of Alabama Press, 369.

[20]   White R. 1993. *'It's Your Misfortune and None of My Own': A New History of the American West*. Norman and London: University of Oklahoma Press, 223; Caddell J. nd. *Texas Cattle Trails*, published on http://www.rootsweb.ancestry.com/~txecm/texas_cattle_trails.htm.

[21]   McCoy J.G. 1874. *Historic Sketches of the Cattle Trade in the West and Southwest*. Kansas City, Mo: Ramsey, Millett & Hudson. Republished online at http://www.kancoll.org/books/mccoy/.

thousand head of cattle each, with horses in proportion', resided. McCoy is robust in his insistence that eastern capital played only the smallest part in the development of the cattle industry. The risk, of long drives to market without a guaranteed price, was borne by ranchers, drovers and traders like himself. Only the First National Bank of Kansas City 'saw, as with a prophetic eye, the future greatness, importance, and the lucrative nature of the livestock trade and its value as a commerce to such banking houses as secured it'. Few other banking houses would take what they deemed 'extreme extra-hazardous discount risks, as they regarded loans to the uncouth sunburned drovers who claimed to have herds grazing on the prairie, somewhere out on the uncertain frontier of civilization'. On the other hand, when things turned bad in the east, so did the cattle market. There was a panic in 1873 'which depressed the live-stock interests of the west more disastrously than any other branch of commerce', and until the National Bank was recapitalised, the industry saw only 'financial darkness and ruin'. After this episode, other banks saw the profits to be made and cautiously ventured vital bridging loans to drovers.[22]

Were these the men, bankers, traders, ranchers and their employees, who caused the Native Americans grief and destruction? Not according to McCoy. If there were any villains in his story, they were the Indian agents. One duty of the agents was to care for tribes confined to reservations and to arrange supplies of beef. 'But in those days an Indian contract was only another name for a big steal and swindle. Not one contract in each hundred made was ever filled in letter and spirit. Often the cattle would be delivered at an agreed average of net weight greater than the actual gross weight, and when delivered on one day would be stole from the government agent at night and re-delivered the next day. Of course the government agent was entirely innocent and was not conniving with the contractor.' Behind the phalanx of self-serving agents were good customers.

However, Indian hostility to the extension of settlement was also known. In 1868, there was 'a determined effort' to reclaim a favourite hunting ground, with raids in north-western Kansas approaching as near as 60 miles to McCoy's new cattle hub of Abilene. There was much scary talk, and reprisals fuelled by fear that the Indians might descend in great numbers.[23] While warriors could dream of holding up European advance, as hunters they knew they were in trouble. Within a very few years, Native Americans

---

22   McCoy, *Historic Sketches*, ch. 16. Brown D. 1994. *The American West*. New York: Charles Scribner, has many indexed references to pioneering cattlemen but few in relation to Indians.
23   McCoy, *Historic Sketches*, ch. 7.

would have no choice but to adapt to European livestock. As they watched the cattle arrive, the native animal they had always depended on for food, clothing and shelter was being wiped out. The destruction of the buffalo would end the hunting economy that sustained the independence of the Kiowas, the Comanches and other peoples, but it was not a plot of the cattle industry. It originated in a complex of developments in the east after the Civil War. There were many restless men with rifles and many tales of easy money. There were new machines needing leather belts and new tanning methods that made buffalo hide ideal for driving the wheels of America's industrial revolution.[24] The employment of Union generals—Sherman, Sheridan and Custer—to impose peace on the frontier ensured that sacrificing a whole ecology, and if necessary many whole peoples, would not stand in their way.

> *Of the 3,700,000 buffalo destroyed from 1872 through 1874, only 150,000 were killed by Indians. When a group of concerned Texans asked General Sheridan if something should not be done to stop the white hunters' wholesale slaughter, he replied: "Let them kill, skin and sell until the buffalo is exterminated, as it is the only way to bring lasting peace and allow civilization to advance."*[25]

The only place for the Plains peoples in this new order was on reservations, dependent on government handouts. In 1874, a large group of Kiowa, Comanche and Cheyenne broke out to re-establish their hunting lives in Palo Duro Canyon. 'The floor of the canyon,' writes Brown, 'was a forest of tepees ... all well stocked with food to last until spring. Almost two thousand horses shared the rich grass with buffalo. Without fear, the women went about their tasks and the children played along the streams.' It was an idyll of the old ways intolerable to the authorities. Brown describes how Sherman launched a many-pronged attack with repeating rifles and artillery against this cohort of a few hundred rebel Indians:

> *Although caught by surprise, the warriors held out long enough for their women and children to escape, and then they retreated under a cloud of dense powder smoke. Mackenzie's troopers stormed up the creek, burning tepees and destroying the Indians' winter supplies. By the end of the day they rounded up more than a thousand ponies. Mackenzie ordered the animals driven into Tule Valley, and there the Bluecoats slaughtered them, a thousand dead horses left to the circling buzzards.*

---

[24] Elliott West in the illustrated reissue of Brown, *Bury My Heart*, 302. Contributing factors are convincingly drawn together in Isenberg A.C. 2000. *The Destruction of the Bison: An Environmental History, 1750–1920.* New York: Cambridge University Press.

[25] Brown, *Bury My Heart*, 296. 'The United States' elimination of the buffalo to coerce all Indians into compliance with the reservation system' is part of the larger case made in Rand J.T. 2008. *Kiowa Humanity and the Invasion of the State.* Lincoln: University of Nebraska Press, 69.

Across the Plains the Indians scattered on foot, without food, clothing, or shelter. And the thousands of Bluecoats marching from the four directions methodically hunted them down, the columns crossing and crisscrossing, picking up the wounded Indians first, then the aged, then the women and children.[26]

The defeated were not killed off, nor were they entirely defeated. Raids into Texas continued as groups tried to reassert their claims and independence. But the weight of official policy, backed and often led by Congress, and mercilessly carried through by a military with no other field for glory, made it hopeless for resistance to continue. Just before more than 300 peaceful Indians, mainly women and children, were murdered by 'a mass of infuriated men intent on butchery' at Wounded Knee in 1890, a writer in the *Aberdeen Saturday Pioneer* called for the army to 'finish the job':

The nobility of the Redskin is extinguished ... The Whites, by law of conquest, by justice of civilization, are masters of the American continent, and the best safety of the frontier settlements will be secured by the total annihilation of the few remaining Indians. Why not annihilation? Their glory has fled, their spirit broken, their manhood effaced; better that they should die than live the miserable wretches that they are.[27]

No doubt, among the audience for these incitements were cattlemen, and small homesteaders hoping to be cattlemen. Some were prominent among the inciters.[28] The Apaches of the southwest mounted raids as the ranchers advanced and often drove off livestock. It took a long military campaign of violence and deceit to subdue them. While there was talk of the most extreme options—'a general policy to kill them wherever found ... if we go in for extermination'—it also made sense to settle them on reservations where they would either raise cattle themselves or be customers, at government expense, for the ranchers' beef. A peace with one redoubtable

---

26 Brown, *Bury My Heart*, 303.

27 Ward Churchill notes that the editorialist was L. Frank Baum, 'who would later attain fame as the gentle author of *The Wizard of Oz*'. Among earlier incitements, Churchill records Colonel Chivington, 'a former Methodist minister with political ambitions', soon to be notorious for the Sand Creek massacre, telling a Colorado audience in 1864 that his intention was to kill all the Indians he came across, including infants, because 'nits make lice'. In 1881, when a US Senator asked a public meeting whether it might not be better to civilise the Indians rather than exterminate them, the Denver citizens replied 'with a shout almost loud enough to raise the roof of the opera house "EXTERMINATE THEM! EXTERMINATE THEM!"'. Churchill W. 1997. *A Little Matter of Genocide: Holocaust and Denial in the Americas, 1492 to the Present*. San Francisco: City Lights Books, 229–31, 244–5.

28 For the long history of Texan warfare against Indian peoples, see Anderson G.C. 2005. *The Conquest of Texas: Ethnic Cleansing in the Promised Land, 1820–1875*. Norman: University of Oklahoma Press. The rancher King Woolsey's genocidal propaganda features in Jacoby K. 2008. '"The broad platform of extermination": nature and violence in the nineteenth century North American Borderlands'. *Journal of Genocide Research*, 10, no. 2, 249–67.

warrior, Cochise, was soon followed by another war, not concluded until the surrender of Geronimo. Lured back from Mexico in 1883, his small band brought 350 head of cattle with them. But Geronimo was not allowed to settle down as a rancher. The cattle were taken and sold to compensate the Mexican owners. Not until his recapture in 1886 did the war end and the fragmentation of his people continued long after he rode in Teddy Roosevelt's inaugural parade in 1905. [29]

In the last decades of the century, there was new hope, and then more despair. In 1885, Texas cattlemen, after overstocking the range, were paying 'grass money' to lease land from the Comanches, led by Quanah Parker, and from other tribes on the reservation. For six cents an acre per year they were running 75 000 head of cattle on one and a half million acres:

> *Though less than market value, grass money did provide about $55,000 a year for the Kiowas, Comanches, and Apaches. Twice a year the cattlemen distributed the grass money. In the summer of 1885 the companies paid each Indian on the Kiowa-Comanche reservation $9.50, all in silver dimes. Many government officials disliked the idea of the Indians leasing their lands rather than farming them, so in 1890 the United States declared the cattle leases null and void and ordered the cattle off the reservation.*[30]

For the Cherokee, too, a future as cattle ranchers was cut off. They had been granted a six-million-acre strip of good grass extending some 150 miles east to west and 60 miles north to south, known as the Cherokee Outlet, a corridor to the buffalo hunting regions on the plains:

> *Toward the latter end of the trail-drive era (roughly 1866 to 1886), cattle raisers from both Texas and Kansas began negotiations with the Cherokee Nation to place cattle legally on the Outlet. The Cherokee Strip Live Stock Association, loosely organized in 1880 and more formally structured in 1883, has been called by historian Edward Everett Dale the greatest livestock organization in the world during its ten-year existence. Despite the wishes of both cattlemen and Cherokee officials, the U.S. government ordered the removal of cattle in order to open the Outlet for white settlement, culminating in the great Cherokee Outlet Opening of 1893. As in the rest of the central plains, the range-cattle era in Indian Territory was brief. In 1895 the open range was declared closed by the territorial legislature, and by the first year of the new century almost all Indian lands had been settled.*[31]

The final blow to Native American autonomy was certainly not initiated by the cattlemen. It came from the mix of activism and ideology peculiar

---

[29]   Debo, *A History*, 219–35. Roosevelt's inauguration was on 4 March 1905. Geronimo died, still a prisoner far from home, in 1909.

[30]   La Vere D. 2004. *The Texas Indians*. College Station: Texas A&M University Press, 217.

[31]   *Encyclopedia of Oklahoma History and Culture*. Available at http://digital.library.okstate. edu/encyclopedia/entries/C/CA077.html.

to genuine philanthropists. They believed the best interests of Indians required a radical intervention in the communal land-holding conventions that in fact were working well. Indian protests were to no avail, nor were the objections of the big cattle companies who did not want to lose their leases. What became notorious as the Dawes Act, more formally the General Allotment Act, was passed by Congress in 1887.

The Dawes Act, said President Roosevelt in 1901, served as 'a mighty pulverizing engine to break up the tribal mass'. Reservation land was chopped into individual allotments of 160 acres for each family head, with further provisions for the unmarried, and for selling off 'excess' land. These sales were meant to pay for education and purchase of farming equipment: everything was put in terms of benefiting the Indians. As individual proprietors, they could even become US citizens. Through every possible forum and negotiation, the Indians resisted. Why should they become impoverished smallholders like the poor whites they saw around them, unable to afford a horse or any cattle at all? They knew the likelihood of falling into debt and having to sell up. The Native Americans, notably the Kiowas backed by the 1867 Medicine Lodge Treaty, took the fight all the way to the Supreme Court—and lost.[32] The policy was forced through everywhere to the bitter end, and always with a 'surplus' of land for sale to new settlers. The 'Five Civilized Tribes', initially exempted, were pressed by a negotiating commission headed by Dawes himself to come to terms. Its report on Indian Territory was blunt:

> *The resources of the Territory itself have been developed to such a degree and are of such immense and tempting value that they are attracting to it an irresistible pressure from enterprising citizens. The executory conditions contained in the treaties have become impossible of execution. It is no longer possible for the United States to keep its citizens out of the Territory. Nor is it now possible for the Indians to secure to each individual Indian his full enjoyment in common with other Indians of the common property of the Territory.*[33]

---

32   President Rooseveld quoted by Sharon O'Brien. 1985. 'Federal Indian policies and the international protection of human rights', in *American Indian Policy in the Twentieth Century*, ed. V. Deloria Jr. Norman: University of Oklahoma Press, 43; La Vere, *Texas Indians*, 220. The story of the negotiations is told in greater and sadder detail in Debo, *A History*, ch. 16, and Ostler J. 2004. *The Plains Sioux and US Colonialism from Lewis and Clark to Wounded Knee.* New York: Cambridge University Press, ch. 10. The negotiations and the context of colonialist policy are powerfully explicated in Rand, *Kiowa Humanity*, ch. 3.

33   Prucha F.P. 2000. *Documents of United States Indian Policy.* Lincoln: University of Nebraska Press, 189–93. Critically, the Dawes Commission insisted on the newly fashionable 'blood quantum' definition of 'Indian' for enrolment, a racist move against the more open cultural practice of the tribes. Chang D.A. 2010. *The Color of the Land: Race, Nation, and the Politics of Landownership in Oklahoma, 1832–1929.* Chapel Hill: University of North Carolina Press, 94.

So migration pressure and US government policy killed the best hope of self-sustaining Indian communities and even the individual enterprises some Indians had started on their own account. The Comanche leader Quanah Parker had promoted leasing to white cattlemen in their best, and then their most desperate, times against opposition from many of his own people. When in 1885 President Cleveland ordered all leases cleared, he persevered with his own herd.

Individual enterprise, like leasing to outsiders, caused resentment among tribal conservatives who saw capitalist farming for what it was intended to be—destructive of all communal traditions.[34] The government could have encouraged Indian ranching by continuing to buy beef grown on the reservations to feed Indians not gainfully employed. Instead they reduced Indian holdings and opened the reservations to immigrant farmers. The Osage, who had also been exempted from the Dawes Act, were legally able to increase their leasing business: 'all or almost all the 819,934 acres of Osage land was under grass lease in 1890'. The boundary of their reservation, with official approval, was fenced and patrolled; its income tripled in the five years 1893–1898. Having taken their case to Washington with enough support to get their own amendment, they found that their reprieve was temporary; 'the homesteaders had more votes and political power than the cattlemen and the Indians had no votes'. By 1906, when their rights were extinguished, legal redress was hopeless.[35] Three years earlier, Lone Wolf, one of the most influential and militant Kiowa chiefs, had lost to the Secretary of the Interior in the Supreme Court. His last stand could not stop the Kiowa reservation being opened to the last great land rush.[36] In 1907, the former Indian Territory was joined with Oklahoma and admitted to the Union. The population of the new state was 1 414 177. Only 5.3 per cent was Indian.[37]

---

34 Iverson P. 1994. *When Indians Became Cowboys: Native Peoples and Cattle Ranching.* Norman: University of Oklahoma Press, 87. Rand observes that individual achievement was by no means incompatible with Kiowa attitudes and cites evidence of cattle ownership, but does not pursue the question of cattle-raising enterprises. Rand, *Kiowa Humanity*, 72, 129–31, 154.

35 Burns, *History of Osage*, 374, 384–8. Burns, himself of Osage descent, also points out the rapid development of property consciousness and constitutional regulation among the Osage. As with other peoples, the more successful Osage ranchers were able to expand by acquiring further grazing land.

36 Iverson, *When Indians Became Cowboys*, 32.

37 Debo, *A History*, 261.

Colonisation, cattle, genocide

Cowboys and Indians did in a sense fight the last great battle in establishing the continental dominion of the United States, though grazing interests brought them close to being on the same side. The war took more than a century and it has taken another century for Turner's thesis of the frontier to be re-assessed in its larger comparative context as a story of conquest and dispossession by capitalist expansion in what might be called second-wave globalisation. As in Australia, Argentina and southern Africa, grazing stock, often financed from far away, was a precious investment demanding security of tenure and military protection. There were always voices arguing that permanent security would best be achieved by permanent removal of the Native American owners of the grazing land and its transfer into private ownership. After the Civil War, the newly strengthened democratic institutions of the United States stepped forward. The US Congress and the Supreme Court finished the job for the pastoralists and settlers by moves to finish off the resisting tribes, not by murder but by a ruthless policy of privatisation. Whether destruction of an independent ethnic group by insistence that it surrender its economic, social and cultural cohesion should be considered genocidal can be long debated. Beyond debate is the fact of a free and autonomous life being reduced to a beggarly dependence, a mere existence. The survivors resisted incorporation with costs seen elsewhere among the indigenous dispossessed: misery, alienation and an endemic culture of self-destructive behaviour. Where collective identity could be nurtured, Native American peoples adapted to individualism more positively, but no less sadly. The life that had formed their world was gone and the world made only mean and short-sighted sense.

This was well recognised by everyone involved in 'Indian removal' and land appropriation throughout the nineteenth century. Jefferson proclaimed more than once that the reliance on hunting would have to give way to a European style of agricultural life if Indians were to survive. 'Jeffersonian philanthropy' was one of his more cold-eyed legacies. Individualist farming, he foresaw, would mean many indebted and then dispossessed Indian farmers. If relentless civilisation was the ideological core, dispossession was the practical effect. Benign and malevolent intentions fused in the policies Patrick Wolfe characterises as 'elimination of the native'. He quotes Mr Justice Johnson, concurring with Chief Justice Marshall's judgement in *Cherokee v. Georgia*: 'The hunter state bore within itself the promise of vacating the territory, because when game ceased, the hunter would go elsewhere to seek it. But a more fixed state of society would amount to a permanent destruction of the hope, and, of consequence, of the beneficial character of the pre-emptive right'.[38]

Wolfe avoids any simplistic verdict of intentional genocide, often enough given voice by contemporary Native Americans, their white sympathisers, and later historians. I am inclined to join him in his caution. Behind the dense reasoning of Justice Johnson there is a recognition of economic and cultural realities as cool as Jefferson's. Regarding the larger history of European expansion in North America, I do not doubt that the relations of genocide ruled as they did in Australia and everywhere settlers took both land and lives. From the first colonists to Jackson's removals, the Indian casualty rate was of little concern. Later, most tragically in California, there were enough episodes of massacre and starvation to make genocide the only appropriate term.[39]

Richard White also sees California as the worst of the killing fields, where 'Indian hunting' ran amok. But he does not talk of genocide. As in Oregon, 'people simply murdered Indians'. In the broader picture, he is forthright about military campaigns: 'the goal of this fighting was the subjugation and not the extermination of Indian peoples'. And about cattlemen: 'Large cattlemen were probably the most prone to violence of any economic interest group in the West', but mainly to assert their tenuous claims against each other. He does not dwell on conflict with farmers or Indians.[40]

What White does put beyond doubt is the appalling devastation wrought by cattle on the environment they, and indigenous peoples, needed to sustain their numbers. The cattle did not displace the buffalo that had sustained indigenous societies, but they very rapidly wrecked the grasslands they took over. By overstocking and overgrazing, the cattlemen caused an ecological disaster. In 1870, in the southern plains, '5 acres of land could support a steer; in 1880, the same animal needed 50 acres to survive'. In the winter of 1885, after 200 000 cattle had been expelled for illegally grazing in Indian Territory, came the horrific losses no-one forgot. Some claimed 85 percent of their herds froze to death. The following dry summer and another severe

---

[38] *Cherokee v. Georgia*, 30 US (5 Peters) 1, 1831, 23, cited in Wolfe P. 2006. 'Settler colonialism and the elimination of the native'. *Journal of Genocide Research*, 8, no. 4, 405, n. 19. See also Haake C. 2007. *The State, Removal and Indigenous Peoples in the United States and Mexico, 1620–2000*. New York: Routledge, 14–15.

[39] In addition to Wolfe's summary of frontier expansion and the key policies of Indian destruction, see Madley B. 2004. 'Patterns of frontier genocide, 1803–1910: the Aboriginal Tasmanians, the Yuki of California and the Herero of Namibia'. *Journal of Genocide Research*, 6, no. 2, 167–192, and Kakel, C. 2011. *The American West and the Nazi East: A Comparative and Interpretive Perspective*. Houndsmills UK: Palgrave Macmillan.

[40] White, *It's Your Misfortune*, 337–8.

winter shifted the disaster north. There the depletion was even worse: a single steer now needed more than 90 acres. The losses, though not as great, caused lenders to call in their loans. Ranchers desperate to offload stock drove prices down. The result was ruin. [41]

'Rawhiding the land' had brought enough quick returns to make sure the cattle boom would recover. And it meant continued pressure to turn public land over to private ownership and exploitation. The idea of a public commons, soon to flourish in the movement for national parks, did nothing to stem pressures on the United States government to take grazing land out of communal ownership.[42] Who would inherit the range? Not the roaming hunters and the buffalo they had hunted. Into the Great Plains came sheep, millions of sheep. They ate what cattle would not and by 1900 had taken over the more northern states of Wyoming and Montana. In the ensuing contest, Indians seemed forgotten. Cattlemen, says White, 'fought this expansion. They believed sheep ruined the range for cattle, and they considered sheep inferior animals raised by inferior men—Hispanics, Basques, and later Mormons'. No-one spoke of bringing back the buffalo.[43]

Andrew Isenberg's study of the buffalo slaughter does not engage with the issue of genocide and is at pains to avoid any simple explanation for the animal and human catastrophe. But that makes all the more striking the complex of factors responsible for the destruction:

> *The arrival in the western plains of livestock and their diseases was a late wave in the tide of European ecological expansion in North America ... Some Euroamericans came west to take advantage of economic opportunities, some to escape the commercialization of agriculture in the East, but in either case the nineteenth-century market revolution was integral to Euroamerican westward emigration. The social, economic, and environmental transformations that contributed to the demise of the bison were not separate categories of change but embedded in each other.*

That the drive west 'produced widespread destitution among the nomadic societies' and 'increased warfare among the plains societies as they jostled for control of the remaining hunting territories' is clearly a fair conclusion.[44]

The relations of genocide, as I have called them—relations that brought death to whole peoples from large-scale historical developments, often

---

[41]   White, *It's Your Misfortune*, 223–4, 344.

[42]   Weaver, *Great Land Rush*, 57 situates American land acquisition law in a long-term comparative perspective. On the push to privatise the range, see Worster D. 1992. *Under Western Skies: Nature and History in the American West*. New York: Oxford University Press, ch. 3.

[43]   White, *It's Your Misfortune*, 118, 222–5. He notes that Congress in the 1870s passed a bill protecting the bison, but President Grant vetoed it.

[44]   Isenberg, *Destruction of Bison*, 110–11.

despite benign intentions[45]—were visible to every witness at the time. Propaganda about civilisation and savages should not be allowed to mask contemporary understanding of how ramified the causes of destruction were and how intractable the problems of saving whole peoples in an era of migration and displacement never before known in human history. The relations, more dynamic and dialectical than 'structures', included those between Native Americans thrown together in the struggle for survival. Here the hunters were literally on the front line. In 1849 the Commissioner of Indian Affairs, Orlando Brown, saw that the dwindling 'chief resource' would bring 'great suffering' and competition between tribes 'in their hunting expeditions and lead to bloody collisions and exterminating wars between them'. His 1851 attempt at setting agreed boundaries failed and the next commissioner, George W. Maypenny, warned that destitution would drive the Indians to 'steal from our citizens or starve'. That would hasten their end. 'Under the existing state of things,' he wrote in 1855, 'they must rapidly be exterminated by the whites or become extinct.'[46]

The later conflict between hunters and cattlemen on the prairies took on a different temper. It was a war to eliminate resistance, not physically to eliminate the resisters.[47] There was plenty of genocidal rhetoric, but the clear policy was to settle the issue by settling the Indians. When they could no longer hunt on the open range, confinement to reservations was the solution. The roaming, independent Indian was a reproachful symbol that had to be exorcised, always with an insistence that this was the only way ahead for the Indians themselves. They must adapt to the new order or disappear altogether. An 1873 editorial in the *Omaha Republican* on the sale of the western part of the Omaha reservation 'for the benefit of the tribe' brought out the pure oil of frontier passion:

> *This is to our mind only the beginning of the end. It seems certain that these Indian reservations are designed to be sold and settled by a white population. The Indian does not take kindly to civilization. He cannot or will not endure constraints. They either*

---

45 Barta T. 1987. 'Relations of genocide: land and lives in the colonization of Australia', in *Genocide and the Modern Age*, eds I. Wallimann & M. Dobkowski. Westport, CT: Greenwood Press, 237–252. Barta T. 2007. 'On pain of extinction: laws of nature and history in Darwin, Marx and Arendt', in *Imperialism, Slavery, Race and Genocide: The Legacy of Hannah Arendt*, eds R. King & D. Stone. New York: Berghahn Books; Finzsch N. 2005. '"It is scarcely possible to conceive that human beings could be so hideous and loathsome": discourses of genocide in eighteenth and nineteenth-century America and Australia'. *Patterns of Prejudice*, 39, no. 2, 97–115.

46 Isenberg, *Destruction of Bison*, 112.

47 The mobility and guerrilla skills of the Indians made a military solution prohibitively expensive. 'One accountant figured that each Indian killed by the army cost the United States $1 million.' Perdue & Green, *North American Indians*, 76.

pass away or become so mixed by marriage with the Whites that their nationality is lost, and they become to all intents and purposes, citizens. We confess that we have but little faith in the ultimate civilization of these roving savages ... They die well. They waste rapidly away before the breath of civilization, but they do not civilize.[48]

'Civilisation', not pastoralism, was the huge engine of European expansion. It incorporated every kind of enterprise and a ruthless, occasionally compassionate, confidence that there was no other way, no alternative future for any group in America. If 'the only good Indian is a dead Indian' gave way to 'kill the Indian, save the man' that was itself a civilised advance, but it did not guarantee Indian peoples—historic human groupings with their own languages, cultures and physical lineages—a future. If they wasted away, it was hardly even a waste; it was simply inevitable and had the advantage of being final. More often than not, frontier rhetoric envisaged the final solution with scarcely a hint of sorrow and certainly without embarrassment. It was noted and forthrightly interpreted by America's most perceptive commentators, including Turner.

While Turner was general and schematic, he also called for more local histories of the frontier. And indeed the large locality that concerns us here, Indian Territory and its neighbours, received a remarkable history in Turner's wake. *The Range Cattle Industry: Ranching on the Great Plains from 1865 to 1925* by Edward Everett Dale was published in 1930 and republished, almost another classic, in 1960. It straightforwardly follows Turner: the cattlemen belonged to 'a much larger movement' of 'successive stages of society—that of the hunter and trapper, the herder, and the pioneer farmer' in a great westward movement. But the detail of negotiations, about the leasing and eventual sale of the Cherokee Outlet, for instance, reinforces the alliances between cattlemen and Indian nations, and the dubious role of the United States government. As noted earlier, the cattlemen sealed a satisfactory lease agreement and then, in 1888, made a much more favourable offer of more than double the US price for the purchase of the six million acres of excellent grazing in the 'panhandle strip'. But both the lease and the purchase were vetoed by administrations looking towards land acquisition for settlement.[49]

Dale was followed by many more fine histories, with major changes in interpreting the West, especially with respect to Turner. They have not, however, changed a stubborn fact of pastoral expansion into Native American territory. It is the striking ability of whole tribes, as well as enterprising

---

[48]   Reilly H. 2010. *The Frontier Newspapers and the Coverage of the Plains Indian Wars.* New York: Praeger, xv.

[49]   Dale E.E. 1960. *The Range Cattle Industry: Ranching on the Great Plains from 1865 to 1925.* Norman: Oklahoma University Press, 136–46.

individuals, to grasp the possibilities of the cattle boom for their own survival and advancement. Whether by running their own herds, or by charging tolls of 10 cents a head for the droving of cattle across their lands, the Indians allied with the cowboys and their masters in the interests of saving their collective existence in the new economy. There were many conflicts. Some between competing Indians, others with white people claiming Indian citizenship or heedless of whatever rights had been negotiated. But pastoralism itself was rarely rejected. That is the story told by Angie Debo about the Creeks in 1941 and by Morris Foster about the Comanches in 1991.[50] It was not the ranchers who had destroyed the buffalo, and the replacement stock they brought into the grasslands was thought by some to offer a stable existence for communities faced with hunger and fragmentation. The cattle deployed in America's West, unlike the sheep in Australia's south, were not instruments of genocide. This 'capital on four hooves' offered survival—at a price. As with the cattle industry in Australia's north, indigenous stockmen found employment for their riding skills and knowledge of the country.[51]

Would cattle, more than any other intrusion, offer a sustainable coexistence? Possibly, but a destructive intrusion nonetheless. Jeffrey Ostler shows that the Sioux were more successful than other ranchers in maintaining their herds through the bad winter of 1886–1887, but were resistant to the expectations placed on them. 'In providing Indians with stock cattle, agents wanted them to behave like expectant capitalists.' They punished those who slaughtered for communal purposes beasts meant to multiply for competitive individual advancement. The cattle became part of the long effort to integrate the Indians into the commercial economy. It was the continuation of Jefferson's vision of independent hunters becoming indebted farmers. Inevitably allied with the relentless advance of railroads and settlers, pastoralism could offer opportunity, and resentment, to individual Indian entrepreneurs, but not security to traditional culture or society.[52]

If gold, not beef, brought Custer's legions to Little Big Horn, the prospectors and soldiers were only the advance guard of 'civilization'. Railways bringing migrants, rather than cowboys driving herds to the railhead, created new

---

50   Debo A. 1941. *The Road to Disappearance: A History of the Creek Indians.* Norman: University of Oklahoma Press, 336–43. According to Foster M.W. 1991. *Being Comanche: A Social History of an American Indian Community.* Tucson: University of Arizona Press, 80, 'Stock raising was the most successful indigenous subsistence venture during the reservation period'.

51   On Australia, see especially McGrath A. 1987. *'Born in the Cattle': Aborigines in Cattle Country.* Sydney: Allen & Unwin. According to Broome R. 2010. *Aboriginal Australians,* Sydney: Allen & Unwin, ch. 7, about 10 000 Aboriginal men and women worked in the pastoral industry until the 1960s.

52   Ostler, *Plains Sioux,* 138–9.

towns and cities, centres of dissipation and disease that weakened Indian communities as they faced a renewed onslaught.[53] The next wave of the 'fierce and irresistible cavalry', this time from all over Europe, sealed the fate of the tribes. From the 1840s, crop failures and the gathering industrial revolution in Europe, with resulting social and political upheaval, brought teeming millions to the United States. In the decade 1841–1850, 143 439 immigrants arrived; in the next decade, spurred by the gold rush, 2 598 214 came; and then between 1861 and 1870 another 2 314 825 entered the US. The extraordinary inflow almost stabilised in the years 1871–1880 with 2 812 191 immigrants arriving, but took off again to reach 5 246 613 in the decade 1881–1890.[54] They did not all stay near their point of entry. Millions of refugees and fortune seekers flooding west demanded both military protection and an end to hostilities, a case eloquently put by the Indian commissioners appointed to settle the tribes.[55]

Indigenous peoples, as James Belich has again pointed out, did not lack resilience or adaptability. 'These peoples could cope with normal European colonization; it was explosive colonization that proved too much for them.'[56] Their resistance to the great rush west won them only truncated reserves, often far from their own lands, but they did not give up on an independent future. The reserves might have worked even as enclosure by barbed wire signalled the end of cattle roaming the range.

The reserves had always had an assimilationist purpose. Their great proponent in the 1870s, Commissioner Walker, saw no hope of survival unless Indians were made to learn white ways. Once the railroad, 'the great plough of industrial civilization', had drawn its 'deep furrow' across their lands, they must also be subject to a 'severe course' in the ways of the new society. Others believed the reserves still protected the Indians from

---

[53]   In some years, death rates exceeded 50 per 1 000. Tuberculosis was the main killer, but measles, whooping cough and influenza combined with poor diet, poor ventilation and alcohol abuse to claim lives. Ostler, *Plains Sioux*, 187.

[54]   They were not typical ranchers. In only five years from 1881–1885, one million Germans arrived at the peak of German immigration. It took somewhat longer, 1881–1920, for two million Eastern European Jews to emigrate to the United States. These figures have been taken from Harvard University Library Open Collections timeline at http://ocp.hul.harvard.edu/immigration/timeline.html.

[55]   See, for instance, NADP Document R872001A. *Annual Report of the Commissioner of Indian Affairs to the Secretary for the Year 1872*, Washington: Government Printing Office, 1872, 3–22, available at http://public.csusm.edu/nadp/r872001a.htm.

[56]   Belich, *Replenishing the Earth*, 181–82, writes: 'Explosive colonization was a remarkable phenomenon—human history's most rapid form of societal reproduction. It created the massive American and British Wests in little more than a century'. Walter Nugent records that physical reproduction was also explosive in frontier society. Even Malthus was astonished at its fecundity. Nugent W. 2009. *Habits of Empire: A History of American Expansion*. New York: Vintage, 221–23, 233–34.

the bracing advantages of individualism. They lost the contest. Regarding themselves as 'true friends' of the Indians, the reformers and their friends in congress determined to end separatism forever. The Dawes Act and all that followed was a catastrophe. If congressional politicians, responding to their land-hungry constituents, had not insisted on fragmenting tribal property into individual holdings, the tribes could have prospered as pastoralists rather than, a century later, as casino operators. The tribal lands were guaranteed by treaty to belong to Native American people in perpetuity. The abrogation of the treaties and the fragmentation of the patrimony into individual plots that could be sold off was foreseen by Indians and legislators alike to be the death knell for independent Native American existence. [57]

Should either dependence or fragmentation be blamed on the pastoral economy? Native Americans struggled and the cattle kings prospered. But Native peoples had also prospered in the new pastoralism once the hunting economy was destroyed. The longhorns that flooded through the territories where the plains peoples had hunted did not displace the buffalo, they replaced them. It was the flood of people who came from across the sea, and then across the mountains, across the rivers and up the river valleys, that displaced the people in possession of the plains.

When it suited them, cattlemen were useful allies to Native American peoples. They helped the Comanches to stall allotment for nine years and retain 480 000 'big pasture' acres in joint ownership with the Kiowas and Apaches for continued leasing.[58] Parties pursued their own interest with whatever arguments, and violence, they could get away with. Cattlemen's associations could sound communalist in defence of the open range even as they were dominated by big ranchers intent on extending exclusive ownership. Against farmer settlers they invoked a right of prior possession, that fundamental right they would not dream of according Indians. Rights were not likely to be argued out as custom or law: rapacious staking out and get-off-my-land shooting was a justified image of the later frontier.[59]

Indian agency—almost the opposite of Indian agents—had shown itself impressively capable of responding to the challenge of new animal staples and a revolutionary commercial economy. Native Americans quickly proved that their own adaptation to pastoralism, mixing individual

---

[57]   Takaki R. 1979. *Iron Cages: Race and Culture in 19th Century America.* New York: Oxford University Press, 181–93, details the rapid transfer of land from Indian to white ownership. Takaki writes of the Dawes Act: 'It promised to be the final solution to the "Indian Question"'. See also Takaki, R. 1993. *A Different Mirror: A History of Multicultural America.* Boston: Little Brown, 231–24.

[58]   Foster, *Being Comanche,* 103–04.

[59]   Weaver, *Great Land Rush,* 56–59; Debo, *Road to Disappearance,* 338.

enterprise and communal ownership, could make a success of ranching. Cattle, equably bovine to whiffs of irony and paradox, presented themselves as the saving grace in the onslaught from the east. A more ideal replacement for the buffalo in the transition from hunting and gathering economy to a capitalist, commercial one could hardly have been invented. The transition had advantages to which even those most reluctant to let go of the old ways could adapt. Rounding up tamer and more securely profitable beasts was perhaps less manly than going out on the perilous and uncertain hunt, but leaders as different as Pleasant Porter and Geronimo firmly grasped that their peoples could stay together and prosper if left alone to do so.

Why were they not left alone? Because of the huge migration of European Americans, far exceeding any expectations, and the confluence of ideological streams rising in the dreams of founding fathers who could not imagine a human tide of such proportions. The individual farmer-citizens envisaged by Jefferson would always have competed with the Indian farmers he hoped to create. But he also created, most dramatically by the Louisiana Purchase, the idea of unlimited access to land even as the Indians were pushed west by the fierce and irresistible cavalry of settlers. They would sweep away the self-sustaining societies of Native American peoples and then their best chance of independent—not dependent—survival.

The culture of dependence that came with the distribution of sale or lease money can be construed as a near-genocidal disaster or as essential to survival of the fragmented tribes.[60] Grass money became a subsistence staple for many families after federal rations were ended in 1901. Some individuals did achieve independence as the Dawes idealists and cynics had both hoped. The cattle herds largely disappeared with allotment. By 1910, only two per cent of Kiowa, Comanche and Apache (KCA) Indians were engaged in stock raising. In 1934, the year of the New Deal Indian Reorganization Act that began to reverse the Dawes fragmentation, only 95 out of 805 KCA households had beef cattle.[61]

---

[60]   Native Americans, proud of survival, may resist references to genocide shaping their present. Rand, in *Kiowa Humanity*, rightly insists that history embrace both genocide and continuity. But the results of societal destruction remain catastrophic: 'There are, of course, some reservations around the country that have struck it rich with gambling or other ventures. But here in the prairies, those riches are only rumors. Half the population over 40 on Pine Ridge [South Dakota] has diabetes, and tuberculosis runs at eight times the national rate. As many as two-thirds of adults may be alcoholics, one-quarter of children are born with foetal alcohol spectrum disorders, and the life expectancy is somewhere around the high 40s—shorter than the average for sub-Saharan Africa. Less than ten per cent of children graduate from high school'. Krystof N. 'Poverty's poster child', *New York Times*, 9 May 2012.

[61]   Foster, *Being Comanche*, 103, 122.

John Collier, architect of the Indian New Deal, understood that economic independence was essential to the survival of Indian cultures. He was aware that the Indian Bureau he would head from 1933 to 1945 had been spoiling the efforts of the Plains tribes to succeed in the cattle industry. 'The Bureau persuaded and where necessary coerced them to sell their breeding stock; and then (in World War I years and thereafter) it pressured all the lands into white leaseholds. It leased the semi-arid grasslands to be broken to the plow, and soon thereafter to be washed or blown away.'[62] Collier persuaded Henry Wallace, Roosevelt's Secretary of Agriculture, to assist re-establishment of the cattle herds on reservations by the purchase of pure-bred stock from drought-stricken white ranchers. Stimulated by this $800 000 investment, the Indian beef cattle industry took off. 'Between 1933 and 1939 the number of Indians owning cattle increased from 8,627 to 16,624, the size of the herds jumped from 167,373 to 267,551, the money income derived from these cattle expanded from $263,095 to $3,125,326.'[63] But even a reformer as historically aware and persistent as Collier was not in the longer run able to prevent further alienation of Indian land and another collapse of Indian pastoral enterprise. The Second World War saw thousands of Indian men leave the reservations to serve in the armed forces and in war industries; those that returned found that the enterprises were no longer functioning and land had been leased to white cattlemen who took advantage of the wartime rise in beef prices. Federal agreements were once and for all 'terminated' by a conservative congress and Collier's experiment in re-constituting tribes fragmented and at odds was pronounced a failure.[64]

There are now sparse Indian reservations dotted where Indian Territory used to be. All over the Great Plains are the separated and diminished locations where Native American peoples have survived successive genocidal onslaughts—physical, societal and cultural—over two centuries. The Kiowa, the Comanche and the other great tribes, all are scattered. Oklahoma has Kiowa and Comanche counties, with few place names to recall the indigenous languages.[65] Only the Osages have a reservation large enough for grazing on an open range. Neither buffalo nor cattle could protect the peoples of the

---

62 Collier, J. 1947. *The Indians of the Americas*. New York: Norton, 246.

63 Philp, K.R. 1977. *John Collier's Crusade for Indian Reform 1920–1954*. Tucson: University of Arizona Press, 122–23, citing annual reports of the Commissioner of Indian Affairs for 1935 and 1940.

64 Deloria, V. & Lytle, C. 1984. *The Nations Within: The Past and Future of American Indian Sovereignty*. New York: Pantheon, 190–94.

65 Thornton, 'Population history', 36, reproduces the Indian Territory map from Hoxie F. ed. 1996. *Encyclopedia of North American Indians*. New York: Houghton Mifflin. There is a map of Kiowa and Comanche counties in a recent comprehensive study of survival markers. See Meadows W.C. 2008. *Kiowa Ethnogeography*. Austin: University of Texas Press, 216.

Plains from peaceful and warlike invasion from the east, from hordes who wanted nothing more than to set up new homes. It was Lincoln, the champion of union and freedom, who took advantage of the cession of the slave states to sign the Homestead Act. But the campaign to open up 'free' land went back to the formation of the United States. Washington described the pressure as graphically as Burke. In 1796 he agreed that policing a line to prevent further settler advances was the right thing to do: 'The Indians urge this; the Law requires it; and it ought to be done; but I believe scarcely anything short of a Chinese Wall, or a line of troops will restrain Land Jobbers, and the Incroachment of Settlers, upon the Indian Territory'.[66]

Washington had fought to establish the American union based on representative democracy and the democratic will of Americans was clear. Lincoln said democracy must not perish from the earth. Many thousands, on both sides, died for the right to decide their own form of economy and society in the terrible Civil War. But when that war ended, the hunters of the Plains paid the price for the new nation, the new economy and the manifest destiny of the United States.

N. Scott Momaday, a Kiowa writer celebrated for the access he has given Americans to a world that survives mainly in memories, says the culture he learned was not fixed or immune to adaptation. It was given to the Kiowas by the Crow on the move southwards. For a century, in alliance with the Comanches, the Kiowa horsemen dominated the Plains and sustained their people with the buffalo they hunted. But they did not believe the world as they knew it was stable or safe from dangers. In November 1833, a shower of meteors broke the stillness of the huge night sky. 'The falling stars seemed to image the sudden and violent disintegration of an old order.' Four years later, as a proud and independent people, they made the first of their treaties with the United States. All were broken. By 1875, the society and culture dependent on hunting was gone.[67] Their great leader Satanta had fought by treaty and by battle to save the world his people had known before the wagon trains, before the cattle drives, before the ranches and the railways. He warned his captors: if they killed him, his warriors would set the prairies alight. In 1878, he killed himself. His life was already a death, confined in a prison built on his plains.

---

66   Quoted in Sheehan B. 1973. *Seeds of Extinction: Jeffersonian Philanthropy and the American Indian.* Chapel Hill: University of North Carolina Press, 269, and Limerick, *Legacy of Conquest*, 192.
67   Momaday N.S. 1969. *The Way to Rainy Mountain.* Albuquerque: University of New Mexico Press, 6, 85–86.

Chapter Eleven

Dispossession, Ecocide, Genocide: Cattle Ranching and Agriculture in the Destruction of Hunting Cultures on the Canadian Prairies

Sidney L. Harring

City University of New York

The First Nations of the Canadian prairies had long and diverse histories of interaction with British, Canadian and American colonialism, but they could not have foreseen the sudden and violent end to their free existence on the open plains in the latter decades of the nineteenth century. The Blackfoot, Gros Ventre, Plains Cree, Plains Ojibwa, Assiniboine, Stoney, Dakota and Sarcee, among others, were of rich and diverse cultures but had one thing in common—their dependence on the buffalo hunt.[1] The Metis, mixed blood descendants of Europeans working in the fur trade, also engaged in this hunt and are recognised in Canada as an indigenous people. By the mid- to late-1870s, the hunt was rapidly failing, and by 1880 the buffalo herds were gone from Canada, replaced first by cattle ranching, then by mixed farming. By 1920 over 600 000 settlers, many of them Americans, had moved onto the Canadian prairies, displacing the remnants of plains Indian societies to tiny, impoverished reserves.[2]

Following British colonial policy, the new government of the Dominion of Canada, created in 1867, sought treaties with plains First Nations in order to open up the west, first to a transcontinental railroad and then for agricultural settlement.[3] Until 1869, the prairies were under the rule of the Hudson's Bay

---

[1] There is an extensive literature on Plains Indian cultures. Key works include Mandelbaum D. 1979. *The Plains Cree: An Ethnographic, Historical, and Comparative Study*. Regina: Great Plains Research Center; Samek H. 1987. *The Blackfoot Confederacy, 1880–1920: A Comparative Study of Canadian and US Indian Policy*. Albuquerque: University of New Mexico Press; Howard, J. 1984. *The Canadian Sioux*. Lincoln: University of Nebraska Press; DeMaillie, R. 2001. *Handbook of North American Indians: Plains*, 13, parts 1 and 2. Washington, D.C.: Smithsonian Institution.

[2] Elofson, W. 2000. 'The untamed Canadian ranching frontier, 1874–1914', in *Cowboys, Ranchers and the Cattle Business: Cross Border Perspectives on the Ranching Frontier*, eds S. Evans, S. Carter & B. Yeo. Calgary: University of Calgary Press, 81–100.

[3] There is a substantial and very contested literature on these treaties, which are still the subject of land claims and litigation. See Treaty 7 Elders and Tribal Council. 1996. *The True Spirit and Original Intent of Treaty 7*. Montreal: McGill Queens University Press; Price R. ed. 1997. *The Spirit of the Alberta Indian Treaties*. Edmonton: University of Alberta Press.

Company, a fur trading corporation chartered by the Crown. In 1869, these lands were 'sold' to the Crown and turned over to Canada in 1870. The region was under weak territorial government as part of the North West Territories until 1905 when the provinces of Saskatchewan and Alberta were created.[4]

These prairie treaties were extensions of British policy applied across Canada, but the scale of the negotiations on the plains was unique. Thousands of native people gathered to meet with formal Canadian delegations at each of these treaty sites and many of the First Nations signed treaties 4 (1874) through 7 (1877). There is a voluminous literature on these treaties which make it clear that First Nations were cheated out of their lands through a series of hollow promises, as well as misunderstandings about how English terms and modern concepts translated into indigenous languages. Especially significant was the failure of Canadian negotiators to adequately explain the notion of fee simple (private) ownership of property which had no meaning in indigenous cultures. In addition, fear of an uncertain future, growing poverty and the spectre of starvation, all due to rapidly diminishing hunting prospects, and deference to the new Canadian state, embodied in the powerful symbol of the British Crown, played their part in inducing Indian chiefs to sign these treaties. While the treaties differed in detail, the main element of each was that First Nations 'sold' their land to the Canadian government and agreed to move onto reserves. These reserves were tiny fractions of their previous lands that could not sustain anything remotely resembling their traditional way of life.[5]

The treaties also reserved for Indians the right to hunt, trap and fish outside of the reserve on their traditional lands. This concession, however, meant little to them as the bison on which they had been dependent were rapidly disappearing from the plains. The extension of railroads west brought an unprecedented level of commercial hunting that rapidly exterminated the herds. For the prairie First Nations, the hunt became more and more difficult and ended abruptly only a few years later. Hunting parties went out in 1879, after meager yields in 1877 and 1878, but found no buffalo.[6]

---

[4] Friesen G. 1987. *The Canadian Prairies: A History.* Toronto: University of Toronto Press, 220–41.

[5] Ray A., Miller J. & Tough F. 2000. *Bounty and Benevolence: A History of the Saskatchewan Treaties.* Montreal: McGill-Queens University Press; Miller, J. 2009. *Compact, Contract, Covenant: Aboriginal Treaty Making in Canada.* Toronto: University of Toronto Press; Morris A. 1880. *The Treaties of Canada with the Indians of Manitoba and the North-West Territories, Including the Negotiations on Which They were Based.* Toronto: Belfords Clarke.

[6] Hornaday W. 1989. *The Extermination of the American Bison.* Washington, DC: Smithsonian Institution Press, is the classic study of the destruction of the buffalo. The end of the Canadian herds is described on pages 504–05. See also Isenberg A. 2001. *The Destruction of the Bison: An Environmental History.* Cambridge: Cambridge University Press.

Indigenous peoples dependent on the buffalo hunt starved that winter. Thousands died of hunger and disease over that, and following, winters.[7] Large herds of American cattle were brought into Canada, beginning in the late 1870s, as the last of the buffalo were wiped out. The Canadian Pacific Railroad reached what is now Saskatchewan in 1882 and Alberta in 1883. Canadian investment companies, some backed by British investors, entered into agreements with American companies to purchase and graze cattle, leasing vast stretches of land in Alberta and Saskatchewan as soon as the Canadian government in 1881 enacted legislation to allow such leases.[8] In 1880, the population of what is now Alberta consisted of about 8 000 Indians and 1 500 whites. Ten years later, there were nearly 30 000 whites and no more than 5 000 Indians.[9] Within barely 10 years, Canada had removed the plains First Nations to small, isolated reserves and incorporated their lands into Canada with a plan to open these lands to white settlement.

Colonisation of the Canadian prairies

Increasingly, students of colonialism and the destruction of indigenous peoples recognise that these processes had global dimensions and cannot be understood simply as localised events. By the 1870s, Britain had had a long history of the destruction of indigenous peoples and the incorporation of their lands into its empire, represented in this instance by the new Canadian government, self-governing only since 1867.[10] It is clear that Canadian Indian policy as it developed after 1867 was based on preceding British protocols, rooted in turn in imperial practices that were playing out across Africa, Australia, New Zealand, Asia and Latin America. Though adapted to local conditions, British imperialism was distinctive through its widespread use of treaties to 'purchase' indigenous land, governing by indirect rule through local chiefs, removing indigenous people to reserves,

---

7   Samek, *Blackfoot Confederacy*, 38–41; Carter S. 1990. *Lost Harvests: Prairie Indian Reserve Farmers and Government Policy.* Montreal: McGill-Queens University Press, 70, 71, 90, 116, 131, 134, 231–32.

8   Elofson W. 2003. *Cowboys, Gentlemen and Cattle Thieves.* Montreal: McGill Queens University Press, 1–22; Foran M. 2003. *Trails and Trials: Markets and Land Use in Alberta Beef Cattle Industry, 1881–1948.* Calgary: University of Calgary Press, 1–28.

9   These population figures are rough estimates, reflecting both the frontier character of Alberta, but also that it was not a distinct administrative unit until 1905. Indians to the north of the prairies were beyond the reach of Canadian authorities, living in isolated bands that were often on the move.

10 The colonies of Nova Scotia, Prince Edward Island, New Brunswick, Ontario, Quebec and British Columbia were confederated as the Dominion of Canada in 1867. The Northwest Territories were added in 1869, with other territories joining later, Newfoundland being the last to do so in 1947.

and provoking colonial wars. Canadian Indian policy after 1867 was deeply rooted in the treaty process, and was in effect British policy, with key decisions made in London.[11]

While acknowledging this British colonial legacy, it is also true that much of Canadian history was intertwined with that of the United States. US Indian policy was also originally British policy but, with the Royal Proclamation of 1763, it took a different direction.[12] While the British, and later the Canadian state, chose to direct Indian policy from central government, the United States de facto devolved much of its Indian policy to the frontier. While nominally keeping federal control of Indian affairs, it in effect left decisions to local and state interests which were generally hostile to Indians and intent on getting control of their lands.[13] The result was a series of extremely destructive Indian wars. Many thousands of Indians were killed and many acts of genocide perpetrated on the American frontier. Entire Indian villages were destroyed, mass forced removals executed, and death through sickness and ill treatment wiped out entire communities. This legacy has had a unique impact on American culture, and helped shape United States imperialism as wars against indigenous peoples have been extended around the globe, initially to the Philippines and Mexico, but now against tribal peoples in Iraq, Afghanistan, Somalia, Yemen, Pakistan and other countries.[14]

---

[11]   Harring S. 1998. *White Man's Law: Native People in Nineteenth Century Canadian Jurisprudence.* Toronto: University of Toronto Press & Osgoode Society for Canadian Legal History, 16–34.

[12]   Harring, *White Man's Law*, 22–27; Samek, *Blackfoot Confederacy*, 1–35. The Royal Proclamation of 1763 recognised Indian rights to their lands west of the Appalachian Mountains and restricted white settlement there. It required that Indian lands be purchased by the Crown before white settlement took place. This is now regarded as one of the causes of the American Revolution because American colonists would not stand for British interference in their move westward. After the revolution, the Royal Proclamation remained at the core of Indian policy in Canada.

[13]   While it is now clear under United States law that Indian affairs are entirely under federal jurisdiction, this was contested by many states, especially in the South, through the first half of the nineteenth century. In addition, American state and local interests have always been powerful and competed with federal authority in the west through the nineteenth century. Harring, S, 1994. *Crow Dog's Case: American Indian Sovereignty, Tribal Law, and United States Law in the Nineteenth Century.* Cambridge: Cambridge University Press, 25–56.

[14]   Drinnon R. 1997. *Facing West: The Metaphysics of Indian Hating and Empire Building.* Norman: University of Oklahoma Press; Atwood P. 2010. *War and Empire: The American Way of Life.* London: Pluto Press. Any analysis of the centrality of violence in American culture needs to begin with an analysis of the Indian Wars. The United States' military expenditure is larger than the next 10 countries combined. The United States is the only country in the world that maintains military forces around the world on every continent with a policy of actively using them to protect American interests.

The impact of developments in the United States was often very directly felt on the Canadian plains. Until the middle of the 1870s, the border between the US and Canadian prairies was open and completely unregulated, with no topographical or other barriers between the two.[15] The first Americans on the Canadian plains were traders, often called 'whiskey traders', who tried to undercut the Canadian fur trade by engaging in quick and independent, but often also corrupt and violent, deals with Indians fueled with cheap liquor. It was not until the summer of 1874 that the Canadian government established a presence on the prairies, sending a detachment of 275 of the newly created North West Mounted Police, commonly called the 'Mounties', to the Alberta and Saskatchewan borderlands.[16] The creation of this police force was a direct result of the Cypress Hills Massacre of 1 June 1873. A party of American wolf hunters had been robbed of their horses in Montana. They tracked the stolen horses into Canada, lost the trail and ended up at two whiskey trading posts at Cypress Hills, now in southern Saskatchewan. Here were also gathered 200 to 300 Assiniboine people. After excessive drinking, a dispute over another missing horse arose. The confrontation culminated in a group of wolfers, whiskey traders and Metis freighters opening fire on the Assiniboine camp, killing 23 Indians.[17] The incident outraged Canadians, who were concerned both about violations of Canadian sovereignty as well as the extension of US-style frontier violence into Canada.

Canadian history presents its prairie frontier as distinct from that of the United States from that period onwards in that this frontier was henceforth policed. Mounties supposedly travelled ahead of settlement with the intention of controlling frontier development, in direct contrast to the violence and disorder of the American frontier. This ideal of the orderly and policed frontier today has the status of a creation myth in Canadian political culture. Reality was very different because such a small police force could not have had more than a tenuous control over the vast borderlands.[18] American cattlemen, for example, ran their herds into Canada to take advantage of the seasonally high grasses, kept them moving, then re-crossed the border

---

15   West H. 1958. 'Starvation winter of the Blackfeet'. *The Magazine of Western History*, 9, no. 1; Dusenberry V. 1954. 'The Rocky Boy Indians: Montana's displaced people'. *The Magazine of Western History*, 4, no. 1, 1–15. Hogue M. 2002. 'Disputing the medicine line: the Plains Cree and the Canadian-American border, 1876–1885'. *The Magazine of Western History*, 52, no. 4, 2–17.
16   McLeod R. 1976. *The North-West Mounted Police and Law Enforcement, 1873–1905*. Toronto: University of Toronto Press.
17   Goldring P. 1973. 'The Cypress Hills massacre: a century's retrospect'. *Saskatchewan History*, 26, no. 3, 89–120.
18   Elofson, *Cowboys, Gentlemen and Cattle Thieves*, vii–xx.

ahead of the mounted police. In addition, Indians from both sides freely crossed the border, dealing as independent nations with both governments. They followed buffalo herds, until their end, also oblivious to the presence of the border. Indeed, the structure of plains Indian society, loosely organised into small hunting bands that could respond quickly to changing buffalo herd movements,[19] was extremely well suited to evading mounted police. Even Indians on reserves easily gave Mounties the slip. The usual modus operandi was for several bands of riders to flee the reserve at night, riding fast with tracks going in different directions to confound mounted police. They would then regroup days later at a planned rendezvous.

The porousness of the border is demonstrated by the experience of the great Sioux chief Sitting Bull. Following his brilliant defeat of the American army at the Battle of Little Big Horn, he fled to Canada in 1876 with 5 000 of his people, remaining there for five years. As he reached the border, he was greeted by Canadian Mounties and produced a medal, given to his ancestors by British authorities as reward for their loyalty in the War of 1812. This represented the second wave of Sioux refugees to seek sanctuary in Canada, the first coming after their defeat in the Minnesota Sioux War of 1863. Thousands of Sioux descendants still live on the Canadian plains. Sitting Bull subsequently returned to the United States in 1881, only to be killed in 1890 when US authorities sought to arrest him, fearing that he was going to flee the Standing Rock Reservation and join the ghost dance movement, a peaceful cultural rebellion against US authority.[20]

Canadian First Nations were therefore familiar with United States Indian policy. They learned about American Indian wars, reservations and treaties first hand, sitting around council fires and speaking to native people from the United States. Indeed, the Great Plains had created a vast plains culture that transcended individual First Nations and languages. These plains, more than two thousand miles north to south, and up to a thousand miles east to west, consisted of flat, open terrain with few natural obstacles. The various plains First Nations, having horses and easily movable teepees, could cover great distances with relative ease. The

---

[19] There is a substantial literature on the social organisation of the plains First Nations, which took similar forms across the prairies. According to Mandelbaum, *Plains Cree*, 290: 'Bands are loose, little co-ordinated units, largely moulded by geographical considerations ... chieftainship is dependent on merit and valor; the power of the chief varies with the personality wielding it'.

[20] Utley R. 2008. *Sitting Bull: The Life and Times of an American Patriot*. New York: Holt, 72–80, 261–300; McCrady D. 1998. 'Living with strangers: the nineteenth century Sioux and the Canadian American borderlands'. PhD dissertation, University of Manitoba, 1–101; Howard, J. 1984. *The Canadian Sioux*. Lincoln: University of Nebraska Press, 1–50.

spread of both plains peoples and their material cultures across the region testifies to this interchange. The use of horses, which had diffused from the south northwards during the eighteenth century, was adapted by each plains nation to their own advantage. The woodland Cree, for example, moved west onto the prairies and adapted to the horse and the buffalo hunt within a relatively short period. Sioux peoples moved from Minnesota and Wisconsin to the Dakotas within a few generations after the mid- to late-1700s. Dene peoples from northern Alberta and Saskatchewan moved to New Mexico, becoming known as the Navajo.

In the 1870s, the easiest access to the southern Canadian plains was through the United States via the Missouri River, the main artery of trade. By the 1870s, Montana was well settled and steamships from St Louis plied the Missouri to various points just south of the border. Beginning in the 1850s, the US government negotiated a series of treaties with Indian peoples living in its northern prairie region. As a consequence, a network of American Indian reservations extended south of the Canadian border well before Canadian authorities were present in the area. Some US First Nations took advantage of this and moved across the border into Canada to escape confinement to reserves. Montana had a white population nearing 40 000 by 1880. The American side of the border was two decades ahead of the Canadian side in terms of white settlement. Indeed, by the 1890s the US line of settlement had moved completely across the plains, resulting in many American settlers or their children seeking land in Canada.[21]

Canada was founded on the fur trade which was dependent on Indians as hunters, trappers, traders and a variety of ancillary capacities, both skilled and unskilled.[22] This thorough integration of indigenous peoples into the colonial economy distinguishes Canada from the United States and many other colonial societies, particularly settler colonies. Some First Nations prospered, adapting their societies to the needs of the fur trade. Until 1869, the Hudson's Bay Company owned the Canadian prairies under British law and employed thousands of Indians in the fur trade.[23] While some were directly employed, most worked independently, hunting for furs, which they traded annually with the company. The company operated through a system of indirect rule akin to that used by the British in other parts of the world. This entailed deferring to the sovereignty of First Nations and

---

21 Hogue, 'Disputing the medicine line', 2–17.
22 Ray A. 1974. *Indians in the Fur Trade: Their Role as Trappers, Hunters and Middle Men in the Lands Southwest of Hudson Bay, 1660–1860*. Toronto: University of Toronto Press.
23 Raffan J. 2007. *Emperor of the North: Sir George Simpson and the Remarkable Story of the Hudson's Bay Company*. New York: Harper Collins.

leaving them to practice customary law as long as they served the economic interests of the colonial power.[24]

The fur trade required a highly mobile workforce and thousands of native people travelled great distances across Canada, meeting and getting to know others as they went about their business. The French, by the late 1600s for example, employed Iroquois and Algonquians in present day Ontario, Quebec, and even the prairies, to carry freight to and from the central part of the continent, the lands north and west of Lake Superior. The Hudson's Bay Company employed Crees from Ontario and northern Manitoba to carry freight as far as the Rocky Mountains and back. This disrupted traditional society, but also opened them up to European innovation and created a colonial settler society built on native labour.

After the American Revolution, thousands of American farmers moved to Upper and Lower Canada, what is now Ontario and Quebec. This aided the colonial economy's shift to agriculture, especially as the fur trade also waned in the early- to mid-nineteenth century as fur animal populations declined due to over-exploitation. A concomitant shift from the fur trade to agriculture in the native economy began in the east, a change reflected in Canadian Indian policy. First Nations in the east were now required to surrender their land and moved to reserves, where they would be provided with basic implements and taught to farm. While it cannot be said that this policy had significant success in Ontario, it came to be the model used on the prairies.[25]

Colonialism and the fur trade disrupted traditional Indian society and set in motion many First Nation population movements. Some First Nations became relatively rich and powerful by serving as mediators between English and French traders and more remote bands. The Cree, Sioux, Ojibwa and others moved west in pursuit of fur or because of population shifts caused by that pursuit. First Nations with access to guns and iron had a strategic advantage over competitors that did not, encouraging further conflict. Indian nations robbed of their lands in the east, moved west, putting pressure on other Indian communities, which occasionally ended in wars. Scarcity of game, the result of over-hunting and trapping, forced some eastern tribes to move west. It also pushed woodland tribes out onto

---

24   Myers J. 2008. *Indirect Rule in South Africa: Tradition, Modernity, and the Costuming of Political Power.* Rochester: University of Rochester Press. There is a voluminous literature on indirect rule as a form of colonial rule which, I argue, was in part formed by earlier confrontations with indigenous peoples. Harring, *White Man's Law*, 16–34.

25   Sample K. 1968. 'Changes in agriculture on the Six Nations reserve'. *Open Access Dissertations and Theses*, paper 4920 available at http://www. digitalcommons.mcmaster. ca/cgi/viewcontent.cgi?article=4920; Carter, *Lost Harvests*, 3–49.

the plains in search of buffalo. As the buffalo disappeared, plains Indians encroached on each others' territories in search of game, further disrupting Indian life on the plains.[26]

By the time the numbered plains treaties 4 to 7 were signed in the mid-1870s, most of the plains First Nations understood that a new order was being imposed on them, and that they were not strong enough to mount effective resistance. They were well aware of American military conquest of the plains to the south. What is more, thousands of settlers following the transcontinental railroad had moved into Montana and the Dakotas, and in Canada, as far west as Manitoba. The interior of British Columbia had already been occupied after a gold rush in 1858. A long history of trade and other forms of interaction with European peoples had given the plains First Nations a great deal of exposure to settlers and they knew what to expect. While some First Nations protested the sale of Hudson's Bay lands to Canada, arguing that it was Indian land, Canadian authorities ignored their demands. Part of the Indians' willingness to agree to the numbered treaties was that they provided some acknowledgement of their land rights and status as First Nations.[27]

Destruction of buffalo herds and creation of reserves

The vast grasslands of the North American prairie provided the ecological environment that supported first, vast buffalo herds, and subsequently, an economy based on cattle farming. American cattlemen settled the west on their own terms, without government regulation. In the open range, they moved their cattle wherever there was good grass, and as soon as the grazing was exhausted, trekked on to new pastures, exploiting the open commons.[28] Since the grass was free and labour rates low, it cost little to raise cattle, making the enterprise highly profitable, albeit economically risky. It was also environmentally destructive because cattle herds grazed the fragile prairie grass down to its roots, causing massive soil erosion. No thought was given to this environmental damage at the time.

The destruction of the buffalo herds had devastating consequences for First Nations of the Canadian prairies. Not only were these herds their main source of sustenance, but entire cultures were based on the seasonal

---

26 Jenish D. 1999. *Indian Fall: The Last Great Days of the Plains Cree and the Blackfoot Confederacy*. Toronto: Penguin. The Piegans, Bloods and Blackfoot made up the Blackfoot Confederacy, each with a reserve in southern Alberta.
27 Ray et al, *Bounty and Benevolence*, 108–11.
28 Jordan-Bychkov T. 2000. 'Does the border matter? Cattle ranching and the 49th parallel', in *Cowboys, Ranchers, and the Cattle Business*, eds Evans et al, 1–10.

migrations in search of buffalo. The respective territories of each tribe were, for example, based on well-established buffalo migration patterns. As buffalo herds were depleted, each nation moved further and further away in search of buffalo, to lands that they had never hunted before and into the territories of other nations.[29] Herds on the Canadian side of the border were depleted before those on the US side. As a result, some Indian nations that had lived in Canada went south across the border to hunt, especially in Montana, where buffalo herds lasted a few years longer. This brought them under the jurisdiction of the United States and in conflict with American settlers.[30] Importantly, the collapse of the hunt destabilised the social structures of First Nations. Many were dispersed, weakening traditional society irretrievably.[31]

The North American buffalo herd which numbered between 20 and 40 million in 1850, was small and scattered by 1879 and completely gone by 1883. The extension of railroads across the United States had divided the herd into northern and southern branches, with the southern herd hunted to extinction by the middle 1870s. Hunters then focused their attention on the northern herd which had always moved freely between the United States and Canada. In this they were facilitated by the US Army, under General Philip Sheridan, who was tasked with ending the wars on the plains. Sheridan recognised that the destruction of buffalo herds served his interests, reportedly observing in 1875 of white hunters that 'they are destroying the Indians' commissary. Let them kill, skin, and sell until the buffaloes are exterminated'.[32] After the 1876 Sioux War and the stunning defeat of his army at the Battle of Little Big Horn, Sheridan wanted the buffalo eradicated in order to force plains Indians back onto their reservations—a goal his army had failed to achieve.

These same herds migrated back and forth across the Canadian border, so that the killing off of buffalo herds in the United States contributed to their extinction in Canada. In addition, the buffalo were hunted in Canada, both by American hunters, crossing a poorly controlled border, and also by First Nations and Metis hunters, selling their hides to traders. One party of hunters had the capacity to kill an entire herd, so the final hunt occurred in

29 Jenish, *Indian Fall*, 113–53.
30 Hogue, 'Disputing the medicine line', 2–17.
31 Samek, *Blackfoot Confederacy*, 38–47; Jenish, *Indian Fall*, 132–42.
32 Smits D. 1994. 'The frontier army and the destruction of the buffalo, 1865–1883'. *Western Historical Quarterly*, 25, 312–38. There is still controversy about the slaughter of the buffalo, including debate over the import of General Sheridan's words. See Robbins J. 'Historians revisit slaughter on the plains'. *New York Times*, 16 November 1999.

a single year.[33] For the Blackfeet, it seems that they were able to hunt buffalo in 1877 and 1878, but were starving by 1879. Further north in 1881 near Moose Jaw, a party of Cree were seen with several carts of buffalo meat, but further east, Cree at Fort Qu'Appelle were starving as no buffalo could be found.[34] By 1883, there were no buffalo left on the Canadian plains and hunger was everywhere.[35] Plains peoples met this catastrophe by following dwindling herds. For thousands this meant moving south to Montana where the buffalo lasted to the middle 1880s. Canadian authorities welcomed this migration, not only because it emptied the Canadian plains for settlement, but also because it reduced the cost of feeding starving Indians on the reserves.[36]

By the end of the 1870s, the plains First Nations were starving on their reserves, created a few years earlier by treaties 4, 6 and 7. Reserves were under the complete control of the Canadian government, backed by their North West Mounted Police and Indian agents. Canadian reserves in the west were created well after their US counterparts. They were also smaller, operating with much less funding and far fewer government employees. Unlike the Canadian government that wanted to settle the plains as cheaply as possible, the American government financed a huge bureaucracy of Indian agents and their hirelings, who ran a system ridden with corruption. The US also fed tens of thousands of Indians, on hundreds of reservations, for many years.

The Canadian government's policy of creating reserves was based on its experience of agriculture as practised by eastern First Nations. A few acres planted with the 'three sisters'—squash, beans and corn—could feed a family, especially when combined with small-scale animal husbandry and reasonable hunting opportunities, which existed through much of the nineteenth century.[37] This model of farming coincided with the dominant mode of northern European farming brought to Canada and the United States by settlers, and was well adapted to North American conditions. Indians throughout Ontario practised this form of agriculture along with an extensive hunting and trapping economy.[38]

---

33 Hornaday, *Extermination of the American Bison*, 492–504.
34 Hornaday, *Extermination of American Bison*, 504.
35 Carter, *Lost Harvests*, 70, 71, 90, 116,131,134, 231–2.
36 Hogue, 'Disputing the medicine line', 2–17.
37 Carter, *Lost Harvests*, is the classic history of Canadian government policy on Indian agriculture. Hurt D. 1987. *Indian Agriculture in America: Prehistory to the Present*. Lawrence: University Press of Kansas, analyses the various Indian farming systems in North America.
38 Waisberg L. & Holzkamm T. 1993. 'A tendency to discourage them from cultivating: Ojibway agriculture and Indian affairs administration in northwestern Ontario'. *Ethnohistory*, 40, no. 2, 175–211.

This agricultural tradition did not, however, extend to the prairies. The Hudson's Bay Company brought some European agriculture to the west, creating gardens around their posts, growing all the food they could, using Indian labour. But the plains First Nations did not adopt agriculture. The buffalo hunt was all encompassing, requiring highly mobile modes of life that made crop growing or animal husbandry impossible, especially since buffalo were hunted in summer when fields needed tending. In addition, the prairie climate was too dry for the type of agriculture practised in the east. Initial Canadian government assessments of the agricultural potential of the prairies, based on eastern models, were that crop farming would not be feasible on the southern plains, because of insufficient rainfall. The Palliser expedition of 1858–1859, sent to study the potential for agriculture on the southern plains, concluded as much.[39] The Palliser Triangle, as the arid region of southern Alberta and Saskatchewan came to be called, still defines the rough boundaries of cattle ranching in western Canada. Modern, large-scale wheat, canola and sunflower farms, among the richest in the world, use new seeds and agricultural technologies unknown at that time.

While the Canadian government was eager to move prairie First Nations to reserves, little thought had been given to how they were going to subsist there. It was simply assumed that Indians would use reserves as a base from which to assimilate into Canadian society and not remain separate or dependent on government aid. Underlying this premise was a racist belief that colonial society was superior to indigenous societies, that indigenous cultures were backward and barbaric, and needed to be eliminated.[40] The Canadian government used all methods at its disposal to suppress Indian culture, including, later in 1884, expanding the Indian Act to outlaw certain Indian religious ceremonies.[41] This was ethnocide, designed to eliminate native religions and ultimately the independent cultural existence of First Nations.

It was not only the reserve system that the Canadian government used to try and compel assimilation. The reserve system was backed by the 1876 Indian Act, with predecessor laws extending back to the 1850s.[42] The Indian Act gave the government virtually complete authority over First Nations. While plains nations were signing the treaties, they were ignorant of the

---

[39] Waiser B. 2005. *Saskatchewan: A New History*. Calgary: Fifth House, 42–44.

[40] Carter, *Lost Harvests*, 15–49.

[41] Pettipas K. 1989. *Severing the Ties that Bind: Government Repression of Indigenous Religious Ceremonies on the Prairies*. Winnipeg: University of Manitoba Press, 93.

[42] Milloy J. 1983. 'The early Indian acts: developmental strategy and constitutional change', in *As Long as the Sun Shines and the Water Flows*, eds I. Getty & A. Lussier. Vancouver: University of British Columbia Press, 56–73.

provisions of the Indian Act that relegated them to the status of second class citizens. Indian reserves were created, under the ownership and control of the Canadian government. The Indian Nations were broken up into 'bands', with each 'band' relegated to its own reserve, destroying their cultures. The status of individual Indians was determined by the Canadian government and thousands of Indians lost their Indian status as a result. There was little means of income on these reserves and many bands went hungry. Indians were not citizens and could not vote. Religious ceremonies were outlawed. Also, a prairie Indian farmer could not, and still cannot, sell his produce without a permit from his Indian agent.[43] This last provision, besides asserting government control of Indian farming, also kept Indian farmers from competing with settler farmers.[44]

The removal of First Nations to reserves where they were supposed to adopt an agricultural way of life was at the core of the treaty process. The reserves were generally small, based on the rough measure of each Indian household of five receiving 640 acres, with plots allocated in proportion to family size.[45] Allotments on prairie reserves were larger than in the east because the land was more arid, but were of similar proportion across prairie reserves irrespective of differences in climate or soil conditions. Considering that this limited acreage had to feed each family in perpetuity, with succeeding generations living on the same reserve, land allocations were utterly inadequate to provide sustainable farms. Even for the first generation, this amounted to less than 130 acres per person. While small-scale crop production might have been possible, it was woefully insufficient for grazing. In addition, provision was made for the Canadian government to supply agricultural implements to families that chose to grow crops, and

---

[43] Indian Act, RSC 1985. S 32(1) provides as follows: 'A transaction of any kind whereby a band or a member thereof purports to sell, barter, exchange, give, or otherwise dispose of cattle or other animals, grain or hay, whether wild or cultivated, or root crops or plants or their products from a reserve in Manitoba, Saskatchewan or Alberta, to a person other than a member of that band is void unless the superintendent approves the transaction in writing'. S 33 makes unauthorised transactions of the above a criminal offence. The Indian Act was originally passed in 1876 and, although it has been revised, is still in force in a version of its original form. It was extensively revised in 1948, when some of the worst provisions were removed. Indians have been citizens of Canada since 1947. Milloy, J. 2008. 'Indian Act colonialism: a century of dishonor, 1869–1969'. Research paper for the National Center for First Nations Governance.

[44] Waiser, *Saskatchewan*, 124.

[45] Price, *Alberta Treaties*, 15. Treaties 1 and 2 had provided only 160 acres of land for a family of five, utterly inadequate for farming in Western Ontario. The Salteaux in Treaty 3 refused that amount, so the government raised it to 640 acres per family. The various treaties of Canada are still the object of land claims lawsuits. It is not at all clear what the government had in mind in providing so little land to plains Indians, when it was clear that they could not live on such small allotments.

cattle to families that chose animal husbandry. But no thought had been given to the viability of farming on such small plots.[46] It thus doomed generations yet unborn to poverty. Canada's policy of assimilation assumed that future generations would not remain on the reserves, but assimilate into the local population.

It took several years for most tribes to select their reserves, and some took quite a while longer. Some reserve selections were rejected by Canadian authorities and tribes moved to other locations. First Nation peoples were not legally required to live on these reserves permanently and many continued to hunt—or attempted to hunt, at least through to the early 1880s. Thousands of native people gathered in the Cypress Hills area, far from their reserves, where they moved freely back and forth across the border.[47] Much of their subsistence of necessity depended on stolen cattle as there was not much else to eat. Indeed, all of the ranches suffered severe loss of cattle each year, with attrition rates of up to 50 per cent being common. While ranchers often blamed Indians for the depletion of their herds, the reality of the open range was that cattle losses were due to a variety of factors including rustlers, severe weather, wolves and cattle simply wandering off.[48]

Reports of starvation on reserves reached the government in Ottawa at the latest by 1879.[49] While the forced cultural assimilation of First Nation peoples into Canadian society—ethnocide—was always at the core of Canadian government Indian policy, it was its reaction to this news of death by starvation that raises charges to the next level, that of responsibility for the mass death of Indian peoples and of genocide. Once Canada had confined Indians to reserves without access to their former means of subsistence, it had a legal and moral responsibility to ensure their basic well-being and certainly to ensure that Indians did not starve to death. The government vacillated on this issue to an extent that today seems incomprehensible. Parliament actually debated whether or not plains Indians should be fed to avoid starvation. One view was that the government had a duty to support Indians since it had required that they move onto reserves and used armed force to keep them there. An opposing view was that refusing to feed starving Indians would help overcome their indolence and motivate them to learn methods of small-scale agriculture sufficiently to feed themselves.[50]

---

46   Carter, *Lost Harvests*, 50–78; Ray et al, *Bounty and Benevolence*, 187–97.
47   Hildebrant W. & Hubner B. 2007. *The Cypress Hills: An Island by Itself*. Saskatoon: Purich, 89–138.
48   Elofson, *Cowboys, Gentlemen, and Cattle Thieves*, 113–14.
49   Carter, *Lost Harvests*, 70–72, 90, 116, 124, 131–34.
50   Shewell H. 2004. *Enough to Keep Them Alive: Indian Welfare in Canada, 1873–1965*. Toronto: University of Toronto Press, 25–92.

The latter view is one that came to inform government policy making, a stance that took no cognisance of the realities of farming or ranching on the prairies.[51] First Nations farmers lacked access to capital, agricultural training and sufficient land for success under difficult conditions. More than 100 years later, this is still the case.

White settlement of the Canadian prairies

By 1879, much of the Canadian prairies had been occupied by American cattle herds. Soon after Indians had surrendered their lands in the treaties of 1874, 1876 and 1877, American ranchers moved cattle en masse onto the Canadian plains. By 1880, at least 200 open-range cattle ranches run by American farmers were operating on the Canadian plains.[52] Ecologically, ranching was possible as soon as the buffalo herds were sufficiently depleted to allow enough grass to sustain cattle. Raising American cattle, simply by releasing them on the open range to graze on free Canadian grass, then rounding them up the next year, was profitable but risky.[53] This type of ranching became possible once First Nations 'sold' their land to the Crown, making it de facto 'open' although it was only in 1881 that there was any formal provision for leasing Crown lands to ranchers. These early ranches had no legal status at all. They were squatting operations on newly acquired Crown land. Montana herds moved temporarily into Canada in the spring and summer in search of good grass and water, then returned to Montana as winter approached for shelter and to take advantage of its warmer weather. Cowboys moved their cattle within this seasonal pattern as the vagaries of grass, water and weather dictated.

In 1881, four years after Treaty 7 was signed, Canada adopted a system of leases for range lands in southern Alberta and Saskatchewan. This formalised what was already occurring, namely, that large herds of American cattle were grazing the open range of the southern prairies. No one consulted Indians inhabiting unfenced reserves, and soon these cattle were eating their grass as well. The Indians, at this time, did not have cattle. They, however, still had herds of horses, which had great value in plains Indian cultures and which grazed reserve grasslands. There was thus growing conflict over grazing as cattle herds trespassed on Indian reserves. Also, Indians stole

---

51 Buckley H. 1992. *From Wooden Ploughs to Welfare: Why Indian Policy Failed in the Prairie Provinces.* Montreal: McGill-Queens University Press, 28–66.

52 Elofson, *Cowboys, Gentlemen, and Cattle Thieves,* 81–100; Waiser, *Saskatchewan,* 41–58.

53 Elofson, *Cowboys, Gentlemen, and Cattle Thieves,* 81–100.

settler cattle in order to survive. This conflict was contained, in part at least, by the North West Mounted Police.

The precise parameters of this confrontation are difficult to define. To begin with, the data is poor. It seems clear that thousands of cattle were stolen during this period, by both whites and Indians. On the one hand, Indian agents had the support of the North West Mounted Police, who responded to complaints of ranchers that Indians and rustlers were stealing their stock. On the other hand, the land was vast and much happened beyond the reach of the police. Detachments were stationed 40 miles apart, leaving on average one officer for every 500 square miles or about 350 people. The open range, on which thousands of cattle belonging to hundreds of ranches grazed, was impossible to police effectively.[54]

Indians, who were not legally required to remain on reserves and were oftentimes hungry, frequently left their reserves for a variety of reasons— including raids against one another, as well as on settler cattle herds. About this time, the Canadian government started introducing cattle onto Indian reserves, while the North West Mounted Police maintained herds of cattle, both for their own use and to help feed Indians on reserves. The first cattle Indians received were meant for slaughter. These cattle were supplied from government herds which had been bought from local ranchers. These cattle were delivered to Indian reserves on the hoof for Indians to butcher. Later, by the mid- to late-1880s, the first stages of Indian farming on the prairies led to the introduction of breeding cattle onto reserves, and the formation of Indian-owned cattle herds.

Open-range ranching never fit with Canadian policy or legal culture, and the introduction of a leasing system effectively ended the open range during the 1890s. Initially, all of the cattle were brought by Montana cattlemen, who took advantage of free Canadian grass. By the late 1870s, Canadians and British farmers were also entering the business, often buying Montana cattle and moving them to Alberta and Saskatchewan ranges. A few tried to improve their Texas-based American herds by bringing breeding stock from Britain or the east. Some very large ranches were created and, for a

---

54 Elofson, *Cowboys, Gentlemen, and Cattle Thieves*, 102–03. He reveals that at its Fort Walsh post, North West Mounted Police, out of the 14 978 miles travelled in 1881, 12 865 miles (85.9 per cent) were for the survival of the post; 1 283 miles (8.6 per cent) for 'Indian issues' and only 830 miles (5.5 per cent) for what was termed 'law enforcement'. Divided by 365 days, this detachment on average travelled less than four miles a day on 'Indian issues' and a little more than two miles a day on 'law enforcement' matters, in an area of 500 square miles and 40 miles from the nearest post.

time, these operations caught the imagination of British financiers.[55] The Canadian Pacific Railroad reached Saskatchewan in 1882 and Alberta in 1883, providing direct access to markets in the east for the first time. Until the railroad arrived, the market for Canadian cattle remained localised, with the Canadian government the leading buyer of beef for both the North West Mounted Police and to feed Indians on reserves. With railroad access to eastern ports, Canada became a large supplier of beef to Great Britain.

Open-range ranching was not well suited to the ecology of the prairies either. Many cattle died from extreme winter cold, and in the exceptionally harsh winter of 1881–1882, most cattle on the open range died of exposure.[56] By the 1890s, Canadian cattle ranching took the form either of specialised, smaller, fenced operations, or as part of mixed farming enterprises together with the cultivation of wheat or other grains. By the 1890s, most of the leases had been sharply reduced in size, and small-scale producers had moved onto leased lands. Canadian law, reflecting the society's tradition of smaller scale agriculture, gave these farmers the right to pre-empt range leases— which they soon did.[57] The wheat boom followed soon after, creating much greater wealth than cattle ranching did, and many cattle farmers themselves moved, in whole or in part, to wheat farming. Cattle ranches continued as smaller operations using the prairie for summer pasture, but bringing the cattle down to sheltered valleys in winter where they could be fed hay and grain. A study of ranching in the Cypress Hills district in the 1960s found that there were no more than 90 ranchers left, compared to about 1 000 mixed farmers—and this in the country that had been the heart of the Canadian open range.[58]

Indians were pushed aside in this process of expropriation that was both violent and illegal. Indian resistance culminated in a war that broke out in 1885, the closest Canada ever came to a full-scale Indian war. What started as a Metis rebellion was joined by Cree and Sioux warriors in northern Saskatchewan and northeastern Alberta.[59] While the rebellion was quickly put down by Canadian forces, the aftermath was devastating for First Nations. They were forced to move to their reserves and remain there. An extra-legal

---

[55] Breen D. 1983. *The Canadian Prairie West and the Ranching Frontier, 1874–1924.* Toronto: University of Toronto Press.

[56] Elofson W. & Bulger J. 2000. 'Nature's fury', in *Cowboys, Gentlemen, and Cattle Thieves,* W. Elofson, 71–98.

[57] Foran, *Trails and Trials.*

[58] Bennett J. 1969. *Northern Plainsmen: Adaptive Strategy and Agrarian Life.* Chicago: Aldine, 182.

[59] Waiser B. & Stone Child B. 1997. *Loyal Till Death: Indians and the North-West Rebellion.* Calgary: Fifth House, 1–145.

pass system was introduced, requiring all Indians to obtain passes from their Indian agent before being allowed to leave the reserve. Passes were routinely denied. The system was entirely illegal, but enforced by local police, in effect imprisoning Indians on reserves.[60] Also, 81 Indians were tried for their 'crimes' in the uprising, charges including treason against the British Crown. Eight were hanged and most were incarcerated in a special prison wing built for native people at Stony Mountain Prison just north of Winnipeg.[61] The experience of prison broke many Indian leaders, who eventually returned to their reserves sick and old, too weak to resist any further white claims to their land.

As the last Indian resistance was swept aside, the Canadian Pacific Railroad brought tens of thousands of immigrants to western Canada to take up farms on lands that Indians had 'sold'. The demographic shift was dramatic. In 1880, Alberta had about 8 000 Indians and no more than 2 000 whites. By 1890, there were as many as 30 000 whites, and by 1900 a total of over 65 000 whites while the Indian population had declined to below 5 000. The census reported that 6 358 Indians lived in Saskatchewan in 1906.[62] The white population of the North West Territory (Alberta and Saskkachewan combined until 1905) was about 25 000 in 1881 and 67 000 in 1891. The white population of Saskatchewan, opened to immigrant and Canadian farmers, soared from a few thousand to 257 000 at the time of the creation of the new province in 1905.[63] First Nations suffered high death rates, confined to reserves without adequate food or means of survival. In the first two decades of the twentieth century, hundreds of thousands more white settlers, mostly farmers, moved onto the Canadian plains. This settlement boom was, however, short-lived. Whites settled the land indiscriminately, including areas that could not be farmed or ranched at all. Subsequently, between 1921 and 1926, 120 000 abandoned prairie farms were forfeited to the Crown. Even before the depression of the early 1930s,

---

60   Barron L. 1968. 'The Indian pass system in the Canadian west, 1882–1935'. *Prairie Forum*, 13, no. 1, 25–42.

61   Waiser & Stone Child, *Loyal Till Death*, 192–237.

62   A note here on the geography of the North-West Territories. White settlement occurred only on the southern prairies and in the mixed forest 'parklands' to the north of the prairie. Most of the territory further north remained boreal forest, unsuited to farming. The Indians that lived there, Cree and Dene, were left alone until well into the twentieth century, retaining their traditional hunting and trapping economy. Tough F. 1997. *As Their Natural Resources Fail: Native Peoples and the Economic History of Northern Manitoba, 1870–1930*. Vancouver: University of British Columbia Press.

63   The population of Saskatchewan grew from 91 279 in 1901 to 492 432 in 1911. This was primarily a rural, farming population. While 461 new homesteads were taken up in 1895, 2 703 new homesteads were taken up in 1900, 19 787 in 1905, and 21 575 in 1910. By 1911, there were just under 100 000 farms in Saskatchewan. Waiser, *Saskatchewan*, 60, 64, 494, 495, 498.

half of the farms and ranches taken up in Alberta and Saskatchewan were deserted. The destructive farming methods and resultant soil erosion of the early twentieth century settlement boom wreaked massive ecological damage to parts of the prairies, and is still apparent today. Much of this land is still unoccupied and owned by the Crown. [64]

By the 1890s, all First Nations on the prairies were living on reserves. While all reserves had some cattle, most were intended for consumption and not farming. Indeed, most of whatever breeding stock they possessed was eaten by malnourished Indians. A small number of breeding cattle formed the basis for reserve cattle herds and some tribes, such as the Blackfoot and Blood, began to create modest cattle-farming operations during this time.[65] All reserves also had small plots, mostly a few acres, for agriculture. While the plains began its wheat boom, the Government of Canada started implementing plans to reduce the size of reserves, and began selling 'unused' reserve land to white settlers, often without any consultation with Indians.[66] Many reserves were also forced to lease grazing lands to white ranchers. Indian agents made these decisions, acting in their legal capacities as trustees of First Nations' lands. Increasingly, native people were forced to work for farmers at very low wage rates. First Nations' agriculture, including ranching, is to this day a minor enterprise on the Canadian prairies. Currently, more First Nations' agricultural land is leased to white people than is farmed by Indians themselves.

Towards a discussion of genocide on the Canadian prairies

Canadians typically reject out of hand any idea that the concept of genocide has any relevance to the settlement of Canada, pointing both to the orderly history of land purchases through treaties, and a deliberate policy of avoidance of the Indian wars that characterised the neighbouring American frontier.[67] Accordingly, there is a small academic literature on genocide

---

[64]   Belich J. 2009. *Replenishing the Earth: The Settler Revolution and the Rise of the Ango World, 1783–1939*. New York: Oxford University Press, 418.

[65]   Samek, *Blackfoot Confederacy*, 79–86. This paralleled the process in the United States. By the early 1900s, many Indian tribes and individuals in the US had cattle herds. See also Iverson P. 1994. *When Indians Became Cowboys: Native Peoples and Cattle Ranching in the American West*. Norman: University of Oklahoma Press.

[66]   Waiser, *Saskatchewan*, 77–78.

[67]   Some general histories of genocide also accept this distinction. For example, Kiernan B. 2007. *Blood and Soil: A World History of Genocide and Extermination from Sparta to Darfur*. New Haven: Yale University Press, has two chapters on the United States, but no references to genocide in Canada—see 213–48, 310–63. The same is true of Cave A. 2008. 'Genocide in the Americas', in *The Historiography of Genocide*, ed. D. Stone. London: Palgrave Macmillan, 273–295.

against the First Nations of Canada.[68] At the same time, however, the term is often used in political discourse by indigenous peoples. This is particularly true of the intense discussion in recent years over the Canadian residential school system for Indian children. The evidence is that Indian children sent to these schools were forcibly separated from their families, and many were beaten, raped and generally abused there.[69]

At the outset it needs to be made clear that few native people in western Canada were killed by either Canadian authorities or by settlers. Events such as the Cypress Hills massacre of 23 Assiniboine by American hunters were rare. Even in the 1885 rebellion, the closest western Canada came to a general Indian war, native casualties are counted in the dozens. It is doubtful that more than 100 native people were killed by Canadian authorities or settlers between 1870 and 1900. This is a commendable record compared to colonial settler societies such as the United States, South Africa and Australia. The Canadian government certainly had no policy of killing native people, and worked to prevent the kind of mass killings that characterised the American frontier. Under British colonial rule and the days of the fur trading economy, native people were incorporated into the economy as valued workers. Subsequent Canadian policy was to force native people to live on reserves in order to open up their lands to white settlement, support them there as cheaply as possible and assimilate them into Canadian society. What then is the argument that genocide applies to the settlement of the Canadian prairie frontier?

What needs to be taken into account in this regard is that genocide and ecocide are often closely related in the destruction of indigenous peoples and their environments. The degradation of the ecology of the plains annihilated the hunting cultures that had been sustained there. Between 1850 and 1880,

68   Woolford A. 2009. 'Ontological destruction: genocide and Canadian aboriginal peoples'. *Genocide Studies and Prevention*, 4, no. 1, 81–97; Jones, M. 2001. 'Genocide, ethnocide or hyperbole? Australia's "stolen generation" and Canada's hidden holocaust'. *Culture Survival Quarterly*, 25, no. 4; Neu D. 2003. *Accounting for Genocide: Canada's Bureaucratic Assault on Aboriginal People.* Halifax: Fernwood; Annett K. 2001. *Hidden From History: The Canadian Holocaust.* Vancouver: Truth Commission into Genocide in Canada; Zannis M. 1973. *The Genocide Machine in Canada: The Pacification of the North.* Montreal: Black Rose.
69   Chrisjohn R., Wasacase T., Nussey L., Smith A., Legault M., Loiselle P. & Bourgeois M. 2002. 'Genocide and Indian residential schooling: the past is present', in *Canada and International Humanitarian Law: Peacekeeping and War Crimes in the Modern Era*, eds R. Wiggers & A. Griffiths. Halifax: Dalhousie University Press; Powell C. 2010. 'The moralisation of genocide in Canada'. Unpublished paper presented at the symposium Prairie Perspectives on Indian Residential Schools, Truth, and Reconciliation, Winnipeg; MacDonald D. & Hudson G. 2011. 'The genocide question and Indian residential schools in Canada'. Unpublished paper presented at Canadian Political Science Association Annual Conference. There is still a remarkable absence of writing on genocide in Canada in scholarly publications and books on First Nations history.

tens of millions of buffalo were killed by both white and indigenous hunters. While the hunting methods and cultural needs of the First Nations peoples alone could never have wiped out the herd, the commodification of buffalo hides made it profitable to organise large scale hunts by white, Metis and Indian hunters on a scale previously unimaginable. In the space of only a few years, the entire species was effectively exterminated. The ecosystem based on the buffalo collapsed, resulting in the starvation of Indians and the opening up of the plains for Euro-Canadian settlement. Not only did Indians die of starvation caused by the wanton destruction of their main food source, but they also succumbed to diseases that became all the more deadly due to their weakened condition. It seems that between 1870 and 1900, the Indian population of the Canadian plains was reduced by at least half.[70]

Disease and alcohol introduced by whites devastated plains Indian cultures. It was in particular a series of smallpox epidemics in the eighteenth and nineteenth centuries that impacted the plains First Nations, both in the United States and Canada, the last occurring in the early 1870s. Starting in Montana, this epidemic wiped out nearly half the members of some tribes there. By the time it spread north, losses were less severe, but still significant. The exact pattern and cause of these epidemics are unknown, but Indian oral histories report deliberate infection, through smallpox infested blankets being sent north as trade goods. While it is clear that such atrocities were not part of government policy, but the work of unscrupulous and land-hungry settlers, they did play a role in removing native people from the Canadian plains. The introduction of alcohol corrupted the trading process and cheated many Indians of their livelihoods. A native hunter, robbed of his furs by a dishonest whiskey trader, had no food to bring home to his family, reducing the life expectancy of his children. Alcohol also killed many Indians directly through alcohol poisoning and violence; or indirectly through long-term decline in health. While there is no data to account for the extent that it shortened average lifespans, alcohol clearly had a devastating impact on both individual Indians as well as on their communal lives.

What is clear is that from the late 1870s through to the early 1900s, most reserve populations declined as more people died than babies were being born. Part of this was due to the ecocide previously discussed, and partly

---

[70] Waiser, *Saskatchewan*, 169–70; Lux M. 2001. *Medicine that Walks: Disease, Medicine and Canadian Plains Native People, 1880–1940*. Toronto: University of Toronto Press. Because the data is inadequate, we do not have precise figures on how many Indians died in this process.

to the heightened impact of disease on a severely distressed population. In addition, the loss of their cultures and confinement to reserves led to depression and alcohol abuse, while new and unhealthy diets shortened their lives. A host of other causes related to their poor living conditions helped kill thousands of Native people. The extent to which this was either planned or the result of government negligence is open to debate. What cannot be denied, however, is that by 1880, the Indian Department in Ottawa knew that Indians in the west were starving. It chose to deny this and failed to act. Since Indians had been forced onto reserves as wards of the Canadian government, that government should have been held responsible for their condition.

The forced relocation of all plains First Nations onto reserves occurred as part of Canadian government policy. The reserve system was an unmitigated disaster and integral to the destruction of First Nations' cultures. While technically Indians were allowed to select their reserves, and many did so, all were relocated onto small portions of their traditional territories. Other tribes were moved hundreds of miles away from their homelands. In 1882, for example, because of the construction of the railway, the Canadian government moved Indians from southern to central Saskatchewan, locations with less arable land and harsher climate. In addition, the prairie is a complex ecosystem with different micro-climates occurring in places only a few miles apart. The migratory life style of the plains Indians exploited these variations using seasonal resources in different parts of their territories for year-round subsistence. Being able to move to sheltered valleys in the winter was an important part of their migratory pattern. Forced onto a few square miles of prairie was not only destructive of their cultures, but spelt death for many. These dire consequences were a direct product of government policy of removing the plains Indians to reserves so that their traditional lands could be re-distributed to white settlers. Being forcibly deprived of their lands had the effect of destroying both their economic base and their social order. First Nations faced starvation immediately after the loss of their land, a consequence patently foreseeable. This clearly opens the door to charges of genocide.

The Canadian government was, however, self-assured of the morality of the treaty process by which it acquired Indian lands. In the narrow, racist and colonialist thinking of the day, the hunting and gathering way of life of indigenous peoples was inferior in every way to the social order of settlers, and needed to be eliminated. The lands left to the First Nations in the form of reserves did not constitute an adequate base to support indigenous cultures. They were not planned as a substitute for the vast land base of the First Nations prior to colonisation. Rather, the resettlement of First Nations on reserves was meant to be a kind of cure for those aspects of indigenous culture intrinsic to their existence on the plains. Indeed, individual ownership of land which was adopted on reserves was meant to eliminate the 'communist' values of the tribes, which supposedly impeded their acculturation.[71]

The land was also the only material wealth that First Nations owned. The confiscation of this asset and its redistribution, either free or at low cost, to 600 000 Euro-Canadian settlers was characteristic of European settler colonialism across the globe. Whites became rich, while First Nations were left destitute, a condition that persists to this day. To deprive a people of their lands, sustenance and way of life today violates international law. To do this in a way that systematically impoverishes them to the point of starvation, and shortens their lifespans considerably, is genocide.

Forced assimilation is an element of the process that needs to be considered separately. Confiscating the land of an indigenous people is analytically distinct from forcing them to live on reserves and abandon their cultures. Theoretically, people who have lost their land are 'free' to move to an alternative environment and onto unoccupied land or beyond the range of settlement in an attempt to preserve their cultures. These options were not available to Canada's plains Indians. Forced assimilation, the official policy of the Canadian government, was based on the assumption that by living on reservations, Indians would become self-sufficient farmers, gain an education, convert to Christianity, inter-marry with colonists and disappear as a distinct people within a few generations. Forcing people onto reserves where they are under incessant scrutiny by government agents and officials, where their freedom of movement is restricted and their cultural practices are suppressed, is ethnocide—the individuals live, but as a different people, their culture destroyed.[72] The final step in this process of ethnocide was the forced removal of native children to residential schools, where their culture could be 'educated' out of them. As has been widely documented, children at these schools were systematically abused. Residential schooling

---

[71] Conservatives in Canada still argue that collective ownership of Indian land is holding back First Nations' development. Flanagan T., Alcantara C. & Le Dressay A. 2011. *Beyond the Indian Act: Restoring Aboriginal Property Rights*. Montreal: McGill-Queens University Press, 13–41.

[72] Pettipas, *Ties that Bind*, 211–31; Tovias B. 2008. 'Navigating the cultural encounter: Blackfoot religious resistance in Canada (c.1870–1930)', in *Empire, Colony, Genocide: Conquest, Occupation, and Subaltern Resistance in World History*, ed. A.D. Moses. New York: Berghahn Books, 271–95.

was ethnocidal to the extent that it deprived Indian families of their ability to educate and socialise their children.[73]

The reserve system was also meant to destroy Indian nations as political entities, replacing them with administrative units referred to as 'bands'. Most First Nations were broken up and placed on separate reserves, each under a head man, a government appointed chief often paid by the government. The Canadian government, through the Indian Act, gave recognition to these bands but not to nations.[74] Individual native people thus had no option but to relate to the government though these bands, and were governed by band councils. Reserves and bands were thus artificial entities of political affiliation forced onto First Nations with the intention of subverting their traditional identities.

The policy of forced assimilation in fact failed because the Indian nations refused to assimilate. The reserves were so isolated and the Indians so determined to maintain their cultures, that it became a system of forced separation, not unlike apartheid. Nevertheless, great damage was done to Indian cultures and the reality of the reserve system is that it has been one of unequal development and damaged communities. Today inhabitants have a far lower standard of living and a much shorter life expectancy than other Canadians. Most native people currently remain separate from mainstream Canadian society, living on isolated reserves. The majority of those who have moved off reserves remain impoverished, without education or skills, and concentrated in a few urban centres. Indians have for the most part been free to leave any reserve, move to the city, gain an education and participate fully in Canadian society—provided they had the resources to do so. When, for example, the North West Mounted Police struggled to mobilise recruits for the Boer War in 1899, the question of Indian and Metis recruits arose. The response was clear: if any young Indian man wanted to use this as a conduit for passing into white society, he was free to enlist.

Because of the relative openness of racial categories in Canada and the government's assimilation policy, many thousands of Indians have passed into Metis or white society. Canada today has tens of thousands of people who consider themselves to be 'Indian', but do not meet the definition of Indian under the Indian Act. There are two categories of Indians in Canadian society, 'status' and 'non-status'. This has resulted in substantial

---

[73]   Milloy J. 1999. *A National Crime: The Canadian Government and the Residential School System, 1879–1986*. Winnipeg: University of Manitoba Press, 51–186.
[74]   Indian Act, RSC 1985, c. I-6, s2.

numbers of people of Indian or partial Indian descent who are 'non-status', desiring official recognition as Indian. In terms of the Indian Act, these self-identified natives are not eligible either for enrollment in a band or for whatever other benefits that might follow. While 'Indians' can, on their own initiative, move off reserves and become non-Indian, the reverse is not possible. This is deeply ironic as it over time has the potential to eliminate Indian status altogether.

Conclusion

Today, First Nation peoples are the poorest in Canada. More than half of them still live on reserves, relics of nineteenth century colonialism. Their lands are legally held 'in trust' by the Crown, supposedly for their benefit. Much of this land is still leased to white farmers, just as it was a hundred years ago. While Canada's First Nations are poor, white settler farmers on the prairies are rich, as the Canadian prairies feed a good part of the world's population. At the same time that these farmers are buying new machinery, expensive cars and living affluent lives, most reserve Indians are living in poverty and subsisting on welfare. Their diet of cheap, processed food is among the worst in the world, and they suffer chronic ill health and considerably shortened life spans.

Property still is the basis of much of the world's wealth and owning land in Canada has been an excellent long-term investment, rivalling returns on the stock market. When the First Nations lost their prairie lands, it was not simply a case of them losing their livelihoods and becoming poor. Their wealth was forcibly expropriated by Euro-Canadians, who saw the potential of the prairies for agriculture, seized the opportunity, and became rich with the help of the Canadian government. The legality of that process is still being contested in Canadian courts. These courts have not been willing to dig very deeply into this past injustice, nor have they been willing to apply the concept of genocide to it. At the same time, Canada proudly promotes itself as a leader in the implementation of human rights internationally. There is a contradiction here that is very painful for First Nations peoples to confront.

Scholars of genocide have engaged in considerable debate around the definition of genocide. Most are heavily influenced by the ideas of Raphael Lemkin, who coined the term 'genocide' in 1944 in the context of revelations of Nazi atrocities. Lemkin's conception has influenced the current definition adopted by the United Nations Convention on the Prevention and Punishment of the Crime of Genocide (UNCG) in 1948, which defines genocide as:

any of the following acts committed with intent to destroy, in whole or in part, a national, ethnical, racial or religious group, as such:

(i)   *killing members of the group;*

(ii)   *causing serious bodily or mental harm to members of the group;*

(iii)   *deliberately inflicting on the group conditions of life calculated to bring about its physical destruction in whole or in part;*

(iv)   *imposing measures intended to prevent births within the group;*

(v)   *forcibly transferring children of the group to another group.*

There can be no question that provisions (ii) through (v) apply to Canada's treatment of native peoples on reserves. Genocide is therefore a relevant legal category for analysis and discussion in this case. Issues relating to genocide are complex, and each First Nation, and each reserve, has its own history. But the relevance of the UNCG definition to this case is too obvious to ignore. Any further analysis requires the type of fact-specific work done by Mohamed Adhikari on the San of the Cape Colony, Raymond Evans on Aborigines in Queensland, and Rob Gordon on Bushmen of Namibia.[75]

Each occurrence of genocide is historically unique and it is pointless to define genocide in terms of one or other prototype, most commonly the Jewish holocaust. Each genocide, whether the Nazi killing of Jews, the Armenian genocide, the annihilation of the Herero people or the destruction of the Cape San by Boer commandos, is distinctive in its own ways. It is not so much the numbers, as the dynamic and intent behind the killing that is significant. Canada had a policed frontier not comparable to any in Africa. But there were also no reserves or forced residential schooling for the San in the Cape Colony, for example. No Canadian military officer ever gave an extermination order as German General Lothar von Trotha

---

[75]   See, for example, Adhikari M. 2010. *The Anatomy of a South African Genocide: The Extermination of the Cape San Peoples.* Athens: Ohio University Press; Evans R. 2004. '"Plenty shoot 'em": the destruction of Aboriginal societies along the Queensland frontier', in *Genocide and Settler Society: Frontier Violence and Stolen Indigenous Children in Australian History*, ed. A. Moses. New York: Berghahn Books; Gordon, R. 1992. *The Bushman Myth: The Making of a Namibian Underclass.* Boulder: Westview; Gordon, R. 2009. '"Hiding in full view": the forgotten Bushman genocides in Namibia'. *Genocide Studies & Prevention*, 4, 29–58.

did in the Herero War.[76] This does not mean that Canadian treatment of the prairie First Nations was not genocide. The reality is that genocide occurred, and occurs, in a wide variety of political, economic and cultural contexts. While comparative studies are relevant and useful in a variety of ways, no incidence of genocide can be defined in terms of any other. It is therefore important that Canada—as should South Africa, Australia, Namibia and other societies—engage in a separate discussion about the destruction of its aboriginal peoples, based on its unique history, in the context of international law.

A final suggestion here. Perhaps unique to the world, in Canada the Crown still owns most of the land. To the extent that a substantial part of the genocide against its First Nations was the taking of their lands and their removal to reserves, the Canadian government has the means to remedy this injustice in that it has the capacity to restore substantial tracts of land to Canadian First Nations. This is especially true of the western and northern parts of the prairies, but less true of the more densely settled areas of the east and southern farming regions. Such restitution would be a good place to start.

---

[76]   Von Trotha's words, which he put in writing, were; 'All the Herero must leave the land. If they refuse, then I will force them to do it with the big guns. Any Herero found within German borders, with or without a gun, will be shot. No prisoners will be taken. This is my decision for the Herero people.' Quoted in Harring S. 2007. 'The Herero demand for reparations from Germany: the hundred year old legacy of a colonial war in the politics of modern Namibia', in *Repairing the Past? International Perspectives on Reparations for Gross Human Rights Abuses*, eds M. du Plessis & S. Pete. Oxford: Intersentia, 437–50. Just as Canada denies that genocide applies to its history, there is an extensive German literature denying that genocide occurred against the Herero. On the meaning of this, see Kossler R. 2009. 'Entangled history: negotiating the past between Namibia and Germany'. *Journal of Contemporary African Studies*, 26, no. 3, 313–39. It might be pointed out here that while it is illegal under German law to deny the Jewish holocaust, it is not illegal to deny that genocide occurred in Namibia. This represents a right wing defense of German military honour in colonial wars which cannot be applied to the Second World War.

Chapter Twelve

Seeing Receding Hunter-Gatherers and Advancing Commercial Pastoralists: 'Nomadisation', Transfer, Genocide

Lorenzo Veracini
Swinburne Institute for Social Research, Melbourne

As well as on existing frontiers, the pastoral invasion of hunting grounds was also played out at the borderlands of discourse. At first, the narratives associated with this discursive invasion were primarily imaginary. They then drew strength from observations ostensibly emanating from remote pastoral frontiers. Eventually, this veritable colonisation of discourse acquired the power of a self-fulfilling prophecy. These tropes, involving disappearing indigenous hunter-gatherers and rapidly expanding European polities, and circulating in the context of a transcolonial global network of ideas, contributed crucially to rationalisations and justifications of genocidal behaviour.

This chapter contributes to theoretical reflection on settler colonialism as a specific social formation by seeing it as fundamentally constituted of two related transfers. On the one hand, the settler collective physically *transfers* to the destination locale and gradually shifts its commitment from a notion of 'home' that is located elsewhere to a notion of 'home' that becomes fixated in the 'new' land. On the other hand, the indigenous collective is *transferred* away, either physically, via military and other coercive measures, or discursively, in ways that critically detach it from its connection to the land—most likely, though, through a combination of both approaches. In *Settler Colonialism: A Theoretical Overview* I presented a taxonomy of indigenous transfers in the context of what I defined as the settler colonial 'situation'. I also argued that indigenous and settler transfers mirror, co-define and are premised on each other, and that an appraisal of 'transfer', including forms of psychological transfer such as the 'indigenisation' of the settler collective, its self-representation as being autochthonous to the land, is crucial to understanding settler colonialism.[1] This chapter draws attention to this latter form of transfer's necessary counterpoint, namely, the 'nomadisation' of the indigenous collective. It argues that representations

---

[1]   Veracini L. 2010. *Settler Colonialism: A Theoretical Overview*. Houndmills: Palgrave Macmillan.

of indigenous hunter-gatherers being displaced by settler pastoralists, the early historiographies of the composite subject matter of *Genocide on Settler Frontiers*, were crucial to 'nomadisations' everywhere. As they purportedly represented the struggle between essentially evolved and devolved specimens of humanity, these occurrences attained cosmic significance.

'Nomadisation' is crucial to 'sedentarisation'—the latter would not be thinkable without the former. In turn, sedentarisation, as a number of authors have pointed out, is crucial to the acquisition of territory and much, much more.[2] Attempts to 'sedentarise' indigenous peoples are ubiquitous in the history of settler colonial projects, and so is their prior discursive nomadisation. *Genocide on Settler Frontiers* focuses on conflicts between settler pastoralists and indigenous hunter-gatherers in a variety of settings. Hunter-gatherers—even if this collective denomination requires a degree of qualification, as it often does not adequately acknowledge active and deliberate indigenous land management practices—were easy to nomadify. In his paper, Tony Barta, for example, aptly quotes Patrick Wolfe quoting Justice Johnstone: 'The hunter state bore within itself the promise of vacating the territory, because when game ceased, the hunter would go elsewhere to seek it'. While invading their lands was indeed a promising prospect, especially if the invasion was to be carried out on the back of rapidly reproducing eco-transforming ruminants, to the point that many thought they were actually promised lands, the global history this book uncovers is relevant beyond the test cases its contributing authors collectively appraise. Indigenous peoples were being nomadified globally as, simultaneously, non-indigenous peoples were increasingly understood as primarily defined by their sedentarisation. Besides, irrespective of what would actually happen in due course, it was indigenous hunter-gatherers and invading pastoralists

---

2   For an outline of the foundational importance of the binary opposite of sedentarism and vagrancy in the development of colonial imaginings see, for example, Pocock J.G.A. 2005. 'Tangata Whenua and Enlightenment anthropology', in *The Discovery of Islands: Essays in British History*, ed. J.G.A. Pocock. Cambridge: Cambridge University Press, 208–09, 215. Pocock has compellingly demonstrated the sway the binary of sedentarism and vagrancy held over eighteenth century Enlightenment thought, to the extent that 'the step into humanity was taken with the acquisition of capacity for exchange, commerce, specialization and diversification' while 'a wandering condition dehumanize[d] or precede[d] humanization'. See Ince, O.U. n.d. 'Capitalism, colonization, and contractual dispossession: Wakefield's letters from Sydney'; available at http://www.academia.edu/1067870/Capitalism_Colonization_and_Contractual_Dispossession_Wakefields_Letters_from_Sydney, accessed 11 March 2013. For a metahistorical reflection on the fundamental distinction between hunter-gatherers and farmers globally, that reverses, like this chapter, received assumptions regarding hunter-gatherers as 'nomads' and farmers as 'settlers', see Brody H. 2001. *The Other Side of Eden: Hunters, Farmers and the Shaping of the World*. New York: North Point Press.

who often had to work things out at first. While *Genocide on Settler Frontiers* focuses on a succession of crucial moments, the stories emerging from these moments produced an invasion of their own.

The experience of hunter-gatherers facing the pastoral invasion of their territories was fundamental in shaping these perceptions. The hunter-gatherers' shared fate—physical extermination, removal and forced sedentarisation (that is, serial observable disappearance, what would be later called genocide)—was thought to be the fate of *all* indigenous peoples. There was debate about whether this should be seen as a good thing. The humanitarians, for example, vociferously complained about this for decades, but there was consensus regarding the fact that it simply was. Conversely, the experience of rapidly expanding and effectively indigenising pastoral settlers was to be the experience of all settlers and those who identified with them. Thus, paradoxically, what went on in remote, seemingly unimportant frontiers contributed significantly to what was widely deemed to be a crucial development in the history of the whole of humanity. That this essentially eighteenth century narrative actually preceded the mainly nineteenth century dispossessions this book outlines should be noted. This inversion, however, does not affect the importance of these actual occurrences. The comparable and ostensible *convergence* of frontier experiences was not lost on contemporary observers. As such, it became one crucial tenet of pervasive global narratives of settler progress and indigenous disappearance.

As the papers collected here reiterate, and Nigel Penn summarises, hunter-gathering collectives are especially vulnerable to physical forms of settler colonial transfer. They were typically fragile in demographic and military terms, even if, as Mohamed Adhikari and Lyndall Ryan demonstrate in their outline of indigenous resilience to settler incursions, this notion needs to be qualified. Again, as many of the chapters collected here point out, the ecosystems on which their economies and ways of life depended were also especially vulnerable. Most importantly, at the discursive level, this is transfer too. Their 'nomadic' lifestyle could be adduced as 'proof' of their non-belonging to specific locations, indeed, by extension, of all indigenous peoples' lack of belonging. Moreover, when hunter-gatherers were pitted against commercially oriented stock farmers, this fragility was compounded with the specific requirements of this particular settler colonial economy: land was used extensively, there was acute competition for limited resources and indigenous labour was often not needed on an ongoing basis. Moreover, while reliance on indigenous labour did vary from case to case, and while this reliance was crucial in determining different patterns of indigenous destruction (a point that emerges forcefully from most of the chapters collected in this book), the specific requirements of settler economies were inherently destructive of hunter-gatherer society. This emerges most powerfully in Jared McDonald's and Ann Curthoys' chapters. The children of hunter-gatherers could be employed on settler farms and lose their indigeneity, or indigenous semi-slave labour could be needed in areas often distant from traditional estates. Mathias Guenther's chapter outlines a very exceptional case indeed. Besides, the pastoral settlers themselves were 'nomads', a fact that recurringly invited anxious questioning. In these cases, the need to separate settler claims from indigenous ones may contribute to explaining instances of auto-referential racialisation.[3]

In this chapter I suggest that the discursive nomadisation of indigenous collectives is a necessary ingredient to processes of settler indigenisation and a necessary prerequisite for undertaking programmes of forced indigenous sedentarisation. Premised on previous, widely accepted traditions espousing a 'sedentary metaphysics', these transfers should be appraised in the context of what New Zealand historian James Belich characterised as the global settler 'revolution' of the nineteenth century, the comprehensive transformation of images pertaining to the possibility of reproducing social bodies outside of Europe. Previously, during the eighteenth century, these attempts had been eccentric. Afterwards, and more and more so as the nineteenth century progressed, they became commonplace. Previously, the reputation of settlers themselves had been highly questionable, later they would become much more respectable. And yet, despite its success, indeed, precisely because it was successful, this revolution needed to address a fundamental paradox—settlers move and yet must be represented as 'fixed', while conversely, indigenous people reside on their ancestral lands and yet must be represented as pathologically

---

[3]   See Guillaumin C. 1972. 'Caractères spécifiques de l'ideologie raciste'. *Cahiers Internationaux de Sociologie*, LIII, 247–74. Guillaumin argues that hetero-referential racialisation ('they are Other and therefore we are normal') and auto-referential racialisation ('we are human and therefore they are not') are structurally different ways of constructing racialised alterities. They are always interweaved and rarely operate in their 'pure' form, she acknowledges. Generally speaking, however, auto-referential racialisation fits in with settler colonialism's 'logic of elimination', while hetero-referential racialisation works better with the colonial necessities of exploitation. Reflection on different systems of racial oppression through the exploration of colonialism and settler colonialism as different social formations is not unprecedented. See, for example, Fredrickson G.M. 1988. 'Colonialism and racism', in *The Arrogance of Race: Historical Perspectives on Slavery, Racism, and Social Inequality*, ed. G.M. Fredrickson. Middletown, CT: Wesleyan University Press, 216–35; Wolfe P. 2001. 'Land, labor, and difference: elementary structures of race'. *The American Historical Review*, 106, no. 3, 866–905. The notion of settler colonialism's 'logic of elimination' is Patrick Wolfe's. See Wolfe P. 2006. 'Settler colonialism and the elimination of the native'. *Journal of Genocide Research*, 8, no. 4, 387–409.

mobile.[4] The 'nomadisation' of indigenous peoples became a crucial way of dismissing indigenous prior territorialisation while undoing it, a necessary component of all processes of settler colonial consolidation. This is why, in the context of the global expansion of settler colonialism as a distinct social formation during the nineteenth century, and in relation to the ideological dimensions of the 'revolution' that underpinned this process, the dispossession and ostensible 'disappearance' of real hunter-gatherers, as outlined by each of the contributions to this book, acquired an importance that went considerably beyond the specific colonial locations where it happened.

Claims

Despite what Locke said and what neo-Lockean authorities continue to argue, the entire world had not once been 'America'.[5] Allan Greer's conclusion that the 'notion of a universal commons completely open to all', and that Locke's 'America' 'existed mainly in the imperial imagination' is ultimately convincing.[6] On the other hand, much of the world was actually *made* into 'America' in specific ways.[7] *Seeing* unappropriated commons everywhere was one of these ways. We now know that this very powerful vision as it was projected onto the 'New World' was created and propagated in order to sustain a specific colonial formation. Locke himself had a vested interest, and the supporters of Lockean notions of property did too.[8] These lands were not unappropriated, of course. Original owners had to be dispossessed so that new owners could claim their 'original' ownership. *Seeing* nomadic

---

4 See Belich J. 2009. *Replenishing the Earth: The Settler Revolution and the Rise of the Anglo-World, 1783–1939.* Oxford: Oxford University Press.

5 For a convincing analysis of a spate of recent contributions emphasising the need to renew social contract as a guiding political category, see Nichols R. 2013. 'Indigeneity and the social contract today'. *Philosophy & Social Criticism*, 39, 165–186.

6 Greer A. 2012. 'Commons and enclosure in the colonization of North America'. *American Historical Review*, 117, no. 2, 372.

7 One of these ways was premised on Vattel's influential argument about the lawfulness of appropriating parts of countries 'inhabited only by a few wandering tribes'. Ian Hunter notes that rather 'than being based in claims about their extra-European savagery', Vattel's 'impairment of the land rights of nomadic peoples was actually grounded in his basic political-metaphysical argument: that civil rights are conditional on the cultivation of republican virtues—including agricultural, commercial and military virtues—in a national *pays*'. Thus Vattel's 'argument could be readily used as a means of expropriating the lands of non-European peoples deemed to be nomadic', as well as to sustain the claims of settlers able to represent themselves. Hunter I. 2011. '"A jus gentium for America": Vattel in the colonies'. Unpublished conference paper, in possession of the author.

8 See, among others, Arneil A. 1996. *John Locke and America: The Defence of English Colonialism.* Oxford: Clarendon Press.

hunter-gatherers was one crucial element in seeing unappropriated commons.

Settlers in the New World—indeed, by the beginning of the nineteenth century, in a global network of consolidating New Worlds—claimed land against all others, including indigenous peoples, distant sovereigns and absentee speculators by doing specific things to it and with it. They 'mixed' their labour with it, reproduced in it by having babies with non-indigenous women, managed subsistence farming on it, or extracted tradable commodities from it. As settlers eventually became many and powerful in the context of the veritable 'explosion' of the 'settler world', reference to how these lands were being used eventually became crucial.[9]

Not only did settlers claim land in specific ways, they discursively dispossessed indigenous peoples in specific ways too. If settler claims were linked to performing acts on the land, indigenous ones were to be dismissed by a demonstration of an indigenous incapacity or unwillingness to perform the same. William Cronon perceptively quotes two early examples of a settler colonial type of dispossessing rhetoric. They could be understood as expressing the foundational codes of a dispossessory logic:

> In his tract defending 'the Lawfulness of Removing Out of England into the Parts of America', the Pilgrim apologist Robert Cushman argued that the Indians were 'not industrious, neither have art, science, skill or faculty to use either the land or the commodities of it; but all spoils, rots, and is marred for want of manuring, gathering, ordering, etc'. Because the Indians were so few, and 'do but run over the grass, as do also the foxes and wild beasts', Cushman declared their land to be 'spacious and void', free for English taking. [Founder of Puritan New England] John Winthrop distinguished between natural ownership and civil ownership of land: 'As for the Natives of New England', he wrote, 'they inclose noe Land, neither have any settled habitation, nor any tame Cattle to improve the Land by, and soe have noe other but a Naturall Right to those Countries'.[10]

The alleged failure of indigenous peoples to use or order the land enabled their animalisation or naturalisation. In turn, this exclusion from what Edward Said would call the 'world of moral concern' deprived them of

---

9   On 'explosive' colonisation, see Belich, *Replenishing the Earth*, 178–83.

10   Cronon W. 1983. *Changes in the Land: Indians, Colonists, and the Ecology of New England.* New York: Hill & Wang, 56. This was not the only rationale. It was either a perception of indigenous nomadic life that justified settler appropriation, or the perception of indigenous settled life that could be constrained within the limits of cultivation and habitation. Settlers could then acknowledge indigenous property rights in the ostensibly inhabited areas while appropriating the 'unclaimed' ones.

political rights.[11] An entirely negative definition of indigenous life should also be noted. In these renditions, indigenous people are primarily defined by their *failure* to perform the ceremonies of settler possession.[12] Claiming land through performance and claiming an indigenous failure to perform—both crucial elements of settler colonialism's performative construction of place—were intimately intertwined. As a result, a settler perception of indigenous lifestyles, and, most importantly, a growing settler capacity to inform the perception of all others became a crucial vehicle of indigenous dispossession.

One consequence of the 'settler revolution' was that 'settlerism' as an ideology eventually became hegemonic. This required intense ideological labour. Perceptions had to be comprehensively transformed. It is important to note that for a very long time settlers were seen primarily as 'horrid colonials'—decultured, alienated, vulgarly acquisitive, nomadic 'white savages'. These images did not disappear with the settler revolution, but became less prevalent.[13] Sure, 'settlement' and fixity had been interpreted positively in European intellectual traditions much earlier. These categories had not referred to settler colonial collectives, however. For an example of this pre-settler revolution system of perception, see Edmund Burke's description of the 'English Tartars' quoted in Barta's article.

---

[11] Said E. 1988. 'Michael Walzer's exodus and revolution: a Canaanite reading', in *Blaming the Victims: Spurious Scholarship and the Palestinian Question*, eds E. Said & C. Hitchens. London: Verso, 166.

[12] On the various ceremonials of possession of different colonial empires, even if she does not focus on the specifically settler colonial ones, see Seed P. 1995. *Ceremonies of Possession in Europe's Conquest of the New World, 1492–1640*. Cambridge: Cambridge University Press.

[13] Of course, confident boosterist assertions notwithstanding, settlers had frequent moments of self-doubt. Stubborn anxieties pertaining to the possibility of reproducing a degenerated social body irretrievably tainted by nomadism never disappeared either. Advocate of protectionism, Victoria David Syme, for example, argued that 'the arts and manufactures of highly civilized nations' should be imported to Australia in order to keep Australians from becoming like 'Bedouins or Tartars', that is, nomadic people. Quoted in Gerhard D. 1959. 'The frontier in comparative view'. *Comparative Studies in Society and History*, 1, 214. Similarly, the trekboers of the eighteenth century were also often represented as 're-barbarised' nomadic settlers. This was before the settler revolution, however, even if similar images never disappeared. See Penn N. 2001. 'The northern Cape frontier zone in South African frontier historiography', in *Colonial Frontiers: Indigenous-European Encounters in Settler Societies*, ed. L. Russell. Manchester: Manchester University Press, 20.

As recently noted in two perceptive articles by Nan Seuffert and John Frow, 'settlement' and 'civilisation' were always intimately related categories.[14] But settlers, by definition, move and are inherently unsettling *vis-à-vis* this 'metaphysics'. They also often 'inclose noe land', as the historical cases outlined in this book, and as Greer's article referred above remind us. In the face of this powerfully resilient paradigm—Condorcet had identified the 'family settled upon the soil' as the basic building unit of the state, while Comte had emphasised how the 'prime human revolution [is the] passage from nomadic life to sedentary state'—'settlerism' as an ideology needed to emphasise the settler's *fixity* despite an obvious and necessary displacement. It also needed to emphasise indigenous *mobility* despite the apparent fact that, by definition, indigenous peoples, unlike their settler counterparts, had not moved.[15]

Settlers for a long time had to contend with a system of representation that perceived them as inherently degenerate precisely because of their mobility. Crucial promoter of the settler revolution, indeed serial founder of settler neo-Europes, Edward Gibbon Wakefield, noted in *A View on the Art of Colonization* (1849) that 'speaking generally, colonies and colonists are in fact, as well as in the estimation of the British gentry, inferior, low, unworthy of much respect, properly disliked and despised by people of honour here, who happen to be acquainted with the state of society in the colonies'.[16] He had set out to change all this, and his theory of 'systematic colonisation' was specifically aimed at what today would be called a comprehensive 'rebranding' of settler colonial enterprises. 'Systematic colonisation' had important precursors in Federalist attempts to settle the 'Old Northwest'. It was not an exclusively British imperial phenomenon.[17] It was a successful

---

[14]   Seuffert N. 2011. 'Civilisation, settlers and wanderers: law, politics and mobility in nineteenth century New Zealand and Australia'. *Law Text Culture*, 15, 10–44; Frow J. 2012. 'Settlement', *Cultural Studies Review*, 18, no. 1, 4–18. Reflection on the foundational nature of a 'sedentarist metaphysics', according to which 'place and roots are given vivid moral and ethical resonance over and above more mobile states of existence and forms of identity', or on what J.C. Scott has called 'sedentarisation', one fundamental drive of all modernising states, is not recent, however. Cresswell T. 2002. 'Theorizing place'. *Thamyris/Intersecting*, 9, 11; Scott J.C. 1998. *Seeing Like a State*. Hew Haven: Yale University Press; see also Alonso, A.M. 1994. 'The politics of space, time and substance: state formation, nationalism and ethnicity'. *Annual Review of Anthropology*, 23, 379–405.

[15]   Both quoted in Noyes J.K. 2001. 'Nomadic landscapes and the colonial frontier: the problem of nomadism in German South Africa', in *Colonial Frontiers: Indigenous-European Encounters in Settler Societies*, ed. L. Russell. Manchester: Manchester University Press, 201.

[16]   Quoted in Bell D. 2009. 'Republican imperialism: J.A. Froude and the virtue of empire'. *History of Political Thought*, XXX, no. 1, 177.

[17]   See Cayton A.R.L. 1986. *The Frontier Republic: Ideology and Politics in the Ohio Country, 1780–1825*. Kent: Kent State University Press.

campaign, and eventually, settlers managed to disavow their present and recent displacements by focusing on a social body 'to come', and, in accordance with a somewhat counter-intuitive logic, by emphasising that they were defined by fixity because they *aimed to be so*, because they were in fact *returning* to a more genuine version of an ancient fixity that had been compromised by modernity's upheavals. And by re-enacting the mythical displacements of their putative ancestors, they were indeed remaining faithful to themselves, an ultimate indication of an uncanny ability to stay put even when moving.

Fixity

The complementary element of this representational equation, an equally necessary element of the settler revolution, also took hard ideological labour. Indigenous peoples had been represented for a long time as essentially redeemable human material. The nineteenth century humanitarians who for a number of crucial decades exercised significant influence over British colonial policy, for example, based their colonial projects on the prospect of transforming indigenous communities into the constituent elements of a worldwide empire of Christian endeavour.[18] The empire of the humanitarians was most definitely not a settler empire, and often vehemently so. Only as the nineteenth century progressed and humanitarian sensitivities entered a long-lasting crisis, did a settler-informed perception of

---

[18] There is a growing body of literature dedicated to the colonial career of humanitarian concerns and their specifically anti-settler rhetorics. See, for example, Comaroff J.L. 1997. 'Images of empire: models of colonial domination in South Africa', in *Tensions of Empire: Colonial Cultures in a Bourgeois World*, eds F. Cooper & A.L. Stoler. Berkeley: University of California Press, 163–97; Elbourne E. 2002. *Blood Ground: Colonialism, Missions and the Contest for Christianity in the Cape Colony and Britain, 1799–1853*. Montreal: McGill-Queen's University Press; Hall C. 2002. *Civilising Subjects: Metropole and Colony in the English Imagination, 1830–1867.* Cambridge: Polity; Lester A. 2002. 'British settler discourse and the circuits of empire'. *History Workshop Journal*, 54, 25–48; Elbourne E. 2003. 'The sin of the settler: the 1835–36 Select Committee on Aborigines and debates over virtue and conquest in the early nineteenth-century British white settler empire'. *Journal of Colonialism and Colonial History*, 4, no. 3; Lambert D. & Lester A. 2004. 'Geographies of colonial philanthropy'. *Progress in Human Geography*, 28, no. 3, 320–41; Elbourne E. 2005. 'Indigenous peoples and imperial networks in the early nineteenth century', in *Rediscovering the British World*, eds P. Buckner & R.D. Francis. Calgary: University of Calgary Press, 59–85; Lester A. & Dussart F. 2009. 'Masculinity, 'race', and family in the colonies: protecting Aborigines in the early nineteenth century'. *Gender, Place and Culture*, 16, no. 1, 65–76; Laidlaw Z. 2012. 'Slavery, settlers and indigenous dispossession: Britain's empire through the lens of Liberia'. *Journal of Colonialism and Colonial History*, 13, no. 1.

indigenous peoples based on an inherent lack of fixity, become hegemonic.[19] But as an anti-settler discourse was marginalised, even if it did not disappear, the fundamental symmetry involving indigenous and settler collectives was retained.[20] The counterpoint to an exogenous and fixed socio-political body 'to come' was to be an indigenous and itinerant socio-political entity discursively located in 'the past'—the prior. It worked and it still does.[21] This was a crucial marker of the global settler 'revolution'.

Thus the settler revolution subverted but also reinforced pre-existing elements of the sedentarist metaphysics. 'Settling' is especially about agriculture and fixed abodes: 'settlement' is crucially marked by permanent homes, literally by mobile homes that at one point became fixed. The settler wagon in a variety of frontiers was indeed a mobile home according to nineteenth century debates pertaining to the ancestral shift from 'nomadic' to 'settled' life, a shift that settler colonial settlement was ostensibly re-enacting. The Swiss chalet, the Muscovite cabin, the Norwegian peasant's hut, and one could add, the English cottage, were descended from the chariot of previously nomadic 'Nordic races'—travelling houses that at one point became settled on the land.[22] On the other hand, as etymologically 'civilisation' is literally about cities (*civites*) and savagery remains inherently linked to the woods, settlers are counter-intuitive civilisers in that they leave the cities and proceed towards the wilderness.

This inversion, however, was certainly not unprecedented. As recently noted by Georges Teyssot, for example, in German medieval tradition and as far as 'settlement' is concerned, urban locales and related notions of urbanity are not as important as the land itself:

---

[19] See Alan Lester's work on the decline and fall of a humanitarian tradition of anti-settler perception and its reverberations in the metropole. Lester A. 2011. 'Humanism, race and the colonial frontier'. *Transactions of the Institute of British Geographers*, 37, no. 1, 1–17. Lester argues that innatist racism emerged not from humanism's crisis, as Anderson argued in *Race and the Crisis of Humanism* when considering how Aboriginal Australians could not be considered fully human by people that had until then entertained universalist notions, but from settler milieus ('assemblages') engaged in confronting humanitarians on settler frontiers. It was a shift that emerged not from within humanitarian ideologies, as a result of unresolved contradictions, but from without: one result of a failure to sustain a hegemonic position in colonial affairs. See Anderson K. 2006. *Race and the Crisis of Humanism*. London: Routledge.

[20] See Veracini L. 2008. '"Emphatically not a white man's colony": settler colonialism and the construction of colonial Fiji'. *Journal of Pacific History*, 43, no. 3, 189–205.

[21] For a telling example, see Goodin R. 2012. *On Settling*. Princeton: Princeton University Press.

[22] Teyssot G. 2009. 'Settlers, workers and soldiers: the landscape of total mobilization', in *Settler and Creole Re-Enactment*, eds V. Agnew & J. Lamb. Houndmills: Palgrave Macmillan, 23.

[I]t is Man's labor on the land that builds the country's landscape, its Landschaft. The landscape is the physical setting that Germans call either 'fatherland', or Heimat, a place where one feels at home (Heim), the homeland. The Land refers to that part of the country in which Germans have established themselves as a farmer (Bauer). Such farmer is a settler (Siedler) and his territory establishes a Siedlung, a settlement or a colony.[23]

Either way, focusing on cultivation—'colonialism' is also etymologically linked to it—or urban life, the notion of civilisation is crucial to a cluster of ideas privileging fixity. Indeed, as Nadine Cattan has noted, 'the history of civilisations has been constructed around the remains of the first sedentary settlements dating from the Neolithic, and rendered possible by agriculture'.[24]

In this representational context, stability and connection to a particular geography are recurrently understood as inherently positive characteristics. As Nan Seuffert has summarised referring to both Liisa Malkki and Penny Edwards' work, and quoting Tim Cresswell:

[If] putting down roots and cultivation were closely associated with civilisation and settling, uprooting from a place of birth was often linked with immorality ... territorial displacement or uprootedness, and lack of cultivation, are not only uncivilised in some formulations, but pathological, involving a loss of moral bearings ... mobility undermines attachment and commitment to place and, since place is itself a moral concept, mobility is 'antithetical to moral worlds'.[25]

On the other hand, as Frow has argued, the 'settled man or woman and the vagrant, the wanderer, are thus defined by their mutual opposition; each depends for its identity on the other'.[26]

In the settler colonial situation, however, it is settler and indigene who depend on each other. Seuffert also mentions Mill's authoritative definition. The opposition between savagery and civilisation was equivalent to the

---

23 Teyssot, 'Settlers, workers and soldiers', 28.
24 Cattan N. 2008. 'Gendering mobility: insights into the construction of spatial concepts', in *Gendered Mobilites*, eds T. Cresswell & T.P. Uteng. Aldershot: Ashgate, 85. Robert Young also suggests that 'culture' has always been intimately linked to 'colonisation', and systematically disjoined from nomadic uses of the land. See Young R. 1995. *Colonial Desire: Hybridity in Theory, Culture and Race*. London, New York: Routledge, 31.
25 Seuffert, 'Civilisation, settlers and wanderers', 15–16; see also Malkki L. 1992. 'National Geographic: the rooting of peoples and the territorialization of national identity among scholars and refugees'. *Cultural Anthropology*, 7, no. 1, 31–32; Edwards P. 2003. 'On home ground: settling land and domesticating difference in the "non-settler" colonies of Burma and Cambodia'. *Journal of Colonialism and Colonial History*, 4, no. 3; Cresswell T. 2006. *On the Move: Mobility in the Modern Western World*. New York: Routledge, 31.
26 Frow, 'Settlement', 7. On the 'vagabond' as a 'cultural creation' and as an 'archetype that reflected the anxieties of the age', see Matsuda M. 1996. *The Memory of the Modern*. New York: Oxford University Press, 121–41.

opposition between 'wandering' over and 'dwelling in': 'A savage tribe consists of a handful of individuals, wandering or thinly scattered over a vast tract of country', he had noted, 'a dense population, therefore, dwelling in fixed habitations, and largely collected together in towns and villages, we term civilised'.[27] The oppositions are stark: 'wandering' equates with a lack of civilisation, living in 'fixed habitations' is *ipso facto* an indication of being civilised. But while settlers move, they maintain their civilisation. Mill, a genuine promoter of the settler revolution, was adamant about this fact. Settlers are different: they do not just move, they move towards fixity. Indigenous peoples, on the contrary, are also different: quintessentially 'nomadic', undisciplined 'wanderers', and 'erratic', they stay where they are, but are seen as forever moving purposelessly.

Ultimately, in these renditions, 'civilisation' is not only about fixity but also, and importantly, about movement—the movement forward through different stages of history, and upward towards 'development', 'progress' and 'advancement'. As well as effectively neutralising the detrimental consequences that sedentary metaphysics had on informing representations of their movement, settler projects were also able to mobilise another crucial discursive strand. Indigenous directionless wandering could be seen as static and 'backward', ultimately a changeless lack of movement. Seuffert thus concludes that 'discourses on civilisation contrasted [the settlers'] purposeful, upward, progressive mobility with notions of directionless, wandering, erratic movement and a static lack of movement often associated with colonised peoples'.[28] In a mirror image of the negative definition of indigenous peoples mentioned above, according to a circular logic that is typical of settler colonial ideologies, the settlers became negatively defined too: '*not* wanderers or nomads, and *not* mobile', that is, not indigenous. The actual wandering of the settler was comprehensively disavowed as the ostensible wandering of the indigene became more and more entrenched. As in the actual process of colonial settlement, by way of related transfers—the spatial dislocations that accompany the movement of settlers and indigenous peoples—and by way of the related discursive transfers that sustain these processes, the settler and the indigenous person had exchanged places.

---

[27]   Quoted in Seuffert, 'Civilisation, settlers and wanderers', 15.
[28]   Seuffert, 'Civilisation, settlers and wanderers', 28.

Nomadism

In the end, as Stuart Banner has suggested, the shifting position of Indians in the 'popular American imagination'—'the Indians had *become* nomadic hunters'—sustained a 'major change in American legal thought … In the early 1790s the land not yet purchased from the Indians was thought to be owned by the Indians; by the early 1820s that land was thought to be owned by the state and federal governments'.[29] His detection of a crucial shift points to an earlier period than that identified by Belich in relation to the settler revolution. But timing is not as important as processual convergence, and similar transitions may have happened at different times in different contexts. Conversely, as the territorialisation of one socio-political body must be replaced by that of another, it is important to note that settler colonial discourse is necessarily interested in emphasising indigenous 'nomadism' beyond nomadism itself. To express its hegemony, the settler revolution needed to shift perceptions of indigenous unsettledness *away* from an assessment of actual behaviour. Indigenous people had to be represented as inherently unsettled *irrespective* of what they actually did; they had to be characterised by an ontological type of nomadism, not just by nomadism. Many of the chapters collected in this book emphasise indigenous agency, spirited initiative and a determination to take advantage of the opportunities offered by pastoral booms and the accommodations that it made possible. We should recover this agency now, and this book constitutes a fundamental contribution towards this recovery—but they had to be dismissed then. Representations of hunter-gatherers at the periphery of expanding colonial complexes had to focus on an inherent incapacity to settle *and*, in an associated discursive trope, to acquire. The chapters by Mohamed Adhikari and Robert Gordon outline dehumanisation and animalisation, with various references to 'brute creation' and 'inferior orders of the creation'. The dehumanisation of hunter-gatherers was not only useful in justifying genocidal brutality on the spot, although it was crucial to it, representing indigenous peoples as eminently 'nomadic' *somewhere* was instrumental to indigenous dispossession *everywhere* in the context of the global settler revolution.

German South West Africa is a veritable laboratory in the context of these discursive shifts, as Gordon's chapter demonstrates. John Noyes has also drawn attention to the importance of late nineteenth century reflections

---

[29]   Banner S. 2007. *How the Indians Lost their Land: Law and Power of the Frontier.* Cambridge, MA: Harvard University Press, 150, 153, emphasis added.

on nomadism.[30] He identifies a 'general trend that had gained scientific currency' by the end of the nineteenth century, namely, 'the relocation of nomadism from the socius to the *psyche, from a social organization based on land use to a particular mental disposition*'. Crucially, he noted how this discursive relocation and the anthropology that sustained it corresponded to a spatial relocation: 'it amounted to a theoretical removal of pastoralists from their land'—transfer.[31] Of course, the settlers were themselves nomadic in this specific colonial context, indeed in most colonial contexts. As Greer has also noted, Germans, for example, had a mythical nomadic past, which they cherished. The settlers were migrating from the metropole to a colonial periphery, a fact that could not be denied, and in the arid conditions of German South West Africa, had developed a farming method not dissimilar from indigenous practices.

And yet, in

> the colonies and ex-colonies, it became important to qualify the idea of nomadism by differentiating pastoralism from white settler colonization. This corresponded to a similar differentiation that was becoming increasingly evident in discussions of nomadism, and which, I believe, was closely related to the psychological shift. This was the distinction between those nomadic peoples who migrate because of an inner strength, a drive that compels them to expand into new territory, and those who move out of weakness, who are driven, forced out of submissiveness and cowardice to abandon their territory. In this view, nomadism becomes a metaphor for colonial struggles: activity becomes a strength of the mobile European, and passivity becomes a determining condition of the non-civilized pastoralist.[32]

Noyes reviewed especially influential theories linking 'nomadism' and reflection on gendered orders. In these representations, masculinity is seen as inherently nomadic and femininity sedentary, while 'settlement' is routinely represented as a dialectical synthesis where truer manhood and truer femininity could develop. It is not surprising that, as settler colonialism can be defined as a process whereby one socio-political body reproduces in the place of another, gender is a recurring site of concern.

---

[30] Noyes J.K. 2000. 'Nomadic fantasies: producing landscapes of mobility in German Southwest Africa'. *Ecumene*, 7, 48, emphasis added. See also Noyes J.K. 1992. *Colonial Space: Spatiality in the Discourse of German South West Africa, 1884–1915*. Reading: Harwood.

[31] A similar argument involving the intimate relationship between anthropology and a specific settler colonial project is presented in Wolfe P. 1999. *Settler Colonialism and the Transformation of Anthropology*. London: Cassell. For an overview of the relationship between anthropology and colonialism, but not settler colonialism, see Pels P. 1997. 'The anthropology of colonialism: culture, history, and the emergence of Western governmentality'. *Annual Review of Anthropology*, 26, 163–83.

[32] Noyes, 'Nomadic fantasies', 49.

Important contributions on the origin and nature of 'wanderlust' and on its pathologisation included Edvard Westermarck's interpretation of the evolution of marriage, and 'Linus W. Kline's theory of sexual nomadism, in which wanderings were initiated by men in search of brides'. Another 'immensely popular reading was given by the Viennese psychologist Richard von Krafft-Ebing', Noyes notes. For him:

> *the seeds of civilization are sown when women cease to be hunted as sexual objects, and begin to exercise choice in the selection of sexual partners. This introduces the art of wooing, with its attendant idealization, modesty and ethics of love. Instead of joining the roving bands of savages to pursue his animal instincts, man learns to appeal to woman's desire. And since woman's desire is motherhood and home, man's nomadic sexuality begins to succumb to woman's sedentary morality. Man and woman bond to form a couple, and the household emerges as the building-block of civilization. This dual process of sedentarization and moralization is for Krafft-Ebing the driving force in the history of civilization.*[33]

Past and present were thus collapsed as a way to turn a spatial type of territorialisation into a psychological one—transfer. Psychology as a disciplinary field was indeed as important as anthropology in this context. In a different paper, Noyes had also noted that the:

> *image of nomadic hordes as a barbaric limit to civilisation drew on a long tradition of regarding wandering as an unmediated response to landscape and environmental constraints, rather than as a rational system of land utilisation. Since the time of antiquity, the social order of the nomad has been discussed as the barbaric negative of the polis, its horror and its repressed sense of community.*[34]

His analysis of 'nomadism' as an intellectual concern and as a discursive practice ultimately emphasises how crucial it was that 'scientific' condemnation—which amounted, this should be stressed, to 'a theoretical removal of pastoralists from the land'—fitted well with the practical process of indigenous dispossession and forced sedentarisation in the settler colony of German South West Africa. Noyes' analysis focuses on the Herero because 'they were seen to be the most problematic group in terms of mobility, pastoralism and forced sedentarisation'. Similar pseudo-scientific discourse portraying indigenous peoples as irresistibly dominated by nomadic desires and enacting a similar 'relocation of nomadism from the

---

[33] Noyes, 'Nomadic fantasies', 64, no. 13; see also Westermarck E. 1891. *The History of Human Marriage*. London: Macmillan; Kline L.W. 1898. 'The migratory impulse versus love of home'. *American Journal of Psychology*, 10, 1–81; Von Krafft-Ebing R. 1947 [1886]. *Psychopathia Sexualis: A Medico-Forensic Study*. New York: Pioneer.

[34] Noyes, 'Nomadic landscapes and the colonial frontier', 199.

socius to the psyche' was being produced elsewhere in the settler world—in Australia, for example—and read carefully everywhere.[35]

He then evoked the 'phantasm of the destructive, erasing force of the hooves of [Herero owned] cattle [which] extends the metonym of the nomad-reduced-to-cattle, who, even in his sedentary moments, is ruled by the blind destructive instincts of the beast'. 'It is this metonym of the beast', Noyes concluded, 'which defines the threshold between the settlement of nomads and the sedentary life of the European'.[36] Animalisation again, a few centuries later—an animalisation linked to a performative deficit and to the perception of an inherent failure to relate appropriately to a specific territory. It is important to note that the Herero later became victims of genocide, a fate that Jews and Gypsies, among others, would also encounter in different contexts. These socio-political collectives were all seen as especially problematic for similar reasons—a perceived extraordinary mobility had also been transferred from the socius to the psyche, while an alleged stubborn reluctance or inability to embrace sedentarisation had marked them in very special ways.[37]

Conclusion: pastoral settlers as 'possessive nomads'

That settlers actually roamed over a vast settler-made commons; that it was this settler commons that represented the greater danger to indigenous property rights; that it was this commons that had made colonisation possible in the first place; that indigenous peoples were actually attached to specific locations, or that they might become so, as various humanitarian movements had argued, had to be vehemently rejected. And rejected all

---

[35] Noyes, 'Nomadic landscapes and the colonial frontier', 204. On representations of Aboriginal inherent mobility, see Anderson, *Race and the Crisis of Humanism*, 79–109. The distinction between agriculturalists and nomads, on the other hand, could be used to discriminate between different indigenous collectivities as well as between indigenous and settler ones. By the mid-nineteenth century the Kabileans of French Algeria occupied a particular position in French colonial thinking. In *Letters from Algiers*, Tocqueville insists on seeing them as putative Europeans. They were indigenous and rooted on the land, unlike the Arabs, who were represented as irredeemably nomadic. See De Tocqueville A. 2001. *Writings on Empire and Slavery*. Baltimore: Johns Hopkins University Press, 172.

[36] Noyes, 'Nomadic landscapes and the colonial frontier', 206.

[37] On German South West Africa as a crucial site in the genealogy of genocide, see Zimmerer J. 2002. *Deutsche Herrschaft über Afrikaner: Staatlicher Machtanspruch und Wirklichkeit im kolonialen Namibia*. Münster, Hamburg: LIT Verlag.

this was, to the point that these now seem improbable propositions.[38] On the other hand, that narratives depicting constantly receding indigenous hunting grounds and incessantly advancing pastoral estates contributed to crucial rationalisations of multiple genocides should be also noted. How could one blame individuals and the peripheral collectives to which they belonged for behaving badly when it was the very unfolding of historical progress itself that produced momentous transformations? At times, of course, it was the governments themselves that behaved badly, as Sydney Harring's chapter on the Canadian prairies and Robert Gordon's essay on German South West Africa demonstrate.

That these narratives traded in specific images depicting indigenous hunter-gatherers and invading pastoralists was significant. True, the nomadic state of the pastoral settler prompted questioning, but this distanciation enabled disavowal too. These images often focused on rebarbarised pastoralists behaving badly. At times, they were not even European settlers, as was the case with the Griqua polities detailed by Edward Cavanagh. The culprits were never the civilised agricultural pioneers of settler colonial rhetoric. Similarly, it was indigenous hunter-gatherers, not the hypothetical indigenous agriculturalists that should have emerged from settler-driven sedentarisation policies, that were forever disappearing. It was the possibility of disavowal that sustained genocidal practices—someone else was doing it. It was not about indigenous peoples, but about hunter-gatherers, and it was not anybody's fault anyway.

That pastoral settlers were nomads, even if of particular kind, should also be emphasised. It was a specific type of non-nomadic nomadism. In a suggestive exegesis of Exodus, Harry Berger distinguishes between 'possessive nomadism' and 'customary nomadism', that is, the nomadism of people that intend to continue their movement indefinitely.[39] This distinction may be relevant for the understanding of the indigenous–settler relationships outlined in this book. Commercially oriented stock farmers can be seen as possessive nomads, and the dyads Berger extracts

---

38 Open-range grazing of domesticated animals would spread pathogens, destroy unfenced indigenous fields, appropriate indigenous commons *and* remain the personal property of their settler owners. See Greer, 'Commons and enclosure', 376. Later Greer also notes that 'running ahead of the enclosed ecumene in many parts of the New World was a colonial outer commons: an area of settler hunting, timbering, foraging, and above all grazing that was arguably a more significant agent of dispossession than the fields and fences commonly associated with colonial settlement'. The 'commons functioned as a prime instrument of dispossession', he concludes. Greer, 'Commons and enclosure', 383.

39 Berger H. 1989. 'The lie of the land: the text beyond Canaan'. *Representations*, 25, 134–35. For a similar discussion of Berger's essay, see Docker J. 2001. *1492: The Poetics of Diaspora*. London: Continuum, 142–143.

from Exodus may be relevant to the processes involved in their expansion: 'the tent against the house, nomadism against agriculture, the wilderness against Canaan, wandering and exile against settlement, diaspora against the political integrity of the settled state'.[40]

Beyond biblical studies, and beyond settler pastoralists, however, Berger's intuition regarding the relationship between agriculture and nomadism may also be crucial to an analysis of settler colonial formations in general:

> *Agriculture creates both peasants and their enemies and defenders. Those enemies and defenders very often tend to be non-agriculturalists—that is, tribes of pastoral nomads. The agricultural system is a kind of vacuum machine that sucks in possessive nomads at the top and discharges dispossessed peasants from the bottom, either into captivity or wandering. There is of course a big difference between the enforced wandering of such groups and the periodic migrations that characterize mobile pastoralism. The mobility of pastoral nomads is not the consequence of loss, failed conquest, or exile; it is their preference, their condition, their basic economic strategy. Let us call them customary wanderers to distinguish them from both enforced wanderers and possessive nomads who take over the governments of sedentary societies.*[41]

Settlers were indeed a tribe of possessive nomads. They were often enforced nomads too as it was the enclosures at home that threw them off the land and forced them into exile.[42] They take over, but are 'sucked in' by a very different kind of vacuum machine, namely, the perceived and manufactured 'emptiness' of the 'frontier'. It is not agriculture *per se*, but agriculture 'to be' that affects them. In this interpretative framework, possessive nomads or enforced wanderers (that is, settlers) are dialectically opposed to customary nomads (namely, indigenous people), who are either nomads or are nomadified in a variety of ways.

This dynamic applies to the settler 'revolution' of the nineteenth century, but it is a more recent phenomenon too. The indigenous person is 'nomadified' in twentieth century settler colonial representations as well. A telling example is provided by Palestinian refugees and displaced people during and after the 1948 Arab–Israeli war who were legally defined as 'wanderers' by the Israeli Supreme Court. 'The Court asserts that a man who *wanders* freely and without permit within the defence lines of the state and within the offensive lines of the enemy does not deserve this Court's help and assistance', it stated in an important judgement. This led

---

40   Berger, 'The lie of the land', 123, 134.
41   Berger, 'The lie of the land', 134–35.
42   See Neocleous M. 2012. 'International law as primitive accumulation: or, the secret of systematic colonization'. *European Journal of International Law*, 23, no. 4, 941–62.

to the consolidation of the legal category of the 'present absentee', someone who is oxymoronically present and non-present at once, the ultimate result of a process of transferist nomadification.[43] While this is a crucial definition, as these Palestinians' 'wandering' was instrumental in justifying their dispossession, this is certainly not a unique case in the context of settler colonial transfers. This correlation confirms that Israel/Palestine could profitably be interpreted as a settler colonial locale and that settler colonialism routinely needs to perceive, represent and indeed produce indigenous non-fixity in order to project its own permanence.[44]

'They die well', proclaimed the 1873 editorial of the *Omaha Republican* that Barta cites. They were the 'evanescent races', Charles Pearson's prophetic *National Life and Character* (1893) would confirm.[45] The counterpoint to the earlier statement, a counterpoint that went without saying, but that the *Omaha Republican* editorialist could have easily added, was that 'we', unlike 'them', progress well. As well as 'offering' their lands, hunter-gatherers offered a crucial contribution to the self-constitution of a global settler identity. Of course, we know that they were not 'nomads', and that they understood their collective existence as bound to specific locations. Besides, it is really a matter of scale, and if we think about it, we are also nomads, as we practice our daily transhumance between home and work, and as we peripatetically spend only *some* of our time in each of the rooms of our houses, perhaps clearly demonstrating an erratic disposition and an innate inclination towards wandering aimlessly. Indigenous hunter-gatherers were *turned* into 'nomads' and became even more vulnerable to extermination. They were nomadified.

---

[43]   Quoted in Blecher R. 2005. 'Citizens without sovereignty: transfer and ethnic cleansing in Israel'. *Comparative Studies in Society and History*, 47, no. 4, 735, my emphasis.

[44]   For a recent analysis of the Israeli-Palestinian conflict as an example of settler colonialism, see Rashed H & Short D. 2012. 'Genocide and settler colonialism: can a Lemkin-inspired genocide perspective aid our understanding of the Palestinian situation?'. *The International Journal of Human Rights*, 16, no. 8, 1142–1169; Veracini L. 2013. 'The other shift: settler colonialism, Israel and the occupation'. *Journal of Palestine Studies*, 42, no. 2, 26–42.

[45]   See Lake M & Reynolds H. 2008. *Drawing the Global Colour Line: White Men's Countries and the Question of Racial Equality*. Melbourne: Melbourne University Press, 86.

Select Bibliography

Abrahams Y. 1996. 'Disempowered to consent: Sara Bartman and Khoisan slavery in the nineteenth century Cape Colony and Britain'. *South African Historical Journal*, 35 no. 1.

Abulafia D. 2008. *The Discovery of Mankind: Atlantic Encounters in the Age of Columbus*. New Haven: Yale University Press.

Adhikari M. 2008. '"Streams of blood and streams of money": new perspectives on the annihilation of the Herero and Nama peoples of Namibia, 1904–1908'. *Kronos*, 34, no.1.

Adhikari M. 2010. *The Anatomy of a South African Genocide: The Extermination of the Cape San Peoples*. Cape Town: University of Cape Town Press.

Agamben G. 2005. *States of Exception*. Chicago: University of Chicago Press.

Alonso A.M. 1994. 'The politics of space, time and substance: state formation, nationalism and ethnicity'. *Annual Review of Anthropology*, 23.

Andersson C. 1856. *Lake Ngami or Explorations and Discovery During Four Years of Wandering in the Wilds of South-Western Africa*. London: Hurst & Blackett.

Anderson G.C. 2005. *The Conquest of Texas: Ethnic Cleansing in the Promised Land, 1820–1875*. Norman: University of Oklahoma Press.

Anderson K. 2006. *Race and the Crisis of Humanism*. London : Routledge.

Annett K. 2001. *Hidden From History: The Canadian Holocaust*. Vancouver: Truth Commission into Genocide in Canada.

Anon. 1878. 'The Bluebook'. *Cape Monthly Magazine*, 16.

Anthony T. 2004. 'Labour relations on northern cattle stations: feudal exploitation and accommodation'. *The Drawing Board: An Australian Review of Public Affairs*, 4, no. 3.

Anthony T. 2007. 'Criminal justice and transgression on northern Australian cattle stations', in *Transgressions: Critical Australian Indigenous Histories*, eds I. McFarlane & M. Hannah. Canberra: ANU Press.

Arneil A. 1996. *John Locke and America: The Defence of English Colonialism*. Oxford: Clarendon Press.

Atkinson A. 1991. 'Chinese labour and capital in Western Australia, 1847–1947'. PhD dissertation, Murdoch University.

Attwood B. 2005. *Telling the Truth About Aboriginal History*. Crows Nest: Allen & Unwin.

Attwood B. & Foster S. eds. 2003. *Frontier Conflict the Australian Experience*. Canberra: National Museum of Australia.

Atwood P. 2010. *War and Empire: The American Way of Life*. London: Pluto Press.

Bach J. 1961. 'The political economy of pearlshelling'. *Economic History Review*, new series, 14, no. 1.

Bank A. 2006. *Bushmen in a Victorian World: The Remarkable Story of the Bleek-Lloyd Collection of Bushman Folklore*. Double Storey: Cape Town.

Banner S. 2007. *How the Indians Lost Their Land: Law and Power of the Frontier*. Cambridge: Harvard University Press.

Barnard A. 1992. *Hunters and Herders of Southern Africa*. Cambridge: Cambridge University Press.

Barnard A. 2007. *Anthropology and Bushmen*. Oxford: Berg.

Baron L. 1968. 'The Indian pass system in the Canadian West, 1882–1935'. *Prairie Forum*, 13, no. 1.

Barrow J. 1801–04. *Travels Into the Interior of Southern Africa in the Years 1797 and 1798*, 2 vols. London: Cadell and Davies.

Barta T. 1987. 'Relations of genocide: land and lives in the colonization of Australia', in *Genocide and the Modern Age*, eds I. Wallimann & M. Dobkowski. Westport, CT: Greenwood Press.

Barta T. 2007. 'Mr. Darwin's shooters: on natural selection and the naturalising of genocide', in *Colonialism and Genocide*, eds A.D. Moses & D. Stone. London: Routledge.

Barta T. 2007. 'On pain of extinction: laws of nature and history in Darwin, Marx and Arendt', in *Imperialism, Slavery, Race and Genocide: The Legacy of Hannah Arendt*, eds R. King & D. Stone. New York: Berghahn Books.

Barta T. 2008. '"They appear actually to vanish from the face of the earth". Aborigines and the European project in Australia Felix'. *Journal of Genocide Research*, 10, no. 4.

Bayly C.A. 1989. *Imperial Meridian: The British Empire and the World 1780–1830*. London: Blackwell.

Beck R. 1989. 'Bibles as beads: missionaries as traders in southern Africa in the early nineteenth century'. *Journal of African History*, 30, no. 2.

Belich J. 2009. *Replenishing the Earth: The Settler Revolution and the Rise of the Anglo-World, 1783–1939*. Oxford: Oxford University Press.

Bell D. 2009. 'Republican imperialism: J.A. Froude and the virtue of empire'. *History of Political Thought*, 30, no. 1.

Bennett J. 1969. *Northern Plainsmen: Adaptive Strategy and Agrarian Life*. Chicago: Aldine.

Bennett M.M. 1930. *The Australian Aboriginal as a Human Being*. London: Alston Rivers Ltd.

Benton L. 2002. *Law and Colonial Cultures: Legal Regimes in World History, 1400–1900.* Cambridge: Cambridge University Press.

Berger H. 1989. 'The lie of the land: the text beyond Canaan'. *Representations*, 25.

Berman M. 2000. *Wandering God: A Study in Nomadic Spirituality.* Alabany, N.Y.: State University of New York Press.

Besten M. 2009. '"We are the original inhabitants of this land"': Khoe-San identity in post-apartheid South Africa', in *Burdened By Race: Coloured Identities in Southern Africa,* ed. M. Adhikari. Cape Town: UCT Press.

Blagbrough J. 2008. 'Child domestic labour: a modern form of slavery'. *Children and Society,* 22, no. 3.

Blainey G. 1980. *A Land Half Won.* South Melbourne: Macmillan Australia.

Blainey G. 2006. *A History of Victoria.* Cambridge: Cambridge University Press.

Blecher R. 2005. 'Citizens without sovereignty: transfer and ethnic cleansing in Israel'. *Comparative Studies in Society and History,* 47, no. 4.

Bley H. 1971. *South-West Africa Under German Rule, 1895–1914.* Evanston: Northwestern University Press.

Boas J. & Weiskopf, M. 1973. 'The activities of the LMS in South Africa, 1806–1836: an assessment'. *African Studies Review,* 16.

Boeseken A.J. 1944. 'Die Nederlandse kommissarisse en die 18de eeuse samelewing aan die Kaap', in *Archives Year Book of South African History.* Pretoria: Government Printer.

Bonn M. 1914. 'German colonial policy'. *United Empire,* 5, no. 2.

Bonn M. 1949. *Wandering Scholar.* New York: Day & Co.

Bonwick J. 1870: *The Last of the Tasmanians; Or, The Black War in Van Diemen's Land.* London: Sampson Low, Son, & Marston.

Boonzaier E., Berens C., Malherbe C. & Smith A. 1996. *The Cape Herders: A History of the Khoikhoi of Southern Africa.* Cape Town: David Philip.

Bottoms T. 2013. *Conspiracy of Silence: Queensland's Frontier Killing Times.* Sydney: Allen & Unwin.

Boucher M. & Penn N. 1992. *Britain at the Cape, 1795–1803.* Johannesburg: Brenthurst Press.

Boyce J. 2008. *Van Diemen's Land.* Melbourne: Black Inc.

Brace C.L. 1868. *The Races of the Old World: A Manual of Ethnology.* New York: Charles Scribner.

Bradlow E. & Bradlow, F. eds. 1979. *William Somerville's Narrative of His Journeys to the Eastern Cape Frontier and to Lattakoe, 1799–1802.* Cape Town: Van Riebeeck Society.

Brantlinger P. 2003. *Dark Vanishings: Discourse on the Extinction of Primitive Races, 1800-1930.* Ithaca, NY: Cornell University Press.

Breen D. 1983. *The Canadian Prairie West and the Ranching Frontier, 1874-1924.* Toronto: University of Toronto Press.

Breuil B.C.O. 2008. 'Precious children in a heartless world? The complexities of child trafficking in Marseilles'. *Children and Society,* 22, no. 3.

Brockmann C. 1912. *Brief Eines Deutschen Mädchens aus Südwest.* Berlin: Mittler & Sohn.

Brody H. 2000. *The Other Side of Eden: Hunters, Farmers and the Shaping of the World.* Toronto: Douglas & McIntyre.

Broome R. 1982. *Aboriginal Australians: Black Responses to White Dominance.* Sydney: Allen & Unwin Australia.

Broome R. 2003. 'The statistics of frontier conflict', in *Frontier Conflict,* eds B. Attwood & S. Foster.

Broome R. 2005: *Aboriginal Victorians.* Sydney: Allen & Unwin.

Brown D. 2009. *Bury My Heart at Wounded Knee.* New York: Sterling, first published New York: Holt, Rinehart & Winston, 1970.

Buckley H. 1992. *From Wooden Plows to Welfare: Why Indian Policy Failed in the Prairie Provinces.* Montreal: McGill-Queens University Press.

Burns L.F. 2004. *A History of the Osage People.* Tuscaloosa: University of Alabama Press.

Buttner K. 1879. 'The Berg Damara'. *Cape Monthly Magazine,* 18.

Campbell G., Miers S. & Miller J.C. eds. 2009. *Children in Slavery Through the Ages.* Athens: Ohio University Press.

Campbell J. 2002: *Invisible Invaders: Smallpox and Other Diseases in Aboriginal Australia 1780-1880.* Melbourne: Melbourne University Press.

Cannon M. 1990. *Who Killed the Kooris?* Melbourne: William Heinemann Australia.

Card C. 2003. 'Genocide and social death'. *Hypatia,* 18, no. 1.

Carranco L. & Beard E. 1981. *Genocide and Vendetta: The Round Valley Wars and Northern California.* Norman: University of Oklahoma Press.

Carter S. 1990. *Lost Harvests: Prairie Indian Reserve Farmers and Government Policy.* Montreal: McGill-Queens University Press.

Cattan N. 2008. 'Gendering mobility: insights into the construction of spatial concepts', in *Gendered Mobilites,* eds T. Cresswell & T.P. Uteng. Aldershot: Ashgate.

Cavanagh E. 2011. *The Griqua Past and the Limits of South African History, 1902-1994.* New York: Peter Lang.

Cavanagh E. 2013. *Settler Colonialism and Land Rights in South Africa: Possession and Dispossession on the Orange River.* Houndmills: Palgrave Macmillan.

Cave A. 2008. 'Genocide in the Americas', in *The Historiography of Genocide*, ed. D. Stone, Houndmills: Palgrave Macmillan.

Cayton A.R.L. 1986. *The Frontier Republic: Ideology and Politics in the Ohio Country, 1780-1825.* Kent, OH: Kent State University Press.

Chapman W. 2010. *Reminiscences*, ed. Stassen N. Pretoria: Protea.

Chennels R. & Du Toit A. 2004. 'The rights of indigenous peoples in South Africa', in *Indigenous Peoples' Rights in Southern Africa*, eds R. Hitchcock & D. Vinding. Copenhagen: IWGIA.

Chidester D. 1996. 'Bushman religion: open, closed and new frontiers', in *Miscast*, ed. Skotnes.

Childers G. 1976. *Report on the Survey Investigation of the Ghanzi Farm Basarwa Situation.* Gaborone: Government Printer.

Chirenje J.M. 1977. *A History of Northern Botswana 1850–1910.* London: Associated University Presses.

Chirot D. & McCauley C. 2006. *Why Not Kill Them All? The Logic and Prevention of Mass Political Murder.* Princeton: Princeton University Press.

Chrisjohn R., Wasacase T., Nussey L., Smith A., Legault M., Loiselle P. & Bourgeois M. 2002. 'Genocide and Indian residential schooling: the past is present', in *Canada and International Humanitarian Law: Peacekeeping and War Crimes in the Modern Era*, eds R. Wiggers & A. Griffiths. Halifax: Dalhousie University Press.

Churchill W. 1997. *A Little Matter of Genocide: Holocaust and Denial in the Americas, 1492 to the Present.* San Francisco: City Lights Books.

Clark I.D. 1995: *Scars in the Landscape: A Register of Massacre Sites in Western Victoria.* Canberra: Australian Institute of Aboriginal and Torres Strait Islander Studies.

Clendinnen I. 2001. *Dancing With Strangers.* Melbourne: Text.

Cloete H. 1852. *Three Lectures on the Emigration of the Dutch Farmers From the Colony of the Cape of Good Hope, and Their Settlement in the District of Natal.* Pietermaritzburg: J. Archbell & Son.

Cocker M. 1988. *Rivers of Blood, Rivers of Gold: Europe's Conflict With Tribal People.* London: Jonathan Cape.

Comaroff J. & Comaroff J. 1986. 'Christianity and colonialism in South Africa'. *American Ethnologist*, 13.

Comaroff J.L. 1997. 'Images of empire: models of colonial domination in South Africa', in *Tensions of Empire: Colonial Cultures in a Bourgeois*

World, eds F. Cooper & A.L. Stoler. Berkeley: University of California Press.

Comaroff J.L. & Comaroff J. 2008. 'Ethnicity', in *New South African Keywords*, eds N. Shepherd & S. Robins. Johannesburg: Jacana Media.

Comaroff J.L. & Comaroff J. 2009. *Ethnicity, Inc.* Chicago: University of Chicago Press.

Connor J. 2002. *The Australian Frontier Wars: 1788–1838.* Sydney: University of New South Wales Press.

Cornell F. 1921. *The Glamour of Prospecting.* London: Fisher-Unwin.

Courtwright D. 1996. *Violent Land: Single Men and Social Disorder From the Frontier to the Inner City.* Cambridge: Harvard University Press.

Crapanzano V. 1985. *Waiting: The Whites in South Africa.* New York: Doubleday.

Cresswell T. 2002. 'Theorizing place'. *Thamyris/Intersecting*, 9.

Cresswell T. 2006. *On the Move: Mobility in the Modern Western World.* New York: Routledge.

Critchett J. 1990. *A 'Distant Field of Murder': Western District Frontiers 1834–1848.* Melbourne: Melbourne University Press.

Critchett J. 2003. 'Encounters in the Western District', in Attwood & Foster, *Frontier Conflict*, eds B. Attwood & S. Foster.

Cronon W. 1983. *Changes in the Land: Indians, Colonists, and the Ecology of New England.* New York: Hill & Wang.

Crosby A. 2004. *Ecological Imperialism: The Biological Expansion of Europe, 900–1900.* Cambridge: Cambridge University Press.

Crwys-Williams J. comp. 1999. *Penguin Dictionary of South African Quotations.* Sandton: Penguin.

Cunningham H. 2006. *The Invention of Childhood.* London: BBC Books.

Curthoys A. 2008. 'Genocide in Tasmania: the history of an idea', in *Empire, Colony, Genocide*, ed. A.D. Moses.

Curthoys A. & Docker J. 2001. 'Introduction—genocide: definitions, questions, settler-colonies'. *Aboriginal History*, 25.

Curthoys A. & Docker J. 2008. 'Defining genocide', in *Historiography of Genocide*, ed. D. Stone.

Dachs A.J. 1972. 'Missionary imperialism—the case of Bechuanaland'. *Journal of African History*, 13.

Dale E.E. 1960. *The Range Cattle Industry: Ranching on the Great Plains from 1865 to 1925.* Norman: Oklahoma University Press.

Day D. 2008. *Conquest: How Societies Overwhelm Others.* Oxford: Oxford University Press.

Deacon H.J. & Deacon J. 1999. *Human Beginnings in South Africa: Uncovering the Secrets of the Stone Age*. Cape Town: David Philip.

Debo A. 1941. *The Road to Disappearance: A History of the Creek Indians*. Norman: University of Oklahoma Press.

Debo A. 1970. *A History of the Indians of the United States*. Norman: University of Oklahoma Press.

Degirmencioglu S.M., Acar H. & Acar Y.B. 2008. 'Extreme forms of child labour in Turkey'. *Children and Society*, 22, no. 3.

Delius P. & Trapido S. 1982. 'Inboekselings and Oorlams: the creation and transformation of a servile class'. *Journal of Southern African Studies*, 8, no. 2.

Deloria V. & Lytle C.M. 1983. *American Indians, American Justice*. Austin: University of Texas Press.

DeMaillie R. 2001. *Plains, Handbook of North American Indians*. Washington, D.C.: Smithsonian Institution, 13.

De Tocqueville A. 1959. *Journey to America*, trans. G. Lawrence, ed. J.P. Mayer. New Haven: Yale University Press.

De Tocqueville A. 2001. *Writings on Empire and Slavery*. Baltimore: Johns Hopkins University Press.

Diamond J. 1992. *The Third Chimpanzee*. New York: Harper Collins.

Diamond J. 1999. *Guns, Germs and Steel: The Fates of Human Societies*. New York: Norton.

Dippie B. 1982. *The Vanishing American: White Attitudes and U.S. Indian Policy*. Lawrence: University Press of Kansas.

Docker J. 2008. 'Are settler-colonies inherently genocidal? Re-reading Lemkin', in *Empire, Colony, Genocide*, ed. A.D Moses.

Docker J. 2008. *The Origins of Violence: Religion, History and Violence*. London: Pluto Press.

Dooling W. 2005. 'The origins and aftermath of the Cape Colony's "Hottentot Code" of 1809'. *Kronos*, 31.

Dooling W. 2007. *Slavery, Emancipation and Colonial Rule in South Africa*. Scottsville: University of KwaZulu-Natal Press.

Dooling W. 2009. 'Reconstructing the household: the northern Cape Colony before and after the South African War'. *Journal of African History*, 50, no. 3.

Drechsler H. 1980. *Let Us Die Fighting*. Berlin: Akademie-Verlag.

Drinnon R. 1997. *Facing West: The Metaphysics of Indian Hating and Empire Building*. Norman: University of Oklahoma Press.

Du Plessis J. 1911. *A History of Christian Missions in South Africa*. London: Longmans, Green and Co.

Dusenberry V. 1954. 'The Rocky Boy Indians: Montana's displaced people'. *The Magazine of Western History*, 52, no. 4.

Du Toit A. & Giliomee H. 1983. *Afrikaner Political Thought: Analysis and Documents, 1780–1850*. Cape Town: David Philip.

Dwyer P. & Ryan L. eds. 2012. *Theatres of Violence: Massacre, Mass Killing and Atrocity throughout History*. New York: Berghahn Books.

Dziewiecka M. 2008. 'Places of the people: the Khwebe Hills in the history of Ngamiland'. *Botswana Notes and Records*, 40.

Edwards P. 2003. 'On home ground: settling land and domesticating difference in the "non-settler" colonies of Burma and Cambodia'. *Journal of Colonialism and Colonial History*, 4, no. 3.

Elbourne E. 1994. 'Freedom at issue: vagrancy legislation and the meaning of freedom in Britain and the Cape Colony, 1799–1842'. *Slavery and Abolition*, 15, no. 2.

Elbourne E. 2002. *Blood Ground: Colonialism, Missions and the Contest for Christianity in the Cape Colony and Britain, 1799–1853*. Montreal: McGill-Queen's University Press.

Elbourne E. 2003. 'The sin of the settler: the 1835–36 Select Committee on Aborigines and Debates Over Virtue and Conquest in the Early Nineteenth-Century British White Settler Empire'. *Journal of Colonialism and Colonial History*, 4, no. 3.

Elbourne E. 2005. 'Indigenous peoples and imperial networks in the early nineteenth century', in *Rediscovering the British World*, eds P. Buckner & R.D. Francis. Calgary: University of Calgary Press.

Elbourne E. 2008. 'Between Van Diemen's Land and the Cape Colony', in *Reading Robinson*, eds A. Johnston & M. Rolls.

Eldridge E. 1994. 'Slave raiding across the Cape frontier', in *Slavery in South Africa*, eds E. Eldridge & F. Morton.

Eldridge E. & Morton F. eds. 1994. *Slavery in South Africa: Native Labour on the Dutch Frontier*. Boulder, CO: Westview Press.

Elofson W. 2000. 'The untamed Canadian ranching frontier, 1874 Eldridge & Morton, 1914', in *Cowboys, Ranchers, and the Cattle Business: Cross Border Perspectives on the Ranching Frontier*, eds S. Evans, S. Carter & B. Yeo. Calgary, University of Calgary Press.

Elofson W. 2003. *Cowboys, Gentlemen and Cattle Thieves*. Montreal: McGill-Queens University Press.

Elphick R. 1985. *Khoikhoi and the Founding of White South Africa*. Johannesburg: Ravan Press.

Elphick R. & Giliomee H. eds. 1989. *The Shaping of South African Society*. Cape Town: Maskew Miller Longman.

Elphick R. & Giliomee H. 1989. 'The origins and entrenchment of European dominance at the Cape, 1652–1840', in *Shaping*, eds R. Elphick & H. Giliomee.

Elphick R. & Malherbe V. 1989. 'The Khoisan to 1828', in *Shaping*, eds R. Elphick & H. Giliomee.

Evans R. 1999. 'Kings in brass crescents: defining Aboriginal labour patterns in colonial Queensland', in *Fighting Words: Writing About Race*, ed. R Evans. Brisbane: University of Queensland Press.

Evans R. 2003. 'Across the Queensland frontier', in *Frontier Conflict*, eds B. Attwood & S. Foster.

Evans R. 2004. '"Pigmentia": racial fears and white Australia', in *Genocide and Settler Society*, ed. A.D. Moses.

Evans R. 2007. *A History of Queensland*. Cambridge: Cambridge University Press.

Evans R. 2008. '"Crime without a name": colonialism and the case for "Indigenocide"', in *Empire, Colony, Genocide*, ed. A.D. Moses.

Evans R. 2013. 'Foreword' in *Conspiracy of Silence*, ed. T. Bottoms.

Fein H. 1993. *Genocide: A Sociological Perspective*. London: Sage.

Fenton J. 1884. *A History of Tasmania from Its Discovery in 1642 to the Present Time*. Hobart: J. Walch and Sons.

Findlay D. 1977. 'The San of the Cape thirstland and L. Anthing's "special mission"'. BA Hons thesis, University of Cape Town.

Finnane M. & McGuire J. 2001, 'The uses of punishment and exile: Aborigines in colonial Australia'. *Punishment and Society*, 3, no 2.

Finzsch N. 2005. '"It is scarcely possible to conceive that human beings could be so hideous and loathsome": discourses of genocide in eighteenth and nineteenth-century America and Australia'. *Patterns of Prejudice*, 39, no. 2.

Finzsch N. 2007. '"It is scarcely possible to conceive that human beings could be so hideous and loathsome": discourses of genocide in eighteenth and nineteenth-century America and Australia', in *Colonialism and Genocide*, eds A.D. Moses & D. Stone. New York: Routledge.

Finzsch N. 2008. '"Extirpate or remove that vermine": genocide, biological warfare, and settler imperialism in the eighteenth and early nineteenth century'. *Journal of Genocide Research*, 10, no. 2.

Finzsch N. 2008. '"The Aborigines were never annihilated, and still they are becoming extinct": settler imperialism and genocide in nineteenth-century America and Australia', in *Empire, Colony, Genocide*, ed. A.D. Moses.

Fitzpatrick B. 1951. *British Imperialism and Australia 1783–1833*. London: Allen & Unwin.

Flannery T. 2001. *The Eternal Frontier: An Ecological History of North America and Its Peoples*. Melbourne: Text.

Flood J. 1994. *Archaeology of the Dreamtime: The Story of Prehistoric Australia and its People*. Sydney: Allen & Unwin.

Ford L. 2010. *Settler Sovereignty: Jurisdiction and Indigenous People in America and Australia, 1788–1836*. Cambridge: Harvard University Press.

Foran M. 2003. *Trails and Trials: Markets and Land Use in Alberta Beef Industry, 1881–1948*. Calgary: University of Calgary Press.

Forrest K. 1996. *The Challenge and the Chance: The Colonisation and Settlement of North West Australia 1861–1914*. Carlisle, WA: Hesperian Press.

Foster M.W. 1991. *Being Comanche: A Social History of an American Indian Community*. Tucson: University of Arizona Press.

Fredrickson G.M. 1988. 'Colonialism and racism', in *The Arrogance of Race: Historical Perspectives on Slavery, Racism, and Social Inequality*, G.M. Fredrickson. Middletown, CT: Wesleyan University Press.

Frenssen G. 1906 *Peter Mohr's Fahrt Nach Su¨dwest Afrika*. Berlin: G. Grote.

Freund W. 1989. 'The Cape under the transitional governments, 1795–1814', in *Shaping*, eds R. Elphick & H. Giliomee.

Friesen G. 1987. *The Canadian Prairies: A History*. Toronto: University of Toronto Press.

Frow J. 2012. 'Settlement'. *Cultural Studies Review*, 18, no. 1.

Gadilobae M.N. 1985. 'Serfdom (bolata) in the Nata Area 1926–1960'. *Botswana Notes and Records*, 17.

Gall S. 2001. *The Bushmen of Southern Africa: Slaughter of the Innocent*. London: Chatto and Windus.

Gallois W. 2013. *A History of Violence in the Early Algerian Colony*. New York: Palgrave Macmillan.

Gann L. & Duignan P. 1977. *The Rulers of German Africa*. Stanford: Stanford University Press.

Gardner P.D. 2001. *Gippsland Massacres: The Destruction of the Kurnai Tribes 1800–1860*. Ensay, Vic.: self-published.

Gerhard D. 1959. 'The frontier in comparative view'. *Comparative Studies in Society and History*, 1.

Gewald J-B. 1999. *Herero Heroes*. Athens: Ohio University Press.

Gifford-Gonzalez D. 2000. 'Animal disease challenges to the emergence of pastoralism in sub-Saharan Africa'. *African Archaeological Review*, 17, no. 3.

Giliomee H. 1981. 'Processes in development of the southern African frontier', in *The Frontier in History: North America and Southern Africa Compared*, eds. H. Lamar & L. Thompson. New Haven: Yale University Press.

Giliomee H. 2003. *The Afrikaners: Biography of a People*. Charlotteville: University of Virginia Press.

Gillett S. 1969. 'Notes on the settlement in the Ghanzi District'. *Botswana Notes and Records*, 2.

Goldring P. 1973. 'The Cypress Hills massacre: a century's retrospect'. *Saskatchewan History*, 26, no. 3.

González O.E. & Premo B. eds. 2007. *Raising an Empire: Children in Early Modern Iberia and Colonial Latin America*. Albuquerque: University of New Mexico Press.

Goodin R.E. 2012. *On Settling*. Princeton, NJ: Princeton University Press.

Gordon R.J. 1984. 'The !Kung in the Kalahari exchange: an ethno historical perspective', in *Past and Present in Hunter Gatherer Studies*, ed. C. Shrire. Orlando, Florida: Academic Press.

Gordon R.J. 1998. 'The rise of the Bushman penis: Germans, genitalia and genocide'. *African Studies*, 27.

Gordon R.J. 2003. 'Inside the Windhoek lager: liquor and lust in Namibia', in *Drugs, Labor and Colonial Expansion*, eds W. Jankowick & D. Bradburd. Tucson: University of Arizona Press.

Gordon R.J. 2003. 'Collecting the gatherers', in *Worldly Provincials: Essays in the History of German Anthropology*, eds H.G. Penny & M. Bunzl. Ann Arbor: University of Michigan Press.

Gordon R.J. 2009. 'Hiding in full view: the "forgotten" Bushman genocides of Namibia'. *Genocide Studies and Prevention*, 4, no.1.

Gordon R.J. & Douglas S. 2000. *The Bushman Myth: The Making of a Namibian Underclass*. Boulder, CO: Westview Press Gott R. 2011. *Britain's Empire: Resistance, Repression and Revolt*. London: Verso.

Gray G. 2007. *A Cautious Silence: The Politics of Australian Anthropology*. Canberra: Aboriginal Studies Press.

Green L. 1955. *Karoo*. Cape Town: Howard Timmins.

Green N. 1981. 'Aborigines and white settlers', in *A New History of Western Australia*, ed. C.T. Stannage. Perth: UWAP.

Green N. 1984. *Broken Spears: Aboriginals and Europeans in the Southwest of Australia*. Perth: Focus Education Services.

Green N. 1998. 'From princes to paupers: the struggle for control of Aborigines in Western Australia 1887–1898', *Early Days*, 11, pt. 4.

Greer A. 2012. 'Commons and enclosure in the colonization of North America'. *American Historical Review*, 117, no. 2.

Guelke L. 1984. 'Land tenure and settlement at the Cape, 1652–1812', in *History of Surveying and Land Tenure in South Africa*, eds C. Martin & K. Friedlander. Cape Town: University of Cape Town.

Guelke L. 1989. 'Freehold farmers and frontier settlers, 1657–1780', in *Shaping*, eds R. Elphick & H. Giliomee.

Guelke L. & Shell R. 1992. 'Landscape of conquest: frontier water alienation and Khoikhoi strategies of survival, 1652–1780'. *Journal of Southern African Studies*, 18, no. 4.

Guenther M. 1976. 'From hunters to squatters: social and cultural change among the Ghanzi farm Bushmen', in *Kalahari Hunter-Gatherers*, eds R.B. Lee & I. De Vore. Cambridge: Harvard University Press.

Guenther M. 1977 'Bushman hunters as farm labourers'. *Canadian Journal of African Studies*, 11, no. 2.

Guenther M. 1980. 'From "brutal savages" to "harmless people": notes on the changing western image of the Bushmen'. *Paideuma*, 26.

Guenther M. 1986. *The Nharo Bushmen of Botswana: Tradition and Change.* Hamburg: Helmut Buske Verlag.

Guenther M. 1986. '"San" or "Bushmen?"', in *The Past and Future of !Kung Ethnography: Critical Reflections and Symbolic Perspectives*, eds M. Biesele, R. Gordon & R. Lee. Hamburg: Helmut Buske Verlag.

Guenther M. 1989. *Bushman Folktales: Oral Traditions of the Nharo of Botswana and the /Xam of the Cape.* Stuttgart: Franz Steiner Verlag.

Guenther M. 1993. '"Independent, fearless and rather bold": a historical narrative on the Ghanzi Bushmen of Botswana'. *Journal of the Namibian Scientific Society*, 44.

Guenther M. 1997. '"Lords of the desert land": politics and resistance of the Ghanzi Basarwa of the nineteenth century'. *Botswana Notes and Records*, 29.

Guenther M. 1999. *Tricksters and Trancers: Bushman Religion and Society.* Bloomington: Indiana University Press.

Guenther M. 2002. 'Independence, resistance, accommodation, persistence: hunter-gatherers and agro-pastoralists in the Ghanzi veld, early 1880s to mid-1900s', in *Ethnicity, Hunter-Gatherers, and the 'Other'*, ed. S. Kent. Washington: Smithonian Institution Press.

Guenther M. 2007. '"Poor Baines has his troubles …"': Thomas Baines and James Chapman afoot in the Kalahari, 1861—deconstructing an imperialist narrative'. *Journal of the Namibian Scientific Society*, 55.

Guenther M. 2010. 'Sharing among the San, today, yesterday and in the past', in *The Principle of Sharing Segregation and Construction of Social identities at the Transition from Foraging to Farming*, ed. M. Benz. Berlin: Ex Oriente.

Guillaumin C. 1972. 'Caractères spécifiques de l'ideologie raciste'. *Cahiers Internationaux de Sociologie*, 53.

Haake C. 2007. *The State, Removal and Indigenous Peoples in the United States and Mexico, 1620–2000*. New York: Routledge.

Haacke W. 2000 *Linguistic Evidence in the Study of Origins: The Case of the Namibian Khoekhoe-speakers*. Inaugural lecture. Windhoek: University of Namibia.

Habermas J. 1996. *Between Facts and Norms*. Cambridge: Polity.

Haebich A. 1988. *For their Own Good: Aborigines and Government in the Southwest of Western Australia, 1900–1940*. Perth: UWAP.

Haebich A. 2000. *Broken Circles: Fragmenting Indigenous Families, 1800–2000*. Fremantle: Fremantle Arts Centre.

Haebich A. 2004. '"Clearing the wheat belt": erasing the indigenous presence in the southwest of Western Australia', in *Genocide and Settler Society*, ed. A.D. Moses.

Hahn C.H. 1878. 'Damaraland and the Berg Damaras'. *Cape Monthly Magazine*, 16.

Hahn C.H. 1985. *Diaries of a Missionary in Nama- and Damaraland 1837–1860*, ed. B. Lau. Windhoek: Windhoek Archives Services Division of the Department of National Education.

Hall C. 2002. *Civilising Subjects: Metropole and Colony in the English Imagination, 1830–1867*. Cambridge: Polity.

Hall S. 2010. 'Farming communities of the second millennium: internal frontiers, identity, continuity and change', in *The Cambridge History of South Africa: From Early Times to 1885*, eds C. Hamilton, B.K. Mbenga & R. Ross. Cambridge: Cambridge University Press.

Harring S. 1994. *Crow Dog's Case: American Indian Sovereignty, Tribal Law, and United States Law in the Nineteenth Century*. Cambridge: Cambridge University Press.

Harring S. 1998. *White Man's Law: Native People in 19th Century Canadian Jurisprudence*, Toronto: University of Toronto & Osgoode Society for Canadian Legal History.

Harring S. 2007. 'The Herero demand for reparations from Germany: the hundred year old legacy of a colonial war in the politics of modern Namibia', in *Repairing the Past: International Perspectives on Reparations for Gross Human Rights Abuses*, eds M. du Plessis & S. Pete. Oxford: Intersentia.

Hartwell R.M. 1954. *The Economic Development of Van Diemen's Land 1823-1850*. Melbourne: Melbourne University Press.

Hasluck P. 1970. *Black Australians: A Survey of Native Policy in Western Australia, 1829-1897*. Melbourne: Melbourne University Press.

Heintze B. 1972. 'Buschmaenner unter ambo-aspekte ihrer gegenseitigen beziehungen'. *Journal of the South West Africa Scientific Society*, 26.

Herskovits M. 1926. 'The cattle complex in East Africa'. *American Anthropologist*, 28.

Hetherington P. 2002. *Settlers, Servants and Slaves: Aboriginal and European Children in Nineteenth Century Western Australia*. Perth: University of Western Australia Press.

Hewitt R. 2008. *Structure, Meaning and Ritual in Narratives of the Southern San*. Johannesburg: Witwatersrand University Press.

Hildebrant W. & Hubner B. 2007. *The Cypress Hills: An Island By Itself*. Saskatoon. Purich.

Hinton A. ed. 2002. *Genocide: An Anthropological Reader*. Malden: Malden.

Hitchcock R., Ikheya K., Biesele M. & Lee R. eds. 2006. *Updating the San: Image and Reality of an African People in the 21st Century*. Osaka: National Museum of Ethnology.

Hoernle A.W. 1987. *Trails in the Thirstland: The Anthropological Field Diaries of Winifred Hoernle*, eds P. Carstens, G. Klinghardt & M. West. Cape Town: Centre for African Studies, UCT.

Hogue M. 2002. 'Disputing the medicine line: the Plains Cree and the Canadian–American border, 1876–1885'. *The Magazine of Western History*, 52, no. 4.

Holland A. 1995. 'Feminism, colonialism and Aboriginal workers: an anti-slavery crusade'. *Labour History*, 69.

Hornaday W. 1989. *The Extermination of the American Bison*. Washington, D.C.: Smithsonian Institution.

Howard J. 1984. *The Canadian Sioux*. Lincoln: University of Nebraska Press.

Hughes R. 1987. *The Fatal Shore: A History of the Transportation of Convicts to Australia 1787–1868*. London: Pan Books.

Hull I. 2003. 'Military culture and the production of "final solutions" in the colonies: the example of Wilhelminian Germany', in *The Specter of Genocide*, eds R. Gellately & B. Kiernan. Cambridge: Cambridge University Press.

Hunt S.J. 1978. 'The Gribble affair': a study of Aboriginal–European labour relations in north-west Australia during the 1880s'. Honours thesis, Murdoch University.

Hunt S.J. 1986. *Spinifex and Hessian: Women's Lives in North West Australia, 1860–1900*. Perth: UWAP.

Hunt S.J. 1987. 'The Gribble affair: a study in colonial politics', appendix to J.B. Gribble, [1886] *Dark Deeds in a Sunny Land*. Perth: UWAP.

Hunter A. 2012. *A Different Kind of 'Subject': Colonial Law in Aboriginal–European Relations in Nineteenth Century Western Australia 1829–61*. Melbourne: Australian Scholarly.

Ingold T. 2001. *The Perception of the Environment*. London: Routledge.

Inskeep A. & Schladt M. 2003. *Heinrich Vedder's the Bergdama: An Annotated Translation of the German Original With Additional Ethnographic Material*. Cologne: Köppe.

Isenberg A.C. 2000. *The Destruction of the Bison: An Environmental History, 1750–1920.*: Cambridge: Cambridge University Press.

Iverson P. 1994. *When Indians Became Cowboys: Native Peoples and Cattle Ranching*. Norman: University of Oklahoma Press.

Jacobs M.D. 2005. 'Maternal colonialism: white women and indigenous child removal in the American west and Australia, 1880–1940'. *Western Historical Quarterly*, 36, no. 4.

Jacoby K. 2008. '"The broad platform of extermination": nature and violence in the nineteenth century North American Borderlands'. *Journal of Genocide Research*, 10, no. 2.

Jeffreys M. 1978. 'An epitath to the Bushmen', in *The Bushmen: San Hunters and Herders of Southern Africa*, ed. P. Tobias. Cape Town: Human & Rousseau.

Jenish D. 1999. *Indian Fall: The Last Great Days of the Plains Cree and the Blackfoot Confederacy*. Toronto: Penguin Books.

Jennings F. 1975. *The Invasion of America: Indians, Colonialism, and the Cant of Conquest*. Chapel Hill: University of North Carolina Press.

Johns L. & Ville S. 2012. 'Banking records, business and networks in colonial Sydney, 1817–24'. *Australian Economic History Review*, 52, no 2.

Johnston A. 2004. 'A blister on the imperial antipodes: Lancelot Edward Threlkeld in Polynesia and Australia', in *Colonial Lives*, eds D. Lambert & A. Lester.

Johnston A. & Rolls M. 2008. *Reading Robinson: Companion Essays to Friendly Mission*. Hobart: Quintus.

Jones A. 2011. *Genocide: A Comprehensive Introduction*. London: Routledge.

Jones M. 2001. 'Genocide, ethnocide or hyperbole? Australia's stolen generation and Canada's hidden holocaust'. *Culture Survival Quarterly*, 25, no. 4.

Jones R. 1977. 'The Tasmanian paradox', in *Stone Tools as Cultural Markers: Change, Evolution and Complexity*, ed. R.V.S. Wright. Canberra: Australian Institute of Aboriginal Studies.

Joyce J.W. 1938. *Report on the Masarwa in the Bamangwato Reserve, Bechuanaland*. League of Nations Publications, C112, M98,VIB, 'Slavery', Annex 6.

Kakel C. 2011. *The American West and the Nazi East: A Comparative and Interpretive Perspective*. Houndmills: Palgrave Macmillan.

Keen I. 2010. 'The interpretation of Aboriginal "property" on the Australian colonial frontier', in *Indigenous Participation in Australian Economies*, ed. I. Keen. Canberra: ANU Press.

Kercher B. 1995. *An Unruly Child: A History of Law in Australia*. St Leonards: Allen & Unwin.

Kiernan B. 2001. 'Australia's Aboriginal genocide'. *Yale Journal of Human Rights*, 1, no. 1.

Kiernan B. 2007. *Blood and Soil: Genocide and Extermination in World History from Carthage to Darfur*. Yale: Yale University Press.

Kinsman M. 1989. 'Populists and patriarchs: the transformation of the captaincy at Griquatown, 1804–22', in *Organisation and Economic Change: South African Studies, 5*, ed. A. Mabin. Johannesburg: Ravan Press.

Kirby P.R. ed. 1939–40. *The Diary of Dr. Andrew Smith, Director of the Expedition for Exploring Central Africa, 1834–1836*. 2 vols. Cape Town: Van Riebeeck Society.

Kline L.W. 1898. 'The migratory impulse versus love of home'. *American Journal of Psychology*, 10.

Koch A. & Peden W. eds. 1944. *The Life and Selected Writings of Thomas Jefferson*. New York: Random House.

Kociumbas J. 1992. *The Oxford History of Australia: Possessions, 1770–1860*. Melbourne, Oxford University Press.

Kociumbas J. 2004. 'Genocide and modernity in colonial Australia'. *Genocide and Settler Society*.

Kossler R. 2009. 'Entangled history: negotiating the past between Germany and Namibia'. *Journal of Contemporary African Studies*, 26, no. 3.

Kuper A. 1970. *Kalahari Village Politics: An African Democracy*. Cambridge: Cambridge University Press.

Kuper L. 1982. *Genocide*. New Haven: Yale University Press.

Laidlaw Z. 2012. 'Slavery, settlers and indigenous dispossession: Britain's empire through the lens of Liberia'. *Journal of Colonialism and Colonial History*, 13, no. 1.

Lake M. 1993. 'Colonised and colonising: the white Australian feminist subject'. *Women's History Review*, 2, no. 3.

Lake M. & Reynolds H. 2008. *Drawing the Global Colour Line: White Men's Countries and the Question of Racial Equality*. Melbourne: Melbourne University Press.

Lamar H. & Thompson L. eds. 1981. *The Frontier in History: North America and Southern Africa Compared*. New Haven & London: Yale University Press.

Lambert D. & Lester A. 2004. 'Geographies of colonial philanthropy'. *Progress in Human Geography*, 28, no. 3.

Lambert D. & Lester A. eds. 2006. *Colonial Lives Across The British Empire: Imperial Careering In The Long Nineteenth Century*. Cambridge: Cambridge University Press.

Lau B. 1987. *Namibia in Jonker Afrikaner's Time*. Windhoek: National Archives.

Lau B. 1995. '"Thank God the Germans came": Vedder and Namibian historiography', in *History and Historiography: Essays in Reprint*, ed. B. Lau. Windhoek: MSORP.

La Vere D. 2004. *The Texas Indians*. College Station: Texas A&M University Press.

Lebzelter V. 1934. *Eingeborenenkulturen in Suedwest-und Suedafrika, 2*. Leipzig: Karl W. Hierseman.

Legassick M. 1969. 'The Griqua, the Sotho-Tswana, and the missionaries, 1780–1840: the politics of a frontier zone'. PhD thesis, University of California, Los Angeles.

Legassick M. 1989. 'The northern frontier to c.1840: the rise and decline of the Griqua people', in *Shaping*, eds R. Elphick & H. Giliomee.

Legassick M. 2010. *The Politics of a South African Frontier: The Griqua, the Sotho-Tswana, and the Missionaries, 1780–1840*. Basel: Basler Afrika Bibliographien.

Lemkin R. 1944. *Axis Rule in Occupied Europe: Laws of Occupation, Analysis of Government, Proposals for Redress*. New York: Columbia University Press.

Lester A. 2002. 'British settler discourse and the circuits of empire'. *History Workshop Journal*, 54.

Lester A. 2005. 'Humanitarians and white settlers in the nineteenth century', in *Missions and Empire: The Oxford History of The British Empire Companion Series*, ed. N. Etherington. Oxford: Oxford University Press.

Lester A. 2011. 'Humanism, race and the colonial frontier'. *Transactions of the Institute of British Geographers*, 37, no. 1.

Lester A. & Dussart F. 2009. 'Masculinity "race", and family in the colonies: protecting Aborigines in the early nineteenth century'. *Gender, Place and Culture*, 16, no. 1.

Levene M. 2005. *Genocide in the Age of the Nation State: The Rise of the West and the Coming of Genocide*. New York: I.B. Taurus.

Lewis-Williams D. & Pearce D. 2004. *San Spirituality: Roots, Expressions and Social Consequences*. Cape Town: Double Storey.

Lichtenstein H. 1928, 1930. *Travels in Southern Africa in the Years 1803, 1804, 1805, 1806*, 2 vols., trans. A. Plumptre. Cape Town: Van Riebeeck Society; first published London, Henry Colburn, 1812–15.

Limerick P. 1987. *The Legacy of Conquest: the Unbroken Past of the American West*. New York: Norton.

Limerick P. 2000. *Something in the Soil: Legacies and Reckonings in the New West*. New York: Norton.

Lindqvist S. 1996. *Exterminate All the Brutes*. London: Granta.

Lindsay B. 2012. *Murder State: California's Native American Genocide, 1846–1873*. Lincoln: University of Nebraska Press.

Loos N. 1982. *Invasion and Resistance: Aboriginal-European Relations on the North Queensland Frontier*. Canberra: ANU Press.

Lumholtz C. 1979. *Among Cannibals: Account of Four Years Travels in Australia, and Camp Life with the Aborigines of Australia*. Firle, Sussex: Caliban Books, first published London: 1889.

Lye W.F. ed. 1975. *Andrew Smith's Journal of His Expedition Into the Interior of South Africa, 1834–36: An Authentic Narrative of Travels and Discoveries, the Manners and Customs of the Native Tribes, and the Physical Nature of the Country*. Cape Town: A.A. Balkema.

MacCrone I.D. 1937. *Race Attitudes in South Africa: Historical, Experimental and Psychological Studies*. London: Oxford University Press.

Mackaness G. ed. 1965. *Henry Melville: History of Van Diemen's Land From the Year 1824 to 1835, Inclusive During the Administration of Governor Arthur*, first published in 1836. Sydney: Horwitz-Grahame.

Macmillan W.M. 1963. *Bantu, Boer, and Briton: The Making of the South African Native Problem*. Oxford: Clarendon Press.

Macmillan W.M. 1968. *The Cape Colour Question: A Historical Survey*. Cape Town: Balkema.

Madley B. 2004. 'Patterns of frontier genocide 1803–1910: the Aboriginal Tasmanians, the Yuki of California, and the Herero of Namibia'. *Journal of Genocide Research*, 6, no. 2.

Madley B. 2008. 'California's Yuki Indians: defining genocide in Native American history'. *Western Historical Quarterly*, 39, no. 3.

Magubane Z. 1996. 'Labour laws and stereotypes: images of the Khoikhoi in the Cape in the age of abolition'. *South African Historical Journal*, 35, no. 1.

Mako S. 2012. 'Cultural genocide and key international instruments: framing the indigenous experience'. *International Journal on Minority and Group Rights,* 19.

Malherbe V.C. 1978. 'Diversification and mobility of Khoikhoi labour in the eastern districts of the Cape Colony prior to the labour law of 1 November 1809'. Masters thesis, University of Cape Town.

Malherbe V.C. 1991. 'Indentured and unfree labour in South Africa: towards an understanding'. *South African Historical Journal*, 24, no. 1.

Malkki L. 1992. 'National Geographic: the rooting of peoples and the territorialization of national identity among scholars and refugees'. *Cultural Anthropology*, 7, no. 1.

Mandelbaum D. 1979. *The Plains Cree: An Ethnographic, Historical and Comparative Study.* Regina: Great Plains Research Center.

Mann B. 2012. 'Fractal massacres in the old northwest: the destruction of the Miami people'. Unpublished paper presented at the Violence and Honour in Settler Colonial Societies Conference, University of Cape Town.

Mann M. 2005. *The Dark Side of Democracy: Explaining Ethnic Cleansing.* Cambridge: Cambridge University Press.

Mann W. 1994. 'Sagacious seers and honourable men: pearling, Aboriginal labour and representations of Australian colonialism', in *Papers in Labour History, 14,* ed. J. Bailey. Perth: Australian Society for the Study of Labour History.

Manne R. ed. 2003. *Whitewash: On Keith Windschuttle's Fabrication of Aboriginal History.* Melbourne: Black Inc.

Marais J.S. 1944. *Maynier and the First Boer Republic.* Cape Town: Maskew Miller.

Marais J.S. 1968. *The Cape Coloured People, 1652–1937.* Johannesburg: Witwatersrand University Press.

Marks S. 1972. 'Khoisan resistance to the Dutch in the seventeenth and eighteenth centuries'. *Journal of African History*, 13, no. 1.

Marshall P.J. & Williams G. 1982. *The Great Map of Mankind: British Perceptions of the World in the Age of Enlightenment*. London: Harvard University Press.

Mason J.E. 2003. *Social Death and Resurrection: Slavery and Emancipation in South Africa*. Charlottesville: University of Virginia Press.

Matsuda M. 1996. *The Memory of the Modern*. New York: Oxford University Press.

Mattenklodt W. 1931. *Fugitive in the Jungle*. Boston: Little Brown.

Maybury-Lewis D. 2002. 'Genocide against indigenous peoples', in *Annihilating Difference*, ed. A. Hinton. Berkeley: University of California Press.

Maylam P. 1980. *Rhodes, the Tswana, and the British: Colonialism, Collaboration, and Conflict in the Bechuanaland Protectorate 1885–1899*. Westport, Conn.: Greenwood Press.

McCarthy M. 1994. 'Before Broome'. *Great Circle*, 16, no. 2.

McCombie T. 1858. *History of the Colony of Victoria From its Settlement to the Death of Sir Charles Hotham*. London: Chapman and Hall.

McCoy J.G. 1874. *Historic Sketches of the Cattle Trade in the West and Southwest*. Kansas City: Ramsey, Millett & Hudson.

McCrady D. 1998. *Living With Strangers: The Nineteenth Century Sioux and the Canadian American Borderlands*. PhD dissertation, University of Manitoba.

McDonald J. 2007. 'When shall these dry bones live? Interactions between the London Missionary Society and the San along the Cape's north-eastern frontier, 1790–1833'. MA thesis, University of Cape Town.

McDonald J. 2009. 'Encounters at "Bushman Station": reflections on the fate of the San of the Transgariep frontier, 1826–1833'. *South African Historical Journal*, 61, no. 2.

McGrath A. 1987. *Born in the Cattle: Aborigines in Cattle Country*. Sydney: Allen & Unwin.

McGregor R. 1997. *Imagined Destinies: Aboriginal Australians and the Doomed Race Theory, 1880–1939*. Melbourne: Melbourne University Press.

McLeod R. 1976. *The North West Mounted Police and Law Enforcement, 1873–1905*. Toronto: University of Toronto Press.

McMichael P. 1984. *Settlers and the Agrarian Question: Capitalism in Colonial Australia*. Cambridge: Cambridge University Press.

Memmi A. 1967. *The Colonizer and the Colonized*. Boston: Beacon.

Mendes A. 2009. 'Child slaves in the early north Atlantic trade in the fifteenth and sixteenth centuries', in *Children in Slavery through the*

Ages, eds G. Campbell, S. Miers & J.C. Miller. Athens: Ohio University Press.

Miers S. & Crowder M. 1988. 'The politics of slavery in Bechuanaland: power struggles and plight of the Basarwa in the Bamangwato Reserve, 1926–1940', in *The End of Slavery in Africa*, eds S. Miers & R. Roberts. Madison: University of Wisconsin Press.

Mentzel O.F. 1944. *A Geographical and Topographical Description of the Cape of Good Hope, Part 3*, ed. H. Mandelbrote. Cape Town: Van Riebeeck Society; first published Glogau: Christian Friedrich Günther, 1787.

Mercer J. 1980. *The Canary Islanders: Their Prehistory Conquest and Survival*. London: Collings.

Miller J. 2009. *Compact, Contract, Covenant: Aboriginal Treaty Making in Canada*. Toronto: University of Toronto Press.

Milloy J. 1999. *A National Crime: The Canadian Government and the Residential School System, 1879–1986*. Winnipeg: University of Manitoba Press.

Milloy J. 2008. 'Indian Act colonialism: a century of dishonor, 1869–1969'. Research paper for the *National Center for First Nations Governance*.

Mitchell J. 2009. '"The galling yoke of slavery": race and separation in colonial Port Phillip'. *Journal of Australian Studies*, 33, no.2.

Mitchell L. 2009. *Belongings: Property, Family, and Identity in Colonial South Africa (An Exploration of Frontiers 1725–c.1830)*. New York: Columbia University Press.

Mitchell P. 2002. *The Archaeology of Southern Africa*. Cambridge: Cambridge University Press.

Momaday N.S. 1969. *The Way to Rainy Mountain*. Albuquerque: University of New Mexico Press.

Moodie D. ed. 1960. *The Record: Or a Series of Papers Relative to the Condition and Treatment of the Native Tribes of South Africa*. Cape Town: Balkema, first published Amsterdam, 1838 and 1842.

Moore R. 1994. 'The management of the Western Australian pearling industry, 1860 to the 1930s'. *Great Circle*, 16, no. 2.

Morris A. 1880. *The Treaties of Canada with the Indians of Manitoba and the North-West Territories*. Toronto: Belfords, Clarke.

Morton F. 1994. 'Slavery and South African historiography', in *Slavery in South Africa*, eds E. Eldridge & F. Morton.

Morton B. 1994. 'Servitude, slave trading and slavery in the Kalahari', in *Slavery in South Africa*, eds E. Eldridge & F. Morton.

Morton F. 2009. 'Small change: children in the nineteenth century east African slave trade', in *Children in Slavery through the Ages*, eds G. Campbell, S. Miers & J.C. Miller. Athens: Ohio University Press.

Moses A.D. 2000. 'An antipodean genocide? The origins of the genocidal moment in the colonization of Australia'. *Journal of Genocide Research*, 2, no. 1.

Moses A.D. ed. 2004. *Genocide and Settler Society: Frontier Violence and Stolen Indigenous Children in Australian History.* New York: Berghahn Books.

Moses A.D. 2004. 'Genocide and settler society in Australian history', in *Genocide and Settler Society*, ed. A.D. Moses.

Moses A.D. ed. 2008. *Empire, Colony, Genocide: Conquest, Occupation and Subaltern Resistance in World History.* New York: Berghahn Books.

Moses A.D. 2008. 'Empire, colony genocide: keywords and the philiosophy of history', in *Empire, Colony, Genocide*, ed. A.D. Moses.

Mostert N. 1992. *Frontiers: The Epic of South Africa's Creation and the Tragedy of the Xhosa People.* London: Pimlico.

Myers J. 2008. *Indirect Rule in South Africa: Tradition, Modernity and the Costuming of Political Power.* Rochester: University of Rochester Press.

Neocleous M. 2012. 'International law as primitive accumulation; or, the secret of systematic colonization'. *The European Journal of International Law*, 23, no. 4.

Neu D. 2003. *Accounting for Genocide: Canada's Bureaucratic Assault on Aboriginal People.* Black Point: Fernwood.

Neville D. 1996. 'European impacts on the the Seacow River valley and its hunter-gatherer inhabitants'. MA thesis, University of Cape Town.

Newton-King S. 1999. *Masters and Servants on the Cape Eastern Frontier.* Cambridge: Cambridge University Press.

Nichols R. 2013. 'Indigeneity and the settler contract today'. *Philosophy & Social Criticism*, 39, no. 2.

Noyes J.K. 1992. *Colonial Space: Spatiality in the Discourse of German South West Africa, 1884–1915.* Reading: Harwood.

Noyes J.K. 2000. 'Nomadic fantasies: producing landscapes of mobility in German Southwest Africa'. *Ecumene*, 7.

Noyes J.K. 2001. 'Nomadic landscapes and the colonial frontier: the problem of nomadism in German South Africa', in *Colonial Frontiers: Indigenous–European Encounters in Settler Societies*, ed. L. Russell. Manchester: Manchester University Press.

Olivier M.J. 1961. 'Inboorlingbeleid en administrasie in die Maandaatgebied van Suidwes-Afrika'. DPhil dissertation, Stellenbosch University.

Orpen F.S. 1964. *Reminiscences of Life in South Africa from 1846 to the Present Day*. Cape Town: Struik.

Ostler J. 2004. *The Plains Sioux and U.S. Colonialism from Lewis and Clark to Wounded Knee*. Cambridge: Cambridge University Press.

Ostler J. 2008. 'The question of genocide in US history', in *Genocide 2*, ed. A. Jones. London: Sage.

Paisley F. 2000. *Loving Protection? Australian Feminism and Aboriginal Women's Rights 1919–1939*. Melbourne: Melbourne University Press.

Palmer A. 2000. *Colonial Genocide*. London: C. Hurst.

Parkington J. 1984. 'Soaqua and Bushmen: hunters and robbers', in *Past and Present in Hunter Gatherer Studies*, ed. C. Schrire. Orlando: Academic Press.

Parkington J. & Hall S. 2010. 'The appearance of food production in southern Africa 1,000 to 2,000 years ago', in *Cambridge History of South Africa*, eds C. Hamilton, B.K. Mbenga & R. Ross.

Passarge S. 1907. *Die Buschmänner der Kalahari*. Berlin: Reimer.

Patterson O. 1982. *Slavery and Social Death: A Comparative Study*. Cambridge: Harvard University Press.

Patterson S. 2004. *The Last Trek: A Study of the Boer People and the Afrikaner Nation*. New York: Routledge.

Pederson H. 2009. 'Frontier violence, Kimberley', in *Historical Encyclopedia of Western Australia*, eds J. Gregory & J. Gothard. Perth: UWAP.

Pels P. 1997. 'The anthropology of colonialism: culture, history, and the emergence of Western governmentality'. *Annual Review of Anthropology*, 26.

Penn N. 1986. 'Pastoralists and pastoralism in the northern Cape frontier zone during the eighteenth century', in *Prehistoric Pastoralism in Southern Africa: The South African Archaeological Society Goodwin Series*, 5, eds M. Hall & A. Smith.

Penn N. 1991. 'The /Xam and the Colony, 1740–1870', in *Sound From the Thinking Strings*, ed. P. Skotnes.

Penn N. 1993. 'Mapping the Cape: John Barrow and the first British occupation of the Cape, 1795–1803'. *Pretexts*, 4, no. 2.

Penn N. 1996. 'Fated to perish: the destruction of the Cape San', in *Miscast*, ed. P. Skotnes.

Penn N. 2001. 'The Northern Cape frontier zone in South African frontier historiography', in *Colonial Frontiers: Indigenous-European Encounters in Settler Societies*, ed. L. Russell. Manchester: Manchester University Press.

Penn N. 2005. *The Forgotten Frontier: Colonist and Khoisan on the Cape's Northern Frontier in the 18th Century*. Cape Town: Double Storey Books.

Penn N. 2007. '"Civilizing" the San: the first mission to the Cape San, 1791–1806', in *Claim to the Country*, ed. P. Skotnes.

Penn N. 2011. 'Written culture and the Cape Khoikhoi: from travel writing to Kolb's "full description"', in *Written Culture in a Colonial Context: Africa and the Americas, 1500–1900*, eds A. Delmas & N. Penn. Cape Town: UCT Press.

Penn N. 2013. 'The British and the "Bushmen": the massacre of the Cape San, 1795–1828'. *Journal of Genocide Research*, 15, no. 2, 183–200.

Perdue T. & Green M.D. 2010. *North American Indians*. New York: Oxford University Press.

Pettipas K. 1989. *Severing the Ties That Bind: Government Repression of Indigenous Religious Ceremonies on the Prairies*. Winnipeg: University of Manitoba Press.

Philip J. 1828. *Researches in South Africa: Illustrating the Civil, Moral and Religious Condition of the Native Tribes*, 2 vols. London: James Duncan.

Plomley N.J.B. ed. 2008. *Friendly Mission: The Tasmanian Journals and Papers of George Augustus Robinson 1829–1834*. Hobart: Quintus.

Pocock J.G.A. 2005. '*Tangata Whenua* and Enlightenment anthropology', in *The Discovery of Islands: Essays in British History*, ed. J.G.A. Pocock. Cambridge: Cambridge University Press.

Pratt M.L. 1985. '"Scratches on the face of the country": or what Mr. Barrow saw in the land of the Bushmen', in *'Race', Writing and Difference*, ed. H.L. Gates. Chicago: Chicago University Press.

Prein P. 1994. 'Guns and top hats: African resistance in German South West Africa, 1907–1915'. *Journal of Southern African Studies*, 20, no.1.

Price R. ed. 1997. *The Spirit of the Alberta Indian Treaties*. Edmonton: University of Alberta Press.

Pringle T. 1835. *Narrative of a Residence in South Africa*. London: Edward Moxon.

Prichard J.C. 1851. *Researches into the Physical History of Mankind, vol. 1*. London: Sherwood, Gilbert & Piper.

Prucha F.P. 2000. *Documents of United States Indian Policy*. Lincoln: University of Nebraska Press.

Pybus C. 1992. *Community of Thieves*. Melbourne: Minerva.

Rafalski H. 1930. *Vom Niemanssland zum Ordnungstaat*. Berlin: Werseitz.

Raffan J. 2007. *Emperor of the North: Sir George Simpson and the Remarkable Story of the Hudson's Bay Company*. New York: Harper Collins.

Rand J.T. 2008. *Kiowa Humanity and the Invasion of the State.* Lincoln: University of Nebraska Press.

Ray A. 1974. *Indians and the Fur Trade: Their Role as Trappers, Hunters and Middle Men in the Lands Southwest of Hudson Bay, 1660–1860.* Toronto: University of Toronto Press.

Ray A., Miller J. & Tough F. 2000. *Bounty and Benevolence: A History of the Saskatchewan Treaties.* Montreal: McGill-Queens University Press.

Reilly H. 2010. *The Frontier Newspapers and the Coverage of the Plains Indian Wars.* New York: Praeger.

Ridley H. 1983. *Images of Colonial Rule.* New York: St.Martins.

Reiner O. 1924. *Achtzehn Jahre Farmer in Afrika.* Leipzig: Paul List Verlag.

Reynolds H. 1981. *The Other Side of the Frontier: Aboriginal Resistance to the European Invasion of Australia.* Ringwood: Penguin.

Reynolds H. 1990. *Black Pioneers: How Aboriginal and Islander People Helped to Build Australia.* Ringwood: Penguin.

Reynolds H. 1990. *With the White People: The Crucial Role of Aborigines in the Exploration and Development of Australia.* Ringwood: Penguin.

Reynolds H. 1995. *Fate of a Free People.* Ringwood: Penguin.

Reynolds H. 1998. *This Whispering in Our Hearts.* Sydney: Allen & Unwin.

Reynolds H. 2001. *An Indelible Stain? The Question of Genocide in Australia's History.* Ringwood: Penguin.

Reynolds H. 2004. 'Genocide in Tasmania', in *Genocide and Settler Society,* ed. A.D. Moses.

Reynolds H. 2012. *A History of Tasmania.* Melbourne: Cambridge University Press.

Richards J. 2008. *The Secret War: A True History of Queensland's Native Police.* St Lucia: University of Queensland Press.

Roberts S.H. 1939. *The Squatting Age in Australia 1835–1847.* Melbourne: Melbourne University Press.

Robinson S. 2008. *Something Like Slavery? Queensland's Aboriginal Child Workers, 1842–1945.* Melbourne: Australian Scholarly.

Rohrbach P. 1915. *German World Policies,* trans. E. von Mach. New York: Macmillan.

Rosenblad E. 2007. *Adventures in South West Africa 1894–1898.* Windhoek: Namibian Scientific Society.

Ross A. 1994. 'The legacy of John Philip.' *International Bulletin of Missionary Research,* 18.

Ross R. 1975. 'The !Kora wars on the Orange River, 1830–1880'. *Journal of African History,* 16, no. 4.

Ross R. 1976. *Adam Kok's Griquas: A Study in the Development of Stratification in South Africa*. Cambridge: Cambridge University Press.

Ross R. 1981. 'Capitalism, expansion and incorporation on the southern African frontier', in *The Frontier in History: North America and Southern Africa Compared*, eds H. Lamar & L. Thompson. New Haven: Yale University Press.

Ross R. 1983. *The Cape of Torments: Slavery and Resistance in South Africa*. London: Routledge.

Ross R. 1989. 'The Cape of Good Hope and the world economy, 1652–1835', in *Shaping*, eds R. Elphick & H. Giliomee.

Ross R. 1994. 'The "white" population of the Cape Colony in the eighteenth century', in *Beyond the Pale: Essays on the History of Colonial South Africa*, ed. R. Ross. Johannesburg: Witwatersrand University Press.

Roux P. 1925. *Die Verdedigingstelsel aan die Kaap Onder die Hollands Oosindiese Kompanjie, 1652–1795*. Stellenbosch: publisher unknown.

Rowley C.D. 1970. *The Destruction of Aboriginal Society*. Canberra: ANU Press.

Russell M. 1976. 'Slaves or workers? relations between Bushmen, Tswana and Boers in the Kalahari'. *Journal of Southern African Studies*, 2, no. 2.

Russell M. & Russel M. 1979. *Afrikaners of the Kalahari: White Minority in a Black State*. Cambridge: Cambridge University Press.

Ryan L. 2006. 'Massacre in Tasmania? How do we know?'. *Australia and New Zealand Law and History Journal*, 6.

Ryan L. 2008. 'List of multiple killings of Aborigines in Tasmania, 1804–1835'. *Online Encyclopaedia of Mass Violence*, ed. J. Semelin. Paris: http://www.massviolence.org/List-of-multiple-killings-of-Aborigines-in-Tasmania-1804.

Ryan L. 2008. 'Massacres in the Black War in Tasmania 1823–34: a case study of the Meander River region, June 1827'. *Journal of Genocide Research*, 10, no. 4.

Ryan L. 2010. '"Hard evidence": the debate about massacre in the Black War in Tasmania', in *Passionate Histories: Myth, Memory and Indigenous Australia*, eds F. Peters-Little, A. Curthoys & J. Docker. Canberra: ANU Press.

Ryan L. 2010. 'Settler massacres on the Port Phillip frontier, 1836–1851'. *Journal of Australian Studies*, 34, no. 3.

Ryan L. 2012. '"No right to the land": the role of the wool industry in the destruction of Aboriginal societies in Tasmania (1817–32) and Victoria (1835–51) compared'. Unpublished paper presented at the Violence and

Honour in Settler Colonial Societies Conference, University of Cape Town, December 2012.

Ryan L. 2012. *Tasmanian Aborigines: A History Since 1803.* Sydney: Allen & Unwin.

Ryan L. 2012. 'Untangling Aboriginal resistance and the settler punitive expedition: the Hawkesbury River frontier in New South Wales, Australia, 1794–1810'. Unpublished paper presented at the Violence and Honour in Settler Colonial Societies Conference, University of Cape Town, December 2012.

Sadr K. 2008. 'Invisible herders? The archaeology of Khoekhoe pastoralists'. *Southern African Humanities*, 20.

Said E. 1988. 'Michael Walzer's exodus and revolution: a Canaanite reading', in *Blaming the Victims: Spurious Scholarship and the Palestinian Question*, eds E. Said & C. Hitchens. London: Verso.

Samek H. 1987. *The Blackfoot Confederacy, 1880–1920: A Comparative Study of Canadian and US Indian Policy.* Albuquerque, University of New Mexico Press.

Sartre J.P. 1967. *On Genocide.* Available at http://www.brussellstribunal.org/GenocideSartre.htm.

Schapera I. 1953. *The Tswana.* London: International African Institute.

Schapera I. 1958. 'Christianity and the Tswana'. *Journal of the Anthropological Institute of Great Britain and Ireland*, 88.

Scheper-Hughes N. 2002. 'Coming to our senses: anthropology and genocide', in *Annihilating Difference: The Anthropology of Genocide*, ed. A.L. Hinton. Berkeley: University of California Press.

Scheulen P. 1998. *Die 'Eingeborenen' Deutsch-Suedwestafrikas.* Koeln: Rudiger Koppe Verlag.

Schinz H. 1891. *Deutsch-Suedwest-Afrika.* Leipzig: Schulzesche Hofbuchhandlung.

Schneider, H. 1981. *The Africans: An Ethnological Account.* Englewood Cliffs, New Jersey: Prentice Hall.

Schoeman K. 1993. 'Die Londense Sendinggenootskap en die San: die stasies Ramah, Konnah en Philippolis, 1816–1828'. *South African Historical Journal*, 29, no. 1.

Schoeman K. 1993. 'Die Londense Sendinggenootskap en die San: die stasies Toornberg en Hephzibah, 1814–1818'. *South African Historical Journal*, 28, no. 1.

Schoeman K. 1994. 'Die London Sendinggenootskap en die San: die stasies Boesmanskool en die einde van die sending, 1828–1833'. *South African Historical Journal*, 30.

Schoeman K. ed. 1996. *Griqua Records: The Philippolis Captaincy, 1825–1861.* Cape Town: Van Riebeeck Society.

Schoeman K. ed. 2005. *The Griqua Mission at Philippolis, 1822–1837.* Pretoria: Protea Book House.

Schultze L. 1914. 'Südwestafrika'. *Das Deutsche Kolonialreich,* 2. Leipzig: Verlag des Bibliographischen Instituts.

Schultze L. 1928. *Zur Kenntnis des Körpers der Hottentotten und Buschmänner.* Jena: Fischer.

Schwirck H.M. 1998. 'Violence, race and the law in German South West Africa 1884–1914'. PhD dissertation, Cornell University.

Scott J.C. 1998. *Seeing Like a State.* Hew Haven: Yale University Press.

Scott P. 1965. 'Land settlement', in *Atlas of Tasmania,* ed. J.L. Davies. Hobart: Lands and Surveys Department.

Seed P. 1995. *Ceremonies of Possession in Europe's Conquest of the New World, 1492–1640.* Cambridge: Cambridge University Press.

Semelin J. 2005. *Purify and Destroy: The Political Uses of Massacre and Genocide.* London: Hurst & Company.

Seuffert N. 2011. 'Civilisation, settlers and wanderers: law, politics and mobility in nineteenth century New Zealand and Australia'. *Law Text Culture,* 15.

Shaw A.G.L. 2003. *A History of the Port Phillip District: Victoria Before Separation.* Melbourne: Melbourne University Press.

Shaw M. 2007. *What is Genocide?* Cambridge: Polity Press.

Sheehan B. 1973. *Seeds of Extinction: Jeffersonian Philanthropy and the American Indian.* Chapel Hill: University of North Carolina Press.

Shelton L. 2007. 'Like a servant or like a son? Circulating children in northwestern Mexico', in *Raising an Empire,* eds O.E. González & B. Premo.

Shepherd B. 2009. 'Pearling', in *Historical Encyclopedia of Western Australia,* eds J. Gregory & J. Gothard. Perth: UWAP.

Shewell H. 2004. *Enough to Keep Them Alive: Indian Welfare in Canada, 1873–1965.* Toronto: University of Toronto Press.

Silberbauer G. 1965. *Bushman Survey Report.* Gaberones: Bechuanaland Government.

Silberbauer G. 1981. *Hunter and Habitat in the Central Kalahari Desert.* Cambridge: Cambridge University Press.

Silberbauer G. & Kuper A. 'Kgalagari masters and Bushman serfs: some observations'. *African Studies,* 25, no.4.

Sillery A. 1965. *Founding a Protectorate: A History of Bechuanland 1885–1895.* The Hague: Mouton & Co.

Sillery A. 1971. *John Mackenzie of Bechuanaland, 1835–1899: A Study in Humanitarian Imperialism.* Leiden: A.A. Balkema.

Sillery A. 1974. *Botswana: A Short Political History.* London: Methuen & Co. Ltd.

Silvester J. & Gewald J. 2003. *Words Cannot be Found: German Colonial Rule in Namibia. An Annotated Reprint of the 1918 Blue Book.* Leiden: Brill.

Skotnes P. ed. 1991. *Sound From the Thinking Strings: A Visual, Literary, Archaeological and Historical Interpretation of the Final Years of /Xam Life.* Cape Town: Axeage Private Press.

Skotnes P. ed. 1996. *Miscast: Negotiating the Presence of the Bushmen.* Cape Town: UCT Press.

Skotnes P. ed. 2007. *Claim to the Country: The Archive of Wilhelm Bleek and Lucy Lloyd.* Johannesburg: Jacana Media.

Smalberger J.M. 1975. *A History of Copper Mining in Namaqualand. 1846–1931.* Cape Town: Struik.

Smith A. 1991. 'On becoming herders: Khoikhoi and San ethnicity in southern Africa'. *African Studies,* 50, no. 1.

Smith A.B. 1986. 'Competition, conflict and clientship: Khoi and San relationships in the Western Cape', in *Prehistoric Pastoralism in Southern Africa: The South African Archaeological Society Goodwin Series,* 5, eds M. Hall & A.B. Smith.

Smith A., Malherbe C., Guenther M. & Berens P. 2000. *The Bushmen of Southern Africa: A Foraging Society in Transition.* Cape Town: David Philip.

Smith D.L. 2011. *Less than Human: Why We Demean, Enslave, and Exterminate Others.* New York: St Martin's Press.

Smith V.W. 1992. '"The most wretched of the human race": the iconography of the Khoikhoin (Hottentots), 1500–1800'. *History and Anthropology,* 5, nos. 3–4.

Smits D. 1994. 'The frontier army and the destruction of the buffalo, 1865–1883'. *Western Historical Quarterly,* 25, no. 3.

Sparrman A. 1975–77. *A Voyage to the Cape of Good Hope Towards the Antarctic Polar Circle Around the World and to the Country of the Hottentots and the Caffres from the Year 1772–1776,* 2 vols., ed. V.S. Forbes. Cape Town: Van Riebeeck Society, first published London: G.G. & J. Robinson, 1785–86.

Stals E.L.P. 1978. *Kurt Streitwolf: Sy Werk in Suidwes-Afrika 1899–1914.* Johannesburg: Perskor.

Stals E.L.P. 1984. 'Duits Suidwes-Afrika na die groot opstande', in *Archives Yearbook for South African History*. Pretoria: Govt. Printer.

Stannard D. 1992. *American Holocaust: The Conquest of the New World*. Oxford: Oxford University Press.

Stockenström A. 1964. *The Autobiography of the Late Sir Andries Stockenström, Sometime Lieutenant-Governor of the Eastern Province of the Colony of the Cape of Good Hope*. 2 volumes. Cape Town: Struik.

Stone D. 2007. 'White men with low moral standards? German anthropology and the Herero genocide', in *Colonialism and Genocide*, A.D. Moses & D. Stone.

Stone D. ed. 2008. *The Historiography of Genocide*. Houndmills: Palgrave Macmillan.

Storey W. 2008. *Guns, Race and Power in Colonial South Africa*. Cambridge: Cambridge University Press.

Stow G.W. 1905. *The Native Races of South Africa: A History of the Intrusion of the Hottentots and Bantu into the Hunting Grounds of the Bushmen, the Aborigines of the Country*. London: Swan Sonnenschein & Co.

Strauss T. 1979. *War Along the Orange: The Korana and the Northern Border Wars of 1868–69 and 1878–79*. Cape Town: Centre for African Studies, University of Cape Town.

Sundermaier T. n.d. *The Mbanderu*, trans. A. Heywood. Windhoek: MSORP.

Sylvain R. 2001. 'Bushmen, Boers and baasskap: patriarchy and paternalism on Afrikaner farms in the Omaheke region, Namibia'. *Journal of Southern African Studies*, 27, no. 4.

Szalay M. 1995. *The San and the Colonisation of the Cape 1770–1879: Conflict, Incorporation, Acculturation*. Köln: Rüdiger Köppe.

Szalay M. 1983. *Ethnologie und Geschichte Zur Grundlegung einer ethnologischen Geschichtsschreibung Mit Beispielen aus der Geschichte der Khoi-San in Südafrika*. Berlin: Dietrich Reimer Verlag.

Tabler E. 1973. *Pioneers of South West Africa and Ngamiland: 1738–1880*. Cape Town: Balkema.

Tagart E.S.B. 1935. *Report on Conditions Existing among the Masarwa in the Bamangwato Reserve of the Bechuanaland Protectorate and Certain other Matters Appertaining to the Native Living Therein*. Pretoria: Government Printer.

Taylor R. 2013. 'Genocide, extinction and Aboriginal self-determination in Tasmanian historiography'. *History Compass*, 11, no. 6.

Teyssot G. 2009. 'Settlers, workers and soldiers: the landscape of total mobilization', in *Settler and Creole Re-Enactment*, eds V. Agnew & J. Lamb. Houndmills: Palgrave Macmillan.

Theal G.M. comp. 1897–1905. *Records of the Cape Colony*, 36 vols. London: Clowes Printers for the Government of the Cape Colony.

Theal G.M. 1911. 'Introduction', in *Specimens of Bushman Folklore*, comp. W.H.I. Bleek & L. Lloyd. London: George Allen & Company, Ltd.

Theal G.M. 1919. *Ethnography and Condition of South Africa Before AD 1505*. London: Allen & Unwin.

Thom H.B. 1936. *Die Geskiedenis van Skaapboerdery in Suid-Afrika*. Amsterdam: Swets & Zeilinger.

Thompson G. 1968. *Travels and Adventures in Southern Africa*. Cape Town: Van Riebeeck Society.

Thornton R. 2000. 'Population history of native North Americans', in *A Population History of North America*, eds M.R. Haines & R.H. Steckel. Cambridge: Cambridge University Press.

Thunberg C.P. 1986. *Travels at the Cape of Good Hope, 1772–1775*, ed. V.S. Forbes. Cape Town: Van Riebeeck Society, first published London: W. Richardson, 1793–95.

Tlou T. 1969. 'Khama III—great reformer, "king" and innovator'. *Botswana Notes and Records*, 2.

Tlou T. 1977. 'Servility and political control: *Botlhanka* among the BaTawana of north-western Botswana, 1750–1906', in *The End of Slavery in Africa*, eds S. Miers & R. Roberts. Madison: University of Wisconsin Press.

Tobias P. ed. 1978. *The Bushmen: San Hunters and Herders of Southern Africa*. Cape Town: Human & Rousseau.

Tough F. 1997. *As Their Natural Resources Fail: Native Peoples and the Economic History of Northern Manitoba, 1870–1930*. Vancouver: University of British Columbia Press.

Tovias B. 2008. 'Navigating the cultural encounter: Blackfoot religious resistance in Canada 1870-1930', in *Empire, Colony, Genocide*, ed. A.D. Moses.

Treaty 7 Elders and Tribal Council. 1996. *The True Spirit and Original Intent of Treaty 7*. Montreal. McGill-Queens University Press.

Turnbull C. 1965. *Black War: The Extermination of the Tasmanian Aborigines*. Melbourne: Lansdowne Press.

Utley R. 2008. *Sitting Bull: The Life and Times of a Patriot*. New York: Holt.

Vamplew W. ed. 1987. *Australian Historical Statistics*. Sydney: Fairfax, Syme Weldon & Associates.

Van den Berghe P. 1970. *South Africa: A Study in Conflict.* Berkeley: University of California Press.

Van den Berghe P. 1972. 'Distance mechanisms of stratification', in *Readings in Race and Ethnic Relations,* ed. A. Richmond. London: Pergamon Press.

Van der Merwe P.J. 1937. *Die Noordwaartse Beweging van die Boere voor die Groot Trek, 1770–1842.* Den Haag: W.P. van Stockum & Zoon.

Van der Merwe P.J. 1938. *Die Trekboer in die Geskiedenis van die Kaapkolonie.* Cape Town: Nasionale Pers.

Van der Merwe P.J. 1995. *The Migrant Farmer in the History of the Cape Colony, 1657–1836,* trans. R.G. Beck. Athens: Ohio University Press.

Van der Post L. 1958. *Lost World of the Kalahari.* London: Hogarth Press.

Van Krieken R. 2004. 'Rethinking cultural genocide: aboriginal child removal and settler-colonial state formation'. *Oceania,* 75, no. 2.

Van Krieken R. 2008. 'Cultural genocide reconsidered'. *Australian Indigenous Law Review,* 12.

Van Rooyen P.H. & Reiner P. 1995. *Gobabis: Brief History of the Town and Region.* Gobabis: Municipality of Gobabis.

Van Sittert L. 2004. 'The supernatural state: water divining and the Cape underground water rush, 1891–1910'. *Journal of Social History,* 37, no. 4.

Van Warmelo N.J. 1977. *Anthropology of Southern Africa in Periodicals to 1950.* Johannesburg: Witwatersrand University Press.

Vedder H. 1926. 'Ueber die vorgeschichte der voelkerschaften von Suedwestafrika'. *Journal of the South West African Scientific Society,* 1.

Vedder H. 1934. *Das Alte Südwestafrika.* Berlin: Martin Warneck.

Vedder H. 1937. *Die Voorgeskiedenis van Suidwes-Afrika.* trans. H. Rooseboom. Windhoek: John Meinert.

Veracini L. 2008. '"Emphatically not a white man's colony": settler colonialism and the construction of colonial Fiji'. *Journal of Pacific History,* 43, no. 3.

Veracini L. 2010. *Settler Colonialism: A Theoretical Overview.* Houndmills: Palgrave Macmillan.

Vergara T.C. 2007. 'Growing up Indian: migration, labour and life in Lima, 1570–1640', in *Raising an Empire,* eds O.E. González & B. Premo.

Viljoen R. 2005. 'Indentured labour and Khoikhoi "equality" before the law in Cape colonial society, South Africa: the case of Jan Paerl, c.1796'. *Itinerario,* 29, no. 3.

Voeltz R. 1988. *German Colonialism and the SWA Company.* Athens: Ohio University Press.

Vogan A. 2011 [1890]. *The Black Police: A Story of Modern Australia*. London: British Library Historical Print Editions.

Von Francois H. 1895. *Nama und Damara Deutsch Sued-West-Afrika.* Magdeburg: Verlag G. Baensch.

Von Krafft-Ebing R. 1947 [1886]. *Psychopathia Sexualis: A Medico-Forensic Study*. New York: Pioneer.

Wadley L. 1979. 'Big elephant shelter and its role in the Holocene prehistory of central South West Africa'. *Cimbebasia*, 3, no. 1.

Waisberg L. & Holzkamm T. 1993. 'A tendency to discourage them from cultivating: Ojibway Agriculture and Indian Affairs Administration in Northwestern Ontario'. *Ethnohistory*, 40, no. 2.

Waiser B. 2005. *Saskatchewan: A New History*. Calgary: Fifth House.

Waiser B. & Stone Child B. 1997. *Loyal till Death: Indians and the North West Rebellion*. Calgary. Fifth House.

Walker E. 1957. *A History of Southern Africa*. London: Longmans Green.

Walther D. 2002 *Creating Germans Abroad*. Athens: Ohio University Press.

Weaver J.C. 2003. *The Great Land Rush and the Making of the Modern World, 1650–1900*. Montreal: McGill-Queen's University Press.

Weber M. 1957. *The Protestant Ethic and the Spirit of Capitalism*. New York: Scribners.

Wells J. 2000. 'The scandal of Rev. James Read and the taming of the London Missionary Society by 1820'. *South African Historical Journal*, 42, no. 1.

West H. 1958. 'Starvation winter of the Blackfeet'. *The Magazine of Western History*, 9, no.1.

Westermarck E. 1891. *The History of Human Marriage*. London: Macmillan.

White R. 1993. *"It's Your Misfortune and None of My Own": A New History of the American West*. Norman: University of Oklahoma Press.

Wilmsen E. 1989. *Land Filled with Flies: A Political Economy of the Kalahari.* Chicago: University of Chicago Press.

Wilmsen E. 1996. 'Decolonising the mind: steps toward cleansing the Bushman stain from southern African history', in *Miscast*, ed. P. Skotnes.

Windschuttle K. 2000. 'The myths of frontier massacres part II: the fabrication of the Aboriginal death toll'. *Quadrant*, October.

Windschuttle K. 2002. *The Fabrication of Aboriginal History: Volume 1, Van Diemen's Land 1803–1947.* Sydney: Macleay Press.

Wolfe P. 1999. *Settler Colonialism and the Transformation of Anthropology.* London: Cassell.

Wolfe P. 2001. 'Land, labor, and difference: elementary structures of race'. *American Historical Review*, 106, no. 3.

Wolfe P. 2006. 'Settler colonialism and the elimination of the native'. *Journal of Genocide Research*, 8, no. 4.

Wolfe P. 2008. 'Structure and event: settler colonialism, time, and the question of genocide', in *Empire, Colony, Genocide*, ed. A.D. Moses.

Woolford A. 2009. 'Ontological destruction: genocide and Canadian Aboriginal peoples'. *Genocide Studies and Prevention*, 4, no. 1.

Worster D. 1992. *Under Western Skies: Nature and History in the American West*. New York: Oxford.

Wright J. 1971. *Bushman Raiders of the Drakensberg, 1840–1870: A Study of Their Conflict With Stock-keeping Peoples in Natal*. Pietermaritzburg: University of Natal Press.

Wright J. 1996. 'Sonqua, Bosjesmans, Bushmen, abaThwa: comments and queries on pre-modern identifications'. *South African Historical Journal*, 35.

Wright R. 2008. *What is America?* Melbourne: Text.

Young R. 1995. *Colonial Desire: Hybridity in Theory, Culture and Race*. London: Routledge.

Zannis M. 1973. *The Genocide Machine in Canada*. Montreal: Black Rose Books.

Zimmerer J. 2002. *Deutsche Herrschaft über Afrikaner: Staatlicher Machtanspruch und Wirklichkeit im Kolonialen Namibia*. Münster, Hamburg: LIT Verlag.

Zimmerer J. 2004. 'Colonialism and the Holocaust: towards an archaeology of genocide', in *Genocide and Settler Society*, ed. A.D. Moses.

Zimmerer J. & Zeller J. eds. 2003. *Völkermord in Deutsch-Südwestafrika*. Berlin: Ch. Links Verlag.

Zins H. 1997. 'The international context of the creation of the Bechuanaland Protectorate in 1885'. *PULA Botswana Journal of African Studies*, 11.

Index

smallpox epidemic, 1713 92
state formation 90–96
subjection of San to forced
  labour 98
Willem Barend 1, 12
Griquatown 22, 61, 91, 92, 94, 95,
  97, 98, 99, 100, 101, 106
Gros Ventre Indians 259
guerrilla tactics 7, 18, 39, 43, 51, 65,
  164

H

Hahn, Theophilus (Dr) 123, 124
Hall, H.L. 1
Hendricks, Hendrick 103, 104
Henry, Patrick 237
Hephzibah mission 76–77
herders
  becoming labour for stock
    farmers 66
  displacement of hunter-gatherers
    by 4
  dispossession of land and
    livestock by 35
  Ghanzi region 152, 153, 154
  Griqua 93
  'Hottentot' 85
  removal of guns from 45
  San 47, 56m 71
  San relationship with settlers
    153
  slaying of by San 7, 41, 73
Herero peoples 3, 23, 110–124, 127,
  130–133, 157, 284, 285, 300, 301
horses
  accessed by Griqua and Korana
    57
  commandos and 43, 44, 46, 165
  First Nations and 264, 265, 273

Griqua 95
Highland Brigade and 203
killed 243
Kiowa 258
as livestock 5, 242, 243, 246,
  264, 273
military value of 14, 15, 45, 46,
  161, 162, 164, 183, 206
Port Phillip District and 207
stolen 42, 81, 104, 108, 263
as transport 11, 219
trekboers and 43, 45, 49
'Hottentot' Code of 1809 70
Hottentots *see* Khoikhoi
  (Hottentot) peoples
Houston, Sam 236
Hudson's Bay Company 259–260,
  265, 267
humanitarianism 24, 25, 52, 72, 76,
  78, 155–157, 167, 169, 180, 182,
  192, 200, 294
hunter-gatherers
  ancestral land 20
  attacks at dawn 18, 46, 165
  attitudes of settlers towards
    women and children 19,
    163–164
  child-bearing 20
  conflict with livestock farmers
    6–7, 162–163
  dehumanisation of 298
  destruction as result of settler
    economies 289
  destruction by colonial pastoral
    farmers
    Australia 159, 174–184
    Cape 159, 174–184
  and disease 16
  displacement by subsistence
    herders 4

U

United Nations Convention on the
Prevention and Punishment of
the Crime of Genocide (UNCG),
1948 2, 84, 209, 283–284

V

Van Diemen's Land 159, 160, 161,
178, 179, 180, 185, 186, 187,
188–209, 213, 214, 216
renamed Settled Districts 19
Vedder, Heinrich 127–128, 132
veldwachtmeesters 42, 52, 166
*Verenigde Ooste-Indische
Compagnie* (VOC) *see* Dutch
East India Company
Victoria 5, 9, 15, 25, 120, 165, 178
see also Aborigines, Port Phillip
District; Port Phillip District
vigilantism 8, 53, 213
Visser, Floris 167
Von Trotha, Lothar (General) 115,
118, 285

W

Washington, George 237, 258
Waterboer, Andries 92, 94, 98
weapons 14, 15, 45, 161, 164, 184

X

Xhosa
land occupation in east 41, 163,
164
truce 167
victories over frontier farmers
166
war threat 169

Y

Yuki Indians 1